# Origins of the Undergr

# Origins of the Underground

*British poetry between apocryphon
and incident light, 1933–79*

ANDREW DUNCAN

CAMBRIDGE

PUBLISHED BY SALT PUBLISHING
14a High Street, Fulbourn, Cambridge CB21 5DH United Kingdom

All rights reserved

© Andrew Duncan, 2008

The right of Andrew Duncan to be identified as the
author of this work has been asserted by him in accordance
with Section 77 of the Copyright, Designs and Patents Act 1988.

This book is in copyright. Subject to statutory exception
and to provisions of relevant collective licensing agreements,
no reproduction of any part may take place without the written
permission of Salt Publishing.

First published 2008

Printed and bound in the United Kingdom by Lightning Source UK Ltd

Typeset in Swift 10/12

*This book is sold subject to the conditions that it shall not,
by way of trade or otherwise, be lent, re-sold, hired out,
or otherwise circulated without the publisher's prior consent
in any form of binding or cover other than that in which
it is published and without a similar condition including this
condition being imposed on the subsequent purchaser.*

ISBN 978 1 84471 078 2 paperback

Salt Publishing Ltd gratefully acknowledges
the financial assistance of Arts Council England

1 3 5 7 9 8 6 4 2

# Contents

| | |
|---|---|
| *Acknowledgements* | vii |
| *Preface* | ix |
| *Chronology* | xv |
| *Introduction: A case that needs to be made* | xxiii |
| The closing of the 1940s; and the prehistory of the underground | 1 |
| Reflexivity and sensitivity | 15 |
| A Various Art and the Cambridge Leisure Centre | 23 |
| Precision and the influence of photography on the poem | 46 |
| Objectivism and the self-investment with modernist legitimacy | 51 |
| The cognitively critical tradition: Madge, Tomlinson, Crozier, Chaloner, Fisher | 56 |
| Secrets of Nature: documentary, group feeling, and propaganda | 82 |
| Avant-garde legitimacy, continued; Neo-Objectivism | 98 |
| The procurement of the information in poetry | 109 |
| West-bloc dissidents, or the history of ideas in poetry | 129 |
| The dissolution of the horizon: New Romantic poetry | 142 |
| Moral man in an immoral society: personalism and authenticity in the 1940s | 153 |
| New Romantic poets | 166 |
| In the land of the not-quite day; or, the frisson of ruins. David Gascoyne | 186 |
| Bad science, pulp topography: Iain Sinclair | 210 |
| Radical toxins and lingering hallucinogens: Counter-culture and New Age | 222 |
| Apocalyptic foreglow, and origins of the Counter-Culture | 236 |
| Peripheral nationalism and collective disloyalty | 254 |
| The 1970s and Left versus Right in the Labour Party | 262 |
| Decentralisation: the ideal of workers' control | 272 |
| Under the ground, into the Crypt | 285 |
| Conclusion | 297 |
| *Bibliography* | 300 |
| *Index* | 308 |

# Acknowledgements

The reviews of John Riley, David Chaloner, and Charles Madge appeared in *Angel Exhaust*. The section on John Hall appeared in *Terrible Work*. The essay on documentary and propaganda appeared in *Shearsman*.

## *Preface*

The background to *Origins of the Underground* is really the story of how British poets became intellectuals. As they retreated from inherited and fixed value systems, they had to think for themselves, and this was a race which intellectuals generally won. You can't just buy in ideas like a small tropical country buying jet fighter planes. What the success of poets seems to turn on is their willingness to use ideas which excite the ideas part of their brains because they are genuinely unfamiliar. Poets who prefer to stick to well-worn and inherited arguments, where they can predict every move, fail for this reason. The area of nearby uncertainty has an odd shape. Obviously, most of the ideas which were new and risky thirty years ago are now forgotten—the risk fell to earth, so to speak. A certain archaeology is needed to retrieve these "casualty" ideas. I admit that I enjoy this sort of digging, and the practice of psychoceramics (the scientific study of crackpots), but perhaps this pleasure pursuit is useful as well. The terrain is made impassable by deep mutual disagreements between different groups of poetry readers (and writers). Going in at the level of ideas offers a possible way of easing these disagreements. Admittedly, it's very difficult to find out exactly what they are.

    Lagging behind rather, critics turn up and have to write history of ideas in order to get at the poems. This is not a finished science but a provisional one. We can remark, even at this early stage, that the histories of ideas which deal with what was being said in university philosophy departments are of no use. Poets use a different set of ideas. Further, the theme is information in general, rather than abstract ideas. More exactly, it is the imaginative rules by which one visualises social processes. The history of what appears in photographs is very important to our subject. Some of the ideas belong properly in the psychoceramics lab. Unless you know something about dear old crackpots like Jung and Olson, you have very little chance of understanding modern British poetry.

I accept that putting the history of ideas on a quantitative basis is an advance—because hundreds of ideas were in circulation, because one idea was more important than another, we would like to measure just how important each one was. I have not tried to do this. I found the *stories* of people like Stephen Tallents, Joseph Macleod, or David Gascoyne captivating. I am aware that lighting a few paths through the vaporous mass of ideas floating around in the period does not amount to a full intellectual history. All I can say is that the extent of such a history would be vast. The studies I needed were not available, but I hope this preliminary and partial study may be useful to other students one day. The selection of lines was guided by curiosity—I am aware that the ones studied may be marginal, but they are more interesting at this date than more central themes which we are all familiar with. And which my colleagues have explained so well.

Reviews of my previous book tended to find it "exasperating" or "infuriating". I apologise for this. You can believe that I knew anger would block the message from being taken in. I wanted to liberate people from anger, but it seems I took their anger off the leash. Examining disagreement does not, in fact, always tend to reduce it. I am unhappy at the territorial metaphor invoked—I am sure that modern poetry is so complex that two readers, well into it, are seeing quite different pictures, freely co-designed by themselves. In fact, this complexity and this suggestibility are the conditions which modern poetry strives for. Francis Berry is a good example of a difficult and suggestive writer— leaving aside the question of misreading of various lines in the poem, two readers surely form different experiences in such poems. If my response is so deeply subjective, it is illegitimate to call it "wrong" all the time. These furies of territorial defence—of litigatory passion and execration—have no *locus standi*.

Unfortunately, this new book is partly about how conservative cultural managers excluded various ideas, styles, and people they disapproved of, and how the stylistic choices of the most gifted poets were influenced by hatred of the cultural managers—so I may shake up the liquors of wrath again. I don't see how I could avoid this without falsification. Cultural products ask people to assimilate but one of the most common responses is to dissimilate. Negative reactions, denial, withdrawal, inversion, are key behaviours. The favoured political pattern in this society is two *opposed* parties. Stylistic choice has to do with rejection, dread of pollution, fear of contamination by being like people you dislike—not *just* with longing and attraction. The same TLS review which found the last book infuriating compared the English literary establishment, at some length, to Stalinism in the 1940s. Once you understand that analogy, huge tracts of the landscape become visible and readable.

The modernity of modern poetry is suited to minimise the territorial investment, the sense of trespass and violation, the barbed wire, the trench lines. It is designed to supply a stable and capacious external space, boundless and yet reassuring, personal and yet full of other people.

I have to point out, given the craving of reviewers to assume the opposite, that this is not a one-volume history of the period—I intend to publish at least two more volumes on the period since 1960. Reviewers wanted a book to be a one-volume history of the national poetry so that they could find it wanting and tear it to bits. This urge had a lot to do with display acts of protection and loyalty –they could not arraign me for omitting their favourite poets (or, themselves) unless I offered completeness. The act of valiant defender can't start unless someone, i.e. me, is doing injustice. It is a parental vision, and involves a modern-sized family, with no more than three children. Critics want to build big green visions of how things really are, with comfortable and lush niches for the poets they want to protect. This rural vision is somehow linked to the English love of landscape painting. It involves solitude—a very small number of poets. It doesn't want to know about one hundred excelling poets. It is a *private* landscape. My book violated this tender vision, its rolling pastureland. Even though it wasn't an account of the national poetry but only of innovation. Much extra material not intended to appear in books is on my website at www.pinko.org.

This isn't a one-volume history either. There are at least one hundred contemporary poets whom I regard as *national art treasures*, and I would want at least 500 pages to explain why. Further, there is already a mass of writing about the period, and, like a footballer, I must "go for space". I am *selectively* gathering unfamiliar information. Describing all the poetry published in the 1940s was not my project. I haven't written about Auden because there is masses written about him. Generally, if you read ten books on recent literary history you do find that they do all say the same things. This makes reading them a wearing experience. I intend to bang on until you complain about me including too much.

[xii]     *Origins of the Underground*

 This book does not follow a progressive line of time. It radiates out from a central problem that the most interesting British poetry is remote from public view.

 In the introduction, xxiii–xxxi, we gloomily describe the problem and quote a lot of poems to show that the occluded is worth de-occluding. On pages 1–14, we look at the exclusion of the 1940s New Romantics, around 1950, as a possible analogy to the exit from the mainstream in the 1960s. We introduce *A Various Art*, a 1987 anthology of uncelebrated writers which we hope to shed light on. On pp.15–22, we go back to the forties to look at self-critical, reflexive poets of that time. On pages 23–81 we look at the school which produced the poets of *A Various Art*, and consider possible influences from the 1930s (Objectivism) and 1940s (Charles Madge). On pp.82–97 we go backwards to look at British State propaganda between the wars, as a set of myths, ruthlessly repeated, which constituted what poets retreated from. We are depressed to see how far it created the school of British documentary, with its appearance of being truthful and left-wing. We return to further discussion of neo-Objectivism, now with a more informed view of the cult of objectivity. Following the theme of photography, and capture of new channels of data, we look on pp.109–128 at the history of the information filling poetry, a dialectic pattern whereby an excess of inflowing data led to changes in the structure of the poem. On pp.142–185 we consider the New Romantic school of the 1940s—a contraction of the radius of interest to the body. a rejection of documentary knowledge, world news, group propaganda, and precision, in favour of intuition and personal myth. Unfortunately, we have already seen that the *A Various Art* school was based on reflexivity and interrogation of visible light—an inheritance of themes just cannot be. The New Romantics were anarchist and pacifist. On pp. 186–209, we look at the haunted New Romantic figure of David Gascoyne, ending up in the 1980s with the occultist magazine *Temenos*, edited by another forties poet, Kathleen Raine. So perhaps the offspring of the 1940s are not the school of Prynne but the New Age. Intrigued, we move on to look, pp.210–221, at Iain Sinclair, who is in *A Various Art* but writes mainly about deluded New Age figures; and, pp.223–235, at the New Age and Counter Culture, social-political movements which may be the poles of attraction which drew poets away from the mainstream and the High Street, and which want to found a new knowledge in special states of awareness. Anarchism? pacifism? distrust of machines? is this a return of the New Romantic 1940s? At pp.236–253 we take a trip back to the 1920s to reveal the origins of the Counter-Culture in certain intellectual currents, largely derived from Symbolism, which influenced the New Romantics and only later gave rise to the New Age. On pp.254-261 we look at the Scottish end of New Romanticism and at avant-garde folk music. On pp.262-271 we move back to the 1970s to examine the struggle between Left and Right in the Labour Party as the source of embitterment which poisoned relations between mainstream and underground factions in poetry, the mutual contempt of pragmatists and idealists. On pp. 272-284, we look at the idea of autogestion, a society with totally decentralised power, as an inspiration for poetry which hyperassociates at every step—the loose joints. We dredge up a link between the forties radicalism of Asger Jorn and the high-riding Situationism of May 68 (he founded it). And are disappointed to find it's over.

# Chronology

1840s — Start of the Occult Revival, an inseparable part of the Symboliste Movement. Driven by opposition to the rise of science and scepticism.

circa 1850 — William Fox Talbot, *The Talbotype applied to hieroglyphics*, an avowedly Neoplatonist project. We ask whether English photographers want to capture reality, or to fix ideal scenes in visual form.

1881 — William Morris sets up his works at Merton Abbey. Start of the Arts and Crafts Movement. Attack on machine production, praise of the hand-made. Village thinking; the back to the land movement.

1889 — Publication of *Lux Mundi*, in which Anglican theologians take on and try to absorb modern science and scholarship, and launch the kenotic strand of theology; whose preoccupation with the Incarnation leads on to the Apocalyptic concern with the human body.

1900 — Founding by Oedenkoven of a Theosophist and Naturist colony at Ascona (Switzerland);

1906 — Start of activities of Otto Gross, leading light of Ascona and chief influence on DH Lawrence.

1909 — Crowley and Victor Neuburg go into the desert to try and put the Neoplatonic "calls" left by Edward Kelley into practice.

1910 — Modernism not happening in Britain.

1912 — Georgian poetry, a reform involving: reduction of verbal complexity, refusal of egoism; lower-class social scenes; crafts and the countryside, physical work; humility; new rhythms, close to speech and dialect. This influence pervades the rest of the century.

circa 1914 — Edward Thomas breaks through into real poetry, his "imagined village".

1915 — *The Dramas and Dramatic Dances of non-European Races*, by William Ridgway; ecstatic culture of the colonised.

circa 1920 — Founding of Surrealism, an offshoot of Dada. Interest in dreams, the inexplicable, the mystic side

[xv]

of Romanticism, the unconscious, European occultism, Protestant mysticism, the cultures of the colonised. Forerunner of Apocalyptic movement.
1920 Modernism not happening in Britain.
1920s Peak of Ascona. Foundation of academic literary criticism, a new discipline, with orientation towards scepticism and precision. Peak of Spiritualist Church, with focus on prophecy and spirit guides.
1923 *Fantasia of the Unconscious*, D. H. Lawrence. Occultist work based on a sun myth.
1926 Debut of H.J. Massingham, key figure of the topographic school; anomalies or buried powers of the countryside.
1927 Film, "Drifters", released. Foundation of British Documentary Movement by Stephen Tallents. Max Plowman's book on Blake. Jack Lindsay's anthology of "bedlam" poetry (the wisdom of madness; the irrational as poetic).
1928–31 Experiment magazine in Cambridge, bringing intelligence into culture; reception of cinema and Surrealism.
1930 Death of modernism as the Depression re-orients the cultivated public towards politics and realism. Start of the "pylons" school in poetry, what the New Romantics sought to abolish.
1931 Objectivist Anthology published in Poetry (Chicago). "Apocalypse" (Lawrence).
1932 *The Projection of England*, by Stephen Tallents. A formulation of a national iconography as a scheme for propaganda; based on the English gentleman, stress on privatisation, leisure, games, tailoring.
1933 founding of Eranos conferences by Rudolf Otto, organised by Olga Froebe-Kapteyn, held in Ascona. Probable peak of pacifism in UK, with a celebrated vote at the Oxford Union not to defend "king and country". Early books by Dylan Thomas, Barker, and Gascoyne.
1934 *Variations on a Time Theme*, Edwin Muir; 2nd edition of *Human History*, Elliot Smith

1936 Start of "organic" farming in England, based on the "bio-dynamism" of occultist Rudolf Steiner. Flourishing of organic farming in the Third Reich.
1935 *Life Quest*, Richard Aldington; first attempt to write the poetry of ideas in England? *Foray of Centaurs*, Joseph Macleod (unpublished 2nd version).
1936 Yeats' Oxford Book of Modern Verse enshrines a history of neo-Symbolism and visionary trances, bypassing anything realist or documentary.
1936 Surrealist Exhibition in London. English Surrealism largely found itself as the Apocalyptic movement. Outbreak of Spanish Civil War breaks up the pacifist line as the Left quite rapidly turns in favour of a "just war". Caudwell, *Illusion and Reality*, places poetry close to dreams and the irrational, talks about 'dream work'.
1937 *Britain and the Beast*, edited Clough Williams-Ellis. A defence of the 'rural amenities' of Britain; articulation of dislike of machines and mechanical modernity, forerunner of the Apocalyptics. Founding of Mass Observation movement by Harrison, Madge and Jennings. Pacifists take to communal farming as a withdrawal from the State. Paris Exhibition; British Pavilion extols virtues of privatisation, leisure, games, good tailoring. John Goodland is formulating the Apocalyptic creed. Start of *Wales*, and a brilliant school of poets, arrival of Anglo-Welsh poetry. Conflict of Tallents and Macleod at BBC.
1938 Berdyaev, *Solitude and Society*, defines Apocalypse in personalist terms. *Famine in England*, a plea for organic farming by the Earl of Portsmouth, evokes one of the four horsemen, and attacks the object-machine.
1939 Huge wave of loyal propaganda produces British sentiments, eclipse of peripheral nationalism until a new boom in the second half of the 1960s. Small nation nationalisms articulate themselves as anti-war because the war was defending the Empire. Recycling of 30s Left imagery, characters, etc. as images of national unity.

[xviii]          *Origins of the Underground*

|  |  |  |
|---|---|---|
|  | 1939 | Pilgrim Trust programme of painters recording old and fragile things. Possible start of the "catalogue of beauties' style —anomalies of the countryside. *The New Apocalypse* published. |
|  | 1939 | "Entrance to Lane", by Graham Sutherland; anomalies or buried powers of the countryside. Basic to New Romantic painting. |
| 1940–50 |  | Flourishing of New Romantic school. |
| 1940–8 |  | *Horizon.* |
| 1940– |  | After fall of France, the U-boat blockade; national energies focus on food and farming; "dig for victory". |
|  | 1941 | 1st issue of magazine "Helhesten", edited by Asger Jorn. Union of Surrealism and local folk mythology. |
|  | 1942 | Helpmann "Hamlet" ballet. The whole set represents the "nightmare of the dying prince". (Archbishop) William Temple, *The Church and the Social Order*, part of the line of social engagement which parallels the documentary movement. |
| 1940s |  | Thriving of neo-Romantic painters: mystic configurations, anomalies of the countryside, visions. |
|  | 1943 | *The Inward Animal*, by Terence Tiller (pp.15–22) |
|  | 1945 | *Marxism and Poetry*, by George Thomson; defines everything except folksong as inauthentic |
| 1945–51 |  | Attlee government; creation of the Welfare State. |
|  | 1946 | Effective stop of Mass Observation. Dismantling of wartime propaganda apparatus. |
|  | 1947 | *In Trust for the Nation*, ed. Williams-Ellis; illustrations by Barbara Jones; "catalogue of beauties" style book about the holdings of the National Trust. Frye's book on Blake. |
|  | 1948 | Formation of COBRA group of abstract artists, with Asger Jorn as theorist. |
|  | 1949 | *New Romantic Anthology.* Last anthology of the New Romantic/apocalyptic movement. |
| 1948–65 |  | Especially dolorous' time for Anglo-Welsh poetry; similar low period for Scottish poetry. |
|  | 1950 | Launch of wonderful Key Poets series of pamphlets. |
|  | 1950 | Termination of Key Poets series by Communist Party leadership. *Contemporary Verse*, Kenneth |

Chronology [xix]

|  |  |  |
|---|---|---|
|  |  | Allott's anthology writing the New Romantics out of history. |
| Eternally, but at least 1951–80 |  | Left-right struggles within Labour party, model for opposition between "idealists" and common sense in poetry. |
| 1950–2 |  | Collapse of institutional bases for New Romantics. |
|  | 1953 | Publication of Eliade's *Shamanism: archaic techniques of ecstasy* kindle an interest in ecstatic religion, reprising themes of Spiritualism. *Script from Norway*, Joseph Macleod. |
|  | 1953 | Barbara Jones book on *Follies and Grottoes*. Anomalies of the countryside. |
| 1950s |  | Cultural crisis of Anglican Church. Switch of values away from inherited literary beauty towards something "live", urban, youthful, and relevant. First generation of English poets not dominated by Anglicanism is maturing. Small-scale dissemination of new ideas about ecstatic religion and personal religion. *Nimbus* (1951–8) features Eliade, Ascona, as well as late New Romanticism. |
| 1956–? |  | K Raine working on Blake's sources, on Neoplatonist lines. She probably links Spiritualism and Neoplatonism? |
| mid-1950s |  | Return of a consumer economy, led by housing and "white goods". End of austerity. Reversion of propaganda energy to advertising—propaganda for the household. |
|  | 1956 | Easter Marches unify pacifist and Christian opinion in anti-nuclear protests; rise of CND. |
|  | 1956 | Russian invasion of Hungary brings about a secession from British Communist Party and a "New Left" whose influence on poetry is disputed. |
|  | 1957 | Formation of Situationist International by Asger Jorn. |
|  | 1958 | A.L. Morton's book on Blake's sources. |
| mid-1950s |  | Return of a consumer economy, led by housing and 'white goods'. End of austerity. Reversion of propaganda energy to advertising—propaganda for the household. |
|  | 1959 | *Songs*, by Christopher Logue. Start of folk boom. |

Origins of the Underground

| | | |
|---|---|---|
| 1959 or 1960 | | Start of British Poetry Revival, according to Görtschacher or Mottram. Unrevived poetry lingers on in a kind of living death (to the present day). |
| | 1960 | *City*, Roy Fisher. 1st publication of the poetry revival. The first English poet to imagine the city. |
| 1961-4 | | "Dog Star Man", Stan Brakhage. |
| | 1962 | *The New Poetry*, anthology. Alvarez intro links inner space to insight into the cosmic order, fulfilling an Apocalyptic programme. |
| | 1963 | *Honest To God*, Bishop John Robinson, radical (bultmannian) demythologising. |
| 1963- | | Jeff Nuttall continues New Romantic line of the dominance of physiology; stress on sound, noun strings, reduced syntactic articulation. Ancestral to the London School. Rediscovery of Objectivism in Britain. Reading of Rakosi, Zukofsky, Oppen, Olson. |
| 1960s generally | | Interest in Blake, ecstatic "altered states", Third World religion, inner space, Jung, personal myth |
| 1965? | | Start of revival of Scottish and Welsh national sentiment. |
| 1966-70 | | *The English Intelligencer*. |
| | 1967 | Craze for psychedelic music. Origin of Counter-Culture (hippies, psychedelia . . .). Fashion for the non-Western. Founding of Grosseteste Review. Origin of Ferry Press/Grosseteste school. *The Society of the Spectacle*, by Guy Debord. |
| 1968-75 | | Era of student revolts. Challenges to inherited academic approaches. Literary criticism becomes more diverse. Links between New Left, Counter culture, and underground poetry remain controversial. |
| | 1968 | *From Glasgow to Saturn*, by Edwin Morgan. |
| circa 1968 | | End of wave of films about the Second World War. Replaced by other configurations. |
| | 1969 | *The White Stones*, by J.H. Prynne. Founding of RILKO |
| | 1970 | *Crow*, by Ted Hughes; apex of myth/inner space/primitive religion current. |
| | 1970 | Publishing of *The Leaves of Spring*, by Aaron Esterson. Discusses young female schizophrenics in the sense |

Chronology [xxi]

of being pushed into the non-secular and compares them to saints; theme of prophecy.
1975 *Quicksilver Heritage*, doctrinal New Age work by Paul Screeton. Describes arrival of metal as ending the Neolithic era of spiritual wisdom—village thinking, continuing the "object-machine" idea. Ley lines and barrows are Neolithic achievements. Describes a Neoplatonist view of energy and pattern. Anomalies of the countryside.
1975 Arguable end of British Poetry Revival, to be replaced by other configurations.
1975 *After Striking the Pavilion of Zero*, John James.
1977 Publication of *The Bloodshed, the Shaking House*, by Martin Thom (pp. 233-5)
1977 *A Lamentation for the Children*, Walter Perrie.
1977-80 Recession of the Underground away from a brief access to the mainstream. Polarisation.
1978 *High Zero*, by Andrew Crozier (pp.70-77).
1979 *Suicide Bridge*, Iain Sinclair. Most successful use of Blake (pp. 210-221).
1981-92 Magazine *Temenos*. (pp. 196-8)
1987 "A Paradise Lost?" New Romantic exhibition at the Barbican. Publication of *A Various Art* (passim).

# Introduction: A case that needs to be made

> the sound has forlorn the lost, horse chestnut leaves across their mouths
> mourn the nights that stop the portuguese
> from changing flowers to musak
> in other tongues our futures rung
> the old uneconomic songs
> proclaimed pandemic
> distinctively white shorelines await
> the brave, the nonchalant, the hysteric,
> servants retreat into a background
> (for the) prophesies of April light
> are noticed to be aiming
> by slow and sure control
> at correct definition
>
> held fast as half strangled elegant cats
> hanging a late grape on a battered straw hat,
> and a cherry glistening, and a raspberry listening,
> to the cream viyella collars of vietnamese sailors
> flying their crafts to mexico
> where snows melting around tangerines
> drift to cool the edges of horse chestnut leaves
> oblivious to the forlorn's lack of imperialese.
>
> (Grace Lake, from *Bernache Nonnette*)

> ah, how the hay smokes
> into papaverous skies
> as we address the heights of the C20th
> in a poplin shirt, all declamatory and tired
> with a suit that seals to rest these soft
> & perfect metals. The organization
> owes everything; is fit to tweak

a neuralgic scene reading Auden
beneath a naked sheet in stormy cupolas
where the coupled latch and larchlap twitter
breaks sleet print through the cigarette
dries trays of warm roses & vocable ash
as hands permitting a multiple
sleepless walk for the uninked signatory
through august hours

(HELEN MACDONALD, FROM 'TUIST')

What is it that damasks the waves of this great bay
as if with a care for each moment within the deep sad systems
of the sea? Stone crop flares on the boulder face
and we walk the high edge, our words leaving no mark,
silent on the more general silence. The great sun
is absconded beyond the waste and we navigate as if
we were the old-time sailors, peering eyelessly to gain
the pressure of invisible land with a facial seeing,
the blind sight of those who move by dark of intuition
and the common surface of their skin.

(NIGEL WHEALE, FROM 'SILENT COAST')

    rich off
    the dead
    strata, he

    is all possible forms
    of gain
    (the hollow sign
    Iron, haematite)

    yet herding
    nomadism
    outstrip
    his double articulation, do not rise
    through the mesh of quantities
    suddenly deferr'd
    until the true season
    comes around, shuffling across the market
    in small coils of gold air, tickets

        Which is
        only the passage
        of their cattle, ankles tied
        to stop flight. Already sold
        before birth
        the blooded calves
        in unwinged music of

*Introduction: A case that needs to be made* [xxv]

> what is to come, kick out
> against this pressure
> of hooded cities, do not rise
> to sudden wealth and love
> the quality of soil
> to leave it
> within the cycles
> of slow animal care, to be
>
> with him in all the
> fading inscription of his thought on
> such a pale sign as he could now
> give to things, in a
> magical world
> girl or boy, blood
> or bone. Disappearing
> he could have the key
> in all his will does not
> pretend to
>
> riding into the arena
> waving the zero
> phoneme
> the finally human unhuman
> bearer of meaning
> in Arabia Deserta for years
>
> (MARTIN THOM, FROM 'FRIGHTENING HAPPY GLOW')

damage might be done to his teeth
or excitation of neural impulses
black things on the horses' mouths
may appear between laboratory and real life
white stimulus wipes out the wave
from individual case histories
not cleaned adequately
while he called out the fluctuations
confined to explaining

(TOM RAWORTH, FROM SENTENCED TO DEATH)

Recording on a slate in the rain:

Give me your hardest hardness
your bitterness, your spleen
Give me the harshest harness
thrown off by beasts used to your harm

your inability, your dreadful shame
your words untouched by human warmth

all liquid innuendoes and brittle slates
quartz-tongue flint-heart, pass me
jagged qualities of your meanest acts
Your silence beginning with O

broken stiles
littering the princedom
neglected ditches
clogged with clarts

locked-up chapels
where lamenting starts

sheepwire stapling
her fells and fields

wild Northumberland
hemmed in, stitched up

more dismay
for me and my fiefdom

(BARRY MACSWEENEY: FROM RANTER)

He is the work of his own dismayed genius.
An amphora found in the city after
excavation crumbles into dust, his mother's
arm. To the applause of crowds
he runs through the dance that will
fire their alien tribunes, who scrape and bow.
His charm is to be foolish as they are
foolish, with his hands in a bowl of acid.
They have travelled so far for nothing but his smile
they can barely see in the earthly light
what children they are. Those he has banished
gather in their nets
while a red tongue licks from a cloud.
These have been spared, in the great waves
they are crushed to infinite sand.
He raises his finger and a new music is born.
An acrobat turns on the stars to scream.

Let blood. Peel off his nipples,
starfish. The philosophic jaw
swings over his tranquil harbour,
midges on its slowly dissolving
yellow screen. Not soft enough
to be wrought as the landing stage
sets up a bright film he saw years ago in

*Introduction: A case that needs to be made*

the bright arena, and bled.
He cannot bear that flatulent music.
(CHARLES LAMBERT, FROM 'HEROES')

Silver moon; thatch; owl on the gable
and twelve silver instruments on the desk
for surgery. Silver moon on the desk,
twelve silver instruments constellate
behind clouds. Ready for the straw
bird in the house of feathers. Mild
fingers set twelve silver straws on
the shining wood. There is a soft
interjection, stroboscopic starlight
and the powers realign. In another
box there are two gold rings.

[ ... ]

White hedonism cut on blue
intelligence and laced
with silver anxiety. Bravo.
It braces milady's cortical
layer to take what could
have been trauma but now snugs
a bee in a comfort. While ants
silkily fidget and moderate
men press on, juddering,
grinning, being temperate
because of the price of beer.
(RF LANGLEY, FROM 'THE ECSTACY INVENTORIES')

A dread of terns takes flight out from
the drear vast wastes of icy paranoiac silence
of magnetic fields. A flurry of the nerves
of earth intelligence. Acute, sheer white
and nightless, even as the solar or soul of
light. A polar midnight.

Try this door into the atmosphere tonight,
And is there no reply? The kinless stranger
with his collar up against the wind walks on
his death programme. No signs except
the Day Original stands flapping by the rowan
like a raven flag. Vacuity.
A barometric fall.

Blackberry eyes. Bleak sky. Black dots
and spots of rain.

(MICHAEL HASLAM, FROM *CONTINUAL SONG*)

I hope these quotations show that there is something alive in British poetry outside the toxic scorched-earth dump estates of Philip Larkin, pop poetry, and Bloodaxe Books. The poets quoted belong to a poetic archipelago, afloat in navigable reaches of magazines, events, and personal contacts, many of whose shores are in Cambridge. I would like to extend the accepted list of classic small presses—traditionally, Goliard, Trigram, and Fulcrum—to include Ferry Press and its paredros, Grosseteste Press. Exhibit Number One is *A Various Art* (edited by Crozier and Longville and published by Carcanet in 1987), effectively an anthology of Ferry Press (publisher A Crozier) and Grosseteste Review (1968–84, editor T Longville), and reflecting the situation up to 1975. By the Cambridge School we really mean contributors to Ferry and Grosseteste. *AVA* remains baffling, less in the detailed course of the poems than in the presuppositions, and in the path by which people reached this exotic and shared style. It seemed worthwhile, therefore, to treat it as a problem in intellectual history and in iconology.

The traditional society (the one which the 1960s are supposed to have ended) had a large category of things you shouldn't say. This affected poetry a great deal; the moments of exclusion are themselves not on record, in an act of nihilation (to use a term from sociology) which forces us to reconstruct undocumented events. In the immortal words of James Jesus Angleton, I'm not privy to *who struck John*, but I can draw a few sketches. In speech, the line between the aesthetic, and the psychologically acceptable (in terms of politics, accent, social attitudes, ethnicity) cannot be satisfactorily drawn. I spent a long time going through the theatre programmes of the Festival Theatre, run during 1933–35 by the poet Joseph Macleod, who was silenced by its commercial failure. What good is a theatre producer with no theatre? Most of the programmes were advertisements; after hours of blocking them out, I underwent a figure-ground reversal and began looking at the ads. One for ladies' underwear was in every programme; I reflected how much easier it was to "sell the space" if you had actresses who were obviously wearing expensive undergarments, and who were obviously (if not visibly) adorned by them; and how many more drinks and meals you were going to sell on the premises (also repetitively advertised) if you had a middle-class audience, and if you made them feel affluent, and if you staged sophisticatedly sexy scenes to make the gentlemen willing to show off in front of their girlfriends. Theatre was all about glamour in those days. The exclusion of real-life problems was (is) basic to the quality of sexy: because that depends on play, and play feelings disappear very quickly where there is anxiety and insecurity. Plays about poverty don't make people feel affluent; plays about the decline of the bourgeoisie don't help you to sell bottles of wine to the good old bourgeoisie. Such factors may have speeded the vocally left-wing Macleod (who was certainly filling quite a few of the special one-and-sixpence seats) out of his lease without anyone conspiring against him. Business failure is bad for everyone and the feelings of anxiety it leaves behind may influence people's feelings and decisions without them being consciously aware of the problem.

So it is with anxious-making speech. The cultural managers (editors and bookshop owners, in particular) are prone to anxiety. Anxiety has a lot to do with money, or so I find. Five-shilling seats are a lot calmer than one and six pennies. Their jobs are hopelessly over-specified; to get publicity, they have to please the media, and the media are selling an atmosphere of affluence and conformism, which they are wonderfully careful of. Maybe I can recover some of the rules of what you shouldn't say; and help explain the careers of so many poets, who when the curtain went up on the rich pageant of literature were mysteriously missing from the stage. Xed from the project. There's nothing down for you. You are not suitable for this position. Macleod's theatre became a costume warehouse. Although the documentation has not been kept, maybe I can identify who shortened the invitation lists.

The initial project—how long ago?—was to fulfil the accepted role of the critic, by locating authenticity in specified traits, and then finding these in the texts of poems whose fixedness and inspectability comprise their charm. Like everyone else who has set out on this Grail Quest, I discovered, after a while, that the factors composing an "authentic experience" were mainly in the mind of the reader, and that the sense of trust is given for arbitrary and fickle reasons (to be exact, reasons which are sociologically conditioned in a fickle way). The conscious efforts of both poets and readers are given over to scanning material records to locate this spiritual quality, or its absence; their success, constant and yet intermittent, is self-referential, their reach circular. It is possible, nonetheless, to find out what traits they are scanning and selecting for.

Most accounts show a kind of centralised cultural oppression in the 1950s and a prehistory of poetic radicalism in the 1940s. AVA is part of the British Poetry Revival, as defined by Eric Mottram in a classic and polemic essay some twenty-five years ago, which began in 1960 and destroyed all previous rules. We use AVA, the broadest and most significant cultural monument of the era, as a staging post where we can examine both an array of causes and an array of consequences. An overall revision of the history of the century's poetry is too ambitious, let alone a journey back to other cultural complexes, of 1880 or 1850, to trace long-term forces and changes. The backward look follows a perception that nothing new has arrived on the scene since 1975, or perhaps slightly earlier; the stability of the present cultural conjuncture gives it a strength which makes its origins worth examining. Was there an alternative? Where are the points of instability? How were the alternatives discredited and contaminated by the stories of the culturally powerful? What are the social supports of various verbal styles? The 1940s offer us the nuclei of: epistemology; sexuality; reflexive and metaphysical poetry; Communist poetry; the underground; the poetry magazine; "celticity" and peripheral nationalism; oral and "performance" poetry; apocalyptic, prophetic, and Jungian poetry. They anticipate the British Poetry Revival even though they were quite unable to inspire it. These nuclei are significantly under-researched, and the complex seems worth description, not because the poetic results are fully achieved but because contemplating the long run of time may make a true awareness of the present arrive more swiftly.

The whole project has taken place within the force field of re-assessment of the 1940s by James Keery, Andrew Crozier, Simon Jenner, and Nigel Wheale, and contact with them (and with Martin Seymour-Smith, who gave me first-hand information on a scene which he took in as a poetry-mad adolescent) made the whole enterprise of reconstruction seem credible.

I found poetry hard to grasp but have gathered knowledge to make it easier; by "construction" from puzzling and inexplicit signs, no doubt much of it misconstruction. This is not the history of poetic activity for which someone should find the "prominent books" of each year (from various bibliographies) and simply read through them. Against this excess of primary data, I can afford to be subjective in offering only momentary flashes, shot at horizontal sections of great interest. I do not give a continuous history of English cinema, politics, propaganda, imperial policy, religious affairs, or political protest, although all of these appear in the book. Printed sources do not secure the information on which I rely, which was acquired by flashes of intuition, over the last twenty-five years, while dealing with poets face to face, listening to them read their work, or looking at someone's personal, yet revealing, collection of books, or scanning the calculated fantasy of some publisher's blurb. The moment when you realise someone definitely isn't going to publish your poems, doesn't even like them, and regards them as naive, is especially full of insight. The explanations I write down are not of "secret codes" but of why one person thinks that an emotion makes it a bad poem, and why someone else thinks an idea makes it a bad poem.

The same poetological idea produces bad poems with one person and good ones with another. Political events, too, are ambiguous, never exhaustively to be judged and described. But I have noticed that what I write about this nebulosity is firm and definite. I think the answer is that I detest vagueness so much that I only ever write about moments that can be firmly defined, and in fact that I have seized these moments, and stored them up, over decades. This method produces a selective and idealised view, while meeting my criteria of good prose.

# The closing of the 1940s; and the prehistory of the underground

The end of the New Romantic style was dramatic, involving the going out of business of the magazines and publishers which were most dedicated to them; an informal but effective ban on the style by the editors of magazines which had formerly welcomed them; the decision of several publishers not to take any more books in this style. A purely conflict-oriented analysis is mistaken, since close scrutiny of the dates shows that the collapse of outlets occurred two years before the "Movement" arrived to make propaganda against them; and the decline of the wartime poetry boom was a broad economic phenomenon, due to a general decline of interest in culture as well as to cost inflation in the printing industry and to paper shortages. Wrey Gardiner's farewell note in the last issue of *Poetry Quarterly* (1952) is most interesting about these business problems.

The style purge of 1950–52 left a number of young poets high and dry. Although their productions of the 1940s had mostly been premature, daring, and underdeveloped, they were unable to get further books out during the 1950s. This created a split between official and unofficial poetry which is currently one of the main features of the scene. The private trajectory of those poets over the following forty years offers a window on public aesthetic, economic, and social-political structures. Even if we detest the Jacobite-style cult of the excluded rightful heirs, and we dislike the New Romantic style itself, we have to suspect that the inability of British poets to write for the market stems from a period of being cut off from it for simple material reasons, of publicity and distribution, and it is clear that a gap between the reading public and the best poets dominates the British scene.

It's hardly a coincidence that the Conservatives won three General Elections during the 1950s.

### The fate of the New Romantics

A while ago, I supposed that there was a whole body of suppressed and obscured work by the NRs, who, having been born in the 1920s, might have produced their mature works during the 1960s. This hypothesis was bound to survive until I had made contact with people adapted to resurrection, a kind of graveyard crew of book dealers, who could reveal otherwise; sadly, most of the "silenced" had simply stopped writing poetry. Glyn Jones has observed that two-thirds of the poets in the 1944 classic *Modern Welsh Poetry* had given it up. Peter Riley's coup in publishing a pamphlet by Dorian Cooke in the mid-nineties merely points to what didn't happen. There are no great books buried out in the desert. (James Keery claims exactly the opposite.)

Further, we have to recognise the small size of the achievement during the movement's heyday. I usually excuse this by reflecting that early excess is often followed by grand maturity; but I can't pretend that anthologies like *Lyra, the white horseman, A New Romantic Anthology*, are great books. Similarly, the prolific public output of Vernon Watkins and Henry Treece, who continued to be published by Faber (which only slowly moved away from being the chief New Romantic publisher), does not show poems we can praise and admire. At least the style survived in Wales.

Further, the NRs who became famous later on had not been at all eminent during the 1940s; Edwin Morgan and Christopher Middleton were not stars in the 1940s, although they were certainly producing in the fashionable style. Hendry's decision to issue *The Orchestral Mountain* straight away, in unrevised form, was a disaster which certainly influenced his fate of having to wait thirty-five years before his next book of poetry was published; it was a poem composed in 1947. Both books demand exception from the generalised condemnation of the style.

Further, the forties poets who went on writing mostly evolved far away from the forties style, which represents a sort of vote against it even by the people who owned it. This certainly applies to Middleton and Morgan. In fact, the anthologies and magazines of the time rolled up quite a few poets who didn't really fit into the period style but who benefited from the outlets.

Further, there is no geometry whereby we could map the new styles of the sixties onto the 1940s style. However, much the new generation disliked the aggressive and conservative cultural managers who had emerged in the 1950s, and who held all the jobs in the 1960s and 1970s, they weren't artistically close to the original victims of those managers, against whom they had campaigned. There are some interesting exceptions to this, which we will discuss later on.

Herbert Palmer's book *Post-Victorian Poetry* shows Sturge Moore, in the 1930s, complaining that he had spent forty years writing while no editor would take his poems. His brother was the Cambridge philosopher, G.E. Moore; his nephew, Nicholas Moore, also spent forty years writing poems which nobody wanted to publish. Was this the origin of the Cambridge School? T. Sturge did slightly better than that, since we have his Collected Poems, in two volumes; the anecdote may have been improved. We think of the Georgians as "low cultural capital", while Moore had "high cultural capital", but one of his long poems was in a Georgian Book. The generalisation, made by Peter Riley, is that up until 1960 poets who stopped being published also stopped writing; if Sturge Moore was an exception to that, it was presumably because he did have high cultural capital, and this armoured him against the opinions of mere editors. This is unfair, because we are implying that a poet working as a journalist in Newcastle, let's say, would have given up because he didn't have the same sociological self-confidence. Already in the 1920s, then, we can see reasons why people certified by the education system, and living in towns where they could gather with groups of equally stubborn, nonconformist, and self-validating people, were more likely to produce original poetry in the long term. The problem whose existence I have implied is that "official" poetry could not be good, nor good poetry be accepted straight away; this is a proposition false in many ways, at many points, but since the reader probably knows about celebrated poetry, we will not halt to prove how much of it, in the 1920s or the 1970s, is good.

The psychology of someone who writes poetry without expecting it to be available in the shops, read by the literary public, reviewed in the well-known literary magazines, etc., is quite different from someone who does have these expectations; it is unusual, perhaps partly paradoxical and founded on fantasies, and calls for explanations. Sacheverell Sitwell is another early example of a poet who withdrew; having been published in his teens (around 1917), famous in his twenties, he withdrew from publishing (perhaps on finding the response too lukewarm?)

but went on writing poetry for circulation among his friends (meantime writing rather a large number of prose books on art history). When a whole book was published for sale in 1973, he seemed like a creature from another millennium. I believe a gap of thirty-six years separates this volume from the last book in which he had included new poetry.

The phenomenon has been obscured by the common and unrelated role of the *soi-disant* genius. Herbert Palmer's book is full of his accounts of poets neglected in their day, not one of whom has been dusted off by posterity, while his central thesis is the worthlessness of TS Eliot and the illusory aesthetic values of his followers. In 1938 — as at other times — there was clearly a whole class of baffled and ignored would-be poets, generating unreadable verse and, in parallel, theories of cultural resentment and of future resurrection, in the transvaluation of all values. Certainly, no one could fault me for reading all the wholly obscure poets he praises, while anyone could blame me for not doing this work; critics are all, like me, afraid of wandering off into the desert to read dozens of volumes which, in the end, prove valueless. This slagheap of unreadable verse is what hides wonderful marginal poets from view. Small publishers do not equip their books with the legend "obscure but really boring", I don't think; no, all the books, some 2000 a year by now, sally forth with the legend "obscure but brilliant and neglected through a conspiracy of metropolitan taste", which consequently is the least credible claim. If I make it (about David Chaloner, Michael Haslam, Ralph Hawkins), how can I be credible? Behind this screen, mainstream editors publish abject and banal books, denounce everything they haven't read, and get away with it. This set-up is remarkably stable.

The question of authenticity comes up throughout, not just as the missing quality which makes such a large part of the poetry audience reject the mainstream but also, incompatibly, as the quality which the mainstream finds missing from "reflexive" or "original" poetry, which they do not tolerate. The concept derives from a finite set of shared symbolic sets, irresistibly convergent for some (so that deviation is inauthenticity) and for others restrictive, so that the measure of poetic virtue is the extent to which a poet modifies these sets. Authenticity seems to be caught up with the area closest to, on, and within the body, space which is very densely banded with emotional distinctions. Poetry (it seems) differs from prose from being closer in, and so more affected by the rules of subjective space, than prose; this intimacy makes the issue of trust urgent. Trust is something we decide, in this region, with life-saving quickness, and without accountability, on the basis of cultural signals (identified with authenticity by a convention) or a pre-rational reading of character.

The forerunners of the underground poetry scene are numerous, if not very similar to it. The word "press" properly signifies someone who has a press and prints books themselves, an offshoot of the arts and crafts movement; it is misapplied to small publishers. A concern with printing goes back to Robert Bridges, who investigated disused print-faces and raised the standards of the time; some of his typefaces were adopted by the Oxford University Press, which is the accolade.

An angle on minority publishing in the early twentieth century is supplied by Timothy D'Arch Smith's fascinating *Books of the Beast*. Smith (in partnership with Jean Overton Fuller) made a living selling occult books to moneyed rock stars, but obtaining them from the private collections of aged occultists, with whom he was on friendly terms. The cross-connection between Jimmy Page, Fuller, Florence Farr, Yeats (a fellow-member of the Golden Dawn with Farr) and Robert Bridges (depicted with Farr, playing a psaltery, while discussing the lack of oral quality of most English verse) is dazzling, perhaps too astonishing to contain much positive information. So far as I know, Page has never played a psaltery. The books were privately published, often in rather opulent fashion, at the time and circulated among some secretive network of cognoscenti. They combined elements, significant in the prehistory of the small press, of heresy, pornography, bizarre learning, and recreational drugs. All of these were to stride to centre stage in the 1960s, and it was some of the most recondite elements of English "high culture" which the new pop culture took on; the Golden Dawn had much more appeal than, say, EM Forster and Somerset Maugham. D'Arch Smith and Fuller published poems by Peter Redgrove at one point. Another occult bookseller called Iain Sinclair appears in this book in a different role.

One cannot read D'Arch Smith's book without realising that occultism overlapped with a cultured gay underworld, whose pursuit of symbolic experience was compulsive and sophisticated. Here, to publish without the full glare of publicity offered security from prosecution, rather than oppression, and the motivation of those interested to track down the books, and pay over the odds for them, was ardent.

The parochial structure of the Church of England implied the dispersion of the graduate intellectuals to every part of the country, with obligations to a district, while its weak disciplinary powers allowed great latitude to individual priests, although of course by eccentricity they forfeited chances of promotion, and their indemnity from punishment only held good so long as their ideas were marked, in special ways, as not being urgent claims to power (and therefore as merely "eccentric"). Vicars in remote parishes studied local antiquities or formed local societies of the curious; the publications were guaranteed small circulation, and the business practices adapted to this were appropriate to small-circulation poetry. The segment of British literature, which is neither populist nor authorised and metropolitan, has been wide for a long time, and this tended to make writing unpopular poetry credible and even rather prestigious as a way of life. The public has had difficulty realising that there are non-mainstream poets who are also not "local" and committed to parish history.

None of these streams had much influence on the unofficial poetry world, which had its own programme. However, they probably did provide practical models for producing and distributing publications for specialised markets and moral ones for saying "no!". The question of why someone would decline to adapt their work to the norms of the day cannot be exactly answered, although we can point to analogies which may have been persuasive. The question of why someone would continue to write, although refused conventional publication, is more acute, especially when it seems that there was a shift around 1960, and that rejected poets before that generally stopped writing. They accepted the rejection of their work as a sign that they were failures; they accepted the response of the "front line" of editors as an unbiased test of the response of readers; they saw being adapted to the market as the index of artistic skill. Probably, they regarded what was personal to them as not being of public interest and they saw themselves as eccentric and wrong in some way. The switch of position is often attributed to Roy Fisher, and to Migrant Press, run by Michael Shayer and Gael Turnbull; and to the moment of 1959, when a rash of small magazines of unorthodox investment sprang up. Once the magazines exist, eccentric poems can reach their reader, and the "negative pressure" around the poet is replaced by a positive one, however sparse or low impact. The exit from the mainstream (as represented by the Poetry Society, the Third Programme, the *Times Literary Supplement*, Faber and Faber, etc.) which took place during the 1960s was based on a doctrine of linguistic purity which was also ethical purity. It implicitly defined what was being left behind as contaminated. But this perception was certainly not shared by the staff of the institutions or by the majority of poetry readers. This rejection, by a segment of British poets, of the known literary outlets in which the audience would have been able to find them, was not well defined or accompanied by a manifesto. The salient fact is the unwillingness of the editors in-post to publish unconventional poetry, and this on its own accounts for the delayed fame of, for example, JH Prynne, Roy Fisher, Andrew Crozier or John Riley. Something much less conscious and clear is why the poets (the ones who later appeared in *A Various Art*) did not retool their styles to make them acceptable. I think the answer would be in a general erosion of prestige of "official" British poetry, due (for one thing) to the non-emergence of any new talent of any significance since Dylan Thomas, some thirty years earlier. The attraction of the Grosseteste poets to American poetry (or *an* American poetry, for example, that of *Black Mountain Review*, the New York School, and the San Francisco school) is one factor among many. The decision to innovate perhaps does not need much puzzling over, and it is the conservative bias of editors which calls for research.

Since 1965, or soon after, there has been a "parallel system" which young poets could admire and seek to join without undergoing crisis and isolation.

We have said that personal style is related to political dissidence and to autonomy. This is a result: we are now going to try and reconstruct the process by which it came to be.

We address the stage when someone is developing both their style, their understanding of the cultural field, and their understanding of their own place in the market. Advice is offered by people who are de facto authority figures. It takes the form of a "no" along with instructions about modifying the product to make it a "yes". The rejected poet (one of several thousand rejected poets in any year) has the choice either of seizing on the features of their style which the managers object to, and developing them to the maximum, breaking through the limits of transgression to reach a new logic, or of losing the features which distinguish them from the standard product, lowering the stakes, and becoming a mainstream poet.

It seems to me that this process takes place largely by proxies: while you are searching for a place, every judgment made by official critics seems personal to you. It either offers a way of changing, or a reason for rejecting your work. Anthologies are turned into battlegrounds where currents of compliance and defiance fight it out. Unconventional poets are turned into heroes because they do not obey the rules laid down by cultural managers. Projective? Yes—but without projection no symbol has any value.

When someone rejects your work, or gives you advice about making it better, this divides aesthetic values into two groups: A, the ones you hold (which you are being told to lose), and B, the ones you do not hold (which you are being told to acquire). The response you make, then, is likely to be influenced by your attitude towards authority. The legitimacy of the conventional is at stake with every line you try to compose. Someone seized by the affect of revolt will emphasize group A and throw away group B. This is where stylistic values become politicised. Because the package of conventional instructions, in around 1960, included "don't think your feelings are important. Don't put ideas in poems. Don't challenge the political system. Be brief. Don't draw attention to yourself. Don't write about conflict. Don't use free verse. Don't be paradoxical", the whole package of moves which violated these instructions came to symbolise daring and independence, and also to symbolise left-wing and libertarian commitments.

My assumption is that this process, from starting to write to publishing a first book, is passionate and uncertain, traumatic and dramatic. This stage is rich in emotions and leaves a permanent trace: a psychic organ, a piece of virtual physiology, which in future makes the judgments about poetic value.

It produces a poet's professional conscience, their awareness of their own limits, their grasp of the reader's limits and possibilities, and their image of themselves as a writer. That is, its features become the landscape, permanent for good or bad. The movement between in and out draws the line which defines the edge of the work and so its shape. The drama of struggling for originality and comprehensibility is repeated every time you start a new poem. Growth is the richest of experiences and is almost inseparable from conflict with authority.

People sometimes expect rejected poets to be unconventional. Study of unsold typescripts, or of little magazines, suggests the opposite: most unpublished or semi-published poets are wholly conventional. Successful mainstream poets are much better worked out than the average amateur. However, within this invisible sector are a certain number of radically original poets. To be fair to the managers, we have to be clear that original poets mature late. That is, when they become famous at the age of 50, they may only have reached a full understanding of their own stylistic space at the age of thirty. There is a specific kind of poem (we should recognise its flavour) of unrealised ambition, written somewhere along the curve, maybe on a sharp upward turn, but not retrievable, fully shaped, or gratifying. Editors should be sensitive about this.

Is rejection part of the growth process? Well, I think it would be dishonest to deny this. The stage of development seems to me much longer than poets care to admit, and the concept of unique complexity (into which no one else has insight), to be rare or tendentious. I think poets need much more tuition and criticism; this is missing because the funds aren't there.

Reaching maturity suggests calm, stability, and security, but of course you can never reach this as a poet when aesthetics differ so much: you can always be confronted by people who vocally reject your works, want to revoke your decisions, and deny your talent. If you comply with one group, you alienate several others.

This process of conflict within the literary world produces emotions which load and overload symbols. Conflict and frustration thus produce a symbolic instrument: it is easy to form political statements with it. This is the "overspill" by which stylistic radicalism, with its anti-authoritarian charge, is so good at expressing radical political dissidence. This is also why conservative critics always define stylistic innovation as "meaningless": they know very well what it means; it makes them angry because it's against them. This surreptitious revenge is as common today as it was in 1960.

Fairly obviously, editors get attacked much more than poets. They are attacked by everyone they turn down. It is difficult to question all accepted values while clinging to your own values as solid gold. There is, then, a drift towards staidness and security by editors and managers, an unconscious tendency to form a poetic Right as a front against the poetic Left of the excluded.

Periods of social unrest also produce artistic innovation. The legitimacy of received ideas in literature dips sharply when moral and political authority is being challenged. It seems that the credibility of the poetic authorities dipped catastrophically in the 1960s and has never really regained the lost ground.

The objection to conventional outlets is that they force you to write in a standard way, but brief investigation will also show that people choose exotic ways of writing in order to protest against the conventional outlets. We see here a tangled connection between reflexivity, marginality, personalism, and the Cold War. Differentiation is a form of competition between ambitious young poets, who have no honours, yet, to distinguish them, and reflexivity is the faculty which permits this differentiation to take place. Mainstream poets must continually revise their poems to make them less intelligent and less distinctive. Underground poets can't bear to do this. Perhaps this is a weakness?

*Occlusion in Scotland*

Around 1948 an amazing series of advanced books of poetry were published in Scotland, but over the next twenty years none of the poets had a successful career, and the degree of their public obscurity reveals the fearful extent of the problems in the world of Scottish poetry. Hamish Henderson published *Elegies for the dead in Cyrenaica* but never published another book of poetry. TS Law published *Whit Time i the Day* but didn't get another book out until 1983. George Campbell Hay published *The Wind Across Loch Fyne*, but never published a second book in English (or Scots), although he did publish to a very limited extent in Gaelic. Joseph Macleod, from a different generation (his first book came out in 1930), did manage to release a book in 1953 but that was his last for twenty years. Douglas Young published *Auntran Blads* in 1946, followed by *Selected Poems* in 1948, but then no more books of poetry until after his death in 1973; his Collected Poems add little to what was available in 1948. Sydney Goodsir Smith is the exception to the pattern; after his first book in 1951, he did stay in the public eye and did go on publishing. Going back a bit, James Findlay Hendry published books in 1942 and 1943, but *Marimarusa*, composed in 1947, had to wait until 1978 for publication. WS Graham also beat the pattern somewhat; having got out three books during the 1940s (including *The White Threshold*, 1949), he was allowed to release another in 1955, although he then had a fifteen-year gap before the follow-up. Sorley MacLean doesn't really fit the pattern, since he was fully developed at the time of the Spanish Civil War, and although it's true that the poetry he wrote in the late 1930s and early 1940s had to wait more than thirty years before being published. All in all, the 1950s were a terrible period.

*The near and the far in Scots poetry*

One question of fact which published accounts seem very careful to avoid is about the extent of the Synthetic Scots Movement; when I was eighteen, it seemed like a whole movement with many members, a vital intellectual agenda, and a claim to predict and control literary history, but longer experience suggested that the movement consisted largely of smoke and wind, overawing its enemies by a series of brilliant feints behind which hid nothing. A movement sounds so imposing, doesn't it?

*The closing of the 1940s; and the prehistory of the underground* [11]

We're a movement and you're just a poet. If there is no anthology of this movement, the reason is perhaps that it didn't have enough members to fill one; its poems were as theoretical as its ideas. I can say now that

(a) Douglas Young and Sydney Goodsir Smith were Synthetic Scots poets who also reached artistic heights;
(b) they were probably not doing this before 1938, and MacDiarmid was the only Synthetic Scots poet from the launch of the movement around 1925 to that time;
(c) William Jeffrey also wrote a few poems in the style in the late 1930s (a dozen in *Sea-Glimmer* and two more in *Selected Poems*);
(d) I am not sure if Tom Scott can be considered as a Synthetic Scots poet; he was writing in the 1940s;
(e) Maurice Lindsay was a convert to the movement around 1946; Joseph Macleod wrote a few poems in a subdued Synthetic Scots in 1946 (at the first Edinburgh Festival); George Campbell Hay wrote a few poems in the 1940s in a style which is at least parallel to the Synthetic style;
(f) Alastair Mackie was a convert to the style in around 1953, although unpublished until much later;
(g) in the 1970s, Walter Perrie wrote poems in what can probably be considered as Synthetic Scots;
(h) in the early 1980s, Robert Crawford, WN Herbert, and David Kinloch began writing poetry in what is almost certainly Synthetic Scots (Kinloch is William Jeffrey's grandson);
(i) MacDiarmid stopped writing poems in Scots in 1938 or 1939. He wrote a few short poems in Scots many years later, in the 1960s.

We need to stress the difference between Synthetic Scots and everyday spoken Scots, because it is easy for foreign observers to assume that all poetry written in Scots is derived from MacDiarmid's theories simply because they find it hard to understand. The propaganda of the movement persistently cites as evidence of its own success poets (such as Albert Mackie or William Soutar) who visibly rejected its ideals. Granted these points (a—i), we can conclude that

> Synthetic Scots is marginal to the writing of poetry in Scots vernacular in general;
> 
> MacDiarmid was too overbearing and put most people off from joining a movement which obviously "belonged" to him and of which he was *Duce*; the movement flourished after he had moved away from it;
> 
> artistically, the Synthetic Scots poets play a role far larger than their scant numbers would suggest. They have been an elite group and exist, as their founder intended, as part of world culture. One does not need to apologize for them.

By my count, most of the poets listed above did not speak Scots as their mother tongue; they belonged to an Anglicised middle class and wrote Scots almost as a foreign language. (This claim refers to: Jeffrey, Goodsir Smith, Crawford, Campbell Hay, Macleod, Lindsay and Kinloch.) Certain ideas exercised a hypnotic and unnatural suggestive influence over them which can also affect the reader. The magnetic affect of Synthetic Scots is related to the extreme difficulty of writing it, which only seems to be possible in short spurts; Perrie, Herbert, and Crawford seem to have given up writing in Scots, while Mackie gave it up several times. Campbell Hay wrote most of his poetry in Gaelic (which he learnt as a teenager).

These statements may be incorrect, since I have had some difficulty piecing together the evidence, and the guiding literature is deliberately inaccurate.

Since the difference between synthetic and unmodified vernacular Scots relates to items of lexicon, rather than to higher linguistic structures, the separation between the two is statistical; for example, in a Synthetic Scots sentence of twelve words, ten of the words may be ordinary spoken Scots, and one could, stretching a point to absurdity, claim that only the exotic words were Synthetic. However, for a well-informed reader, the separation is rather clear and unambiguous. The lexical differences correlate with differences of tone, reference, and subject matter, which in fact demand the wider vocabulary; the modern style in poetry cannot be used in Scots unless one consents to use words which are not the everyday coin of Scots-speaking communities. This is true because Scottish speakers have, since the late sixteenth century, used English for the prestigious semantic fields; one cannot write about theology in Scots, because the Church of Scotland has used the King James Bible and the English tongue; if however one translates the needed words into Scots (saying "the laird" for "the LORD" would be a terrible solecism) one is already using Synthetic Scots, and what one said would have a wholly uncolloquial ring. The transitions by which, for example, Scottish lawyers came (by 1820?) to discuss Scots law in Scottish law courts in English, are chronologically complex, although all follow a constant pattern.

MacDiarmid was an astute polemicist, successfully disguising from the literary world that the vast majority of poets writing Scots had no interest in his ideas and even disliked them. Consider Albert Mackie (1904–?)

> Alba was there in smilin cheeks
> And poored-oot pennies o' the puir,
> In moist-nebbed bairns wi'shinin breeks
> And bare-shanked wee-things on the flair:
>
> In gnurly men wi'rowed sark-sleeves,
> Smokin on balconies at their doors,
> Cuttin black baccy in their nieves,
> And lauchin whiles wi'lusty roars[.]

Again:

> My ain wee doggie-dainty FLINC:
> I miss ye mair than folk would think,
> For aye ye were a heartsome link
> Wi' happy hours
> In woodlands spent, whar rabbits jink
> Mang bushy bowers.

This is by Pittendrigh MacGillivray (1856–1938), a hater of MacDiarmid. Such Lallans poetry was wholly non-synthetic; Synthetic Scots virtually vanished during the 1950s.

I used the phrase *modern style* but this conceals quite a few problems. Modernity in 1905 could mean writing like Kipling: colloquial, lower-class in subject matter, closely tied to work and physical experiences, narrative, recitable. This vein has been popular in Scottish poetry ever since then. Again, many people think that the "modern" today is pop culture, so that Liz Lochhead is modern. The word needs a closer definition, and I would suggest *intellectual, inquiring,* and *striving to be original* as essential qualities. Rejecting ordinary experience and recording extraordinary experience obviously have implications for subject matter, potential audience, and emotional quality; they prevent sympathetic circularity and affirmative culture. They have implications, more than anything else, for vocabulary. Wider choice in the minimal units correlates, I would argue, with even wider choice in the construction of phrases, lines, sentences, etc.; someone like Liz Lochhead writes like someone chatting in the checkout queue at the supermarket. In fact, the wish to write lines never heard in the supermarket correlates entirely with the wish to use lexical items never heard in the supermarket. This is why vernacular, or realist, Scots has poetic implications as well as merely lexical ones. MacDiarmid can hardly be said to have won: the cheerful daily poetry of Liz Lochhead or Jackie Kay is far closer to Albert Mackie.

The occlusion probably had quite different motives in Wales, Scotland, and England, but the downward curves in the three countries show a very similar shape. Perhaps it's fairer to emphasize, instead, the positive quality of the 1940s: war made the population more prone to exaltation, to longing for eternal values, to high-flown language, and to collective rituals crossing class boundaries. Poetry could satisfy these desires and was less effective in a period of peacetime reconstruction and then of revived consumerism.

# Reflexivity and sensitivity

Poets such as Terence Tiller, Alan Ross, and FT Prince stand as representatives of the positive potential of British poetry in the 1950s, while the living death of The Movement was occupying the public sphere. It is significant that none of them appeared in Lucie-Smith's anthology of *British Poetry Since 1945*. They also represent the potentiality of a manner which has not abandoned syntax and verse movement, or the lyrical speaking subject; a humanism surviving amid alienation and cynical shock effects. They seem to have largely been written out of the record; but after all they are some of the counter-evidence which any protagonist of the avant-garde would have to deal with in a debate on poetics. The avant-garde does not have a monopoly of intelligence: the forward movement of intelligence in verse can also be claimed by a different strand, of post-Metaphysical, academic, logical, and oratorical poets, of whom Auden, Empson, Terence Tiller, and Geoffrey Hill are examples. Conversely, the more complex poetry of the seventies and later decades does not have unthinkingly to be assigned to the avant-garde tradition, but can also be looked for in this poetic line, mediating the influence of great thinking and arguing poets of the past, such as Donne, Milton, or Wordsworth. One can divide modern poetry, not only into mainstream and experimental but into intelligent and naïve.

Terence Tiller (1916–88)
*Poems* (1941); *The Inward Animal* (1943); *Unarm, Eros* (1947); *Reading a Medal* (1957); *Notes for a Myth* (1968); *The Singing Mesh* (1979)

A brainy boy of low social origins, Tiller went to Cambridge to study History, and put his development as a writer before anything else. He went to Cairo to teach, before the war, and spent the war there. The English-language university at Cairo was part of a Foreign Office attempt to draw the Egyptian families of landowners and notables, i.e. the political class, into the British ambit, and so away from the Italian, French, Russian, or indeed Egyptian, ambit; it anticipated later CIA forays into culture (and universities of the Middle East). As GS Fraser remarked in 1944, poets resident in the Near East did not pick up the perfervid New Romanticism which spread in Britain but practised a kind of classicism. He was published in the Middle East magazine *Personal Landscape* and put out a series of books through the Hogarth Press, which implies John Lehmann. He was one of very few survivors of the 1940s who went on publishing, but he did not then take-off into a higher level, a more autonomous and exalted work; his achievement is puzzlingly complete in those wartime poems. We can detect, what is not quite there, a shadow of a subsuming myth or psychodrama, in the heading to the last section of *Notes for a Myth* and the preface to *The Inward Animal*; the latter claims an overall plot to the book, which is, I submit, not there. The wish to write public poetry, raised to the level of myth, emptied of self and at a profound level of the psyche, is not carried out in his work. Instead, his reputation vanished after the fifties, just as his publications became sparse. He worked for the BBC for many years, producing programmes or writing radio plays.

Few poets could have less of a biographical myth. (He is mysteriously missing from one series of Middle Eastern Theatre anthologies, retrospective and of the time; due to some vagary of factions, scarcely unfamiliar to a student of poetry. His absence from other anthologies presumably follows similar political fault lines.) His work has instead a considerable cunning, obliquity, and grace. He represents one of the currents of English-language poetry which ignored modernism but pursued other poetic lines (the seventeenth century, in this case) without pastiche and without forfeiting intelligence. It is easy to rush into a room waving the merits of modernity about one's head and be stopped short on finding that poems by Tiller, FT Prince, or Geoffrey Hill, are better and more complex than the modernist ones. Perhaps the solution to the crisis in which we are all plunged does not lie in dutiful modernism but in some stylistic mix more exacting and difficult to invent. He is missing from all the landmark anthologies of the last fifty years, although not from Stephen Spender's pamphlet *Poetry since 1939*, which is what incited me to read him. Here is what Spender says:

## Reflexivity and sensitivity [17]

"Two young poets of promise are Terence Tiller and GS Fraser. Both of these poets share the tendency which seems almost inevitably associated with the universities of Oxford and Cambridge. They are clear, transparent, intellectual poets writing from their heads rather than from their hearts or their bodies, analysing their passions and conscious of many difficulties in problems of sex and life. Their obscurity, unlike that of the poets who are followers of Dylan Thomas, comes from a too great intellectualisation, a too minute pursuit of their own sensitive reactions, their own inner complication and subtle ideas."

This is upsetting, because it points to a progression away from introversion, which did away with all fine distinctions and ignored all the problems; surely this kind of male interrogation of the emotions represents a sexual conscience and would have been a preparation for a well-founded reply to feminism, when that came along, rather than hostility, denial, incomprehension, blank silence, etc. English poetry of the mid-century was remarkable for its distaste for exploring feelings, and the revival of poetry seems likely to come from a return to emotional self-interrogation which is precise, tender, and optimistic, free from a kind of comic cynicism or blenching adornoesque despair. After all, if you are going to write subtle poetry you have to refine your coarse emotional reactions first. Tiller seems to have devoted much energy to writing poetry which was sexy and romantic at the same time:

> Lithe as fire, lithe as the tongues of the blown tree
> delicate as the lilacs the feather-boned-and-breasted:
> loosen as they do, unbound in the soft of the breeze,
> nets for its ghostly flesh, and their sweet cups tasted.
>
> ('Spring Ceremonies' from *Notes for a Myth*)

Analysis of the words *loosen* and *cups* suggests an erotic sense which is modulated to evoke attention, tenderness, and tranquility. Compare

> Moon...
>       darken her eyes and hair,
> darken the roses upon mouth and breast,
> but wake her skin with silver: and for him,
> bathe his unfolded strength and ardency
> in the live ichors of your floods, that he
> may wield a body built in every limb
> as if of seraphim.
>
> (from 'Prothalamion' from *Notes for a Myth*)

The archaisms (*that he may, ichor*) grate, but surely this is a balanced and collected way of writing about sexuality, in an era of low-affect, didactic, prurient, or touristic writing about the subject. One would wish to take part in such a scene. His poetry is contained and sustained, never putting a foot wrong. Its voice is sensitive, fastidious, angst ridden, serious, weighted and balanced. It is decentralised: the figure of exile, in the Egyptian poems, is typical, he writes about the destiny of individuals, unable to build the City but able to make each other happy if they are emotionally pure and honest. His idea of love is complicated, but not pessimistic. The word "sex" is frequent in his poems of the forties. He seems to have concentrated on the long cadence: poems animated by a rhythm so deep that it sustains the movement for several pages. As in a building, large scale calls for lightness of construction; melodramatic gestures are impossible. A more complicated verbal task involves our attention more profoundly. It also serves, perhaps, to get beyond the unsubtlety of existing words for emotions and explore the ambiguity and changeability of real-life emotions. Although Spender says that Fraser and Tiller were over-complicated, it seems plausible to me that they could have pushed this complexity much further; this would have involved the disruption of the containing boundaries that pass for elegance in English verse, but might have led English verse into the future. What if the reader had trusted and followed Tiller, in pushing out the boundaries of sensitivity, and thus changing; following also Charles Madge and WS Graham; would this reader not have been ready to read and understand the new poetry of the 1960s, for example Roy Fisher and JH Prynne? Tiller was just the opposite of the New Romantics, and his notes on poetic technique, published in *Personal Landscape*, are single-mindedly a refutation of the NR position.

One of the duties of poetry is to find delightful and persuasive ways of saying I love you, because people go to poetry for fine language and that is the most difficult occasion for fine language. It is not impossible that the topic of character entered Western poetry because of protracted uncertainty and interrogation of what exactly the feeling called love is, under this pressure to write love poetry which was true and beautiful. It might be that the personality of the male poet has pervaded the poem for the last four centuries, not as an objective psychological project but as a reverberation from the declaration of love, saturated in intents of self-adornment; and that shifts in the understanding of love would make this personality project disappear from the stage, its task complete.

## Reflexivity and sensitivity

A treatment of the theme of reflexivity in modern poetry can hardly start elsewhere than with Tiller's poems on mirrors, in *The Inward Animal* (1943). There are four of them. The visual event, catching the speaker's appearance in glass, is a temporary equivalent (not quite paradox, not quite allegory) for self-consciousness in general. The mirrors are an example of a limited stimulus field, held to be useful in constructing works of art, as remarked by Victor Turner and by Christopher Middleton in "Notes on a Viking Prow". In "Egyptian restaurant", the poet drops a stone into the reflection (perhaps in a pool? or simply in imagination?) which is itself reflected in the mirrors (which we imagine surrounding the room), to show "the circling crowd of jewelled ghostly Us." Logically, he should say "Uses". The room is full of noise, glare, and rushing activity; the waiters "are lost in brightness, fall in tiny pieces". One of them clutches the last malaise, "the knowledge that he is" and his sadness is reflected in the mirrors. The empty reflections are, then, more beautiful than the real human; but why? because of colonial oppression? or simply because of human frailty? In "Street Scene", the next poem, the shop windows show "a thousand simpering yous", just like the us-es. The displays and the crowds are all projections of the basic "you". A statue in the next square remains constant although the light shifts (so is not a reflection); the speaker now describes a "you" (presumably a loved person?), who appears in many images in his inner street of windows; but is unstill. The last turn is unclear but presumably points both to the inadequacy of observation to the person being observed and to the inconstancy of the observer; the poem is less afraid than "Egyptian Restaurant" but is still oscillating: the oscillations may offer the possibility of being more adequate in relationships. In "Elegy II: Shop Window" there is no mirror imagery, but the theme is incommunicability, setting out from "the confused magnificence of love". We (the human subject in general?) "build the mosaic of a filtered world", i.e. build a model of something complex from small pieces of information, hindered by the limits of our perceptual equipment. The glass of the "mosaic" is a link to the mirror imagery of other poems. We protect ourselves from the excess wildness and roaring of the outside world. Poets tell lies: that is, I suppose, artistic beauty takes these filters and barriers further. In "Piscine" (swimming pool) both water and limbs have lost their reality, dissolved into each other. Two (facing) mirrors reflect each other infinitely; in a phrase of difficult optical interpretation, "touching or breaking planes" are bound to "single selves" or to mosaics. The scene seems to have shifted here, with the word "selves" towards the theme of mutual understanding: the self is isolated or else passive in a terrifying stretto of mutual reflection and re-reflection. In the last stanza, the speaker appears physically, floating in the swimming pool and watching a "luscious" diver whose dive breaks the "infinite imagined depth" of air and water. The reflected image is a symbol for self-consciousness, with the implication that the action of self-consciousness is to check and correct behaviour. The serially repeated images are the slight variants on the basic act, which offer the possibility of change, and which resemble the *fins écarts* which Bourdieu identified as typical of bourgeois cultural preferences. The use of reflections disqualifies automatic, inflexible, and instinctive behaviour and promises a way out of compulsive drives; it was unacceptable to the New Romantics who are in fact promising just the reverse. The resistance to Tiller (and the latest book on the Egyptian scene of the 1940s simply uses him as a foil whose blunders show up the brilliance of Keith Douglas and Lawrence Durrell) has complained about his intellectuality; but the de-emphasising of gratification and instinct in his account of love can be read quite differently, as a recognition of the difficulty of knowing a woman (as opposed to just having sex with her), and of the work that has to be done to unlearn drive-controlled and selfish behaviour patterns. The "inward animal", as the Foreword explains, is the new life, or new living person, brought forth through pain and difficulty. The intelligence is part of a transformatory project; the book is about the "impact of strangeness" which destroys a "customary self". This anticipates the critique of (naive) awareness of a later decade. What people expect of a poet is sensitivity, and this draws our attention. The word *sense* means touch and this can only refer to the skin. When we refer to the responsiveness of tracts of skin, the sexual resonance is obvious. The sensitivity of poets is a promise of delicacy, applied as much to the literal tracts of skin as to the virtual area of emotional vulnerability and responsiveness, which becomes much larger in moments of intimacy, which requires so much protection, and which is so precious to us. It is the charge of his images of moonlight, petals, and water.

So it seems that reflexivity and finesse could be symbolic allusions to sexual sensitivity, and that the famous missing love poetry could be found in this shifted form, wrapped in the metaphorical and oblique as its vulnerable nature demands. Further, that the self-questioning and rapid movement of philosophical poetry could be allusions to virtues in a relationship, where someone has mastery over their primitive and selfish drives, and complies with the other's wishes rather than asserting their own programmes. No wonder he hated the New Romantic poetry in which subjectivity was blind and incapable of learning.

Tiller's self-doubt not only anticipates the claims of feminism, as they emerged in the 1970s, but also supports them in the assertion that there was a gap between the complexity of modern life and the simplicity of men. He cannot rescue the honour of English poetry, since after all he was set aside by the makers of opinion, but surely he points ahead to a whole strand of 1960s poetry which was reflexive and self-critical and preferred the fine to the gross. The stress on the limits of the observer starts to dissolve the captured reality caught in realism and points forward to the interest in epistemology and phenomenology which took off in the 1960s. Tiller's preoccupation with mirrors is comparable to Madge's concern with the disengagement of 3-D vision from the 2-D image offered by the eyes, and both anticipate the concern with light which appears in poets like David Chaloner and Denise Riley.

## The Grosseteste-Ferry school, a table

### Key dates
late 1950s enthusiasm for Pound among some Cambridge students (Prynne, Langley, J Riley, etc.)
1959 first issue of *Migrant* magazine
1960 *City*, by Roy Fisher, from Migrant Press; the first modern book of English poetry
1963? Prynne's visit to the USA and friendship with Charles Olson and Ed Dorn
1964 first issue of *Resuscitator*; first identifiable magazine of the school
1968 student revolts; peak of the Counter-Culture
1969 publication of *The White Stones*
1971? reduction of intensity of interaction of the poets; stabilisation of styles
1973-5 general collapse of counter-cultural optimism. closing-in of boundaries.
1982 start of monumental and fastidious series of Collected Poems from Allardyce, Barnett

### Some anthologies
*the new british poetry, Conductors of Chaos*

### Magazines
*Resuscitator, The English Intelligencer, Grosseteste Review, Poetry Review* (in Mottram's editorship), *Ochre, Perfect Bound, The Blue Room, Equofinality, constant red/ mingled damask*

### Some publishers
Grosseteste Press, Ferry Press, Allardyce Barnett, Paladin, Equipage, Reality Studios

### Some poets other than those in *A Various Art*
RF Langley, John Temple, Nigel Wheale, Barry MacSweeney, Wendy Mulford, Rod Mengham, Denise Riley, Martin Thom, Michael Haslam, Grace Lake, Tom Lowenstein, Geoffrey Ward, John Wilkinson

### Some key American sources
George Oppen, Carl Rakosi, Charles Olson, Ed Dorn, John Ashbery, Frank O'Hara

# *A Various Art and the Cambridge Leisure Centre*

### What happened in British poetry in the 22s?

Geoffrey Moore's British Council pamphlet on *British Poetry Now*, for 1957, says that "For ten years after the war, British poetry seemed to be dead on its feet.": a remarkable statement for an official publication of the body engaged in promoting British culture but not necessarily an intemperate or out-of-date one. Surely the era where Kingsley Amis, Donald Davie or Philip Larkin could achieve national eminence has something of the cadaver and of blue-black skin tones about it. This confusion about semantics and self-presentation was the fore-shock of a whole new social order, brewed by working-class prosperity and mass higher education, and exploding onto the world scene in the 1960s. Eric Clapton, Eduardo Paolozzi, the New Left, the mini-skirt, Nicholas Roeg, John James, JH Prynne: we are talking about a quantitative and qualitative breakthrough, and the historian is permitted a modest pride. Görtschacher identifies 1959 as the year of take-off: in that year, a huge lump of chaos fell to earth and what was alive died or vanished. Relevantly or not, the poetic establishment in 1958 was dominated by Oxford graduates.

Life has been hard on successive waves of poets who believed, before the 1960s, that they were demotic, non-moralistic, empirical, technophile, modern, etc. The conservative 1950s deserve some credit for having generated, if only by pent up rebellion and loss of self-confidence, the radical sixties and the start in growth of the universities.

In the early sixties, the paranoid theme (sketched by Moore) was popular; British poetry was obviously dead but what was new was a joyful optimism, a confidence that a new start was possible and that

[23]

those present in this room including me are going to get it under way. Americanism is the starting-point for the renewal of 1959, or of 1965, or whenever it was. Outbreaks can be traced, sometimes, to individual teachers, such as Tomlinson at Bristol, who were au fait with the most advanced US poetry. The map of British poetic factions was partly a result of which American models they had chosen to follow. There is a whole theology around this, which I find fatiguing, but let's just note that the stylistic scatter between Ginsberg, Zukofsky, Stevens, Olson, Ashbery or O'Hara produced a whole geography as it re-scattered at the English end. American poetry post the 1950s hasn't had the same impact at all. The trip to the USA became an essential; Andrew Crozier went, in about 1964, to Buffalo, and rediscovered Carl Rakosi and persuaded him to come back to poetry; Prynne went to the USA too, hung out with Olson and Ed Dorn, and revolutionised his style. There was a touch of the laying on of hands about avant-garde poetry at that time, due I think to the extreme scarcity of books and information; if you decide that the official books are talking death, you try to find the True Tradition vested in living people, they become gurus until their lesson has been imparted, and many misrecognitions can occur. Some people decided *they* were gurus and this caused damage. This near-Gnostic True Tradition fantasy inspired the whole small press world of the sixties and seventies. This world had few products more eminent than *Grosseteste Review* (1967–84), the creation of Tim Longville and John Riley. This began essentially as an English Objectivist magazine, gazing at the USA, and gradually became devoted to something much more local, unidentifiable, and unexpected, something which hadn't really existed in 1967 and sometimes called the Cambridge Leisure Centre, although that isn't very appropriate, and "English Objectivism" isn't wholly descriptive either. Most readers will know this group through *A Various Art* (1987, edited by Longville and by Andrew Crozier, the publisher of Ferry Press books, who had co-edited *The English Intelligencer* with Peter Riley), which is useful and widely available. It includes poems by Longville, Crozier, JH Prynne, Roy Fisher, John Seed, John Hall, Anthony Barnett, Andrew Crozier, John James, Douglas Oliver, Peter Philpott, John Riley, David Chaloner, Veronica Forrest-Thomson, Nick Totton, Ralph Hawkins, Iain Sinclair, and Peter Riley. The anthology represents a Timenow of about 1975. This is the British response to the generation of American poets who included Olson, O'Hara, Ashbery, John Wieners and Dorn, as well as to Carl Rakosi and George Oppen, the generation of 1931.

## A Various Art and the Cambridge Leisure Centre

The appearance of *A Various Art* created, although slowly, a considerable stir in English poetic circles. It was the acceptable face of the underground. It gave the lie to the mainstream myth that the small press scene consisted only of lumpish primitives, heedless spontaneists, self-alienating rock musicians without guitars; it showed a delicacy, reflexivity, and sensitivity which turned on a whole market sector of intellectuals who had given up on modern poetry. The history of poetry consists, no doubt, much more of the progress of the lie of the cultural managers that the excluded poetry was less intelligent than they were, than of the internal course of poems and poets. But the audience is missing an account of the aesthetics behind that peculiarly light and fastidious style and of the history which led up to it. No reviewer was available to point out that almost all the poems included had been written before 1975, and that the anthology was a retrospective of an already closed era, whose publishers and magazines had disappeared.

As James Keery, the best student of the subject, has pointed out, AVA is a counterpart and denying response to *Children of Albion*, a dreadful 1969 anthology of "poetry of the Underground in Britain", which portrays the same generation of sixties anti-traditionalists, and overlaps with *AVA*. Crozier's participation (along with James, Roy Fisher, and Chaloner) in *Children of Albion* offers a fascinating contrast with his later reputation as someone "academic and difficult" and editor of the "hermetic" *A Various Art*. However, Crozier hasn't changed all that much. The new coolness and impromptu animated both anthologies. Horovitz (editor of *Albion*) strode off to become a kind of ageing DJ figure, peddling no-hope teenagers as if enough youth and ignorance batched together could bring back the sixties. There is a useful analysis of *A Various Art* by Allen Fisher (in *Reality Studios* #10). Fisher remarks on shared imagery of blood and light, on the basic aim of originality and unofficiality, the use of *sprezzatura* (a feigned indifference and negligence of address), the ambiguous relation to a civic discourse. *AVA* is an incredibly clever selection, made so as to make everyone look the same, and it reads more like a book than an anthology ever can, but I don't understand quite how this was done, nor why. Evidently this is the way to make anthologies.

The intelligent writers of the sixties, the ones most directly influenced by pop music, worked out the implications of the new sound; they were especially associated with a firm called Ferry Press, run by Crozier; the most significant names were Crozier, John James, and David Chaloner. These are not difficult writers. Books published by Grosseteste Press included titles by John Riley, Anthony Barnett, David Chaloner, Roy Fisher, Ralph Hawkins, John James, Tim Longville, Douglas Oliver, Peter Philpott, JH Prynne, Peter Riley, Nick Totton, and John Hall; Ferry Press's books included titles by Peter Baker, Anthony Barnett, Peter Bland, David Chaloner, John Hall, Martin Harrison, John James, Steve Jonas, Douglas Oliver, Peter Philpott, Peter Riley, John Temple, Lewis Warsh, and Nick Wayte.

### What happened in British poetry in the 60s?, or, byways of Balkan ethnography

Wolfgang Görtschacher's *Little Magazine Profiles 1939–93*, the best and most thorough book on modern British poetry, states that there were 2000 poetry magazines in the 1960s. The social basis for this was the giant expansion of higher education from the late fifties onwards, giving rise to a new literate class of largely working-class origin, unable to identify with the existing literary system, and eager to devise new worlds of its own. This expansion and walk out gave rise to what Eric Homberger, in his 1977 book *The Art of the Real*, describes as a "balkanized" environment. It also produced a symmetrical reaction of suspicion, exhaustion, and dread on the part of conservative littérateurs who saw their expertise being swamped and who have periodically issued edicts stating that "nothing interesting comes out of the small press scene and consequently I haven't read any of it". I believe 90% of the good poetry comes out of the small press scene. The cultural managers have a myth which is organic, in the sense that it serves to protect their power and prevent knowledge not controlled by them; it is that all new British poetry was post-Ginsberg, i.e. flabby, sloppy, wacky, and kinky. Output has not decreased since 1977, rather the scene has become ever more diverse and with ever lower visibility and transparency. *AVA* covers one constellation of poets from the small press scene out of dozens. The total number of new poetry books and pamphlets published in Britain since 1960 is roughly between 25,000 and 35,000. I can list about 120 names of poets whom I consider significant but any survey is partly aleatory. There are no wide arms of the sea separating this archipelago from all the others; everything in England is organised in gradual transitions.

The scene in Scotland and Wales saw a very similar expansion of higher education and of the poetry audience, but preliminary analysis suggests that a formal breakthrough was not attained in the poetry of those countries because the climate of optimism and expectations of radical change was channelled into nationalism, and this (in a suggested interpretation) pointed the poets backwards, towards identifiably local schools and forms, and towards an imagined community to be addressed in easy and simplified terms. Reverence for the national past was also reverence for the past; the nationalist intellectual atmosphere had a strongly conservative and religious tinge. Ideals of self-realisation and formal experiment were thus blocked by significant factions within a rather small and closely knit poetry audience; the internationalist New Left current in England produced a rather more fertile atmosphere. Due caution makes me add that the most radical poetry from the upland and outland parts may simply be invisible to me.

Jonathan Green's fascinating *Days in the Life: voices from the English underground 1961–1971* reveals the strong anti-verbal prejudice of key members of the Counter Culture. The new immediacy didn't work in words, which demand conceptual thought and moreover were more deeply furrowed by the markers of social class. Disliking the message, the formers of taste rejected the messenger. Clothes and music and hair were easier to change and scrub free of the past (to be exact, of the fifties and its Tory governments). Instant poetry proved to be instantly forgettable. The new poetry was a lot longer developing than the new dress and the new pop music; it was not therefore any less significant in the long run.

If you looked at all the poets who began writing in the sixties, good and bad, you might find that most of them believed in spontaneity and direct address because that was the flavour of the decade. Nothing distinctive here, and the idea of a "Cambridge Style", i.e. the Ferry and Grosseteste poets, may therefore be unable to float. If everyone's busily being empty-headed, the most interesting ones will be those with enough work ethic to actually practise their dance steps or their poetry, as the case may be. Perhaps the Cambridge scene happened because it was where working-class hedonism met a Hegelian belief in flux. It drew in poets from all over the country. The poets in *A Various Art* and *Grosseteste Review* are simply the good poets to have emerged during the sixties; the cream of a halcyon decade.

The staple of left wing propaganda or fantasy was no longer an unemployed worker, honest and hard done by, object of pity of a middle-class looker who dominates the design of the imagery without being visible in it. With the Welfare State, career opportunities, full employment, strong unions, and nationalised industries, Socialism had half-way arrived, and to appear miserable was to threaten the case for the full-on

Socialist ideal. The central figure is now the working-class dandy, a phrase which brilliantly sums up John James, David Chaloner, Tom Raworth, or Barry MacSweeney (although the best recent clothes poems are by Denise Riley in *Mop mop georgette*). The new figures, drawn directly from life, were just strong, parading, optimistic, rather tetchy people. Wrapped in fab gear, the poetry in question ripples with egalitarian flaunt. This new style king (or queen) wasn't invented by Ferry Press, or Grosseteste Press, or even in poetry but could hardly be missing from poetry, as the usual histories make out.

The arrival of a mass consumer culture preferring fun meant that any presented scene in which people didn't seem to be having fun, or to be offering it, immediately turned people off. The good life was out there somewhere! The poets of the Fifties had lost touch with fun just because it was a low priority for them. Sex had existed for George Barker and Christopher Logue but they were off camera. Logue in particular used, then, most of the devices which became clichés in the sixties, proving, much against my will, that they were good ideas.

Peter Riley has stated that the Cambridge School came to an end in 1970. This is a reasonable cut-off for the Ferry Press group but leaves out the rest of non-dead English poetry. Someone curious to grasp the overall shape of modern English poetry would read through the whole Ferry Press list. However, they might be equally well advised to read all the Equipage pamphlets. In terms of Cambridge, *A Various Art* stops short of the generation who were students in 1968, a landmark year for Left culture; it now seems very eccentric to have left out Denise Riley, Michael Haslam, and Martin Thom. (Nick Totton was included, inexplicably.)

## Some convergences

The most obvious mannerism is a constant reference to "light" as a noun endowed with agency. The human figure is constantly reduced to an outline within a visual plane, both accepted and delimited by it. It occurs to me that this derives from Antonioni, whose characters are always dominated and deified by the space around them. Envy of visual art, seen as more opulent, classless, and free, is also a powerful spur. But the concern also goes back to Charles Madge (1912–96), the only Left intellectual poet of a previous era, whose rigour and isolation make him the ancestor of this grouping in so many ways: the emergence of three-dimensional space from flat planes was one of his preoccupations. It is linked to the piercing of illusory versions of social process to release more integral and inviting ones; the former appearing as merely a picture. The painting appealed because it seemed to offer a sign surface capturing a complex simultaneity given by the order of things and not by the painter's ideological burden. The painter was seen as passive and sensitised; the lens of the camera was a more convincing candidate.

The most pervasive element is direct address. The wisdom about life, which had still formed the poet's stock in trade in the fifties, is systematically dissolved, because it was seen to inhere to a bourgeois civilisation of fixed social roles and property relations, repressing the individual. The belief that the pre-existent was bad was a commonplace when the pre-existent was a composite of the Tory administrations of 1951–64, Donald Davie, the Empire, the City of London, and what was then called "the class system". The scorn for, and explosion of, existing linguistic tropes drives everything. The presence of the past, the "ruins, churches, and castles" whose absence disconcerted poets in nineteenth century Australia, was identified with social and religious reaction, with ossified habits of the emotional life, and with timeworn poetic procedures. The new poem starts from a linguistic vacuum, trying to translate its energy into a new world of forms. The new poems resemble the view of a camera, which cannot see the past. The contemplative merging of past and present is replaced by simultaneity, a continuous present experienced as an immersing and exciting multiple flow. The containing frame could either be an experiencing self or a place.

The starting point was perhaps close attention, that is, the imperative taught by academic study of poetry to pupils. Because poetry records consciousness, this became close attention to the mechanisms of consciousness; because poetry records behaviour, this means searching the bases of behaviour. Persisting in this curiosity led, almost inevitably, to philosophy because a community of philosophers has been asking such questions for centuries, with cumulatively improving methods. Reflexivity is the key word but this is only an extension of the act of verbalisation: to put any experience into words, you have to ask yourself what it is. Enhancing verbalisation always means enhancing the questions you ask, and enhancing the answers always means discarding the old ones. The real work of the school, a part of their core assets for which we are compulsively attracted to them, is in finding a link between the difficult questions of introspection and existing bodies of knowledge. These seizures are always moments of delight. They are like having a difficult physical problem and finding a branch of mathematics, already mature, which allows you to model the processes. In fact, the energy graph sags a bit when the poet is not finding matches between personal experience and formal knowledge. Analysing moments of experience very closely is depressing, so a key move is to depict experience serially: this floods the traditional limits of the poem and sets up a system with high indeterminacy. The central practice of direct address is a function of this: the poem discards finished knowledge from the past in order to record things that hadn't happened when the poem started. The classic example of this is John Hall's book *Days*, but the device is quite generally used. The promise is to surpass available self-consciousness by making more awareness available, making new patterns visible; excitement flags, of course, when this does not happen. Questioning one's experience was a symbolic gesture of willingness to take part in a new society just as the self-satisfied use of finished knowledge, in mainstream poetry, signalled that knowledge was a form of property and status and was not subject to interference.

Wendy Mulford's untitled documentary prose piece (in *Ochre* 4, 1976) records the events of a day as if through a camera, following the model of Mass Observation's Day Surveys of the 1930s. The hope is that unconsidered, unedited collection of detail will reveal underlying patterns made invisible by hardened literary procedures. This is bound to remind us of the documentary film movement, perhaps even of when we saw specific films, like *Night Mail* or *Fires Were Started*. The real, once found, is supposed to burst and disperse the conventional. Other examples of immediacy are:

> What we want indeed! He comes in
> and states exactly what he wants,
> a bacon sandwich and cup of tea.
>
> Tho the actual reason I like to come here
> is that it offers that strangulated feeling
> I get with places stuck in the back streets
> of some obscure &
> complex provinciality—a certain lift
> of amazement that people live and
> eat their lives out
> so far from hope.
>
> (PETER RILEY, FROM *"at the café"*)
>
> Our loss of courtly grace cohabits
> With a loss of hope in the land,
> not just the government
>
> (FROM *"in the pub"*)

This is a crux because, although it appears to be *le regard concret*, immediacy, in real time, it also strongly enjoins the idea of a moral community, which would govern the design of buildings, the training of workmen, the moral standards of entrepreneurs, etc., and which becomes indignant at the exposure of built squalor. The trope of beautiful countryside being turned into third-rate housing and impoverished communities is found in Georgian poetry; the suppressed origin of English leftist poetry, of course.

In blatant defiance of the anti-teleological line implied in direct address, the CLC tends to a theological binding of events and their values. In allusion to the Screaming Me-mes often uncovered in modern poets, we could speak of Screaming We-we-weness. This is a direct continuation of the collectivist, moralising poetry of the past. The Welfare State could only survive if there was a broad communal consensus among taxpayers and voters. The new freedom of individual behaviour was accompanied by a wish to constrain government behaviour, not only preserving a social control board whose balances were complicated and fragile but making those controls more precise as time went on. The cafés don't really appear as mysterious objects of enquiry but as a way in to literary political tropes of stunning familiarity and patness. The arch tone is a way out of this. As Roy Fisher has remarked, we live in a country where every meadow, every building, is invisible beneath centuries of moral literary allegories. It's startling how few British poems are thoroughly free of the stock figures and design values of nineteenth-century religious prints. The arrival of the camera at least provided, via snapshots but above all through advertisements, a new commonplace imagery.

The poetry frequently takes in conceptual structures, for example Freud, usually as modified by Melanie Klein and the British School of psychoanalysis. The Kleinian art historian Adrian Stokes is a revered background figure. It would be easy to write off a school tied to Cambridge as being academic, whereas direct address is the central quality of the poetry in question. The belief that human situations are repetitive enough to allow general, codified, knowledge of them of course contradicts the notion of the "continuous present"; repetition, trauma, and illness return. At the same time, this represents the added value hoped to make the recording of everyday life less banal than a soap opera, or than the poetry of Philip Larkin. Perhaps equally important have been Heidegger and Maurice Merleau-Ponty, but their emphasis on the mystery of the ordinary surface of experience could fund a lyric-documentary poetry of the everyday.

The use of deictics follows from the conception of the poem as a system of argument, unveiling the truths found by the phenomenological gaze, unfolded with cumulative force, and offered to the reader for civil examination and perhaps disproof. Assertions are prevented from being apodictic by exposing the deduction chain that leads to them. This mastery of argument belongs especially to Prynne, Andrew Crozier, and Riley D. The apparatus of argument frequently appears, elsewhere, to be a kind of postiche. A trademark is the syntactic pronoun: for example *therefore* is an implied pronoun, in its *there* component, which marshals and exposes a whole run of foregoing text as a unit, a quasi-noun. A similar parsing applies to *so, or, nor, rather,* in special contexts. This implied cumulation, carry over, contradicts the tenet of the continuous present. It stakes, though, a claim to be superior to anecdotal domestic realism, which is the staple (commercial waste) English poetry.

The tone is full of puzzles:

> The evolution of the principle optic
> fibre is far from complete, we know
> enough to admit as much, but
> prediction is tentative. You see
> intermittently through silhouettes
> of trees to where across the valley
> the darkness relieved along the crests
> of the next hills is streaked
> with falling stars.
>
> (FROM HIGH ZERO, BY *Andrew Crozier*)

This tone can be arch, infuriating, inexplicit, and baffling. It follows from the unrehearsed approach, discovering things without a preset theme, and from the montage which was mandatory in the 1960s. The idea was to bring in generalised knowledge while still remaining casual. Allen Fisher, in his important review, talks about *sprezzatura* as a guiding principle. This is a kind of studied negligence. Again, this casualness pervades all the new poetry of the sixties; the poets in *AVA* point away from it because of their interest in ideas, which implies a certain connectedness and obstinacy in piling up data but they would be as terrified as Brian Patten or Adrian Henri of the past-boundness, moralising, and didacticism found in the academic poets of the 1950s. The archness, like the unruffled procession up the aisle to *we*, conceals the transition from the particular to the general, an operation which, like a river crossing under fire, frequently turns out badly.

The admission of systematic knowledge always contained the latent threat that the voice of the self would be disproved and dispersed. This would possibly supply the basis for the collapse of the existing social order; the Marxist element in the group never repented. This turn would also restore the malevolent spectator who invisibly structures the shot so as to undermine the figure it makes visible. Pessimism about subjectivity is important in the poetry of JH Prynne, Peter Riley, Tom Raworth, and John Wilkinson; more ominously, it is also a reason for rejecting the mainstream of English poetry, identifying it with triviality and inauthenticity. The critique of awareness is also "the rejection of the poem expressing the awareness of persons who have not conducted a critique of their awareness", and the scare-word "naive" is heard a lot hereabouts, in ensuing territorial struggles. This leaves unsolved the question of what replaces individual experience as the content of poetry. The imperative of close attention makes the entry of philosophy into the secure world of the poet inevitable: a servant which becomes a master, since a philosophical poet who is bad at philosophy is a bad poet. The increased status of the Ferry Press poets since the late 1980s is due, first to the common imperative which makes thousands of people see philosophy as a way of writing sophisticated poetry, secondly to their obvious mastery in finding philosophy which wasn't out of date and in fitting it into verse without lurches and incongruities.

The CLC is also the supreme site of modern love poetry and romanticism, particularly in the work of John James, Denise Riley, Andrew Crozier, and Michael Haslam. It represents the moment when the everyday incomprehension of the Absurd lost its despairing affect and became joyful curiosity as well as the brilliance, fastidiousness, and evanescence of English sixties pop, the authentic equivalent of Traffic, Cream, The Beatles, and The Small Faces. This could be a point of contradiction, underlining that there never was any constitution to which anyone signed up. But this dual optic seems quite usual, saying for example that "delight expressed in advertisements is inauthentic but when I express delight it is authentic". Is there anyone who would not sign up to this?

By piecing these foibles together, one can locate a distinctive, caricaturable, CLC tone; immediately recognisable, for example among the student poets in 1970s magazines such as *Blueprint*, though hard to quantify. It seems otiose to go on and disqualify various poets for not uttering in the Cambridge tone. *AVA* is an extraordinary anthology because it selects poems to isolate and accentuate certain characteristics and creates a new appearance.

Wendy Mulford (1941–) published *Selected Poems 1968–78* (with Denise Riley), *Late Spring Next Year: poems 1979–85*, and *The Bay of Naples*. Other poems are in *Out of Everywhere*. After belonging to the Communist Party for several decades, she became a High Anglican and married a vicar. She was part of the milieu of Cambridge poets in the mid-sixties, when it was still a close-knit group, before disillusion set in. Feminism is the theme of many of her poems. A documentary poem in *Ochre* 4 listed all the events of a day; the idea was that existing methods of associating themes in art were stereotyped, and a return to unedited juxtaposition would uncover new patterns. Other poems have a deliberate slightness. The unmediated intimacy with the poet, working in a domestic language without heights, is perhaps meant to break through worn-out verbal structures and revive them. Mulford has an ability to select strong concepts in the taste of the times: the conceptual documentary poem, the feminist poem, the sophisticated hedonist poem, the mystic and spiritual poem, but a depleted interest in the verbal structures that would capture these concepts and put them on the page.

## John Hall, *Else here*

Hall wrote:

> & on the bright face is
> all fair? how does the light
> shine back from the desert spaces of
> the sands & the gleaming ice-caps? I sense the green
> darkness of the latitudes of my origin
> as I move about now
> in the clarity of these northern cities & call it
> my fortune to be talking of origins
> in the grasslands of my own life
> which may have been the grasslands also
> of this species

The sixties saw the acceptance of the Continental Drift theory partly because new photos from space, showing "the sands & the gleaming ice-caps", made people realise the planet was one object; geography was a way (for the Ferry Press poets) of talking about the origins of society (from the African savannahs to the cities of northern Europe) just as location in space was a way of talking about the origins of consciousness. Hall was writing epistemology as myth, and his volume is part of the Etruscan books series, an impressive archive dealt by an erratic taste. Their volumes with three, usually disparate, poets are uniquely resistant to reviewers (but see *Terrible Work* 9). The one with Helen Macdonald's poems is a must have. However, I can't believe that anyone's taste is quite this shaky. *Else here* is a selected poems going back to 1968 and including notably much of the 1973 book *Days*. One supposes that the act of memory takes in a limited length of experience, and that self-awareness is limited by this "clip length" so that using paper to record much longer durations is an unprotected exit into a new awareness, destroying the stylisation of an act of consciousness (which resembles the stylisations of literature). So the plan of "Days" is to open up a new awareness by inspecting a paper trace by recording involuntary acts to shift the balance between voluntary and involuntary. *Couch Grass* partly resembles *Change: a Prospectus*, Tony Lopez's 1978 book. In it, a field going through an annual cycle is a metaphor for new behaviour, growing day by day, and vulnerable as it grows. The purpose of wider showing, at that time, was to bring about a long-term change in social relations: deepening the perceptual field in space and time was just a rehearsal for far more uplifting shifts of awareness. This project was short-circuited, in more conventional poets, by the imperative of impersonating oneself so as to sell to the audience that commodity which is the poet's personality. The outward project, therefore, resorted to demolishing artistic practices, cutting through authoritative self-assertion by unsteady consciousness. Even if you like writing self-similar poems for five years, doing it for twenty-five years surely makes doubt attractive. (I began publishing in 1978.)

## Ralph Hawkins (circa 1950?)

consider these combinatory elements in sequence
perceived as discrete units

thanks to this lineage of ready-mades
events co-lapse to release realizations
of the interpretive mind
the interaction of cities with prominent sites
the container & the contained (*jism & ruh*)

the plateau regions on the apron of majestic mountains
the judicious placement of points of reference
gateways built in the mouths
points of arrival & departure
(haven't we been here before)
bridges & roads deepen the combinative axis
the groin yearns towards the Logos

I have not learned from experience
I have followed neither the line of fortune nor the line of desire

I have studied the imprint left upon the mattress
I have attained the possession of a shadow
I have yearned for the coming synthesis
I am unwilling to compromise with the dialectic
I reject the mechanical softening of contradiction
*We could just kiss and kiss and kiss?*
You could give up and live your life (!)
I take no pleasure in what the world cares for
*I have built a house of osmanthus wood*
*I have planted an orchard of orange and pumelo*
I will cross that gate when I open it
(FROM "SKINNY PROTRUDING MISMATCH",<br>
*so far as I am concerned his best work*)

Note the self-describing allusions to the way bits of language are linked together. This is notoriously completely different in China (the source of much of the imagery) from Western Europe, where the continual use of logic can be related to the government's reliance on a published law code and argument in court. His books include *Well you could do*, *The Word from the One*, *Tell Me No More and Tell Me*, *At Last Away*, *Writ*, and *Pelt*. And of course *Skinny Protruding Mismatch*, which was published as *The Coiling Dragon The Scarlet Bird The White Tiger A Blue & Misted Shroud*.

woke up, back to ordinary consciousness
Harris took the bondage applicator off
Oh he looked unhappy and lachrymal
a bit too much colonic irrigation
words were sweeping through
the city's sewer system
there seemed to be leakage everywhere
I walked the markets
they serve night-shift workers
brewed from a type of millet
small eats booths and windows
first slit of light
organdie, blood sucked orange lips,
silks with dragon prints
cobbled stone walks
back alleys
drains
the civet cat,
hare, hanging duck, snake, wasp nest totems
taken between the lips
sucked and lolloped
happy as a pog in shit

Compared to the rigorous and rationalist image of other Grosseteste poets, Hawkins' poems always give the impression of turning up late and being drunk when they do arrive. They minimise the gap of "constructive effort" between the basic seeking of pleasure and pleasurable sensations and the "mediated" pleasure of the poem. They have a lot in common with the work of John James and David Chaloner; however, all the poets in *AVA* have in common that quality of direct address which, in other essays, I have associated with the "eternal present" of filmic narrative and with the jettisoning of the past in 1960s culture. The phenomenology of these poets involved a gaze turned unwaveringly at immediate experience, in the belief that if philosophy was not solving problems from within that experience then it was facing artificial problems. Hawkins, though, is not aiming at consistency or at results you could swear to. Hawkins is Welsh, a miner's son, and studied at the University of Essex, where he also taught for a while. Crozier and Ed Dorn were at Essex before that time, which is possibly the link between Hawkins, American-derived open forms, and *Grosseteste Review*. He started with the pamphlet *English Literature* in 1978. One of his classes at Essex included Kelvin Corcoran, Ian Davidson, and John Muckle. He edited the magazine Ochre in the late seventies and then *Active in Airtime*, co-edited with Muckle, in the mid-nineties.

He does not bother with stage setting. Each poem launches us into a series of "direct experiences" from whose course we could work out the shape of the self experiencing them. We could either take the individual events and fit them into our own self-experience, or we could take each book as constructing a new "shell self", a role we can both play for a while. Hawkins is not asking how experience happens but by describing the course of a self he answers the question anyway. The course is one of attention, constantly switching on and off, jumping between planes; Hawkins' method is to eliminate whatever is not interesting and his poetic line is as rapid, sporadic, shifting, polyvalent, slight and self-reversing as consciousness itself. We could describe his work as anarchistic because it does not confirm any of the classificatory and causal judgments of our law-abiding society and experiences absolutely no urge to replace these with a new set of rules and values. However, any other antinomian description would do, and he has obviously been tempted by certain Chinese poems, Daoist or Zen, which display a similar scepticism and hedonism:

> write ten wishes & then ten whys
> ten drunken ways

> his poetry is all from there
> known for poverty, cold
> & heavy winter snows
> colloquial & metrically free
>
> (FROM "PELT")

An avoidance of specified causal connections is, as a matter of fact, a feature of Chinese poetry. On the spectrum between intimacy and institutional formality, Hawkins is at the intimate extreme; concerned with textures close to the skin, he has found it natural to write about food, as in *Coiling Dragon*

> we have red and watery fresh peeled
> round eye lychees from Furhou
> from shady cool Piguang some sour tart,
> from Songyang
> sweet sweet luscious
> yellow orange green tangerine and
> some supple supple soft quite quite white
> crystal crushed flat persimmons.

This fineness of texture makes his work elusive and endlessly variable. Intimacy can lead to rigour and a sense of duty, or, as here, to looking at reality so close-up that the features you are looking at shift and then shift back as you watch them. Because he offers low-level flakes of experience, they can be combined into many different higher-level patterns; their failure to achieve consistency must be a feature of their design. It is possible that their success depends on the consistency within a single book, as especially in *Coiling Dragon*, and on the degree of separation of the virtual self in the poems from the sociologically real poet R. Hawkins.

> from the paper
> he wanted to play a cultural piano
> the way some play with syntax
> he didn't know an adjective from an adverb
> now you kids listen, ciao
> I am not rewriting the Maximus
> but learnin to talk proper
>
> (FROM "BUT IT MAY BE SO")

The "piano" implies that the poet can hit a number of keys at will, meaning a detachment from preset sequences, which might include personality patterns or else poetic conventions. Is he being completely frank in describing his own work, or is this a bluff and a joke? The inability to distinguish parts of speech links to the line about learnin; the sarcasm about linguistic authority may also be saying that classification of parts of speech is itself tied to a narrow kind of writing in which each occurrence is predictable; further that the rules of speech help us to translate states of mind, and that the uncertainty of the latter is too great to let us fix the rules. People who cannot name the parts of speech can still express themselves using words. The stanza is a "shadow" of a debate about the frustration of cultural diversity by rigid schools, about the failure of exams to detect the creativity of working-class children; it alludes to the inhibitions around "written culture", which is something barely present in Hawkins' poetry, recognisable as oral in style. The stanza seems to imply the presence of a teacher, but the poet's distaste for this role leaves the definition of the situation unspoken. Anyone who did seize this role would be an object of ridicule.

The removal of conventional connections leaves a vast space for originality: his style is located in the edits, the jumps. The complexity of possible patterns to be assembled from the poet's "flake" style makes it convenient to reflect on the old displaced style of English poetry, in which situations were pre-selected to fall into certain patterns, in which both motives and results of actions were absolutely certain, in which the judgment of the reader was unambiguously prescribed, and where the behaviour of the poet in staging the inherited situation and condemning the guilty was presented as integrity. This scene could be based either on the Christian religion or on patriotism; the two were combined in the idea of the Anglican parish. Everything is held together by rigid lines of causality; everything is an exemplification of a pattern long familiar to everyone. To make obligations quite clear, what each person wants must be simplified and made wholly predictable and fixed. In Hawkins' world, none of this applies; this is signalled by the absence of causal indications in his syntax and the unspecified relationship between the various clauses within a poem. In this world, states of mind are indefinite and interactions between people are unpredictable. Patriotism and piety are notes that cannot be struck. There is no valid law code and no one, even the poet, can demonstrate authority by pronouncing judgments based on it. We can suggest a link between this style and the rise of a non-Christian group of educated and literate people, sixties hedonism and permissiveness, the increasing porosity and mobility of society, and historically old strata of distrust of authority and judgment among the working class. However, as we recall the features of this secure poetry, which after 1965 seemed so utterly out of date, we realise that its jettison left an empty space whose features, temporary or deep, require a new effort of observation and naming.

Older poetry had a documentary value because it had to prove to the reader that they were moral and wise; the poems correlated with agreed verbal accounts (for example in the newspapers and in Parliament) and were confirmed by them. Hawkins cannot be used in this way; his poetry does not converge, avoids work of any kind, and he has a low guilt quotient. This is psychologically very rewarding for the reader. Shaking off these deeply pleasurable feelings for a moment, we wonder why poetry should be an act of duty, and what use to anyone else reading poetry could be.

Hawkins and John Seed are younger than the other poets in *A Various Art*, and began publishing late in the seventies, as opposed to the mid-sixties. There isn't an obvious progression towards them, but the diversity within the group may have led to a misinterpretation of certain poets (as, simplistically, "people trying to write like Prynne"), just as it signifies, for many readers, that *A Various Art* is a whole world: just as the Introduction says, they are the best poets of a generation. I accept that this doesn't amount to a description.

I was curious to relate Hawkins to Welsh poetry. The attempt quickly showed how much he resembled the other Grosseteste poets. I did find one poem about Wales (in *Without & Within*). However, it is quite fruitful to compare him with John James and Peter Finch, also South Welsh and non-conservative poets.

### An Even Break: Anthony Barnett (1941–)

"The poet [AB] quotes himself in a range of particular distances, stripped of all contextuality and commentary, refined to a totalized musical construct. It is a naked poetry, cut off from its occasions but remaining ungeneralized, in which units of language are isolated from each other and only form a discourse as a sequence of suspended moments or self-sufficient and complete notations in themselves". Peter Riley

∽

"In this way lyric poetry slows down experience to measure its properties, and comes to act as a scale of value [ . . . ] For Barnett, this morality-in-language is the purpose of the lyric. Each moment is different from another. And this fight for understanding finds its usual form in love with all its hardness and fury where relations are most concentrated and vulnerable. The poetry, therefore, reveals the risks and benefits which constitute love". Simon Smith

~

These comments come from a 1993 book about his poetry, edited by Michael Grant, which includes extensive interviews. They strike me as unlikely; Barnett's poetry is suggestive but the shapes which it suggests cannot be fixed, as much as this, and measured as a set intent. Barnett, a sometime professional jazz musician, is better known for his typography and book design, which excel anything else I have encountered in the world of poetry. He has stated that Milford Graves represents all his ideals for percussion, so listening to a Milford Graves album, perhaps with the New York Art Ensemble, might be a good introduction to Barnett. It's only fair to point out that Graves, like Sunny Murray, is one of those drummers who have thrown away the idea of time and a beat: this is physiologically arduous music to listen to, because the unconscious adjustment of your body time to the beat of rhythmic music is disturbed and thrown into question by timeless music. When the structure of appetite and physical rhythms are so upset, it's like an exit into a new life. The experience of revolution might feel like this; the forces of habit can wear out, it's certainly possible to learn how to walk, breathe, and eat in a new way. Perhaps it's only when habits are torn away that you become completely conscious. Free jazz is politically radical, but it also gives even greater scope to subjectivity, primarily the musician's, but also the listener's: like or dislike is very violent. Barnett, in poetry, is certainly interested in plunging back to basics; he's actually trying to write as if he were seeing the world for the first time.

> White
> of the Northern bird _
>
> What white?
>
> White ice,
> crystals,
>
>
> besides, the
> black lake, blue-gray lake,
>
> Because of the water-dark,
> May sun.

Speech-like,
beside

bleak prayers of ice
breaks, before morning;

the morning
where your voice is transmitted

is silenced.

("Drops", from *Blood Flow.*)

He is attempting the suspension of time, probably the suspension of other faculties as well. Free jazz is part of the epistemological project, it identifies a human essence which continues to function when every learnt response pattern and symbolic structure is torn away: even if the stripped down consciousness is reconstructing the patterns of art from memory to protect itself from the unbearable onslaught of mere sound. There is some link between the death of the beat and the use of the ocean making the body weightless, and of the Arctic ice, stopping metabolism, in WS Graham's poetry. Barnett's poetry is perhaps in the virtual "container" which once contained Graham's poetry. Barnett's problem is, after forbidding what is known and concentrating on what is seen, which has to be added to the page dot by dot, how to build something complex and alive enough to move on its own. When I say "move", that sounds as if I were talking about a tune, which as we know free jazz doesn't have, but poems are not free jazz. His poems exist in a mist-wreathed mystery, he is gawping, as if he does not understand. They also remind me of TS Eliot's "Song for Marina" (*Ariel Poems*), the landfall on an unknown shore, every sensation registering itself separately but never amounting to security or recognition. The meaning in the words is more of a neurological state than a landscape; a sense of anguished alertness and insecurity. This is also the state in which one encounters a new poet, building a temporary world, a toy world; at this point you have pure subjective choice. The tunnel of visibility down which one gawps and peers can either be the channel through which an unknown world enters the poem or the hole through which the inner pressure of the poem drains away.

Count the repeated words in the quoted poem. All his work has the same simplicity of syntax; I annoyed the poet by comparing this to rock and roll, but the real reason is that the pattern of causal and associative links, assumed by syntactic relations, does not exist in this "primordial" landscape but comes about only as the result of experience and represents recognition, or naturalisation, which is what the poet is trying to escape from. When a large number of very simple stanzas are connected together, they do acquire complexity and life. The problem with the poet gazing at a stone as if he'd never seen one before is that the reader actually has seen one before. At this point the whole situation depends on very delicate unconscious prompting, the suggestiveness of the poet's linguistic means. Dissociation—the dazed look—may have quite different psychological meanings. At worst it is a *voulu* feyness, as the poet intones "Stone. Rain. Mist. Tree."; at best it is the poet discovering twenty new things about a stone, or a wave, and evoking their undiscovered being without even giving them their right names.

There is a question about philosophical complexity, since Barnett uses simple words rather than complex classificatory lines and simple sentences rather than complex qualifications in syntax. This is part of an "asset analysis" in a competition for poetic eminence which is simplifying and misleading. Certainly Barnett is a problem for a classification which would make *A Various Art* "philosophical and academic".

Barnett at least points us at the mystery without introducing premature rationalisations or even abundant details to distract us from the central point, giving us an apparent wealth to secure and dull us. Barnett's work needs protecting from those who too brutally ask "what does it mean", of something like "The history of theatre/ is that of absence./ It is unsound./ It is not wanted in this,/ where climate would be displaced" (from *Fear and Misadventure*), since after all it is pretty clear what his procedure is getting at, and he's hardly alone in trying to go back to the beginning of the mind and of naming. No, the poems don't need specific meanings. I don't find Barnett's turn of phrase gripping or evocative, but I also couldn't explain what "Song for Marina" actually means, or why its phrases are so infinitely haunting.

Most of the poets in *A Various Art* have published little since the anthology came out, but Barnett has produced two full-scale volumes; *Little Stars and Straw Breasts* and *Carp and Rubato*. He has done much translation work. After fruitful discussions with the poet, I would like to make it clear that the "Mist Stone. Rain. Tree." line was not written by Anthony Barnett but is instead an airy, mimetic, and fictional realisation of barnettian stylemes composed by Andrew Duncan. The poet points out that the reader has not seen the stone in his poem ever before, whatever stones the reader's previous experience may encompass.

Milford Graves uses 'poly/nanorhythms' rather than not using time at all.

## The resistance to the CLC

The ambition and high quality of the group discussed could hardly go without arousing criticisms. One mental map of poetico-linguistic space shows two significant Left Modernist groupings, one in Cambridge (inspired by Prynne) and one in London (inspired by Eric Mottram). I don't subscribe to this identification, which is normally followed by a furious denunciation of the Cambridge end for lacking in reverence to the London boys, and being more famous than they are. In a small country with good transport, the city is too leaky to be a closed, self-similar, cultural unit. Yes Virginia, there is a London avant-garde; it is too much like people with bags over their heads banging their heads against the wall and making a lot of noise but making few articulate sounds. Their poetics are too much like someone excitedly playing you an American single they've just bought from the shop and too little like someone making their own music. Nonetheless, the rigorous editing of Clarke and Sheppard did produce an interesting collective statement in the form of *Floating Capital: new poetry from London*, a sketch of the London scene at the end of the eighties, but strongly reflecting the 1970s, no bad thing. Clarke's response to the CLC is in this sardonic aside from the recent *Obscure Disasters*: "in summer's/gold insularised charges light/not visions beneath flowering/meadows surplus to hieratic/for Byzantine dialectical bombast/in orange metropolitan prints/ such that commonly each/lurid in outline embellishment/misted between pastoral and/immensity aestheticist tribal delights" (etc.) Note the parody of deictics.

The young Marxist poet Andrew Lawson wrote, in *Fragmente* no.3 (1991) a fascinating essay on *A Various Art* under the guise of "On Modern Pastoral", which has now become an accepted term, as brilliantly summed up by Denise Riley in her satirical "Pastoral":

> Gents in a landscape hang above their lands.
> Their long keen shadows trace peninsulas on fields.
> Englishness, Welshness, flow blankly out around them.
> Hawks in good jackets lean into the wind, shriek 'lonely I:
> This sight is mine, but I can't think I am.
> Those pale blue floods of watered silk have flounced indoors, I hear
> their flick of vicious fans. I'll land and stow my feathered legs
> and walk to find a sweet interior of beer' — These men are right.

Lawson states that "Philosophical pastoral, meanwhile, flourished in the small windy city of Cambridge during the late 1960s and 1970s ... The residual desire for community in the Cambridge pastorale is itself a form of nostalgia: for small artisan cultures". His position is interesting but presupposes the superiority of misery over happiness as the subject of poetry. The style in question has nothing to do with nymphs and shepherdesses but instead with sixties pop and up-to-date optimism. In fact, the fineness of Lawson's objections is due to his proximity to the group, not to a deep gap between him and them. I imagine that his own poems are produced by a small group, of one person, and by artisanal methods, without use of heavy machinery. They are admirable, nonetheless. I don't want to suggest that everyone published by Ferry and Grosseteste is one of the great and the good; on the contrary, an evening spent with the works of Doug Oliver, John Wilkinson, or Veronica Forrest-Thomson might be one to avoid.

I don't want to claim that the scene around the *Grosseteste Review* was the only significant and exciting one in the nationwide flowering of poetry which took place in the sixties and early seventies. In other cities in Britain, there were other scenes and other experiments; often, these produced poor results at the beginning but reached the highs as they followed a difficult experimental discipline. The reception, by the editors of the anthology, of poets who emerged in the 1970s is more patchy and more in question, although they succeeded with, for example John Seed and Ralph Hawkins. The project of investigating the mysteries of consciousness means that poetry is not closed in itself but shares a great deal with activities such as conceptual art, psychoanalysis, and sociology.

## *Precision and the influence of photography on the poem*

Pound said that the most precise art was good, in a 1913 essay. The Imagist creed talks of "the exact word". Obviously I can't quote Eliot directly without selling my household goods to pay off Faber's, but in Choruses from *The Rock* there is a passage about the slimy mud of words, the frozen snow and frozen rain of verbal imprecisions, inexact words and feelings, and then the idea of words as behavioural jerks that cover up thoughts and feelings not actually happening. There is no doubt this was intimidating to young poets, and that it rang in their minds as they were trying to design poems. In "East Coker" there is a strikingly similar passage, where he talks about imprecision of feeling. Michael Roberts, in the introduction to the *Faber Book of Modern Verse* (1935), made "technical accuracy" the keystone of modern poetry, raised above other virtues. We may well suspect that young poets of that period were impressed by these admonitions and afraid of writing imprecisely.

Precision in the setting of words in the line was part of the general programme; this acted to stimulate vers libre, but also encouraged regular rhythms, as a way of defining the place of the syllable more exactly. A moment of precision pleases the reviewer. Why? Is this a reminiscence of the photograph? The stress on resisting social suggestion and becoming cold and steady, as a condition of autonomy and the fruit of education. A glass lens. But detachment also contains the seed of another possibility, that of political and moral reform, a new consciousness filling the space made empty by primary detachment. Poets who are

## Precision and the influence of photography on the poem [47]

detached both from primary and secondary social orders are unsatisfactory.

The impact of the photograph lay in its relationship to memory. If the ability or willingness of someone to describe the appearance of something is n, the photograph offered n + 1. Of course perception is trained, and so observation can be made sharper and more systematic. All the same, the photograph competed with memory, and even with consciousness of the present at any moment, and this success drew writers into a game where they were competing with the photograph, or with everyday awareness (and its limits). Literature before machine recording stuck to certain conventions, more or less the same ones that people used when remembering scenes: objective and replayable records threatened to demolish these conventions, so that literature had to quicken its pace to compete. Eliot's remarks about imprecision of feeling could give rise to, at least, precise recording of feelings. The reader may care to take part in this book by spending fifteen minutes writing a description of a scene that they saw or took part in yesterday. Things we recognise perfectly well (and I hope the exercise doesn't disprove this contention) prove very hard to remember in any detail. Memory is largely reconstruction, using rules of governing behaviour, rules for the structure of objects and places, which are something like right. If the writer deliberately describes things which breach these rules, the reader may find this effortful and perplexing.

Critical knowledge of literature could seem to differ from subjective impressions in the same way that photographs differ from vague visual memories. The outside edge of poetry seemed, in the 1930s and to university students, to be at the universities. The university library could well be the equivalent of the panorama, or of the vision scenes of *Faust*. Once the data presented in poetry were changed, by a critical process, away from the data of everyday awareness, they were chained up to a process which was structurally unstable: because universities are there to guard the advance of knowledge, knowledge has to advance while there are universities. We could view the "knowledge state" inside poems as an exclave: like the costumes of the leading lady in films, following a logic which is detached from that of the film, dated by being in fashion all the time. The project of reflexivity has quite unreliable results in poetry.

The new pattern casts something in the role of vague and out of date, and this little drama is one being played out all over the century, wherever we look. How can a poet guarantee that he will not be cast, by a critic in a review containing several works, as the one who is vague and hopelessly left behind? Well, one tactic would be to make propaganda against other poetic factions (implying that your faction is really up to speed), and another is to write in demonstratively precise terms (at the expense of whatever artistic qualities, thrown away and neglected). The poet could strive for grade n + 2 of precision.

We find that the pressure to achieve more precision in poetry took three basic forms. The first was the elimination of the subjective language of previous generations, to give the clipped style generally regarded as modern. The second was an attempt to get away from conventional, repetitive, and self-serving accounts of events, and to write something like documentary. The third was the introduction into poetry of ideas, inevitably critical because they were competing with conventional accounts of experience, and likely to be politically controversial because most lines of new thought do not end up justifying the existing power order.

All of these have influenced the basic structures of poetry. The first two (especially) have left a mark on the microstructure of the poem; that is, you can recognise them even in a single line of poetry; if you compared a thousand pages of twentieth century poetry with 1,000 pages of Victorian poetry, you would find the effect of those two lines confirmed in the majority of the poems you looked at; and if you looked at a thousand amateur poems of recent years (say in the entry for an open competition), you would find very many of the poems showing their effect. These reforms have permeated, not only the way a few cultivated poets write, but the way the common run of poets writes. In fact, what we call a naive poet is one who has not noticed that these reforms are worth studying. So prevalent are they, as axes of competition, that we are allowed to wonder how much they add to the reader's pleasure, as they furbish the writer's self-esteem. Further, one can date poems by the kind of precision and objective observation they affect. Provincial poems are those which cultivate the breakthroughs of decades earlier than the ones they were written in.

The piercing of new precision either raises the pious reader to a new level of acuity and noticing or depresses them by destroying a subjective mood to which they had become attached. However much some photos offer a breakthrough moment by the clarity with which they show an outside world already familiar to us, there are thousands of technically perfect and unblurred photos which do nothing for us at all. Equally, the exposure to poems of the standard academic style (from the 1950s to the present day), with moments of clarity and accurate observation, carefully framed and made distinct by leaving other qualities out, made one (rather early, say by 1974) aware that this artistic formula could fail. The line of purging could bring about not so much the emancipation of the poem from elaborate convention as the exit of the genre of poetry from the literary map.

The justification for a poem may often be a moment of insight or fresh observation that it preserves; not always enough to preserve the poem, it is structurally the reason for selecting that moment, from the flux of consciousness, for recording. To those familiar with English middle-class mores, it may recall the practice of asking children what they notice about some object or feature of the landscape, a game fraught with the possibility of noticing the wrong thing. Conventionally, grandparents pronounce themselves satisfied when the child-victim has noticed something and verbally made this available. The trouble with these precepts taught on the mass scale in classrooms is that they turn into conventional rules for attacking a poem, and are applied because they are familiar, even though they offer no way of making the poem better and encourage people to write the same poem as thousands of other people. Aiming for the known prejudices of the English graduate seemed to make sure the poetry-reading market would buy what you were selling but in cold fact produced poems which were boring to write and which bored the reader. The project of teaching yourself to write good poetry is much more complicated.

The third solution to the imperative of precision involves prolonged thought, and so is not available to the ordinary poet. The cognitive models it offers as starting-points for poems can be classified as philosophy, anthropology, psychology, and sociology, although these are just convenient labels for a mass of possibilities, realised or unrealised. The propaideutic course for modern British poetry would include, then, study of British traditions in philosophy, anthropology, etc.– a desirable learning outcome which we are going to point to, in a mixture of joy and languor, without attempting to satisfy.

William Empson's *Seven Kinds of Ambiguity* (1929), in which precision is consistently sidelined, is a riposte to this line. Precision is a concept that grows imprecise as we look at it and in proportion to the length of time we look at it. Where is there a record of the object more precise than the poem, against which we could lay the poem to measure its degree of imprecision? What exactly is the result of abolishing metaphors, as Zukofsky sought to do, from the poem?

It is rewarding to contemplate the poem which Tom Harrisson wrote on Malekula, in Melanesia, in 1934, and to compare it with the poems which the other anthropologists, Martin Thom and Tom Lowenstein, wrote in later decades. Harrisson founded Mass Observation (with Charles Madge and Humphrey Jennings) on his return to England, and it is also rewarding to set his description of kava drinking on Malekula with the MO book on pubs (in Bolton, and mainly written by John Sommerfield) which he arranged on his return. The discussion of collective representations always leads quickly on to the discussion of myth and the unconscious. Harrisson's poem was printed (only) in his wonderful book *Savage Civilisation*, made even more covetable by the evocative and stable orange cover of the Left Book Club. The whole Mass Observation movement seems like a plausible source for the Cambridge poetry which emerged in the 1960s. A room in Blackheath where Harrisson, Madge, and Jennings were meeting in January 1937 might be a founding moment of the Cambridge School where documentary, surrealism, and montage are dominant techniques, and their combination allows new things to be said about the collective identity. The concern with the fabric of daily life may come out of Day Surveys rather than out of Henri Lefebvre (or rather, Lefebvre appears as a resipiscence, a light which shines on what was already there and wakes it up). With Jennings, we may be looking back to an earlier founding moment: the Festival Theatre, Cambridge, under Joseph Macleod's guidance, where in around 1932 Jennings was assistant art director and an odd combination of poetry, documentary, and the unconscious was the nightly fare. The Cambridge poems seem to presuppose a bustling scene around them which they do not explain or describe, but which they are commenting on; this scene, if we could reconstruct it, might be something like a Mass Observation project, with a combination of numerous scenes from daily life and a number of people exchanging complex ideas (about the scenes), and with whom ideas can be exchanged. We apparently have (shared) access to all kinds of files but not just any files. The files which are actually there form the rules of the game.

# *Objectivism and the self-investment with modernist legitimacy*

The heritage of Georgianism isn't hard to find: it's everywhere.
    Objectivism appears here largely as a metonym for the struggle for avant-garde legitimacy. It seems to me that it was in the 1950s that a nostalgic and heroic theory of modernism emerged in the British poetry world, setting aside general principles of poetics in favour of the cult of certain constellations around the First World War, raising them to endlessly relivable fantasies, while their real content, for example the poems, was set on one side. This game could take the form, for example of defining the badness of official poetry (and most unofficial poetry, too) by observing that it wasn't avant-garde. In that decade, poets who decided that Eliot and Pound towered above all other English poets were faced with the awkward need to acquire modernism themselves and the more pleasant prospect of sitting in judgment on other people's avant-garde credentials. (It was always those two, never Edith Sitwell.) The word could perhaps only acquire a definite meaning within such language games; the difficulty of discovering what its meaning was suggests that there was no fertile matrix buried in 1915 and waiting to be uncovered, and that the problem of writing a good poem in 1958, or in 1995, demanded everything except re-enacting 1915. Modernism is today a self-referential word; like *courtly* or *stylish* or *measure* it gives off the scent of something desirable, is part of a shared game. As a matter of fact, the siting of the chief poetic virtue in a founding moment situated in the past is classically conservative, an English trick to reduce poetics to antiquarian loyalty.
    The prime local monument, or asset, or telling blow to be made in debate, came to be Basil Bunting (1900–85). The central fact about Bunting is his lack of an œuvre; he published a single slender volume in

the 1930s (in his thirties), but it was not good (*Redimiculum Matellarum*, i.e. "a necklace of chamber-pots"); the following *Odes* (not published until the 1950s) were not good either. He also published in 1931 in *Poetry (Chicago)* an assessment of modern British poetry which reveals him to have been arrogant and vindictive. It's basically "I never authorised these people to write poetry". Anyone who gives a book a Latin name is arrogant; anyone who calls his book "A necklace of chamber-pots" is immature and pedantic as well. Bunting built isolation around himself by his outright contempt and it is this emptiness in which his inability to write flourished. His first excellent poem was written in 1951. His first book publication in Britain (actually a pamphlet) came when he was sixty-five. I think this is extremely unfortunate; the calmness of an old man towards human phenomena is hard to tell apart from indifference. No one is surprised that the works of Bunting's old age are so tranquil and uneventful but his career up till the age of fifty is as a failure, and this is what impresses us most. Any claims to know about poetic technique must be offset by inability to write poetry, which is usually what they are being set up to disguise. If the English literary atmosphere since the late nineteenth century has been overwhelmingly one in which poetry was felt to be too difficult, and silence indicated sensitivity and moral grace, Bunting has made his contribution to it. The fact that he was ignored scarcely makes him a rebel. Personally, I feel that the great impact of a poet on spiritual life, even more than the poetry, is the proof that it is possible to liberate all one's energies in a constant direction and indeed that these inhuman and almost geological energies do exist; Hughes and Redgrove have changed my life in a way that Bunting never could. He is to be praised for not having published bad poetry in his early decades, but this has to be faced up to his failure to publish good poetry either. Even Harold Macmillan didn't publish slews of bad poetry; or Joseph Stalin. Far too much has been attributed to the quality of Bunting's silence by people whose cultural merit consists largely of keeping silent themselves.

It was only when he shed the influence of Ezra Pound that he became sufficiently humble and human to actually write poetry. When he had calmed down sufficiently, he wrote poems of the first water. His achievement is virtually confined to two long poems, "The Spoils" and "Briggflatts", along with a few passages of the Odes. I must say that these are splendid, especially the former. "The Spoils" is dated 1951 (but perhaps written 1945); "Briggflatts" was published in 1966 and written (according to *Poetry Information*) the previous year. The ideal of a poetry which gives a string of precise sensuous details, in a spare diction and with a sinewy rhythm, has been soiled by hundreds of poets who think they're doing it; but Bunting could bring it off, and his word images are compelling enough that we are receptive to the symbolic structure of the poems, although this is shimmering, persistently evading resolution. It is this dialectic of preciseness and elusiveness which gives these poems an abiding interest. In "The Spoils", for example we start out with the passage about "These are the sons of Shem", based on chapter 10 of Genesis: this is a figure closer to 3,000 than 2,000 years old. We can presume that the speakers, Lud, Aram, Asshur, and Arpachshad, then correspond to the peoples of Lydia, South Mesopotamia, Assyria, and (somewhere else), as provinces of the Persian Empire; quite what the sense of what they say is, I cannot say. The fifth son is missing. This portrait of Empire then has some bearing on the British Empire, portrayed in the second half of the poem as fighting for its life in the Second World War; what bearing, cannot be made out. As soon as the matrix of the poems inspires us to see pictures and frame meanings, it does not matter that it does not also close the process by guaranteeing a definitive interpretation.

Bunting wrote "Briggflatts", "an autobiography", because he was excited by the response to his poetry in Newcastle, especially from Tom Pickard, who, with Gael Turnbull and Michael Shayer, published "The Spoils" as a pamphlet in 1965; Bunting worked on the same regional newspaper as Barry MacSweeney. His encouragement of young local poets was important within the limits of his understanding. We can hardly call him neglected, since acclaim followed very rapidly when he actually wrote anything good. On the other hand, he doesn't appear to have written anything significant after 1966, despite the acclaim for "Briggflatts".

Another prop to his elitist version of himself is the idea, emitted in interviews that "what I write is like (Classical) music" and "what I write is like classical European poetry (and no one can write without knowledge of several European languages and deep culture)". These were self-deceptions of a kind which he professed to be without. Essentially, they are claims that his silence has a huge value and that his most crabbed and scanty writing should be revered. The obvious retort is "studious—always reading—not interested in real people, withered old stick, disdain, not many feelings except reactions to someone else's art". The thinness of his style may be as much from self-regard as from physical feebleness and apathy. He may well have known a lot about Dante and

Persian poetry (and Zukofsky), but this is of no use to us, what counts is knowing how to write. Poetry which is hushed and still and like Sunday afternoon is not interesting, it has to have more energy than the rough-and-tumble of business life, or business is going to be more exciting.

Bunting's technique, and his influence, cannot be assessed without going into the history of the American Objectivist movement. This is also the history of the school of Pound and a great deal in modern English poetry depends on this. Certainly, many of the traits which poets take for granted, and which confuse ordinary people altogether, come from this stylistic heritage, divided among so many people. The cunning refusal of conservative critics, over forty years or even sixty, to explain what these traits of style were for and why they weren't merely mistakes, is sad. We could go back eighty years, to the original Imagists group, with TE Hulme, FS Flint, and Florence Farr, before Pound was on the scene; but I presume this is a primal scene, which any student of poetry will have a pin-up of in their bedroom. A piquant sight is Miss Farr, with a psaltery, reciting a selection of old English poems to Robert Bridges (a certain amount of editing has been done about Bridges' part) and exclaiming that things had been alright up till the Augustans, but had gone dead after that, and that poetic life was to be uncovered simply by reciting the poems. So we have a bridge of silk: a fatal judgment which defines some poems as live and casts others into the bottomless abyss. You would not want to belong to the latter group. This image, which proved exciting for Pound and Bunting, was wholeheartedly taken up in the 1960s, and the search for proofs of life directed poetic thinking at that time. In *Poetry (Chicago)* in 1931 there was an anthology of young poets, edited by Louis Zukofsky, who reluctantly gave them the name Objectivists and wrote a crabbed and obscurantist essay explaining what it meant. Largely, they were a continuation of the Imagists, and their principal influences were Ezra Pound and William Carlos Williams. Because of the economic situation in America in 1931, there was a strong Marxist element in their work. The originals had strayed away and political or administrative reasons wished it that the second generation called themselves Objectivists and not Imagists. The only holdover was William Carlos Williams, but the group revered Pound. We now have an anthology of these poets: *The Objectivists*, edited by Andrew McAllister. I don't understand why the original Objectivist poetry worked; I find this mysterious. I think Lorine Niedecker's work really excellent. I also like Carl Rakosi a lot. I admire the closely related WC Williams. But Charles Reznikoff's volumes are some of the dullest ever written, Oppen is too eccentric to be forceful, and Zukofsky is bafflingly undermotivated.

Also, this second group was American, except for Bunting. They evolved far and fast and created a new overall sound, which can't be broken down, but a few traits can be described, such as parataxis, preference for the concrete detail, interest in Left politics, avoidance of the traditional music of English verse, very close focus on rhythmic units such as feet or parts of lines as if that would prevent the verse from going dead, plainness, avoidance of metaphors and most forms of ornament, avoidance of generalisations and "commonplace truths", unease at describing states of mind, reliance on juxtaposition instead of marshalled argument. A lot of things happened in America and by the 1950s these poets had gone underground. A new follower of Pound, Charles Olson, was active. There was some kind of Poundian scene in England in the 1950s, with names like Peter Russell, Peter Whigham, Denis Goacher; they were paranoid, extremely right-wing, and poetically quite sterile. It had a magazine called *Nine,* wonderfully summed up by Christopher Logue as *"catacombs financed by saccharine",* referring to the right-wing sugar family which funded it (and a magazine really called *Catacomb).* However, there were also some students at Cambridge who, inspired possibly by Donald Davie in his Caius period, were developing an interest in Pound, in Objectivism, and in Olson and they proved to be carrying the future in their bones. Known names include Michael Grant, John Riley, Tim Longville, Roger Langley, and JH Prynne. Olson's influence on the new English poetry was quite crucial. The neo-Objectivists of the 1970s (and following years) in England don't bear a close resemblance to the Objectivists, but the latter must be understood as the stylistic source; why there is such a discontinuity with the English poetry of the 1950s. The possible exception, halfway across the discontinuity, is Charles Tomlinson.

## *The cognitively critical tradition: Madge, Tomlinson, Crozier, Chaloner, Fisher*

There is a difference between seeing a pretty picture and setting two pretty pictures side by side. One of the divisions between high and low in poetry is that between facts and rules, where the higher poets discuss the rules themselves and the mass of readers do not recognise that this is height. One of the central features of AVA is the critical approach to experience and in particular the criticism of the complex of simultaneous acts of judgment and interpretation which compose perception. The kind of rules which are being discussed include those brought to bear when reading poems: the cognitively critical approach is not explained within any single poem but is part of a skill which readers bring to it. The skill is something which one acquires inside the poetry world, and the argument is, as well as reflexive, cumulative: it progresses with each new poem of significance, this is a yardstick of significance, and we do well to approach new poems through the cognitive poetry of the past as a knowledge network. Poets in this network include Charles Madge, Terence Tiller, Charles Tomlinson, Roy Fisher, JH Prynne, Andrew Crozier, David Chaloner, Denise Riley, Allen Fisher, Tom Raworth, and RF Langley. The analysis of vision was being developed in the 1940s by poets like Tiller and Madge.

The critical line will probably remind us of the line of investigation carried out by documentary film, where the function of photographic record is always, implicitly, to criticise both personal memory and the public memory of organised written records, with their links to institutional power. The conflict between film and other types of record is part of the atmosphere which influences poetry. A turning point in the thematics of Left poetry is Joseph Macleod's 1953 *Script from Norway*, a poem in the form of a film script about the making of a documentary film. One of the characters remarks that the story of the making of the film would be more interesting than what actually got on screen; an insight which Left poets of the 1960s took up en masse. *Script* is still a book-length work in which the interaction between the industrial interests providing the budget for the film, their prejudices as explained to the producer, and the inspirations of the scriptwriter actually looking at Norway, is set out in detail; later poems display essentially the same process, but at blinding speed, within short passages. Context has become inexplicit, as the "dominant non-verbal" which you are just "supposed to know". Macleod shows camera crews photographing, not reality, but what their employers want to be shown. What is not visible doesn't show up on film; analogy, the meaning of the visible, is tightly controlled. Everyone, since the arrival of television sets on a mass scale, has become expert in noticing how filmed scenes are "faked" and influenced in their meaning by the means of representation, for example music and editing. We may well doubt how much similarity there is between the documentary movement (including its continuation in TV documentary and quasi-documentary) and the critical line in poetry.

The sensory deprivation chamber, variously prepared, in a series of experiments from 1950, shows us what a subject perceives when there is nothing to perceive. Donald Hebb, the leader of the experiments, was a follower of the gestalt school of psychology and was well placed to analyse the dynamic behaviour of the brain in interacting with the underdetermined surface of the world. His book, like that of a less eminent follower of the gestalt school, Merleau-Ponty, was called *The Organisation of Behaviour*; the letters of his contract are widely rumoured to have been the CIA, as the issue had a great deal to do with successful interrogation and resistance to interrogation, hot topics in the flap about "Communist brainwashing". Where the CIA leads, up to date artists follow; we can ponder how much the experimental cognitive set-up, with its inlets and outlets rigorously controlled, influenced the set-ups of conceptual art; the extension of the work of art to an overall environment seduced the 1960s, notably in the playrooms set up by drug users for their trips. Certainly the poetry of the 1960s inclined to start from zero and try to build up with few elements. The themes of interrogation and suggestibility were central. The new poem was a game in the sense that the rules could be written down and counted although each play was unpredictable.

The insight that the observer was as well worth studying as the observed object, as factors in the observation, is common to phenomenology, gestalt psychology, sensory deprivation studies, structuralism, and to the interest in "language games" which followed Wittgenstein. Indeed, it could also come from watching documentaries and wondering about their grip on truth, from becoming disillusioned with an ideology once believed in, or even from taking many psychoactive drugs.

Being critical sounds pretty exciting, and few poets would own up to being uncritical. The dividing line between poets who are genuinely critical, and those who are conventional but imagine they aren't, became important in the 1960s. We could imagine the traits: conjecture about society; walking away from centrist politics; walking away from conventional rhythm; criticising everyday awareness and knowledge; as occurring separately, but in fact they structurally reinforced each other so much that they all occurred together; and someone who wasn't doing all of them stuck out as conventional. This structural implication merged leftism and radical poetics, so that they weren't perceived as separate things, and there was one overall signal, eagerly fought over and readily recognised by the informed readers, to whom it was all — important. Conjecture became more attractive in an era of rapid social change, and, in such an era, to insist on realism and actuality seemed exceptionally boring and inhibited.

### Grids, perspectival space, and rules of deduction: *Of Love, Time, and Places; Selected Poems*, by Charles Madge

Charles Madge (1912–96) published two volumes (*The Disappearing Castle, The Father Found*) with Faber in his twenties; this, published 1994, is his first volume of poetry since 1941. The impact of Auden was decisive on his poetic voice, as was his conversion to communism at about the same time. Rejection of his third volume in 1946 (! this is a rumour rather than something in print anywhere) was, along with the rejection by the same publisher of new material by Lynette Roberts, part of the preparation for a dull and conformist era in the 1950s. An outsider and bearer of the hopes of those who were satiated and disgusted by the main line of stultified English poetry, he was from then virtually invisible, apart from sporadic appearances in *Nine*. Seymour-Smith's *Guide to Modern World Literature*, published in 1973, discusses two long unpublished poems by Madge, "The Storming of the Brain" and "Poem by Stages": "The resultant poetry is a major revelation, and should be made available without delay". The present volume includes "Poem by Stages" — not the other poem. His technique is extremely advanced, to say the least, incapable of an orthodox link or phrasing. It would be simple to

## The cognitively critical tradition: Madge, Tomlinson, Crozier, Chaloner, Fisher

review him with a fanfare, as a grand old man, but this is not that kind of magazine.

The profession of sociology opened a more urgent everyday way of living and thinking and moreover promised more rigorous solutions to the problems of human nature and politics. Madge's style increasingly, and from the first, placed the demand that the language of poetry should be as precise as the standards of academic discourse, under the penalty of regression and infantilism. One can conjecture that this scepticism made satisfactory formulations out of reach and wiped out the superficial rewards of posing the self in poetry—whether as a rebel, or as man of the world, or as a sensitive spirit. Still, it did not become implausible itself; probably, most people today would agree with him; poetry, clinging to an old-fashioned definition of what is poetic, has not kept the key to a magic kingdom but excluded itself from the concerns of intelligent people. Madge's poetry shows an evolution from self-righteous sinking of other people's philosophies of compromise, to austere unhooking of the cherished truths; at no point does he scatter around the bonbons which would console a self-indulgent poetry audience for their brush with objectivity:

> For a moment I was naked on the wall, hung there
> Flat, with a drain pipe to hold on to
> And all parcelled out in bricks and mortar
> As a grid set up for reference purposes.
> I cannot say how long arrested motion
> Kept me in shadow under the guttering eaves
> Or whether I walked away with all my windows
> Blazing to the uplifted light, blinded
> With the idea of sight. I was divested
> One moment, that was it, of guise and fashion.
> I was not, no shape hid me, in mere pain
> Of existence I was laid out by length and breadth,
> And then, look, I drew on the matted cowl
> And was expelled into the three dimensions
> Walking and talking, nodding to acquaintances.
> And there were drawn upon all identities
> At once their dull or gleaming surfaces.
>
> ("POEM BY STAGES", XII).

What this reminds me of is Piers Plowman; an eschatological narrative of being thrown into social being, rendered here as the closing and rebirth of pictorial space. In any case, this style has under-developed narcissism and highly developed wish for precision. Whereas the poetry audience's secret longing is for just the reverse.

"Poem by Stages", in forty-eight parts, written in "January-March 1949", resists interpretation: the arrangement of junctures is quite unforgiving, the consolation of a possible convergence dissolved in a thorough polyvalence and scepticism. Close analysis shows a striking number of religious themes. The putting on of the "matted cowl" (xii, above) oddly recalls the *anapausis tou endumatos* of certain Gnostic texts, the mortal body seen as a "garment" whose divestment throws the soul into a place of nothing and potentiality. This would incline us to re-interpret the "disappearing castle" of 1937. Hints at the end of the poem suggest that the whole is addressed to a new-born child—the son found, perhaps, and that the themes are the taking on of flesh and worry about the future as a repetition of a dark human past.

*The Disappearing Castle*, his 1937 book, referred to the castle of the feudal noble as the imaginary home in which the poet, lingering over a thousand years or so of patronage and upward identification, attempted to make his language native. The disappearing castle is also the Grail Castle, in *Aufhebung* and visible only at certain junctures: the goal of the search. Madge did not really describe the university as the poet's emergent new home.

The most frequent theme, it seems to me, in this selection is that of the emergence of binocular vision and of recession; the volume includes two poems by that name and makes unmistakable references to the theme on pages 38, 65, 84, 95, 99, 128, 166. The point of departure is the assumption of consciousness: "The strain of man upright in the flat world" but also the prevalence of illusory, surface, scenes: "The walls of the maelstrom are painted with trees". It has multiple values, relating to the contention between an illusory pictorial space with recession, and an abstract, objectless, but engulfing and sublime, picture plane, in the painting of that time and also anticipating poetry's shift of interest, massively since the mid-seventies but already with early Raworth or even early Roy Fisher, away from the morality of behaviour being represented to the rules which govern how verbal models are organised. For Madge at that time the theme meant, however, the dialectic, and he was seeing a scene from two sides in that sense: "After the revolution, all that we have seen/ Flitting as shadows on the flatness of the screen/ Will stand out solid" (p. 128). Because this is also a temporal perspective, the object imagined is the future socialist state: because it is intermittently visible, it is like the Grail Castle:

> This window by a curious trick can see
> Workaday things and a white rising planet.

*The cognitively critical tradition: Madge, Tomlinson, Crozier, Chaloner, Fisher*

> It looks both in and out and on each side
> Is outside. There's no house for such a window.
> [...]
>
> This is the problem of our understanding,
> Facing the window with transforming panes;
> The plant or sparkle of a star emerging
> Inversely with the drawing of our gains.
> ("Philosophic Poem")
>
> By external astronomy
> I bend towards the side of light,
> Conjecturing with strain of eyes
> The edifice, the future thing,
> Vanishing, wandering.
>
> ("Binocular Vision")

A line on p. 58 rather explicitly points the castle also at Saint Teresa's Castello Interior; the fourth line of "Philosophic Poem" is based on Rilke's "Wo gäbe es ein Äusseres/für so ein Inneres?" Confusingly, the layout of the Castle Teresa had in mind is also an exercise in perspective, showing the mind as convergent walled zones receding from a Centre which is the eye of God. This is the first Panopticon.

The value Madge assumes in the pantheon is as a precursor of certain contemporary currents: by his rejection of the demands of orthodox taste and publishing; by his elimination of the personal voice in favour of more intransigent sources of information; by the indeterminacy and internal polyvalence of his mature work; by his cultivation of the long poem; by his critique of language, of self-awareness, and of social structure; by his foregrounding of the rules of art; by the provisional nature of his answers, with scepticism becoming the hero, the space within which events unfold. If one were to look for a local precursor to Prynne and Allen Fisher, it would be Madge on whom one's gaze would rest.

∼

Charles Tomlinson is a poet who has a preoccupation with the limits of visual information and whose whole attitude could be said to be critical. The rigour of his scrutiny is in fact the source of his poetry's appeal. Tomlinson developed an interest in phenomenology in the 1950s, and quotes Merleau-Ponty's *The phenomenology of perception* as one of his stimuli. The tenuous succession which leads from Empson, in the 1930s, through Tiller and Madge, certainly passes through Tomlinson, before reaching writers like Prynne, Crozier, John James and Peter Riley in the 1960s. An interest in shifting visual effects is mainly found in his early poems (in *The Necklace*) but points forward nevertheless to the exploration of perceptual anomalies which flourished in the poets of the sixties. Where it seems to differ a good deal from Madge and the poets of *A Various Art* is in his handling of argument: he brings philosophical conclusions into the poem like someone dumping a dead rabbit onto a table. We see nothing of the process of argument, and the poem does not offer itself as an oscillation between two possibilities. He slights either the pleasure of philosophising or the capacities of poetry, but in either case his poem is founded on what he slights. He draws the cord tight around its neck. These aperçus are reminiscent of the animal skulls which, as he describes in *Eden*, he drew so obsessively in the 1960s; they have lost their heat and their capacity to move. His poetry is precise, and expresses doubt about what other people believe but lacks a sense of inner doubt. The preferentially visual approach acted to exclude the register of language which describes argument and reasoning.

Tomlinson appears a heroic figure in the atmosphere of the 1950s because of his intellectual intensity and avoidance of moral lessons, and articulated the defects of that poetic atmosphere in a biting way. However, in retrospect he also appears too close to the 1950s because of his dislike of conjecture, because of the moral lessons he draws too easily, because of his lack of interest in ideology except as a kind of sin. In the more excited atmosphere of the 1960s it seemed as if he had written off the imagination along with emotional projection. The intense focus on cognitive distortion during the age of ideology, say 1933 to 1956, had revealed the importance in thought and language of arbitrary and collusive symbolic systems which cannot be subjected to simple truth tests; this move from simple finicality to describing the creation of values and inventing new ones is the step which Tomlinson did not carry out, and which launched the sixties style.

## Birmingham engulfed by pattern: Roy Fisher

"'I shall have to do research', Dougal mused, into their inner lives. 'Research into the real Peckham. It will be necessary to discover the spiritual well-spring, the glorious history of the place, before I am able to offer some impetus.'

*The cognitively critical tradition: Madge, Tomlinson, Crozier, Chaloner, Fisher* [63]

Mr Druce betrayed a little emotion. 'But no lectures on Art', he said, pulling himself together. 'We've tried them. They didn't quite come off'". (Muriel Spark, *The Ballad of Peckham Rye*, 1960)

A central idea in explaining Fisher (1930–)'s technique has been *ostranenie*, a term introduced by the Formalist and former student at the Saint Petersburg Oriental Faculty, Viktor Shklovsky. "In order to restore to us the perception of life, to make things sensuous, to make stone stony, there is something we call art. The aim of art, to give us a sensation for the thing, a sensation that is seeing and not just recognition. In this art uses two devices: defamiliarisation of things and complication of form, to make perception more difficult and to prolong its duration. For in art the process of perception is an aim in itself and must be prolonged". The idea should be related to surrealism and montage, where objects or scenes are thrown into a drastically new context. One could argue that they are all concerned with the faculty of association, which is being upset and disconcerted. The artist is opening up an empty space in which the work of art can take its course; if the reader simply imposed their already existing associations, they would perceive nothing new and the art would be stifled. The danger is that the disconcerting art will prove to be a chain of empty paradoxes, like Mannerist poetry, which succeed in invalidating themselves, and becoming predictable, in short order. Defamiliarisation (a translation of *ostranenie*, which literally means "making strange", from *stranniy*, strange) shears away the predictable run of plots (and metre, inevitably associated words, trains of ideas, etc.) but has rapidly to refill the razed space with an ample flow of perceptions. This might be the associative process itself, foregrounded by the demonstration that it is wrong and conservative, made into an object of study. It might be of consuming interest to study the procedures of perception and memory, which are usually hidden by the tranquillising flow of information. But in Fisher's case the plenitude which refills the razed, and latent and charged, space is the city of Birmingham, made visible once the scenography of sentiment, contempt, and myth has been demolished. Fisher has said his hometown is "like a science fiction empire, and when I wrote about it I hardly ever called it by its name". English literary sensibility is insensible to Birmingham, and the country's second largest city is virtually undiscussed in literature; Fisher enthusiastically lists the feeble evidences of novels by Walter Allen and a poem by Louis MacNeice. We have methods for dealing with large industrial cities but they are unrevealing. (It is curious that this prejudice applies also in the mass media; dramas and comedies are not set in Birmingham, its accent is disliked and therefore little used by actors, it lacks an image.) The drama of Fisher's life is that of someone painting a pre-Raphaelite picture of a mediaeval scene, with models in authentic garb, which he is painting in minute detail, who by chance looks out of his window and sees a modern industrial city stretching away, and wonders what would happen if he looked at that and painted only what he could see. The mediaeval painter was not Fisher himself but the English poetry scene as it was in the mid-1950s, or slightly earlier, which had a problem with source material, because it found the real England unaesthetic and improper. It may be unfair to call rhyme a mediaeval device but it's literally true.

Thirty-five years later, I'm sure it's still true that many people regard Birmingham as unaesthetic. I think you have to have a strong interest in how English society, especially in its buildings, machines, and town layouts, works in order to enjoy Fisher. You show what's there and find the cultured audience would prefer it wasn't there. If my informants are correct, there are remarkably few poets in Birmingham, few poetry magazines, few readings.

Shklovsky wasn't trying to invent something but rather to analyse something which he thought of as an artistic universal. I have a record by Johnny Cash, a performer using traditional genres with rather strict rules, where he exhorts his guitarist, Luther Perkins, "Play it strange, Luther!". Art has to be strange, this isn't some whim of a disaffected minority. Any poetry is riddled with devices for making its surface puzzling, glimmering, ornate, original, and so attractive.

Fisher's approach is related to the insights about the difference between primary perception and awareness which are laid out in books like *The social construction of reality*, by Peter Berger and Alfred Luckmann, and *The intelligent eye*, by RL Gregory. In a normal poem, there are warm rhetorical devices which instruct the reader how to interpret what is happening; Fisher cuts these out, in order to demonstrate that they are there: he gives us glimpses of what the world might be like before verbalisation. These glimpses may be illusory — how on earth could we recognise a shot of a pre-verbal world? — but they are the modern sublime. We are cast back to the beginning of things; we hold as it were an object from millions of years ago, or from very far away, in our hands, and we are inside the object. The specific experience of Fisher's poetry is not what he tells us but the range of hypotheses which we form in reaction to his dissipation of convention and context. It would be misleading to say that work such as Berger's or Gregory's — and much

*The cognitively critical tradition: Madge, Tomlinson, Crozier, Chaloner, Fisher* [65]

like it—supplies an argument for Fisher; their rigorous separation, of the irreducibly real from what is interpretation and socially agreed fiction, washes away most of the justification which exists and opens a million possibilities for art. His exposure of meaning as collusion is also an attack on the cultural and political discourse of London, which by social collusion reduces Birmingham to a fixed emotional flavour, and silences its voice. You can't get back to a pre-verbal self, but you can wander around Birmingham and destroy a particular set of cultural myths about a place.

Fisher has said, in an interview with Robert Sheppard, that his work is "political in the sense that—and this is the didacticism I suppose—the world is made particularly in its social manifestations, in its economics, by mental models. [ . . . ] the human mind makes the world. The investigation of this organism that makes the world is of paramount interest. If we do not know how our minds work, and how our appetites work, and how our senses and our rationalizations are interactive [ . . . ] we're very poorly equipped to interpret the forms by which we live, i.e. the political dimension of the world. All I ask for is to have the imagination regarded [ . . . ] as politicized because the imagination will make the world. And if it isn't my imagination, it is Margaret Thatcher's imagination. She is a deeply imaginative woman. Rhodes Boyson is a deeply imaginative man. They have visions of the world. They have interpretations, rationalizations. [ . . . ] I am, if anything, a specialist in those processes". There is a certain irony in this, because the imaginative processes of Thatcher or Boyson (a ludicrous Far Right educationalist and politician) are, clearly, saturated by obsolete and kitsch sets of imagery and investigating them is to project an unwavering beam onto some pretty ancient artistic properties. It's like using a very modern camera full of intelligent chips to photograph some 1930s semi-detached house which only had forlorn reminiscences of real architecture.

Fisher goes on to say more about these means of interpretation: "You can see the extraordinary range of collocations or combinations that can be made. I don't think that it matters whether you turn the prism so as to give many colours or you turn the prism so as to produce optical chaos. What you have is a prism. What you have is a brain, or language. You can do any bloody thing. [ . . . ] And I don't think you're under any moral injunction to make only convergent patterns".

Fisher's external career has been one of slow progress from a start in the 1950s where he was very frustrated with the English literary scene, and couldn't get published, apparently because he wasn't writing in rhyme. The small press and unorthodox scene that was getting going in the late fifties was designed for poets like him, and he emerged in the light of day with *City*, in 1961 (this is a different text from that included in the 1968 Collected Poems). Three books followed from the classic small publisher Fulcrum, then one from Carcanet, followed by apotheosis around 1980 with a Collected Poems from Oxford University Press. There were no belated apologies; it's so expected that professional makers of taste will get everything wrong that it seems unnecessary for anyone to apologise. Conversely, in fact, one should recognise that publishers like Carcanet and OUP do publish some important books. Perhaps it would be arrogant of me, too, to expect to spot the significant poets before they turn fifty.

Eric Homberger's interesting treatment of the formalism of the fifties (in *The Art of the Real*) sheds light on the origins of Fisher's formulations. He quotes Donald Hall at p.87: "'I have come to think that all human action is formal; all personality is an aesthetic structure, a making something exist by statement: like saying a word. Symmetry becomes the root of morality, conduct, and judgement, and reality is a terrifying chaos outside form glimpsed only occasionally, and never, of course, understood without a translation into form'". (*Poetry from Oxford*, ed. Martin Seymour-Smith, Fortune Press, 1953.) Hall is isolating form and using it as a window to look out into the Unnameable with; this is comparable to Fisher's interest in conceptual tools, also assuming a certain non-identity between the world and human pictures of the world. But Fisher does not find it terrifying. Monsters are rare beasts (unless in a poem by Ted Hughes). The argument that metre has to do with primary categorisation and perception is distinctly odd. The belief that symmetry is the basis of morals is so startling that it might be the subject of a Fisher poem.

∼

"'If art is a window, then the poem is something intermediate in character, limited, synecdochic, a partial vision of a part of the world. It is the means of a dynamic relation between the eye within and the world without. If art is conceived to be a door, then that dynamic relation is destroyed. The artist no longer perceives a wall between him and the world; the world becomes an extension of himself, and is deprived of its reality. The poet's words cease to be a means of liaison with the world;

*The cognitively critical tradition: Madge, Tomlinson, Crozier, Chaloner, Fisher* [67]

they take the place of the world. This is bad aesthetics—and incidentally bad morals.

The use of strict poetic forms, traditional or invented, is like the use of framing the composition in painting: both serve to limit the work of art, and to declare its artificiality: they say, 'This is not the world, but a pattern imposed upon the world or found in it, this is a partial and provisional attempt to establish relations between things.'" Richard Wilbur, (from: *Mid-Century American poets*, ed. John Ciardi, 1950, quoted by Homberger at p.86).

∽

Fisher was by no means a wild man, an isolate. These are the poets of the formalism, with rhyme and strict metre, which Fisher was violently hindered by and reacting against at the outset of his career, yet what they are saying, in these two examples, seems remarkably close to what Fisher believes about poetry. They wish to freeze the artificial relationship of concepts to perception; Fisher wishes to radically draw attention to it, his "turning the prism" round every way corresponds to their "window", fixed in place. It's ironic that, while Fisher's American influences turned English conservatives against him (but got him published in *Origin* in the 1950s), the *chefs de file* of the formalism around him were also American.

Something else contemporary with Fisher's debut was Pop Art, as executed by Hamilton and Paolozzi. The kitsch structures which Pop painters were ostentatiously putting into their paintings correspond to the structures which Fisher was carefully filtering out of his poems in order to produce something mysterious and unadorned. Both techniques show the artist surrounded by highly integrated systems of interpretation and dramatisation with which he is quite at odds and which serve to hide the real nature of the world. Fisher's rigorous interrogation is the successor to poets, of the 1930s, for example who opposed this corrupt scenography of the everyday with a finished oppositional politics, equally scenographic. Fisher, unbeholden to any faction and its iconography, is quietly dismantling the story of the everyday as if it were a motorbike he wished to strip down. The problem, no doubt, is the lack of obvious gratifications for the reader.

Anthropologists are accustomed to study the behaviour of illiterate tribes in terms of cosmology, that is, as a complement to their material culture and their practical relationship to Nature, their attribution of symbolic values to the world, and the system of associations and categories which ties phenomena to those values. It interested people, a few decades ago, to ask how the irrational, religious world view of pre-literates had become the rationalist, scientific world view of the West; an early answer to this was to study the pre-Roman, or Dark Ages, cultures of northwest Europe—giving us the interest in celticity and shamanism. Another response was to single out the irrational elements of Western thought and behaviour. Fisher is trying, by obstinately identifying elements of the physical world and social behaviour, to isolate the cultural process by which social reality is composed. What is the English cosmology? Look at the tabloid newspapers to identify it. Class and religion and saucy sex must be uppermost. The diversity of events can easily be fitted into these repetitive stories, which the public buys every day. The moralising which Fisher has spoken of is a stage flat behind which every new event gets hidden, which disguises its real nature and restores the onlooker to satisfaction and indifference. Yet this is an artificial literary system, it may be more dramatic than the verified facts, but it is as unreal as the apparatus of Classical mythology. Its stock components might be found in finished form as far back as Wesley, perhaps even earlier.

The reason why anthropologists are sent off to the Philippines or New Guinea to do fieldwork is that any society in Britain is too complex. Anthropologists give up: is there any ground for believing that anybody understands British society, a thing with fifty-eight million moving parts? Discourse builds boxes which can be dealt with because they are protected from the complexity of reality; occasionally someone has to come along and demolish one of the walls, to let the puzzling, diffuse grey mass of reality flood in. In such a populous society, the first question is what evidence to ignore; the answer being, at first, to ignore what contains the maximum of interpretation and the least of unfiltered primary data. Moralising is a distraction; the attempts, both Left and Right, to make a link between literary style and ethical or moral goodness are largely false; the parallelism does not exist.

∽

"What I resist [ ... ] is the connotation of what is for me bourgeois—the social democratic outlook of bourgeois guardianship. [ ... ] that there was an arena of informed debate about the true nature of British culture and that it might be found in the New Statesman or an Encounter article [ ... ]

*The cognitively critical tradition: Madge, Tomlinson, Crozier, Chaloner, Fisher* [69]

on the whole you'll find me to the left—or further out—of those people. Not so much in terms of any programme but in terms of distrust of elites and those who constitute them. And I believe that the British forum of articulate culture-bearers is a self-deluding group". (From the interview with Sheppard.) There is an acceptable way of reducing social events to a verbal form; Fisher is saying that it's not a true account, it's a self-referential verbal form, which serves to efface possibilities and restore the mind to calm and apathy; Victorian public opinion ran on sentiment, but contemporary public opinion runs on something more up to date but essentially similar. The empirical project hasn't yet managed to model the chaos of reality, because it has been arrested by a more powerful current of control and fabulation. What Richard Wilbur says, above, about the artificiality of verbal forms, is memorable here; if these systems are artificial, how can they also be accurate accounts of the motives, and the effects, of the behaviour of real people? The Pharisaism of the cultural moralists is their criminal impersonation of goodness and knowledge. The opinionators couldn't wait for the nature of society to be properly understood, because they had to carry out the function of defining who was bad, and who was good, beforehand. This premature assignment of moral values is important, because it accounts for a great deal of literary criticism, of discourse about poetry, and of the poetry which I don't write about: because it is part of "bourgeois guardianship". Perhaps the thing we most look for—or I most look for—in a book is the goodness of the author; the methods of conventional English verse are striving to signal decency that is their function; their failure is that the methods are too self-protective, insufficiently analytical, to decide whether the poet is a good person or not. Perhaps imposing a moral test is a way of reducing the diversity of the world to monotony. Perhaps, if there is no moral test, there is also no need of a judge, of authority, or of tradeable forensic knowledge.

The question of goodness resolves itself, in prose, into the way the writer conducts an argument; fairness will stand for goodness. This is where Fisher's character comes out: in the massive fairness of his interrogative method, in the scrupulousness of his procedures.

Fisher's course, as described in his interviews, has involved a constant exit from romanticism; emotional rebellion is edited out and only cognitive criticism is allowed to stand. His rhythm has to do with the speed at which information can be assimilated, it is didactic, as free of superfluity as a bicycle frame, but dispassionate. This marks him as a transitional generation; although a major poet, he solved his own contradictions in too ruthless a fashion, and the romantic tendency must now have its head.

### Andrew Crozier and the influence of the observer on the observation

Crozier (1943–) has, so far as I know, pursued an orthodox career as postgraduate student and Eng Lit academic (at Keele and Sussex). In a fascinating interview included in Peter Ryan's informative doctoral thesis, Crozier gives a lot of details about his inclinations and early steps, stating that he began writing seriously in 1963, after the Cuban Missile Crisis which ended his preoccupation with nuclear disarmament. In the mid sixties, he was associating very closely with Prynne, John James, Wendy Mulford, Barry MacSweeney. He edited (1966-8) the magazine *The English Intelligencer*, which was planned as a poetic conversation where poets would be sent poems, comment on them, and perhaps take part in a shared journey into the unknown. Many of the poems in *A Various Art* first appeared there. It was he who rediscovered the Objectivist Carl Rakosi and persuaded him to re-enter literary life. I feel that his earliest work (first book publication 1967) is more haphazard and less integrated than what he has written since about 1970; it often deals with travelling, which was disturbing and distracting to stable awareness. The instability of the poet cut open the observer-observed link by destroying the (fictional) fixed viewpoint from which "accurate" knowledge is gained; the poems show both the camera and the object being filmed in motion, so that we have to interrogate both to resolve the data which appear. His poetry has a low emotional temperature; Crozier is a cool writer and does not engineer either climaxes or sites of tension or drama. He does not prefer crises, growth, conflicts of interest, or points of uncertainty. A peak was reached with *Pleats, Moving Parts*, and *High Zero*, between 1975 and 1978. He was not noticeably affected by the "hangover" and ebb of illusion of the mid-70s. He has (like James and Chaloner) been less active since about 1983, perhaps because the dialogue with other poets, in which he always worked, had stopped or altered in nature. His collected poems, *All where each is*, (the phrase is from an Olson poem) came out in 1985. Since then there has been the sequence 'Free Running Bitch', which appeared in *Conductors of Chaos*.

I find it difficult to explain the texts in detail. There are problems in quoting because the context of the whole work is so important. I am rewriting this text now, aware that an early version was in existence in

*The cognitively critical tradition: Madge, Tomlinson, Crozier, Chaloner, Fisher* [71]

around 1995; this is symptomatic of a simple problem, that I haven't really grasped Crozier's poems in the way I have grasped some of his contemporaries. It follows that his interviews (shortly to appear in a book edited by myself and Tim Allen) are a better source. Perhaps a critique of my earlier assertions will be helpful.

Tomlinson believed that by staying very still and looking at things which weren't moving, one could freeze out error. Crozier has concentrated on the effect of serial shifts of state and site of the observer, and of the observed. Some Crozier devices are: the surreal cut; the pun; legato; visual puns. One recurring theme is the direct apprehension of light:

> As I wrote that I saw the sunrise
> an aurora flashing crimson behind a building
> in the blue dawn
> then the disc's rim itself, I saw it rise
> above the roof's edge, the image on my retina
> of steel cut with a blow torch;
> the disc still rose, in four minutes
> it was detached, crimson gone,
> the whole sky lit with it
> and my eye
> dazzled, cannot see these words. I know
> the earth whirling on its axis
> against the direction of the sun ...

(from *Loved litter of time spent*, 1967), which has parallels in each of his books: to examine objectless light clarifies how light is stained by objects, and so brings us information about them. The free metrics and the attention to concrete detail link it to the Objectivists, who had a considerable influence on Crozier at that stage. In 1967, this gesture might be linked to an Objectivist insistence on concreteness, fidelity to the passing moment, with the underlying hope that this acuity would get rid of a baggage of expectations, poetic or cognitive, to reach a pristine layer of non-social meanings. The careful separation of appearances from reality could also point to the central tradition of European philosophy, and later versions of the same trope come closer to the image of the Cave in Plato's *Republic*. The climax might be

> Though we would rob nature
> of her profusion this arch the roof of the world
> echoes prodigally down the corridor, its facings rendered
> an exactly repeated tracery of magic in

cardinal numbers, at each diurnal arc
a hanging lamp mimics our sun.

(FROM *The Veil Poem*)

Perhaps this should point us towards phenomenology, which laid stress on the influence of the observer on the observation event, and on the perplexing simplicity of the original data of perception, patiently exposing the complexity of the processes of deduction and supplement by which they are turned into the data of consciousness. A typical product of this curiosity is the under-interpreted poetic passage; which may annoy the reader a great deal; all the verbal devices which eliminate the ambiguity of what is out there are themselves eliminated. The intent may be to foreground the whole apparatus of deduction and expansion. If all goes well, we recapture a glimpse of a separated world where unmediated sense-data and abstract perceptual rules appear as two separate entities. The act of stripping optical or auditory data of their agreed meaning is therefore hard and exacting work as well as being the opposite, the undoing of work. The catchphrase might be that perception and awareness are incompatible and impossible to compare. The uncovering of the code of deduction rules underlying perception may be claimed as one of the overarching intellectual projects of the past seventy years or so; the writings of R.L. Gregory give a somewhat more up-to-date and intellectually satisfying account than Merleau-Ponty.

Crozier writes poetry which is not anecdotal because it is philosophical:

Light is in the curtains
like a bright veil of numbers
that rises in folds over and over

and the calculus of persistence
undogmatic and fluent in it changes
draws back with the weave
in a white rinse.

(FROM *High Zero*)

This mentions real curtains, with a real weave; but is not anecdotal. We have to mention privatisation as a theme here; let's briefly note that privatisation has been an important trend in Western European life since the 17th century, that it is a mark of "progress" tending to separate Western from Eastern (or Southern) Europe, that the Dutch took it very far very early, and that it is closely tied up with the rise of reading. Lancelot Andrewes' *Preces privatae* (published 1648) could be a key work in the growth of Anglican domestic piety and the domestic genre, which so much influenced the habits of reflection, and therefore of reading and of writing, in England. The specific radius of Crozier's address is small, intimate; it is like chamber music, but it is also very accurate. Self-analysis and self-criticism must precede political action, if it is important that we know which the better policy is.

Philosophical passion is, like sexual passion, extremely hard to fake convincingly; this is an era of bad philosophical poetry, where poets pretend that something complex is going on in their heads. The conditional failure of philosophical poets like Kathleen Raine, Norman MacCaig, or late George Barker is due to their lingering in antique philosophical questions, neglecting the modern group which are unfortunately the only ones unresolved enough to induce the reader to think critically. Often, in modern poetry, the informational value of the text depends on the complexity of the questions opened and made uncertain within it. For example, a communist poet cannot open questions about history or politics because he already knows the answers. Poems depicting proverbial and timeless truths do not arouse thought and have no intellectual content. Crozier's poems reach an apparent maximum of intellectual potential; this could not be increased without introducing problems or assumptions which would reduce the net value. The emotional content of his poems describes the desirability of a marriage and of a contented domestic life; a conclusion which is likely to be right, since so many people do desire those things.

True thought is impossible unless in the presence of true uncertainty. One can only write intellectual poetry on subjects on which one has not reached a settled opinion; the value of modern poetry presumably does not lie in the information it furnishes, but in the opportunities for speculation and formation of hypotheses which it furnishes.

This poetry is observant and contemplative, not at the same time, but in the flickeringly rapid alternation of two trains of information in fastidiously ordered relation to each other:

> Another tarmac scab
> under the grey lake which wrinkles:
> the great skin of water
> closed by the old wound of the moon.
> Like a broken path to the horizon
> the world is in braille
> and enlarged accordingly
> until its brilliance is dimmed
> into the tactile surrounds
> of an auditory tightrope

> the yawning sea of fallen expectation
> now the object is bright and opaque
> like marble in sunlight. The grain
> runs through the mountain to emerge
> running at its foot in the surf
> which foams in fragments heaped up
> like beds of rubble. Half way along
> only the air is visible
> and frightful, not half fast enough
> for anything but a low-pitched green
> blur no farther off
> than it looks. Black out
> in either direction
> and fall like Icarus.

These visual images are not necessarily from the same scene. The marble grain is in a quarry in Carrara, shown in a drawing by Ian Potts which was on the dust cover of the original edition of *High Zero*. It does not contain any green.

The debate about Crozier accuses him of being a "pastoral" poet of ample torpor and complacency. He values smoothness in a poem; he is never jagged, ugly, overbearing, or defiant; stress is always laid on the conduction of the text, the gentle leading of the reader from line to line and from syllable to syllable. These poems have great civility; their burden of meaning is too great to allow abrupt jumps and shock montage. The act of intense focussing on the text is not brought about by some imperious act by the poet, treating the reader as a servant, but by showing something so attractive and open that focussing on it is involuntary—and voluntary. Radical artists have not always been kind to the consumer of art. In intellectual matters the timing and arrangement of ideas and evidence are crucial, and this is why Crozier disposes his text in such a concerted and highly engineered way.

The name of Langley occurs, as a poet who also likes to start from perceptual anomalies and also worked to achieve this precision of timing and capacity to sustain complex meaning in an unresolved state, carrying it like sail without lapsing into the didactic (knowledge we don't possess) or the banal (knowledge we do possess). I find that the capacity to write sustained legato passages, where a meaning is carried on for a long period, gradually being added to without becoming finished and so disappearing from the live area of awareness, is closely related to the ability to sustain ambiguous intellectual propositions, where the equal balance of the two sides prevents resolution and consignment to a storage area of finished truths, and calls for thought.

This capacity is linked to particular skills in metrics, the formulation of propositions, timing, and the use of complex syntax; and points to a power implicit in these skills and denied to poetry when it is the advocate of the self.

∼

In interview, Crozier explained to me that he wrote *High Zero*, a grid of 24 24-line poems, by writing 24 first lines, 24 second lines, and so on. He said, "I have *High Zero* as a kind of theatre in which certain knockabout characters can be rapidly led on and led off"—the different things said in the parts are spoken by these characters, not by a central I-character, whether lyrical or philosophising. The construction of the poem so that horizontal links compete with and complete sequential ones, tends to arrest movement within the poem: it was deliberately constructed so as to be a unified, equal surface, like a painting. The visual art he was relating to was evidently conceptual art, the most promising radical art of the time. I am inclined to relate this to the journey poems of his earliest work. Visual art had to get over its historical commitment to frozen moments of time, fixed in unified and static works of art. The invasion of time was therefore related to the invasion of the conceptual, in which the perforation and as it were emptying of the pure pictorial field were the source of excitement and of resentment. *Loved Litter* has the poet in incessant motion. The later poems dissolve the single point of view and move on to a much more complex, time-based, account of awareness.

The simultaneity suggests that there is no past in the poem: it is a total present, like a painting. To be exact, the poem contains time, but creates its own context from a willed emptiness; its parts are the entire and exhaustive context for each part. The emptying is an act of optimism: the poem is a kind of pure time, untainted by compromise. This emptying also resembles the basis of a relationship, where you lay down your set habits as part of the act of sharing. This suggests that the psychological context of the poem is exchange with other poets, with the heroes who founded English poetry anew with *The English Intelligencer*: as Crozier confirmed in interview, the High Zero title comes from *Striking the Pavilion of Zero* (by John James) and *High Pink on Chrome* (by J.H. Prynne). He used elements from these works as the structural 'rules' of his own work: enforcing improvisation, the creation of a 'pure time' at the behavioural level.

It is usual with conceptual art to make documentation available to the spectator. Crozier was surprised that I hadn't spotted the 24x24 grid on which *High Zero* was based. Conceptual art was also based on an intense discussion between artists—it has the special qualification that it doesn't belong to an individual 'personality' but to a group. This group authorised the language of the works—not special words, of course, but special procedures and semantic structures—and now, of course, is not there to be interrogated, or indeed joined. The capturing of intimacy and private experience, one of the great achievements of the art of that time, can now seem wilfully obscure:

> A dish covers the meanings of fishing a
> River under which a Welsh poet wrote
> His novel subject being sensitive last year
> Scooped delicacies on which a fellow spirit
> Gets up a poem set with little thorns.
> Take the charred entrails in, with hairs singeing.
> Art for short, perhaps ...
>     ("ROSEBUD"; THE WELSH POET IS CERTAINLY JOHN JAMES).

There is a problem of breaking the circle: the works of the Ferry-Grosseteste poets provide the context in which each single work becomes understandable. But, if you can't understand any of them, this not helpful—it seems like a wall with no door.

Crozier made a classic definition, in *Literature and society 1945–70*, of the genre of domestic anecdote as the staple of modern English poetry, and something almost wholly without interest. However, this own poetry is attached to his wife, his home, his friends. His domestic poems are set in real places (mostly around Lewes, which he never seems to have left for very long). Perhaps only in this way is it possible to study the observer and the observed as independent but cooperating factors in the observation event.

A series of isolated, self-contained, successive instants may satisfy a camera but apparently cannot sustain consciousness at all, which only breathes through its ability to step outside time and compare past states with present, and to plan future moments of behaviour. The picture, or the pictorial, have been important releasers of such reflexivity, not especially because ultimate reality is vouchsafed to painters, but because an artificially frozen present-moment permits complex logical operations through its steadiness; which experience certainly lacks. The link with visual art stopped the narcissistic flow of the voice; the bounded area of the painting seems to be less suggestive, prompting, illusionistic, more

*The cognitively critical tradition: Madge, Tomlinson, Crozier, Chaloner, Fisher* [77]

external, than the poem, and encouraged thought about fundamental questions more readily. We have seen the primacy of the visual in Madge and Tiller. It is also true, of course, that art students are forced to think about art, while British poets are essentially self-taught amateurs.

Perhaps I could return to the idea of 'low temperature' which I asserted earlier. This would seem to follow from the suppression of the primary narcissistic flow—as with Madge and Tiller. Crozier's works are not sequences of hot emotions, precisely because they are projects: because you are not allowed to play the tunes familiar from childhood, you can invent new tunes, with a more complex organisation.

I shall return also to the notion of being philosophical. It is more accurate to describe these poems as 'conceptual art projects'. Where philosophy implies the isolation of objects permanent enough to allow permanent truths to be uttered concerning them, this is not happening inside these poems: they are purely transient, that is, complete within their own boundaries. Equally, they are not organised as arguments in which opposing propositions are weighed up.

A satisfying book about the Ferry/Grosseteste school would be possible only on the basis of letters written by most of the poets during the formative years, and also (probably) of interviews with the principal figures.

**An elaborate but two-dimensional backdrop:** *The Edge***, by David Chaloner**
*Duane Eddy in the yellow light of late summer.* First sight of Chaloner's poems was in magazines of the north-west (*poetmeat*, 1966), part of that mid-sixties scene of open forms and a cool manner. He represents in poetry the working-class fop, a typical figure of the era; self-confidence expressed itself here not as swagger or bluster but as comprehensive refinement and languor. He appeared in *Children of Albion*, along with John James and Andrew Crozier, underlining the point that the Ferry Press group, as collected in *A Various Art*, were the most skilled users of the period combination of coolness and direct address, which doesn't yet come off in *Albion* but was smoothed and deepened to reach perfection in the seventies. The first book publication credited in his own list is in 1973; the seventies produced several pamphlets, climaxing with the full-length *Hotel Zingo* (Grosseteste Press, 1981). Chaloner brought off the rock and roll obsession with style and cool, recording the charm and malaise of English summer afternoons and the melancholic poise of the pop dandy:

> the surrounding area prepares itself
> summer lifts over our heads

> like an unrehearsed speech
> here again
> chorused from ascending flashes
>
> milky light polishes
> the ornaments of pretence
> removing the matter of degrees
> of this and thatness
> of yes we do and no we can't
>
> to forget and continue
> as though nothing has happened
> (from "Hotel Zingo")
>
> The view from the window
> dilates the fluid stages of first light,
> the handsome and compelling hours
> where birds forage and invent a sky
> in the filigree of tangled shrubs
> (FROM "SITTING ON THE SIDE LINES", IN *HOTEL ZINGO*)

As in other writers linked to the Grosseteste name, light appears as an independent agent; in Chaloner, as a peculiarly wayward and sulky one, a kind of rival fop:

> you cannot tell the time by the grey light
> in the window
> the frame outlines a response
> tempting permutations of coincidence
> it would seem that someone has forgotten
> to switch off the light
> the underside of the yellow lampshade
> a white ellipse of proof
> in order to belong to what exists
> both elements
> light, therefore lampshade, and window
> thus time, extend the dimension
> that is our sense of dawn anticipated
> an uneasy not working, but content
> you observe the static lucidity of crystal sky
> cool air pressed flat against the eye
> ("INTERIOR: MORNING", FROM *PROJECTIONS*)

Chaloner, who works as an interior designer, is preoccupied with style and detail, as if he were designing and drawing himself: "The fundamental ease of a firm line/ meticulously detailed, perfectly terminated,/ existing within the boundaries of shrinking days" (from "Pact and

## The cognitively critical tradition: Madge, Tomlinson, Crozier, Chaloner, Fisher [79]

Impact", from *Hotel Zingo*). He seems unconvinced that the shadows and irregularities which suggest the visual world to be three-dimensional are in fact anything more than hatching by a supernal designer: "an elaborate but two-dimensional backdrop/ rises slowly into the flytower". This preoccupation with marks signifying the edge of planes is perhaps really directed at the markers at the edges of a social frame, things of peculiar importance in an England apparently being led away, in the 1960s, from "matters of degrees" to unenclosed free openness (*espace lisse*) by class mobility, where the rules of the game were becoming conscious to the players. New leaders of fashion did not bring about a new socio-economic order. Inventive attention to clothes and hair gives the dandy an autonomy, which is illusory or accessory when he is enclosed in a much larger picture, full of objects and rules right outside his control. Control over the generation of meaning cannot be seized by individuals. How aching the swell of optimism:

> bending cutting and glueing the cardboard scenery
> for the systematic fabrication of a landscape
> where we will settle down to solve the logical
> sequence of all that is imposed
> on the pattern of so much we have yet to
> fully understand
> the openings are within our range
> by the time we are prepared and aware that
> to go back to our former selves is to remain
> and to advance is to accept what is offered
> and the chance to rework destiny with clear headed
> abstraction
>
> ("14 April 1971", from *Chocolate Sauce*)

An important influence in the eighties has been what I would think of as postmodernism, possibly in fact the American LANGUAGE poets, as an interest in foregrounding the rules of the form being used, making the artistic illusion conscious. Chaloner published a pamphlet with the Rhode Island avant-garde press Burning Deck as long ago as 1977. It seems that the detached, stylised self-adornment of the Pop era has flowed on into an unquiet self-awareness; the poet is no longer in control but sees his own figure reduced and constrained by genre rules. The poet is in a situation, physical or artistic, which is increasingly rundown and in poor taste:

> No further action abandoned.
> The leak in the lean-to roof, abandoned.

> The cracks in the ceiling that spread while
> you are away, and I'm not looking, defying
> the plasticity of vinyl paint, abandoned.
>
> (FROM A POEM FROM *Trans*)

*The Edge* is a revelation, an advance into radically different subject material, which however amplifies and continues the themes of all his poetry. The edge in question is Alderley Edge, a scarp in Cheshire. A note at the end says: "The events and experiences that inform this work are interpretations of my father's anecdotal recall. After a short period in a cotton mill he worked as a farm labourer through the 1920s and 30s. [ . . . ] The underlying dissatisfaction and frustration with conditions that he accepted as unalterable, in an archaic and feudal system, remained with him into old age. He maintained that landowners and tenant farmers exercised choice preference for non-union men who would not cause trouble. This suited his migrant nature but certainly contributed to exploitation". Chaloner's concern with silent commands, frame markers demarcating paths of social appropriateness, now extends to the organisation of space by boundaries and property rights, not just recession and luminosity. He evokes the order of farms in terms of geological origins, of space being sucked out of nothingness:

> Land economics confound
> The transient labour force
> Whose trade is erased
> Farms surrendered to ruin
> Signify audacious outposts of failure
> Erosion wounds exposed through ground cover
> Reveal their millstone grit
> And glacial junk united
> Beneath a tangled shawl of barren excess
> Low cloud delivers fine rain
> Anointing Three Shires Head
> Upper Swineseye, Red Brook, Spittle House

The narrative element has been reduced almost to a painful extent: the domain of this long poem is the search for meaning, disquieted by a glimpse of the origin of meanings—the invention of private property. What's done cannot be unsaid. A projection of the wish for allegiance and security into the past uncovers a primal erasure, his father was an illegitimate foundling, expelled from the order of succession to suffer the groundless being of the landless. Chaloner's gaze into the English rural order is steady enough to reveal a central horror:

*The cognitively critical tradition: Madge, Tomlinson, Crozier, Chaloner, Fisher*

Glistening rush of boundless light
Where recurrent images laden with truth
Continually move away
Tracking the flawed course of unnatural lineage

# Secrets of Nature: documentary, group feeling, and propaganda

### Myth, propaganda, and documentary

A thesis: that the formally radical poets of the 1940s were anarchist-pacifists, that the radical poets of the 1960s and 1970s were Marxists or otherwise too far Left for the policy-makers of Labour. That the departure from the centre, where everyone understands what is being said because it is wholly predictable, is a flight away from social control. That the popular media, regulated by managers and financial interests in a way which just doesn't exist in the underground, project ideas at people, with a huge suggestive power, which support the existing political and economic structures, and which seem ridiculous when you "sober up". That a certain set of ideas is the "organic" ideology of the political system, in the sense of one which serves its specific needs, and which changes precisely as those needs change. That British imaginative productions incorporate a national myth, or ideology, which to anyone from another country seems repetitive, coercive, pedantic and so boring, and false. That the awesome accuracy and power to record reality, of modern media like photography and broadcasting, are not used to record reality critically, but to suggest ideas to the population, at the service of sectional interests and not dependent on truth.

So much the thesis put in deliberately crass terms, since an accurate treatment of it would take hundreds of pages. The reason why an alternative, occluded line of poetry formed must lie in this region of concepts. Questions like, whether the flight from the centre is just a form of the "privatisation of experience" which is one of the most common (even central) processes of modern times, and whether the

## Secrets of Nature: documentary, group feeling, and propaganda

rejection of the mainstream is political or stylistic, will have to wait. I haven't done the research to find out whether a few hundred small press poets were all Marxists or anarchists, although I know in some cases that they are right-wing or sceptical about politics. Disliking certain styles often turns out to be the result of disliking certain people, which leads us back into "real" experience, although on a spatial scale which we do not normally call political. However, it is time to get down to detail, although only on one plane of this multi-planed problem.

The territory of twentieth-century poetry has been bounded by the rise of other information media, most of them less highly coded and more accessible to the broad public. Poetry exists in the area bounded by the main audiovisual stream of British culture and its history takes place within that area. This relationship defies treatment in print, partly because the main evidence is audiovisual, and partly because it is too intimate and fine-scale. It is attractive to simplify it; the evidence is everywhere, and it is quite easy for the reader to switch the television on and ask how is this different from poetry? Or, could this theme be treated in verse? The increase in crude availability of information did not simply make people better informed, because the overall virtual scenes being put out by illustrated newspapers, radio, film, and television included emotional suggestions and assimilable behavioural models, where the "informative" element could seem peripheral. All these media were as good for propaganda as for documentary. These two, supremely successful, genres, offered poetry a dazzling array of possibilities but they were not taken simply as assets to be seized on, and it is the withdrawal of poets from these public styles of signifying which is most striking. The chastity of Imagism, and its offshoot Objectivism, was a guide for this withdrawal.

Various publications in the drift of "post-imperial" criticism have questioned the interest of Britain or British people as subjects for literature. This is perhaps the most fundamental question in contemporary taste, although for someone in Britain the answer is quite easy to find. Any line of a book is interesting partly because it relates to a larger situation, and we care about the line because we care about the overall situation, or not. The core of British writing, it seems, is an intense self-regard where projective identification swamps accuracy. So, the core of fine writing in Britain looks suspiciously like propaganda. Whereas everyday awareness is about *me*, the gaze of culture is directed at *us*. The artistic form of this is often a series of historical tableaux (a pageant), or a kind of lawsuit where someone is accused of crimes, in government or out, which afflicted the commonweal.

We don't have a mythology like the Greeks, and our myths don't take the form of narratives. The "new mythology" takes the form of repeatable scenes of symbolic intent, taught by audiovisual means, and made attractive by high points. These feature in advertisements, rock videos, album sleeves; it is fair to suppose that variants of them feature in the fantasy life of the audience, where they are appropriated, re-edited, repeated. The constant of which the "myth" consists may be a set of relationships, rather than a place, or a named hero. The role assumed by poetry is to be secondary to these primary event sequences; as the sermon is secondary to the Bible text, or lesson, it studies, and uses different procedures. The modern poem has often set out from the belief that the contents of consciousness are inaccurate, and this theme took over from the religious precept of trying to make the congregation better people.

The First World War saw the plunge of the government into propaganda, both at home and abroad, and so the teaching to everyone of a set of patriotic images and reasons for fighting. A distribution of imagery, in fact. After this point, poets could restage these repeatable scenes, manipulate them, but could only turn to new and personal imagery at the risk of widespread incomprehension. People with no experience of any other country could now tell you what the "British way of life" was. The final, crisis year of WWI saw the climax of a conflict within His Majesty's Government between two different notions of how to make propaganda abroad, in which the tabloid version, led by two newspaper proprietors (Lords Northcliffe and Beaverbrook), defeated the sober Foreign Office version, which aimed to reach a much smaller audience (of "makers of opinion"). There is an odd symmetry between this struggle, to inject populist patriotic violence into the message, and the reform of poetry in the 1920s, which saw patriotism and the heroics of Empire definitively thrown out, and the unconscious decision to direct poetry only at a minority. Sir Henry Newbolt, the symbol of out of date (and naval) poetry for a new generation, had chaired a committee on propaganda during the war, which called for changes in official storywaging. The link between relaxation of truth (in favour of emotion and partiality) and totalitarianism is obvious. The implications for poetry of stepping up the demands for truth (for precision, concrete observation, relation of local data to general principles, etc.) are less obvious. The sense of being deceived is potent, clinging, immersing, agonising; disillusion is one of the major themes of 1920s literature, a hangover from a vanished imperial fantasy so bad that it felt like theological remorse and conversion. The experience of real deception, that is by super-patriotic newspapers breathing out hatred of the Hun, and adulation of "the British way of life", by the swollen pride of a "super-power", for four years of total war, brought a fear of deception. Perhaps modernity in English poetry (so different from modernism) has a lot to do with this new wish for precision.

The documentary film in Britain was started by John Grierson at the film unit of the Empire Marketing Board (1927-1933), in Oxford Street. So the most influential line of 1930s British cinema (certainly the one which meant most to the intellectuals of the nation), and which invented techniques used daily by television, not only for documentary but also for fiction film with a "realist feel", was being paid for by government money, allocated with the aim of creating a "British image" that would produce political and commercial influence.

Stephen Tallents was the ideas man who persuaded the Civil Service to restart the course of propaganda which had been pioneered in the Great War and abolished, as a corrupting factor which damaged the credibility of official utterance, straight after it. At the Empire Marketing Board, there is good reason to think he organised some of the key scenes of "national mythology" but thematically this only developed the propaganda of the Great War period. James Lees-Milne described him as "well read but uncultivated". Anyone trying to find the official imagery of propaganda, hoping to create a reference list of preset "scenes" which could be used via "cross-matches" to analyse modern poetry with, will find valuable material in EMB posters and in the films of the documentary movement. One favoured theme was continuity, as in a poster about Empire trade which shows "John Bull's Emporium, established 450 AD". All the posters project the robustness of what they show, whether trees or locomotives. When the Empire collapsed, its robustness was no longer apparent. The continuity implies that conflict is absent (or indecisive), as is after all necessary for the sustenance of friendly relations and long-distance trade. The Empire was based on credit and on long-distance trade to far-away markets; so all the parts of the commercial network had to be robust. The posters had also to project a sense of security which relaxed people into a consuming mood to compose the market. The request for trust raises the question of authenticity which we search for in the texture and design of the image because that is all we have to go on. The posters were beautiful, and it is hard to find poems which are *more* beautiful.

Planners could foresee that the combination of Japan, Italy, and Germany could create virtually insuperable problems for the Royal Navy in wartime. Images of Britain were therefore used to persuade the White Dominions to supply resources essential for a worldwide naval strategy; images of the Empire were being used to persuade the consumers of Britain to "buy Empire goods" and so strengthen colonial economies which would supply bases, raw materials, and recruits in wartime or, more subtly, to persuade the electorates that imperial wars were good for them. The first worldwide radio broadcast was in 1930, on the occasion of the Naval Conference, at which imperial naval disagreements were argued out; the BBC Empire Service began two years later. The susceptibilities of the imperial cause between 1914 and 1939 (if not earlier) much resemble the susceptibilities of the Cold War Lobby between, say, 1946 and 1989, and the techniques of the Cold War were already in use in the earlier period even if the technology was continually progressing. Democracy was a problem for the small elite groups which produced military and foreign policy, and the worldwide span of the empire was the point of strain: not only was warfare necessary to keep the "super-state" in being, not only was this mixture of hugeness and militarisation the very thing which gave the elite their exciting power (and generated the secrets they shared), but also it required an integrated strategy of awesome complexity (subject therefore to spoiling at any point), and called for a world-spanning system of bases. The radius of the naval-military organism was dangerously wide: the time for dissemination of decisions was dangerously long; this meant that consulting Dominion Prime Ministers during hostilities was infeasible. The decision of the Dominion governments to build their own navies (with their own tax revenues), under their own control, was much against the wishes of the planning elite in London (although they could hope to recoup by having the long-distance units under a unified imperial tactical command). However, this exposure to the strong autonomous reason of Dominion electorates (some of them disloyal Irish, some of them disloyal working-class socialists) was only a variant on the dependency of Imperial policy on the British electorate who had quite inappropriately been given limited powers to interfere with the business of State. The policy-making elite therefore had to develop a narrative fit to build alliances with several different electorates, alongside the similar (but in content quite different) narratives to sustain alliances with their peers inside the elite, with foreign allies, with the world of finance, with trading and manufacturing interests, etc. What

Tallents had realised was the need to put over this narrative in modern forms (films and posters, to start with), and for a new profession of propagandists, free from the stylistic phobias of the traditional civil service (which he called "monk-like"). His project will remind us of thousands of demands on poets to start talking to a broad audience.

The problems of the political elites in the Dominions seem insoluble, in retrospect. Grierson, of course, went to work for the Canadian Film Board. A political party ruling Australia could decide to cut the imperial link; this brought immediate problems in marketing wool and lamb, undefined problems with British financial and trading interests controlling so much debt and credit in Australia, long-term problems in framing a Pacific defense against Japan, and unpleasantly close scrutiny of these problems by pro-British elements at home. Or, they could stick with the motherland, which meant a sophisticated media policy, armed with a plausible line on everything, to cover over the public problems which the British link kept on causing. This media line produced a sensitivity which most probably inclined politicians to co-ordinate events and news releases, where the concerting obviously had to happen "backstage", i.e. before the release of news. The fragility of long-term worldwide alliances produced anxiety and of course resentment against loudmouths who asked awkward questions (of the "why were all those Australians at Gallipoli" and "why is India British" type). The Empire was based on cover-ups. Foreign policy and economics were truly very complex and based on collusion: very few people understood them (they are the classic terrain of hostility towards the electorate) and irritation was frequent. The gap between "you just don't understand the game" and "you are right but you are a contumacious threat to our game" is very hard to draw, although of course it is the essential line in the whole landscape.

Politicians have a lot to hide. Their followers also want it hidden and these include the officers of culture. The fact that poetry has, for a long time, been divided between the "ideologically loyal" (who are allowed access to conventional publication) and the "ideologically disloyal" (who can only publish through small presses and are denounced as "obscure") is not controversial. We ask, instead, why "public affairs" could come to be of such pressing concern that they became the primary issue in poetics (and stylistic differences were their derivatives); the answer is surely in the very tight structure of the policy elite, and the power embodied in the knowledge they owned; a structure which intellectuals found irresistible. No other information could develop this compacted affective charge. The idea of developing an alternative economic philosophy appealed partly because so many of them were being asked to make films, or write bright articles, justifying the one actually in force. We have to wonder whether the appeal of the inexplicit in poetry, with its rich flavours of exclusion, initiation, and collusion, is not based on this primary collegiate collusion, where imperial policy was made. What could be more seductive than the implied secrets of Auden's early poetry, reading like a Graham Greene novel with the plot left out?

Carroll Quigley's version of twentieth century history is that British foreign policy was being produced by a semi-secret "Round Table" which included imperial businessmen, politicians, and Americans. This is unproven; but, awkwardly enough, the other interpretations are essentially similar. Foreign policy must be the product of groups of specialists ("lobbies", if you like) in the regions and languages concerned; it must consult businessmen, since it is largely about trade; it must be long-term and involve alliances with overseas interests; it can only be worked out by setting basic assumptions, which may be wrong, but which allow concrete plans to be detailed and criticised. It is the pursuit of national self-interest, and it does involve money and warfare. Short-term alliances are poor assets, but long-term ones require long-term commitments, shielded from politics. Politicians, and the citizens, can set policy imperatives but cannot exercise detailed control unless they take the time. Foreign policy issues were largely kept out of Parliament, because after all every Foreign Ministry in the world read Hansard. Secrecy promoted ignorance and ignorance justified secrecy.

The dispute about propaganda during WWI was precisely about the value of restricting efforts to the "policy-making elite". The Foreign Office's case was that efforts sufficient to reach the mass electorate in the USA (for example) would have provoked a backlash of resentment at British interference; whereas addressing the elite involved small-scale efforts, and could be done simply by publicising facts, with no element of illicit deceit. This applied also to persuasion in Rumania, Argentina, Australia, etc. The 1918 decision of the politicians, to let the newspaper bosses handle the matter instead, can be taken as the point where the partnership of government and media began: the media are now the link between the politicians and the mass electorate. There is a split between the language (and knowledge base) of the elite and that of ordinary people. To adopt the latter implies that you are ignorant and that the information you impart is of low value.

When Stephen Tallents went from the (closed) EMB to the Post Office, he took the film unit with him, and they became the GPO Film Unit (at 21 Soho Square). We have to ask what is the relationship between the earnest left-wing integrity usually associated with Grierson and his pupils, and the demonic cunning embodied by Tallents and Reginald Leeper, who led the continuation of wartime propaganda into the struggle for influence between the wars. British propaganda is generally assumed to have been more effective than German in both wars, that is, better at propaganda than Hitler.

We tend to forget what Robert Hewison has emphasised, in *Culture in the Cold War*, just how many British writers were spending their working days in making propaganda; in an era which starts in 1939 and goes on until the 1960s. The complex comprising the World Service, the British Council, and "public relations" parts of the government (such as the Ministry of Information and the Crown Film Unit) all goes back to the political insecurity of the Empire between the wars and the far-sighted schemes of Tallents. An institution like the Fuad I University at Cairo goes back to Foreign Office money and a wish to have the small dominant stratum of Egyptian society well affected towards the British. Without the modern naval base at Alexandria, on Egyptian territory, the war in the Mediterranean would have taken quite a different course. The British Council was founded by someone called Reginald Leeper, then at the News Service of the Foreign Office, who in 1940 became head of the Political Warfare Executive; different offices which were all part of "projecting the nation". Political warfare is what was renamed to psy war and then to psy ops. Tallents would have had this job but was fired (from the "shadow Ministry of Information") after his dummy news releases justifying the Munich Agreement didn't come up to scratch. The appeal of the documentary idea, which seemed to get away from the worn-out patriotic imagery associated with the old ruling order and find an untainted source of compelling images, is impaired when one realises that the films were being financed by large corporations to promote their own products, and that the exceptions to this commercialism were more directly government propaganda.

Anyone who looks at the spokesman statements up to about 1960 of the profession of teachers of English, for example when pronouncing on the purpose of the English degree course, will notice how much attention was given to promoting English values, and how many of the jobs for graduates were outside Britain, for example in Africa. Caution is needed in tracing the limits of this drive, which was thoroughly similar to the efforts of the Empire Marketing Board and British Council; it was probably more important as a way of appealing to politicians for funding than as something which individual teachers were truly drawn to. It must have declined very sharply as the Empire dissolved. There was a temporal segment of literary enthusiasts who thrived on Newbolt, Noyes, and Kipling, and read them aloud to their pupils, but there must have been relatively few teachers qualifying after about 1922 who would reinforce it. My impression is that the output of the new English degree courses of the 1920s and 1930s were utterly unsuitable for glorifying a capitalist Empire based on war and disenfranchisement of the coloured races. When Hitler came along, they couldn't write propaganda without feeling sick at heart. In the Empire, though, they must have taught unconscious racism, and indeed the whole project of teaching English literature to African, West Indian, and Indian pupils is a clear example of that.

I wonder if WS Graham would have written "The Nightfishing" if Grierson hadn't made "Drifters", twenty years earlier, and established the concept. I wonder if Auden's 1930s poetry is, essentially, a huge collection of shots suitable for a documentary that never got made, and if his (temporary) interest in social reality wasn't a reflection of Grierson's ideas. The enigmatic quality of that poetry is perhaps due to the author's basic lack of participation; he is just accumulating brilliant shots to be fitted into a filmic concept by someone else. I wonder if Lynette Roberts' amazing poetry about a trans-polar air service (in *Gods With Stainless Ears*) would have been written without the World In Action film (made in Canada, by a film unit headed by Grierson) on this very subject.

British literati, never mind Irish or Australian ones, didn't really want to work for the government. One of the main currents in 1940s poetry is a resistance to the collective life, including the one represented (innocently, you would have thought) by His Majesty's Government. This oppositional strip was criss-crossed by the shifting fortunes of the socialist or Marxist line, and the anarchist line, itself much weaker than the Christian element, represented at that time by pacifism and personalism. It correlates with the refusal to bear arms: some 60,000 people registered as conscientious objectors during the hostilities. This disloyalty didn't do the literary any good in the eyes of His Majesty's trusted servants, people disposing of much greater amounts of power than young poets. The links between being critical, and being more or less unpublished and unread, were being forged at that time.

Political discussion is almost entirely about things which cannot be seen. Part of the interest of art is that it makes these virtual objects firm and visible, so helping the transition from personal symbolism to collective symbolism—a transition which is inevitable and never made with complete success.

It may be that there are two ways of thinking about the world, one which is modern, quantitative, standard in units, steady, and so on; and one which is based on pictures and empathy, perhaps on fantasy, cannot get away from single concrete instances, which changes every time the observer's mood changes, which knows about texture but is vague about dimension, and so on. Presumably political thought includes processes from many points along the spectrum between these two poles. Perhaps unfairly, I have revealed that I think one of these is much better than the other as the information which a government uses; however, the quality of this information is fragile, since it relies on the accuracy of so many sources which are being integrated and rolled up, and one strand of modern political thought has as its founding asset the inaccuracy of this mediated knowledge extending over millions of people and as its stock in trade the list of policy errors which reveal the partiality of this knowledge.

Propaganda can be divided into two parts: the factual part and the emotional part, which consists essentially of a group feeling which the consumer is invited to join. The Empire posters offer us an imagined community. The factual part is easy to deal with and verbalise, but inessential: the speeches of Hitler and Goebbels contain relatively few lies because they simply avoided issues of fact which did not suit them. The group feeling part is the psychological equivalent of marching in step: it means that, when listening to a piece of patriotic music, your emotional impulses are going up and down in time with the music and so also with many other people. We would obviously want to include (patriotic) music, rallies, processions, and fiction (e.g. films) as propaganda, but we have an awkward problem in defining them as false due to their lack of referential meaning. I do not know if this group feeling is undifferentiated, or if it has a complex internal structure. It resembles self-directed, personal subjectivity, generically, as walking resembles climbing.

The interaction between the two channels is decisive. A film without music is less emotionally effective, so the music adds value to the (rational) words and images but also the "real" content defines and directs the music. It is a convention (so far as I know in all countries) to have news bulletins and political speeches unaccompanied by music: to add music would be quite a solecism. The music undermines the words, makes them less credible and more involving. The original binding of propositional meaning and affective tone together may be re-usable: the imagery "stamped" in some public issue of values may re-appear in other contexts and still be successfully caught by the audience. In the EMB posters we have an extraordinarily careful match of the rational form and the emotional value; we imagine that smoothing the "splashes" from this match takes up much of the time of the painter.

One of the key skills in politics is in directing attention towards things that can be verified and in arranging an evidence system in which the witnesses at inquiries, before select committees, and indeed in law courts, give valid answers to questions and the policy process confines itself to such questions. Although we cannot get rid of ideology, it co-exists with the evidence system and deserves to lose ground to the latter both within government and in the course of an individual life. But so far as politicians, and voters, use their imagination, it works like the imagination of a poet, and by collecting political pictures and poems we can come to hold ideology in our hands.

When poems are views of collective fantasies, and parts of a durable virtual world, their meaning can only be brought out by study of political imagery; that is, of sources which are not usually included in literature courses and which have no literary value.

Since the narrative offers us participation in a group feeling, we respond by wondering if we want to take part in this group. When we watch a war film that puts a small group on screen, we look at the quality of interaction within the group and we like to judge it as realistic or inauthentic. This is a difficult area; the zero view is that we cannot qualify group feeling as true or false, as it is a mere bubble. Films made about the Second World War in the 1960s are quite different from ones made in the 1950s or 1940s. Even if we detect unreality (and call it sentimentality or schmalz), it is hard to say whether our reaction means rejection of the emotion or of the accuracy. Also, it is hard to get from the small group pattern to the government and the whole socio-economic structure. Any judgments in this area have to be made with a light touch. However, the attention which the audience gives to such issues encourages us to believe that we can pick up and manipulate such virtual and fragile objects; and the attention which propagandists, scriptwriters, etc. gave to them at the time confirms that such decisions were conscious, and points out to us what they were. The projection of "English identity" into events in small groups, or between two people, was so much a concern of propagandists that we do not need to guess about it.

Poets tend to walk out of the prevailing group feeling, to go into isolation, and to try to create a new group feeling in symbolism, which uses means generically similar and specifically different from the official ones. This does not explain why the occlusion began in the 1940s. In fact, many more poets write in a conventional style than in an unconventional (and so easily occluded) fashion. What I believe happened is that the pressure of war on a fatally overstrained imperial state made the national version of truth overdetermined: it was suddenly more difficult for thinking poets to reproduce it and more difficult for cultural managers and their political bosses to swallow anything else without undermining themselves. The system recirculated its output to its input, but had a slow leak.

The significance of the Objectivist style may now appear more clearly. Imagism was a watershed in British and American poetry. It was a purging from poetry of elements closely associated with it. If we ask what was purged, rather than what was retained, the answer is probably "signs inducing group feeling, sympathy, shared purpose, pathos, sentiment". Historically, this distaste for generous group feelings may be linked to the excess of them let loose by propaganda during the Great War. From excess to disgust. The "watershed" claim needs to be qualified: there was a significant trend towards greater precision and closer control of language between the wars, signposted by the rise of Practical Criticism and the New Criticism and this remains even if we dismiss Imagism and its successor, Objectivism, as factors. The line of close linguistic control and distaste for emotion has become a brandmark of academic poetry, not of all poetry in general. Emotional poetry is still being written, but is of low prestige.

There is an obvious problem with dates, namely that Imagism predates the First World War by five years. However, the psychological myth of the Empire was already very big in the tabloids and popular culture and presumably annoying to intellectuals; the naval race between Britain and Germany was much in the news, and an aesthetic structure of 1909 could easily have been adapted to quite different purposes fifteen years later.

Imagism seems to have been a defining challenge for poets, inducing a crisis which individuals could experience as much in 1965 as in 1920; poets who survived this crisis emerged with a much more original and reflexive style. The crisis may situate the distinction, often made by observers, between "naive" and "self-critical" poetry. The location of this line often seems fickle, arbitrary, and meaningless.

Documentary film has also encouraged greater precision, and made the composition of perception, as a mixture of sense data and of projections based on group feeling, more obvious. Perhaps the use of the camera for this, as opposed to thousands of other cultural projects equally feasible, derives from a collective wish to eliminate propaganda and suggestibility, very much like Practical Criticism. Alternatively, the photographic record progressively destroyed collective representations conceived in visual terms, which embodied the emotional contract of imperialism, and poetry changed because of this destruction. Or, one could attribute the disturbances in the collective imaginary to class conflicts, the upheaval of the oppressed. It would be interesting to give a comparative weighting to these factors.

Going through a course based on Practical Criticism ideas, especially one continued over five years (from O-level to graduation) or even longer, encourages irony, detachment, and sober language ("no rhetoric"). However, interviews with poets show that some of them resented this influence and even that they only began to like their own poetry once they had recovered from it. So, quite a few educated people write poetry which is not ironic or detached. The line between "hot" and "cold" poetry was once chronological, is partly a difference of social class (uneducated versus educated), but is, as well as these, also a matter of personal choice.

The images used to project Britain were in fact images of Britain and their forfeiture meant a loss of language which is comparable to the loss of a shared religious cosmology with the decline of faith. No one can generate an image which is recognisably Britain and yet not similar to the discourse of the government and of advertisers. To put it another way around: no one can develop a symbolic expression of authenticity which cannot be copied and turned out over and over by the creative people in advertising agencies. Every shot in the documentary movement was learnt and copied by admen; after all, that is what they went to film school to study, and that capacity for glossy imitation is what admen cultivate. The agencies were perfectly content to recycle images of working-class solidarity to sell products to working-class consumers; a face redolent of pessimism and integrity could be used to tell you that the product it was endorsing was value for money and would last a long time.

How was poetry going to recapture shared imagery? Simple evocation of the images came to seem subservient and reactionary; registering criticism of them demanded a serious reform of poetic language, to become one level more critical and sharp, and to include an internal critique of what the "main level" was saying. Recognition that the central imagery was virtual apparently destroyed the claims to reality of the poem based around it; selection of unauthorised imagery confused the reader, since its meaning had to be explained rather than simply remembered from a comfortable common pool.

The documentary approach had a great allure for poets. Charles Madge wrote, in the 1940s, two long "documentary poems", although so far only one has been published. He was a sociologist by profession and a founder of Mass Observation and was a friend of Humphrey Jennings, who contributed to some important non-fiction films of the Crown Film Unit. Madge was the first poet to extend political rebellion into a criticism of the rules of representation used in "display objects" (films, novels, posters, etc.) of the order in being. This shift defines the ability of poetry to define a territory for itself in the new landscape: while film is rich in data, poetry is rich in ideas. This is certainly a problem for poets who aren't intellectuals. The perceptualist critique is a response to the dominant audiovisual culture which both recognises its dominance, and withdraws poetry, and uses the poem in order to criticise the "display object" as an artefact and as an instrument of power. Reflexivity and marginality are here combined; the reflexivity comes from an original sense of sickness and doubt, and the marginality then follows from a failure to obey Tony Blair's instruction to "tune in to the dominant reality principle".

References to the artificial nature of the images on show are a staple of advertising, which flatters the intelligence of the audience (and perhaps of the copywriters) in this way. Directions where advertising cannot follow are the framing of complex propositions and the slowing down of the narrative segments, so that the characters dwell with us, and acquire some kind of moral reality. These directions were therefore available for poets, although only for gifted ones; the artistic results offer the reader some difficulty and have been unacceptable to the official magazines and publishers. If your poem is not instantly consumable, it's not going to appear in *Poetry Review*. This tendency is what people sometimes mean by "reflexivity": the deepening of the conventional scenes and of the verbal gestures by which they are evoked.

Another group which, in the 1930s, was trying to bring greater precision to acts of the imagination, is the Euston Road School. Painters such as William Coldstream, Victor Pasmore, and Graham Bell were trying to create a valid equivalent of the visible world, not something dominated by subjectivity and so visibly invalid for other people. One of the students at their school was Humphrey Jennings. The attempt at painting without fantasy involved a stress on frequent checking of proportions, catching the distorting effects of subjectivity in their most basic state. This is reflexivity: the resistance of the conscious mind to the febrile activity of the sensibility. The project involved an endless non-losing chain of correction gains, using reality as the incorruptible witness, to produce the ultimately credible image. A profusion of squaring marks, each recording yet another check of the image against the source object, is the trademark of their work in its unfinished state. It is hard to read about this project without thinking of JH Prynne and his endlessly painstaking attempts to drive out subjectivity and increase the accuracy of registration of the poem. However fertile this group is as a source of ideas about British culture in our period, the resultant paintings up to say 1945 are not especially attractive; the pioneering work did not go to waste, and sorting out the longer-term aesthetic results, for example in the work of Euan Uglow, is something I do not have space for.

No amount of facts can amount to a critical statement because these are two absolutely different categories of utterance. Poetry which merely records experience is trapped in a world of appearance. Poetry becomes political only when it includes conjecture and criticism of what is real. Poetry which fulfils these minimum conditions leaves the populist register and straight away sounds like the discourse of the policy-makers, because the ratio of fact to analysis is also the factor which makes a poem stylistically high or low.

The landscape of quiet, moderation, exchange, of the survival of ancient and fragile objects, is the expression of a wish. Through the cracks, we notice that there is a quite different British political tradition of ultimate force; that wide sections of the electorate definitely were militarist, that the First World War was fought partly through a blockade which brought starvation to German women and children, that the Empire came about through a series of contests of arms, that it was upheld by naked force in emergencies, that democracy was for Whites only, that area bombing of cities full of civilians was one of the means by which the Second World War was fought, that obtaining nuclear weapons was a principal goal of government after the war, etc. No single political value has a central place in the national tradition. I have chosen extreme selectivity because the full picture is wholly confusing. This range of different values means, at least, that poets have a real opponent to take on, when they commend a particular attitude.

## Avant-garde legitimacy, continued; Neo-Objectivism

A certain malaise in the back of the head is suggesting to us that the Objectivist demand for precision is alarmingly like the preference for exactitude associated with IA Richards, Leavis, and what is known as the new criticism, or the Cambridge School of criticism, which produced the Practical Criticism method standard in sixth forms when I was at school. What exactly is the difference between the "neo-Objectivist" Cambridge school and the average English academic writing poetry? I would prefer to point to the works than to engage in an exhausting and possibly elusive attempt at definition. However, we should be aware that there is within the chaste groves of the avant-garde an anti-Cambridge tendency which classifies them along with the academic mainstream. Conversely, it seems quite reasonable to me to regard *A Various Art* as the product of reading Eliot, Empson, John Crowe Ransom, *The Verbal Icon*, and so on and to claim that the one offers no more difficulties than the other.

Zukofsky, Reznikoff, and to some extent Oppen, can be described as documentary poets. Their attitude to rhythm is like documentary because it favours the spontaneous against the staged, it holds its own result to be natural, with convention stripped away. Their choice of subject matter, very consistently, is what is left after the rejection of conventional literary topics; although not gratifying, and not aesthetic, it is held to offer the kick of reality. Like many of the documentary filmmakers, they were socialists, and the puzzling tone of their poetry is due to the absence of what they consider to be reactionary received ideas, the matter of collusion and shared sentiment which is, apparently, holding the revolution back. All of this must have seemed quite palatable to someone who had been formed by years of Practical Criticism.

One of the features of the contemporary scene is poets of crassness and orthodoxy employing tame critics or blurb writers to badge them as sophisticated and experimental; an act of generosity which abuses only the reader. The conformists have a gnawing envy of the underground. I am claiming the knowledge to distinguish between "legitimate signs of intelligence" and "illegitimate signs" and this is a fraught issue; for me it's obvious that David Chaloner is sophisticated and James Fenton is a klutz, but other observers may disagree. The most sensitive line in the world is that between "poets it is OK to put in a small press magazine" and "poets it is not OK to etc." When I was editing a small press magazine, I was constantly trying to find good poets who broke the rules of avant-garde good practice, because I disliked the prejudices of my audience and I wanted to annoy them as much as possible. Poets play on magazines the kind of hard focus of someone choosing going-out clothes; if it doesn't suit their ideas of chic, they don't want to be involved. If you put in a broad range of poets, the most fashion-conscious poets will boycott you. "I'm chic, you're not". Perhaps it's a mistake to select poets on the basis of who publishes them but in the absence of informed reviewing it's the most cost-effective way.

One certainly should not take the word modernist (or its relatives *linguistically innovative, avant-garde, experimental, alternative*, etc.) as given, and search for its British representatives but instead realise that there is a group of real people with a group feeling and self-recognition for whom words are frequently found and taken up. The words take their meaning from the actuality.

It is hard to define the contribution of the Imagist heritage to British poetry. Presumably the most palpable trace is the arrogance and sense of special destiny which damaged Pound's mind so much and which evidently contributed to the indifference to public rejection which made the British Poetry Revival possible. However, the original simplicity of Imagism disappeared in the development of Objectivism, which expanded out in many different ways; and the adaptation of Objectivism which happened in England in the 1960s expanded the model in so many new ways that the source is irrelevant.

If this formation turned out to stand for, not the infinity of possible new poetries in distinction to the few familiar possibilities of the conformist mainstream, but simply the battered loyalists who have absorbed certain strands of the poetic heritage and clung onto them, it would lose its edge and dissolve. Innovation is held, when the incantations work and the invoked spirits descend, to carry not merely a new set of formal possibilities, closed by virtue of clarity of definition, but by metonymy all possibilities of formal variation and the possibility of never being bored ever again. An exotic holiday does not merely take us to a place, where we are caught in a set of finite possibilities, but opens up our senses, washes away our fatigue, and re-animates the intellectual possibility of Place in general. This is what I can hope for, as the new issue of *shearsman* or *fragmente* thumps on the mat, and what I know *Poetry Review* or *Stand* will never do.

Perhaps the fantasy of superiority is the wine and the poems are just the food. We have to dwell on this fantasy because it has been so influential in the reception of poetry; the props and the roles are still on stage, the music goes on playing, even when the play has ended. It offered an assignment of roles: giving to one person a separate and special destiny, to others the role of idiots, saying "You can be the idiots. Here are your idiot costumes". For this reason, it is jealous of its own standing and unwilling to form alliances. It bears ominous resemblances to the bearing of groups possessing "old culture" towards groups with new culture, originating from the peasantry or proletariat but elevated by democracy and public education. Monarchists and reactionary aristocrats, the enemies of the Republic, were not the least creative group in nineteenth century Paris, which did so much to form the rules of twentieth century art. The mass output of graduates in the 1960s put the traditional bourgeoisie into a panic; it also swept away the right-wing elitists, so that the Poundian heritage was seized by the newly educated and by the Left. In fact, the fantasy of achieving cultural superiority through verbal procedures was a reflection of the drive to acquire higher education.

The fantasy of superiority converted many people whose poems remained sketchy and feeble precisely because of this fantasy.

The notion *English poets influenced by Objectivism* can also be phrased as *English poets in whom the influence of Objectivism vanishes*, as the difference between *The Objectivists* and *A Various Art* is so striking that a comparison is only possible through laborious historical reconstruction. The new poetry was legitimated, by a notional ritual of inheritance, before it had come about, but after a while it was legitimated by itself. The influence of *A Various Art* on younger poets had nothing to do with those predecessors. Memory is made possible by stiffness and the decline of change; poetry remembers so much that the continuity of a line is erased constantly, daily, amid the fabulous excess of new patterns oscillating and transforming. This, alone, would cast serious doubts on the genealogical project, the salvation theology of progress bigots, who believe that if A is more advanced than the rest of the world and I am more advanced than A then I am more advanced than the rest of the world.

The severe Objectivist model may account for a complete loss of connection with the local, British, poetry of the 1940s and explain why this lush local style did not make a comeback in the generous 1960s. An interest in poets like Lynette Roberts, Nicholas Moore, and JF Hendry came much later, as part of the development of the underground.

Readers in what is known as mainstream taste have been faced, every year since 1959 or so, with the claims of the avant-garde to excel the mainstream (and indeed to de-legitimise and mock it). The ritual whereby such a reader selects a touted avant-garde book, has a bad experience with it, and decides not to go on or to adjust their sights, has been repeated thousands, perhaps millions, of times. Success is never as simple as just persuading people to read the work; too much can go wrong. If I have not been especially generous to Bunting and Tomlinson, it is partly because they played, for too long, the role of the public alternative and disappointment with their work dissuaded many people from ever trying "the avant-garde" again.

Although the future opened up as an infinitude at every moment, the moments which became past forfeited this multiplicity to become finite, composing a pattern which the literary historian can read. Although thousands of people dreamed of writing poetry, it is possible to say that, in the 1960s or the 1950s, only a dozen or two dozen managed to write and publish significant books. This orderliness disguises, nonetheless, the dwelling within the books, as their claim to interest, of captured multiplicity, shimmering within the apparently fixed and frozen form of the words. Every significant poem opens up as a future, not as a past; its significance both appears and disappears as we read it. The poem presents us with serial incomplete states, whose incompleteness provokes us to gather the information which the poem releases. The poem, exciting us by its suggestiveness and shimmer, converges on a state where it can no longer suggest or shimmer. Awareness of, and willingness to exploit, this temporal curve, may make many poets seem to converge in a line of historical transmission, when the truth is that their insights were independent.

One strand of English poets welcomed the minimalism of the Imagist line because they wanted to write tinkly little poems in which anything except birdsong and old churches had been excluded as "insensitive". Quite a difference! I'm talking about poets like Richard Caddel, Tony Baker, Harry Gilonis, Harriet Tarlo, often in the lists of Pig Press. A kind of statement of this position was made in Caddel's anthology of 26 *New British Poets* made (confusingly) for the magazine *New American Writing* (8/9, 1991). Although he managed to include several authors from other directions, the bulk of this anthology is spindly, fussy, little nature poems; a different version of what the modern tradition is. The new nature poetry can pass as non-bourgeois because it is mainly about things and does not use hypotaxis, hard words, or structures of argument. The use of short lines, scattered phrases, simple syntax, etc. adds up to an absolute paucity of linguistic relations. Caddel's team often come from the North-East, which not only has a great deal of beautiful countryside but also the phantom presence of Bunting as an excuse for it all. They represent a different version of, and claim to, the Objectivist heritage than Ferry Press and Grosseteste. Caddel's (implicit) definition of the Authentic as solitude, contemplation, absence of theorising, is bizarrely an expression of disaffection with the economic system. The retreat into poems about birds and flowers is an occult expression of resentment at London, which is felt to define the terms in which economics, politics, etc. are discussed. Actually the most populous parts of the North-East are "rustbelt", an area of heavy industry and mining, which are both run down (like analogous areas in Germany, France, and the USA). The sensuous detail which fills these poems is meant to be the taste of purity after shedding the illusions of urban life; a nature walk, with shy accounts of sensitive responses to dear little woodland things, a soundtrack of a string quartet, a few allusions to literary classics, and good taste throughout. No conflict, no personal relations, no large energetic things, no problems with identity. I am also reminded of Dark Age hermits, who were equally unable to deal with modern life, and sat in caves relating to mice, limpets, berries, thrushes, and things like that. Some of these, of course, lived in the North-East and adjacent regions.

It may be that Bunting's style is in some way regional; but clearly George Oppen did not come from the North-East of England. Bunting's influence helped at least three excellent poets in the region: Barry MacSweeney, Colin Simms, and John Seed.

**The Worm and the Coin: John Riley, Selected Poems**
Riley (1937–78)'s debut was *Ancient and Modern*, in 1967; it shares a lot of features with other new poetry of the period but is not of great significance in itself. He shows great interest in the rhythmic value of each word and phrase, dissecting the sentence into endless short lines; presumably he was close to American poets in the Imagist-Objectivist

tradition such as William Carlos Williams, Carl Rakosi, and Lorine Niedecker. Already the furniture of the traditional contemporary English poem—cluttered, reassuring, Anglican, benign—has been thrown out. It's apparent that Riley had a problem writing striking phrases or lines, was not naturally insistent, and only loosely connected the parts of the poem.

A lot happened in the late sixties, and 1970's *What Reason Was* is a much more significant book. The title comes from a quotation from Vladimir Solovyov: "So far, love is for man what reason was for the animal world: it exists in its rudiments or tokens, but not as yet in fact". It would be malicious to connect this to philosophies of love floating around at the time. Riley began learning Russian during National Service in 1958 and was received into the Russian Orthodox Church in 1977; evidently he had absorbed a great deal of Russian literature in the intervening years. Names he mentions in his Collected Works include Zhukovsky, Khomyakov, Rozanov, Mandelshtam, and Khodasevich, apart from Solovyov, who was a Symbolist poet of some importance as well as a mystic and theologian. (Russian Symbolism is rather different from the French variant.) Slavophiles and Acmeists feature, but not exclusively. No one can develop a more than touristic interest in Russian culture without becoming an anti-communist; Riley's reaction took him to some pretty queer places. One of his early poems is called "Apophatic Icon"; since apophatic is the way of defining God which proceeds by stating what He is not, it is hard to see how an icon could be such: a picture of what God is not? Nonetheless I suspect that a kind of shamefastness and solemn avoidance of the central truth is important to Riley: he writes in a negligent way, about domestic or natural details of no great interest, because to write about the important things you have to be ordained as a theologian. Such truths as matter are vouchsafed by God, using the words of God, and these are not idly to be spoken through secular lips. There is a point in his writing at which he starts to speak in elevated language of the things of great import; these poems, such as "The Poem of Light" stand out from the rest of his work. This does not mean that his domestic poems are not about theology. There is in fact a Russian tradition of intimate, as if casual, lay, religious writing, owed to VV Rozanov (1856–1919) and in particular *Fallen Leaves* (*Opavshiye listy*, 1913–15). This was something of a lost book for seven decades and is now very influential. (Rozanov's secretary was the great Viktor Shklovsky, one of my models.) I might compare Riley's poetry to that of Viktor Krivulin (b. 1945), Orthodox, much influenced by Rozanov, and with the same façade of casual details and indifference. Rozanov's work was original partly because it dealt with life outside the monastery, for lay people, where for example sexuality is important and not merely a violation of orthonomy. His studied ordinariness may also have to do with his writing in Russian, whereas religious writing had until recently been in Church Slavonic. The title also means "fallen pages", notes on domestic routine (*byt*) written without concentrating and let fall without bothering. There is no argument in Riley's work: it would be very hard to explain how the different parts of a poem support each other, still less the different parts of a sequence such as "Twelve Poems"; this casual structure is paradoxically owed to the underlying total system of coordinating symbolism which Orthodoxy supplies. Riley avoids argument, and other rational procedures, as part of the programme of love and contemplation, which reason could only interrupt. It's hard to imagine how a book of poetry could illustrate the surpassingly beautiful thought of Solovyov's; Riley scarcely gives us a legendary of love, but proceeds apophatically, giving us simple objects to induce a calm state in which the guiding thought can possess us and alter our attitudes. The main obstacle to love is pride, and the techniques of modern poetry all act to increase that; Riley is writing in a humble way. There are no clever phrases. Ulli Freer has been equally concerned to purify his poetry of tokens of power and rational structures; similar motives have animated John Wilkinson. Negligence and inanity are favoured traits here. The lack of surface incident in Riley's work reminds me of what Anton Ehrenzweig says, in *The Hidden Order of Art* (1966), about analytic perception: "From the undifferentiated mosaic of the visual field we are compelled to select a 'figure' on which attention concentrates while the rest of visual data recedes and fuses into a vague background of indistinct texture". For syncretistic perception, however, he posits de-differentiation, "the 'full' emptiness of unconscious scanning", and "the empty-eyed control of inarticulate inflections and handwriting. The artist's vacant unfocused stare pays attention to the smallest detail however far removed from the consciously perceived figure". Riley's empty surface is reminiscent of near-contemporary figure-ground inversion in Op Art and in systems music and possibly of the striking-out of the history of the State to look at millions of households.

The dispersed coherent message is a paraphrase of the Scriptures, such as the words of hymns usually are; a way back to a royal, authoritative, ceremonial kind of language:

*Avant-garde legitimacy, continued; Neo-Objectivism* [105]

> In imagination a building, moving with the seasons,
> Moving on its axis, and in the courtyard a tree,
> Revolving with the motion of the planets
> And answering each heartbeat in token of the time
> When time, with sun and moon, stands still.
>
> And by the courtyard crystal fountains, peonies and Mexicans
> And music
>       echoing the spheres of silence
> Upon an instrument of ten strings, and upon the psaltery;
> Upon the harp with a solemn sound.

The whole passage derives from the description, in one of Liudprand of Cremona's accounts of his embassy to Byzantium in A.D. 968, of mechanical scenographic effects in the throne-room of the palace of Magnaura; its physical details, but not its meaning, refer to the mechanical toys made for the Emperor; but some lines come directly from the Psalms. The poem continues:

> Rain will fall and not fall: the dream
> Of Byzantium interpreted and re-interpreted:
> Eternity will swallow time and art
> Become what is. Art is the building, moved in, breathed in,
> All creatures move in this, and praise the motive, re-inhabiting.
>       (FROM "THE POEM AS LIGHT")

The "dream" has a peculiar importance for the Orthodox Church; when he describes the eternal building of art, it is the form of the real, temporal Byzantium which he chooses to clothe it in. Fedotov remarks, in *The Russian Religious Mind*, "another mighty influence helped to shape the Eastern cult: the imperial palace. Many of the court ceremonies and adoration formulas, the silk and gold vestments, were adopted by the Church. Even now [ ... ] the Constantinopolitan palace still lives in every Orthodox Church, particularly in the Cathedral". Riley's longest poem is "Czargrad", which means "city of the emperor", and is of course Byzantium again. I would hesitate to describe the structure of this, except to say that it is a loose series of reflections, in a mood of remarkable serenity, on the growth of the City of God and the visibility of a benevolent order in the changes of Nature:

> naked phenomena dark, evenings, mornings
> and
> the
> palaces the colonnades the prospects, domes, winter
> dreams, rhythms of the world's desire
> slanted sun circles to eye's limit

> though the City is partly corruption, decay
> a world of greys and greens and white under cloud
> no nearer no further than fifty thousand years ago
> by steps each of which is stable in itself
> the City, jewelled in time
>          I hear the sky go by
> constellations, star seams in a darkening world
>                                 (FROM "CZARGRAD")

There are in fact two systems, one revealing itself through time, stored in writing, and called History, and one revealing itself to our senses, cyclically, and called Nature:

> The scent of bluebells is fresh, and lilac, immediate:
> With all the insistence of decaying sense
>
> Our time came to me. How fine to swim in that pool.
> The fallen sun, falling, takes even that colour away.
>
> The moon is on fire, mad with harvest
> And the spring crops are scarcely out of their holes.
>                       (FROM "A CYCLE")

Both are types for a higher world: Byzantium, the successor to Jerusalem and Rome, predecessor to Moscow, is a type of the Heavenly City. This is never explained. The City appears perhaps as a token of the just life which is only possible in a just society, radically denying the validity of the individual ego and of artistic endeavour in an unjust society. The presuppositions of Riley's work are fallenness as well as the necessity of love:

> a city
> of squatters, drum
> of the dancing bear at morning, past noon
> both man and bear asleep in ruins, the bear's paw
> delicate. easy
>         a formulation
>
> dome after dome and dome within dome
> was. is. the caves within made
> no space made all space having
> rhythm and line and necessity
> and duty perhaps in the poem one recites by heart
> even to no auditors but beauty
> a paradox in the very soft breezes
> not apparent     for all
> that one lives
>         and is grateful
>
>                                     (FROM "CZARGRAD")

The universal availability of fragments implying the cosmic order is reminiscent of the standard design of the Emperor's head, issued as a model to craftsmen throughout the Empire: available, but subject to powerful laws and interdicts. A coin would show an authenticated image of the central godlike power; one can dig in the garden and find such an image, tarnished and buried in earth (as memorably evoked in *Mercian Hymns*). The Russian coin, kopek, contains the word for "spear" because its design was originally based on a Macedonian coin showing Alexander the Great as a mounted spearman; the design comes from the third century B.C. The North re-enacts the culture of the East; Riley digs in the garden but finds the cosmic order there.

The late poems published for the first time in his Collected Works show an even freer attitude to the connection of ideas and images. Some Orthodox theologian was shocked at Western theology because it was so disputatious: it used structures of logical argument the whole time. There is some link between the rules of evidence used in law, and in theological debate, and the kind of rules structuring arguments in daily life, and also in poetry. In an autocracy, where the government is not accountable to the people and is not bound by any laws, argument may well be a neglected skill; civil and ecclesiastical authority do only utter their wishes; it is the status of the person speaking which justifies statements. At the risk of simplifying millennia of history, I could guess that the Western church tradition is much more permeated by law courts, logic, and arguments between two parties, and also the Western personality structure is; Riley's poetry is Eastern in its lack of logic and argument. Since the faculty of association is mysterious, it may well be that the ostensible structure of ideas in organised poems is not the real one and to that extent a false mediation.

The effectiveness of his work obviously depends on our willingness to receive the message soaked into its peakless constancy, which has to do with goodness and love and is probably the one we most want from poetry. Since we identify these qualities rather early in childhood, they are not complex, and there is little inquisitiveness needed to locate or discover them. His gesture is indirect but homogeneous: the humble or apophatic approach locks us into the contemplative pose, the absence of event lulls us into a trance. It is very direct in its purpose and makes one suspect that much of what is going on in modern poetry is a distraction, fulfilling only a second-order purpose which fruitlessly burns up energy. As for the Orthodox Church, the research which I have occasionally had to do into its past fills me with horror and nausea. It is a persecuting church. As for Orthodoxy in action, events in Tuzla, Sarajevo, Bihac and Srebrenica in recent months give a vivid picture. There is an alternative to the tradition of civil rights and conflict governed by law. *Starry-eyed, eternal, fat on the blood of innocents.*

# The procurement of the information in poetry

Because poetry is made up of information, and this information has an existence outside poetry, we can write part of the history of poetry by writing the history of the objects or the knowledge which poetry includes.

Reading is an act of memory. One of the economic limits to poetry is the limit of detailed memory. My impression is that language is a symbolic key to access memories that already exist. The reader processes it by referring it to stock scenes, adding detail where told to and where relevant. Difficult poetry is what asks us to imagine more and remember less: it is depressing how hard we find it to create new ideas. There is no such thing as an infinite resource.

Poetry uses up information the whole time, and replacement data has to drain in from somewhere to keep the whole space from collapsing. The problem may be simply one of economics; governments have gone to great lengths to collect rich detail usable in propaganda stories; the raw material for any other kind of story offers procurement difficulties. A poem is made of information, and this is like a mortgage, where the hope of acquisition gives way to the sense that someone else owns your home. A classic snatch of dialogue about poetry goes: "You should write about shared myths so that everyone would read your works"; "But we start out by forbidding all the shared myths from the poem, because they embody capitalist values". In twentieth century Britain we find the lyric impulse modified in several ways by new information. For example:

subjective experience + realism about the life of the poor
subjective experience + information derived from science and social statistics

subjective experience + info derived from photography
subjective experience + info derived from theorising about original data
(exit from compulsion; return to a world of ideas resembling subjectivity)

This is a schematic account of a complex process. The schema does not allow us to make generalisations about the impact of changes in commonly available information during the twentieth century. It may be wrong to assume that all poets started out from an interest in subjective experience, modified by later impacts; some may have started out instead with a dry and realistic tone. It leaves out, for example the role of religion, the conflict between political philosophies, and the conflict between feminism and residual masculinist ideologies. We are using a deliberately narrow focus here, a limiting frame.

In about 1993, I arranged to meet the critic Martin Seymour-Smith in a pub in Chalk Farm, near Camden, for high-level poetic discussions. On the walls were a wealth of theatrical prints from the early 19th C including a favourite of mine, *Claudian's Gothic War*, a splendid coloured print of an engraving of an epic Roman production. I was impressed by the awesome packing of the visible space. Not just the drama and opulence of the figures, but the density and clarity of organisation of the spectacle with its many component parts, evoking an endlessly deep penetrable space. It made one think of the poet as visual thinker. Of the cost of staging the spectacles, or of visiting the far-off lands. Of the industrial project which went into assembling so many things into a visual pattern, so that the spectator could look into an unhindered, opening space and find everything susceptible to his eye. The objects so lusciously offered are so full of meaning that we can think of the poem as a recollection of that meaning.

The print you see is the product of at least two painstaking and complex efforts—the second is the engraver taking the likeness but the first is the producer or stage manager arranging for the sets and costumes to be built and for the objects to be organised and marshalled on stage. (To be accurate, there would have been a drawing made for the engraver to work from—the print would show *del et inc*, for delineavit and incidit.) The poet gets these more or less for free. One has to speak of the accumulation of wealth here—the basis of the poem is not the poet's ingenuity but the immense free stores of data which the poet taps into. Those productions evoke the whole wood and brass splendour of Victorian engineering—the wonderful social constructions which saw thousands of workers coordinated in sites building railways or building dams on the Nile. A production like *Claudian's Gothic War* would further have drawn on a long archaeological project in which scholars reconstructed Roman costume and object culture. This project started with the Renaissance and had by 1830 or so become the operating knowledge of stage designers and historical painters—who would have used the same costumiers. (Of course, the source of the play is in a poem— Claudian's panegyric, dated to AD 402, to the Vandal general Stilicho. I'm glad they credited Claudian.)

During the nineteenth century, a personal and subjective art was enjoying huge success. French models of Symbolisme were imitated in most parts of Europe. But in parallel a geometrically correct, illusionistic art, producing organised equivalents of apparent space was flourishing, through disciplined drawing and photography. Two lines were developing in the same historical period.

Looking at those precisely packed lithographs makes one wonder if an effort of visual organisation is at the basis of a poem, a complex collection and setting out of people and objects in a stable imaginary space; and so that this visual assembly precedes the verbal pattern which constantly refers to it, and is dependent on it. That is, the poet is also a visual thinker. Perhaps poets fail or succeed according to their technique for calling up and organising visual ideas.

The prints were proof that the torrent of visual data preceded the arrival of photography. The limit drawn around a poem is not what the poet can see, but what the reader can see. It is no use me having a vision on my own. If I have a vision based on a photograph which the reader has seen as well, that is when I can write a poem which he will understand. Thus, the abundant availability of information liberates poetry.

So much raw data—which a poem can only with great pains reproduce —imposes an effort on the reader which is quite unsuitable. But if I use words to snatch up from the stores of memory a deep image—the economics work out. The whole enterprise of poetry takes place between the opposite banks of worn-out images and of images so new that the reader cannot properly grasp them. The history of poetry could be written via the history of shared images.

The process of reading a poem includes assembling a copy of this visual setting, using cues in the verbal script; an effort which can be either successful or unsuccessful If we think specifically of 'Mediterranean Year', a poem by Francis Berry, we can see that it is pushing up against the limits of what we can comfortably and reliably assimilate. Clearly, the verbal pattern is a secondary act, following the primary act of 'seeing' the elaborate mythical pattern, taking place over four seasons in a calendrical cycle, which governs the poem—and in a sense exists outside it. When I typed this poem up for inclusion in an (abortive) anthology, I made discoveries about what it said which were new to me—even though I had read it two or three times before, and owned the book for many years. The poem is not expanding in a vacuum, it is doing work to pass tests which compare it with something potent and already 'there', in a space which is cognitive but not yet verbal.

The acute limits of memory can be reduced, locally, by training. Let me cautiously advance the idea that the basic unit of "controlled memory" used by the poet during the poem (different from the "immediate present" and from "inner memory") has ceased to be the sermon (=stereotyped "length" of behaviour plus memorizable moral lesson) and has become a photograph, or perhaps a length of film. A discontinuity in poetry around 1960 could relate to the impingement of new technology (with vastly improved means of reproducing and replicating colour photographs) rather than to heroic hypotheses of poetic "backroom boys" creating new ideas from thin air. It could be compared with earlier shifts in the library of images available to the poet and to the readership, such as the spread of cheap mass-produced engravings (chiefly from Antwerp, and in the sixteenth century); or the arrival, around 1820, of effective colour lithography, again revolutionising the available image stock. People devour these images whenever they are allowed to; it is hard to believe in archetypal images when it is so easy to believe that we simply remember images from the visual library.

The world of dream preceded any graphics technology. Much of this book is concerned with the Apocalyptic school, who regressed from formal and public images to a primary stream of the imagination. There is a key contrast between poets who rely on the primary flow of dreams, and those whose preferred 'spectrum band' is in the post-processing of visual images, for example in the critique of media images. The Apocalyptics were at pains to dissociate themselves from other English poets, whose work was close to newspapers and seemed to rely on photographs and documentary films. They took the Book of Revelations as their model. Already in the 1$^{st}$ C AD (as the presumptive date of *Revelations*) there was a bipolar relationship between prophetic writing - drawing on dream, trance, the unconscious—and rational prose discourse, whether history, inspired by the language of the State, or logical inquiry, inspired by Greek philosophy. *Revelations* is structured as an alternation of elaborate visual images and explanations of the images.

Anything so primary needs explanation. Evidently dreams consist not just of pictures but also of meanings, an implicit knowledge which we experience along with the pictures. The Apocalyptics had a problem with the explanations. Poetry is always tempted by purity, by the wish to eject anything which merely helps you to follow what is going on. Bunting had complex semantic schemes for his poems, which unfortunately he omitted from the poems. If you read the schemes, for example in Victoria Forde's book, you realise that the essential meaning of the poems has been excluded from the text and cannot be recovered from it.

Poetry is now dependent both on the visual flows which precede the poem and on the prose exegesis which records the substance of the poem. This at least gives some justification to a book like this one. But surely the fastidious ideas about diction which make a poem incomprehensible are a sign of weakness, and better poets can deliver something complete in itself—unlike *Briggflatts*.

The attention of the 19$^{th}$ C was taken up with historicism, explained at the outset by Hegel with his reduction of everything to time-bound processes: nothing is happening without changing, everything which exists is decaying under the assault of time. The whole past of European literature was being resurrected and printed, the visual art of the whole world was being made available by cheap lithographic printing, imperialism and the institution of museums were making an unspendable wealth visible. Everything was re-animated by curators and philologers; everything was dead, and the inheriting artist had to pass through death in order to acquire these ghostly panoplies. Their shared imaginary was chains of form such as fossil sequences or the Indo-European languages, and they tended to impose successive and evolutionary schemas on phenomena where they are invalid, for example in anthropology or forms of government.

There was a generalised topos in the nineteenth century of a vantage point from where far more data could be seen than was normally available to a spectator on the surface of the earth; thus transcending the ordinary limits of the human body and its relationship to incident light and sound. A focus of this topos was the Irving production of Goethe's *Faust*, which made such a parade of all the corners of the earth and all the stages of history central in the attention of the cultured world, and which appears (more or less disguised) in a number of poets of the succeeding decades. The parade topos, corresponding to the diorama, seems strange to us because we are so used to its successor: the unrestricted wealth of photographic images supplied by television, magazines, films, and posters. We still like the same sense of endless spectacle, but our wishes are satisfied in slightly different ways. If someone aged fifteen cuts pictures out of the colour supplements and makes a pin-up board of them, we are entitled to think of Mephistopheles, showing Faust the far corners of space and time; and also of the poems that fifteen-year old might write, and whether the same tenacious principles (of scanning, identification, capture, montage, preservation) are operating to generate the poems. The line demarcating in from out, guarding someone's favourite images from those they pass over, may be crucial for poetry, representing the dominance of style in an age of virtually perfect availability of images.

I have elsewhere given reasons for thinking that the impact of Marxism was that of a new sublime coign of vantage, a point from where all human history and each part of the world could be seen in one single, dizzying perspective. Otherwise, we may think of the complex of museums in South Kensington which resulted from the Great Exhibition of 1851; the whole world apparently attainable within a square mile. Contemporaries compared the Exhibition to the mighty gallery shops of the West End, with their oceans of glass and their stunning range of goods.

How much can we see? Clearly, there is an economics of information; quantity infiltrates the poem at many levels, and the pace of a poem is decisive. Not only do large blocks have to move at the right speed but also lines and even phrases do. This "pace" can only be measured in information, for what else could it be that is moving slowly or fast. Staging and marshalling information is the problem which faces a poet at every step. Most people who try to measure the amount of information in poems come to the same result. Poetry does not offer us new information but persuasively arranged social stimuli to a different way of associating ideas, a richer connectivity based on the impression of leisure and of the absence of functional demands. Value shifts away from the particular associations of ideas and towards the level and freedom of associations. We are interested in public sets of associative paths, because it now seems that the poet is relying on these, and that the sheer wealth of links within the poem guarantees the recurrence of the stock material. After all, association is based on memory, and we remember what is already there, in the cells. A poem with associative tracks which no one can find is like a piece of music which no musician can play: it will remain unheard.

In historicism, architects, painters, and poets engaged technically and by training with the past; writing in the serial perspective which makes each element of language mortal, which offers continuity but soaks everything in self-destroying flux. Variation emerges as an immanent quality of form but is what destroys every form. The climbing to this perspective brings a double-headed gift: one head is godlike power and the other is the awareness that everything you do is a fiction, a set of conventions, and is crumbling from within as its own metabolism turns it to ashes. The sight of historical transience succeeds and replaces theology, as thought reaching out to the denial of the self; almost as a repair job, restabilising the whole by replacing a missing structural element; replacing eschatology, sacred cosmology, and so forth. If you see a sequential set of twelve forms in time, with yourself as the thirteenth, you are bound to see the fourteenth; and yourself crumbling and worn out. Poetry cannot evade the arrow of time by a Linnaean cumulation and cataloguing of detail. But there is a way of feeding this awareness back into the poem and cheating transience. Transience could have been frozen in a frame, caught by the constancy of its evacuation.

In the 1850s, George Meredith wrote a series of poems to great poets of the past. The sense of being on the Marble Cliffs, close to the great ones of the past and far from everyday reality, was quite palpable to Swinburne, who wrote a series of sonnets to Elizabethan dramatists and practiced quite a few different historical styles. William Watson (1858–1935) was, it seems to me, the last poet who had the sense of being able to talk to the illustrious dead and to take on their styles as if banqueting at the same Elysian table. His prolonged dialogue with them is matched by his choice of archaic vocabulary. The slightly younger Stephen Phillips shares the same imagery (*A Vision of Judgement* is precisely a kind of Irving-like panorama in which world history streams past the poet-narrator's eyes), but is even harder to take seriously. Watson's attack on 'fashion' is more than mere resentment: he believes that he can fly back almost three thousand years and simply occupy what he finds there. But the awareness which haunted him must have been that primary innocence was unattainable for someone like him, except fictively through proxies such as primitive characters (variously, gypsy, barbarian, peasant, or Bronze Age Greek): and that he could only drink at the feast of the great if he dared a new style, where knowledge of the past was turned into a virtue. His solution was dialogue in verse with the dead, a museum-style surfeit of the very best things from the best eras of the past, as in this extract from a poem on the death of Tennyson:

The swords of Caesars, they are less than rust:
The poet doth remain.
Dead is Augustus. Maro is alive;
And thou, the Mantuan of our age and clime,
Like Virgil shalt thy race and tongue survive,
Bequeathing no less honeyed words to time,
Embalmed in amber of eternal rhyme,
And rich with sweets from every Muse's hive;
While to the measure of the cosmic rune
For purer ears thou shalt thy lyre attune.
             ('Lachrymae Musarum')

Virgil came from Mantua, and the assumption that the reader will know who the Mantuan was conjures up an in-group of the knowing and loving which is very flattering. The projection, that Virgil, Tennyson, Watson, and the reader too, are picnicking together in some endless landscape of the beautiful and poetic, is so attractive that it is bound to come back in some form. One step more would have turned this knowledge into literary theory, and made the formal properties of art into the subject matter of art. The bit about *sweets from every Muse's hive* is also reminiscent of the display of a West End shop. The poem shows Tennyson hanging out with "godlike spirits [. . .] in speech of Athens, Florence, Weimar, Stratford, Rome", and this sense of being on top of the Marble Cliffs, being shown the aerial perspective, dealing with the great dead is intoxicating, but offers an alluring danger: that the reader-collector endowed with these dazzling historical perspectives will find all forms becoming transparent and time-bound, and him- or herself unable to use any of them with conviction. Who goes among the dead is like the dead. The idea of progress in an art implies that the new generation absorbs the practices of the older one. The system whereby Biblical and Classical imagery was available to the European artist, ahistorically and as it were transcendentally, had lasted for an extraordinarily long time, but was undermined partly by several dozen other formal and mythological traditions becoming (deceptively) available. The poet could satiate his greed on these without ever becoming satisfied or nourished. The late

Victorians were suffering from an excess of analogies: drowned in a tradition which went back to the earliest Greek poets and had lost its 'time now' marker, they tried to be the heirs to all of European poetry. Another solution, available to such plethoric and many-sided geniuses as Browning, was to pilfer history at a hundred different points, rushing through the museum of styles without destroying them. The moment when overflow was reached, for example when someone in 1895 was writing a sonnet sequence with full awareness of fifty previous sonnet sequences in different languages, and was determined to excel them, is an early version of complexity. At the point where too many analogies were available, the stored knowledge magically sank back to zero. The elaboration and infinite-toyshop historicism of the Victorians was lost; destroyed. The issue of continuity, situation on a line of time, and cultural promiscuity, has remained acute since that time. Even Watson, in 'An Apologia' (1895), was stirred to defend his own impersonality and conservatism. This is why people are uncertain about tradition now; everyone reads Milton, but nobody knows where they stand in relation to him.

One solution was a kenosis, using the term developed by Peter Fuller, an emptying-out of knowledge, so that the poet shed the awareness of history and buried himself in a limited style, which however had consistent internal rules and prevented the abysses from opening up. The movement which swept away these billowing thousand-year-stares, and condemned Watson to a kind of sumptuous tomb for the last decades of his life, was the Georgian Revolt; the Georgian poets, believed in immediate physical realities and developed an ideal of the continuous present, imitating peasant speech. Watson was probably referring to them in 1913 when he rebuked 'those who cultivate a gratuitous ruggedness'. Modernism is more interesting, but it seems to me the Georgian solution—stress on moral values, on communal feeling, on physical objects, on country walks, horror of ideas and complex language, preoccupation with animals, nostalgia for folklore, modesty, shy belief in moments of oneness with Nature and of social hope, egalitarianism—has marked English poetry much more profoundly; it was the expression of a radical Liberalism which was at that time also producing the first sketch of a Welfare State and of an institutional compromise between owners and workers. Important parts of this solution were taken up by the Left.

Apart from poems containing sets of data which exist outside the poems, apart from readers perceiving poets as parts of series and defined by their relation to the rest of the several series, there is the poet perceiving their poem as a data object. Or, reflexivity. One of the key ideas about the modern state of literature is that reflexivity is increasing all the time. This idea was articulated to me by the poet and editor John Muckle, who I believe had given a series of lectures on the theme. I think it is one of the fundamental truths which explain what has been happening in English literature in the last 40 years or so. However, we need to consider what reflexivity is. If you watch your reflection in a mirror, as a dancer might, you can see where your motions are awkward or misconceived, and this will guide you towards perfection. The force of the metaphor as applied to literature is that you can see mental processes as if in a mirror. An observer watches the person writing and removes the clumsiness and guides them towards perfection. And clearly writers can improve — they can watch themselves and put themselves in the role of the listener to the text. But to understand this properly, we have to dismantle the idea of perfection. A dancer can see what is imperfect because it shows a loss of control, or is physically straining and dangerous. But perfection in mental processes would imply that there is a right way of carrying each of them out — which we cannot accept. Reflexivity in writing would imply seeing into the mind of each reader and predicting their reactions, so as to control them (and satisfy). If we look at poetry of the past 40 years, it has obviously missed a mass audience, and obviously a large number of people have had the experience of reading some modern poetry and just not "getting" it. This must mean that poets are not successful at predicting audience reactions. So, *the increase of reflexivity has gone hand in hand with a decrease in the ability to pitch the flow of sense where the intended listener can catch and follow it.* This does not make sense. Surely delivering an utterance which flies past the head of the listener without ever reaching them is a sign of naivety — of immaturity, inability to stand outside yourself, over-excitement, getting hot and carried away.

Perfection is only a cogent concept when there is a single norm to achieve; but in fact modellness works in all directions. 80 different people may have 80 different ideas of perfection.

There is a set of rules for the conduct of language which rewriting allows you to fulfil more correctly. A tacit rule is not to use any substantive more than once in any poem. So, for example, just before a reading I discover that I used the word 'spiral' 3 times in a 40-line poem, then spend several minutes frantically rewriting, at a pub table. A sign of my early poems might be the re-use of key words, words I was in love with.

If you see lots of poems, as an editor, you realise that you could improve most of them by simply applying rules of conduct: deleting repeats, putting the ideas in a clear order, and so on. All of these improvements are unimportant if you haven't got a strong poem concept in the first place. If you haven't got that, there is no point bothering with manners and amenity. Also, neat organisation goes along with detachment, and can straightforwardly be a symptom of disengagement, boredom, and vacuity on the part of the poet.

Perhaps we have to discard the idea that reflexivity is a quality which a poet either has or has not, and redirect the idea towards the use of literary models. Maybe the Victorians were much more reflexive than we are. Watson wrote that poem about Tennyson in a sublime style, something consciously artificial, difficult, inorganic, and yet rich with references to a Classical past. Poems then had much tighter norms, in metre, diction, use of genre, etc., and were much more impressive demonstrations of bending personal impulses towards sublime and public norms. Perhaps modern poetry is excited and confused because our models are confused. The possibility of writing like the Greeks and Romans vanished sometime during Watson's career. But you have to have some idea of stylistic perfection in order to guide you as you compose the poem. This is inevitably going to be an individual, inevitably a poet, because our growth processes are directed by imitation and direct perception of people, a human process. This is blurred by the fact that several models are, almost inevitably, involved. It's never just Blake, just Lawrence, just Prynne. But there is such an internalisation process, and the human constellation which any poet perceives is something vital to the poet they become. There is of course a latent theory of history in these perceptions. Modern poets may be writing with reference to a poetic ideal which is not shared by the reader. In this way, self-consciousness and the ability to foresee and conform to the reader's reactions might go in two different directions.

Perhaps Watson did not represent the whole Classical tradition, but simply a childish fixation on Tennyson. Tennyson was a national saint when Watson was growing up, but Watson was fifty years younger, and that mass audience simply wasn't around for long enough to keep Watson prosperous. The linguistic island he was on dissolved. Perhaps the scene we have is an archipelago of shared poet-schemas and shared scene-schemas, or Sites, and rather than seeing an "era" shifting we have to track the fortunes of 30 or so different islands. If you go back to the 1890s and start amassing evidence, it's rapidly obvious that there were lots of other possibilities than luxuriant Tennyson knock-offs.

I can visualise the process of quality controlling a poem through transparencies. I see an imaginary screen on which you can superimpose different Schemas which do not hide each other, and look at differences between them. The poet may have a very strong image of their favourite poem, and be able to apply the images as a way of checking that the new poem satisfies—that its colours are vivid enough, so to speak. If you can summon up several different schemas, probably the memory-images of what other poets do, you can check different aspects of your poem. This process could also be a way of checking that the way you write is original —i.e. if you sound too much like your heroes, you have to pursue your own style further along its latent axis. This total process of summoning up schemas and carrying out comparisons is what we mean by reflexivity.

I envisage the act of self-examination as being dependent on the kind of medium that people have as a model. We have just taken part in a discussion of photography, where we explored the influence of the photograph, and especially of documentary cinema, on the English poem. The connections are difficult to trace, because after all there are many kinds of information floating around in our society, and language is something adaptable, which can absorb or imitate all of them.

The scheme of ascent through technical improvement was sabotaged in the case of literature, because antiquity, the authorizing knowledge for Victorian literary scholars, shows a quite different shape across time: the Homeric epics appear at the beginning of written record (technically, just before), and nothing like them comes afterwards; and there were no great tragedians after Euripides. A pessimistically minded classicist could reflect that poetry sank downwards after the 5th century BC. The whole profession agreed that the decline was a shift from poets, seen as primary or early, and towards scholars, collecting and commenting on texts: men like themselves. This guilty self-knowledge provides, perhaps, that resistance to thought which is such a feature of modern British poetry.

The end of creativity in Classical mythology seems grossly to coincide with the arrival of mass literacy, made possible by the alphabet. A breakthrough in access to information brought an increase in scepticism and critical thinking. I think it is possible that the spread of cheap printing in the 19th C brought a similar advance. This, I believe, occurred in waves as new media technologies kept arriving. The public became more perceptive about congruity. They were aware of the date at which a poet was writing. The hoarded stock of special poetic words, not part of the spoken language, came to seem ridiculous, and was slowly jettisoned. While there is a history of data *in* poetry, the poem itself can be inserted into a series of forms, so that the poem becomes merely a sort of data. By the time you've done this it's obvious that poets too can be arranged in a series and that this series can be sorted according to time. This awareness of congruity leaves William Watson as a miserable fag-end of Tennysonian fullness rather than as a semi-divine spectator of the 2000 years of history. It is a moment of breach. All the precious internalised objects are lost.

There is in Meier-Graefe's history of the dwelling (*Geschichte der Wohnung*) a curious remark about the layout of fishermen's houses in the old regions along the North Sea coast of Saxony. The sea gave up many strange objects, and those which could be preserved without rotting were kept, by these fisher families, on a shelf above the fireplace. The echo with the role of the mantelpiece in English homes will strike many of us. But also, the impulse to collect and preserve. Each family had a small collection, we suppose, but this is the small version of the great collections which marked out great families; just as the small house, with the *Flett* and so on of the regional architecture, resembles the great house which nobles constructed for themselves. Once the collections were large enough to have a room to themselves, the room was called a cabinet (like *cabin*), and in fact a cabinet of curiosities. Or, in German, rarities. Some early versions of these collections were in pieces of furniture rather than small private rooms; things like map-chests or the chests where engravings are stored. Once someone had a large collection of strange objects, they organised them in series. The knowledge embodied in this ability to classify, distinguish, and relate was called science. Later science added a grasp of processes as well as shapes. In order to grasp an anomaly, you have to understand the series which it interrupts: the series came before the collecting. The lexicon of a language embodies such series, such relations and distinctions. Indeed, we can imagine a museum as a diagram of a certain lexicon. There is an intimate relationship between poetry and collecting. In a museum near my home, the Museum of Playthings Past at Kedleston, there is kit for an *object lesson*: actually, a lesson where children were asked to handle objects so as to acquire the knowledge embodied in their physical qualities.

We are back to the limits of memory here: a poem can only evoke objects which the reader has already learnt. It is hard to get the lexical richness of poetry away from the range of developed objects which are found, naturally, in the local great house. A feature of any great house would be that it was stuffed with objects which functionally resemble those found in cottages, but which realise those deep shapes in a wider variety, often with more elaboration, and especially with a wider range into the past and into different geographical origins. The richer poetic lexicon would, in thousands of instances, prove to come, equally, from different languages or regions and from older phases of the language of the country. It may be that books can only come about as consequences of physical collections of objects and expertise; of traps that catch knowledge. So transparent and collectively grasped are the relationships between the qualities of object and the qualities of men that we find it possible when looking at an object to say whose household it belongs in—what kind of person. The connection between gifts and status—between the status of the gift and the status of the recipient—is something we grasp very accurately; a homology whose grammar we grasp as a sign of adulthood. Our society is organised around the acquisition of signed objects as a stuffing, filling, and broadcasting of the self. But a poem made of language partakes of similar histories or industries of elaboration, attenuation, defiance of the norm, recursive excelling of features which are originally functional.

We can easily grow to think of the Great Exhibition, and its successors, as things that imitated and replaced the object-series of the great houses. Equally easily, we can think of the art of photography as a sort of Great Exhibition that could be printed, multiplied, and carried home, and even broadcast into someone's home. We might say that after a few thousand years of dependence on the aristocracy poetry recently became dependent on the electronic media.

We have said that poets have limited imaginations, and have had new possibilities opened for them by the arrival of cheap and abundant visual imagery. However, it is perhaps the information available to the reader which poses a more acute limit to the growth of the poem. Clearly, conventional schemas are vital to poetry. They don't *need* explaining. You can hitch a free ride. The need to explain situations is an economic limit which applies across a wide range of poems. Poets simply have to make the right choice. If you explain too little, running new information too fast, you write a *difficult* poem.

This is widely reported as a reason for avoiding modern poetry. If you explain too much, with new information arriving very slowly, you write a *banal* poem. This is less reported, but evidently banal poems outnumber difficult ones by a factor of 100, perhaps by much more than 100. This error is, then, harder to avoid than the error of difficulty.

These vexing problems to do with the relation between the poet and the public information wealth could be obscured—covered in dazzle, as it were—by redirecting the poem at the public subject, the subject of British society. This disarms critics—who are too eager to vent their own opinions to think about other things. It justifies the use of collective imagery. It moves the test of success or failure to the area of the sociological imagination—something not all poets have.

If all this is true, it suggests that there is a natural overlap between poetry and politics: both discourses use the same stylised public scenes as the evidence with which to construct complex (but publicly comprehensible) statements. We can study both discourses by looking at the sites where the shared scenes are promulgated and taught—in the hypothesis, the scenes are repetitive and few in number. Political ideas can only go so far without being referred to experience, discussion can only go so far with experiences which only one of the speakers knows about. We can clarify poetry by accessing a secular canon of true situations in the same way that access to the set of stock Christian scenes or the stock Communist scenes clarifies poems written by Christians or Communists.

The detection of these shared symbolic sites as units in the inventory of cultural behaviour allows us to deploy evidence from other realms of culture and use it to illuminate poems. A simple example would be 'Spain', which is more interesting than Auden's other poems because it takes a logical structure from a book by V Gordon Childe, who was good at thinking. Let me take this detection as an example of the kind of *reconnection* operation which I am pointing to in modern poetry. In comparing the site and the poem, we have to compare entire sets: not only does one element match another element, but each element in set A matches an element in set B, and the relationships within set A match the relationships within set B. We are always asking the question does this match that, but also looking at both sets in their entirety. We are saying A is to B as A' is to B'. This is what I mean by finding oblique connections between sets of data. Auden's poem about the diffusion of culture is paralleled by a poem by Richard Aldington, of three years earlier, on the same subject. We could go through the exercise of mapping Aldington's poem onto Auden. This might involve us in reading Grafton Elliot Smith and V Gordon Childe. Connections between the two poems are oblique—connections *within* either poem are straight, or structurally stated. Anyway, this kind of matching and transforming and reconnecting plays a major role in modern poetry. Tracking it exactly would be a large project. It occurs to me that what I am doing in this book involves reconnection rather a lot—something which I find enjoyable and which I hope the reader does too. Does thinking about poems contribute to understanding them? I hope so. Other shared sites are the Imagined Village and the Documentary. It is perhaps clearer if we talk about roles rather than sites. Clearly, there are roles such as the Prophet, the Documentarist, the Moral Accuser, the Ethnographer, the Avantgardist, which do not properly belong to a single poet, but to many.

The appeal of the primary sensuous and pictorial element in poetry seems to me underrated. A poem may perfectly well be a visual work—the product of visual imagination and visual organisation, the *ordonnance* of images. The extent of the images available to the public is fabulous and inexhaustible: the poet addressing such a public is like someone let loose in the Museum at Alexandria, with its acres of artworks. Evidently, that first Museum was the product of one dynasty of Diadochic tyrants wanting to outshine the other such dynasties of the east Mediterranean world. As we said, the primary acts of accumulation and collection gave rise to stores of images which could then be reproduced and distributed. The poet's relationship to this public stock of images is benign and enduring. At some level a poem is simply a concatenation of images, a journey from one to the other.

The rippling torrents of data are organised into stories, and the stories imply roles and identifications which are thick with energy but also rigid and predictable.

The first problem can be seen even within the title of one of the cigarette card series dug up by JM MacKenzie: picturesque peoples of the Empire. Even the word *of* is problematic. Would these peoples themselves say that they were part of the Empire, or that the Empire had replaced their own history? Does not the term *picturesque* imply a single perspective on the human subjects of this information? One which reduces them to aesthetic objects at the expense of their humanity. As for peoples, this too implies an administrative perspective within which one can say *The Somali is cruel but courageous* or *The Bengali is educated but talks too much*. That is, it reduces the human subject to an example of a type, obeying official knowledge, and without the qualities of character and personality which all humans possess. And the word Empire implies a whole epic of militarism, expansion, consignment of weaker peoples to the rubbish tip of history, the triumph of commerce, of manly and heroic deeds, of rage against fifty or sixty peoples who claimed land whose title deeds were held by the Empire, which you might not want to take on at all. The cigarette cards, which take you round the world, which were meant as educational, are fraught with problems. Swimming out of this swamp of bad knowledge to the surface and the air is not at all simple. Obtaining clean data is one of the more complex operations. The fabulous stocks of data, which we have already been so excited by, do not break cleanly into good and bad data. This problem can be summed up by the word teleology, and this already exposes a second problem, which we could call the tragic arrival of ideas. In a later chapter, we will discuss how British poets slowly and reluctantly took on the handling of ideas. Of all the people who read poetry, the proportion who want ideas to feature in poetry is amazingly low. The reader would generally prefer flowers, hedgehogs, brooks, that sort of thing.

The next problem has to do with investment in stories. If you break up these complete stories, you invite the wrath of the interests which put them together in the first place. They may have preferential access to the owners of the magazines you write for, or to the bit of the government that runs something you are part of, or the broadcaster you work for, or the owners of the magazines that might not review your work. It's a bit hopeful to think that these wealthy, powerful, and well-connected people are going to give lavish publicity to dynamic sequences of poetic images that don't favour the wealthy and powerful at all. In fact, this whole area may bring a satisfactory answer to the question of "why is the most interesting poetry occluded and repressed". Or, "why does mainstream poetry exist at all". It would be naïve to think that the government is the chief vested interest in the country. To put it another way, poor people do not own newspapers.

Does the whole literature occur within an English or British ideology of vivid self-directed myths which it simply reflects and reproduces? does it exist outside the society which produced it? This could imply that breaking out of the code lets you step outside the social structure.

"The Briton is cruel but talks too much." So much 20th C British literature recounts obviously inaccurate stories about what is typically British. To anyone outside the charmed circle of patriots, the content of British culture may seem like narcissism, brief flights of thought endlessly circling back to self-love.

The critical poetry we mentioned breaks out of the circle. But ideas may simply seem like broken pictures. The action of interrupting the agreed stories may simply break the verbal link between writer and reader. The poet is, as it were, ripping the film in two and stripping down the projector into its components. The audience may want to think—but there is no picture and they can't see what they're thinking about. They may not be able to think about what the picture shows, or how it was composed. They want to share—but there is no longer a picture for them to share in. Whereas, the proprietary stories have a wonderful flow—everyone knows how they go. The radical poet may be showing a fragment of something new rather than anything complete. The problem of obscurity in poetry is linked to the process of damaging the orthodox and central stories.

The question of whether poetry can really be beautiful once it has escaped from the primary pictorial virtues is one that can be posed as we look at poetry of the Underground. Poetry is not really a substitute for critical theory. The project of starting again, when the machinery breaks down, with mere wood and clay, is heroic. Even when it is applied to breaking down the linguistic inventory of poetry, it may remind us of the Imagined Village: back to the peasant base and its virtues.

Once the Virtual Museum has been distributed, the act of seeing and constructing oblique associations between different sets of data may become the central act of poetry. The didactic act of explaining the familiar becomes naïve and low-status. By oblique I mean relationships not built into the conventional knowledge, but which nonetheless pass a test of meaningful, insightful, stimulating, and so on. This mapping can only follow a mastery of both sets of data. It is not something cranky or part of a childish denial that what other people know is real. It draws on a deep penetration into the real and brings real-world relationships back to life.

This operation may not have been central to $18^{th}$ or $19^{th}$ C poetry. It has been central to $20^{th}$ C poetry. It provides a test for saying whether a set of words is worthy of being a poem. Naturally, there are other artistic practices around, and it would be irrational to pay attention to this test when applied to a poem belonging to a different artistic world. This shift puts intellectuals to the fore ahead of naïve and pictorial poets. It may bring us to a restricted market position where poems are only going to be read by intellectuals. The building of new associations is a specific pleasurable sensation and when it catches may shift us into an altered state where the whole world appears in a new light.

The English family structure is the absolute nuclear family. This means that offspring move out of the family home on adulthood, and normally make a living in something other than the family business. Conflicts with parents are intense at a certain stage of adolescence, but become obsolete on moving out of the family home. They are hard to resurrect later, and generally strike people as not belonging to adult existence. Landlord, employer, and parent are three different people. This means that a preoccupation with defying authority in the realm of the symbolic strikes the English poetry reader, generally, as exciting but immature and also factitious. It does not exert a fascination which long survives. The conflict is expected to be resolved by moving on (and finding something more fulfilling to do) rather than by a dramatic confrontation (and the overthrow of the resented authority). This means that the line of conflict between authorised knowledge and personal or valid knowledge can only play a certain, limited role in the economy of poetry.

I spoke of transparencies above, but perhaps we could translate the image into a binocular superimposition device. We were there considering how the poet compares themselves to other poets, and this is certainly an area which develops mapping and transformation skills. This whole area of roles which can be carried out by more than one person without essentially changing is one which practices insight into analogous (but different) sets.

One of the verbal features of $20^{th}$ C English poetry is the paradox. This is not a mystery -it derives from the revival of the Metaphysicals launched by Grierson, and from the adoption by one of the dominant waves of academic English Literature of the Metaphysicals as a favourite source of poetry. Using paradox is a tic with British poets— it's one of the things I missed when translating German and Dutch poetry. I'm very fond of it. It points precisely to the identification of two sets of data, and the mapping of one onto the other, which we have just pointed to. It points to the organisation of data sets in classes structured by means of analogy; and reveals a flaw in that semantic structure. We could say that metaphor is a valid analogy, and paradox is an unsuccessful analogy. It maps back on to the binocular device we were talking of just now. Two sets of data—and a discrepancy. Which perhaps hides deeper structural problems with the knowledge we think we have.

# West-Bloc Dissidents, or The History of Ideas in Poetry

Poetry is not just concerned with faithful reporting of sense-data, as encouraged by competition with photographs. It also deals with ideas—the larger patterns which are not directly accessible to the senses. The idea that "being an intellectual means your poetry departs from the plane of daily experience and of shared experience so that you go further into silence and incomprehension as you accelerate" seemed plausible for years after it was already true that "being an intellectual means you can write poetry which is wonderfully complicated, precise, original, involving, and modern". The story of the century is the recovery of Donne and Shakespeare as *intellectuals*, for whom ideas were the vital substance of poetry, and the achingly slow adaptation of modern ideas to poetry.

Whereas careful listing of facts is widespread in modern poetry, dealing with ideas is specific to the underground, which is constituted by its difference from conventional and hegemonic beliefs. To propose this opposition sets up winners,—and losers too, those who are passive and unreflective. We can't expect the losers to concur with the judgment, and so the question of whether fear of ideas is due to submission to instituted authority, to lack of intelligence, or to a well-founded aesthetic choice (whereby poetry is rightly brainless like song lyrics) is controversial. We could settle it either by group violence or at the level of ideas. The pre-eminence of ideas is a feature of poetry since 1960 (i.e. of underground poetry), and we want to discuss not only what was its forerunner up till 1960, but also what is the sociological fabric which sustains it.

Structurally, poetry has more words than pop music. If it goes on for longer, it is helpful for it to have more intelligence, as well. Poetry which is no more intelligent than pop music has a problem justifying its existence. This direction of questioning is the one I think poetry has been going in over the last forty years (? seventy years) (? one hundred years). The faction which defines such self-questioning as inherently anti-poetic can therefore be defined as anti-modernity. We can also describe them as wielding the dominant ideology—what teaches us that *introspection is bad*. This resistance to ideas parallels the history of Christian resistance to textual criticism, medicine, psychology, evolutionary biology, and all the rest.

Clearly, what I am proposing as excellent poetry is also unpopular. People associate intelligence with competitive testing in which failure is all too possible—the poetry of ideas is associated with the genre of dreams about anxiety in exams. The association of poetry with two super-competitive universities, Oxford and Cambridge, does not exactly help.

Ideas have to do with power. The national dislike of ideas, a few decades ago, had to do with the success and status of Britain, in the world, and of a class, numerous although in a minority, in the country. The successful are conservative; they dislike speculation. "Intellectual" was a dirty word in England. Someone's attitude towards ideas depends on their attitude towards authority. Conversely, one may feel that ideas without power are flimsy. The intellectual life, in intellectual poets, prefers a state where many ideas are available, and where there is a constant flow of new ideas which implies a short life for each. Apparently ideas lose their aesthetic quality as they take power, and we come down to drafting legislation and accommodating pressure groups. Laws are not so interesting to read as poems.

These modern speculative ideas are closely related to religious doctrine, propaganda, and moralising, sets of data or procedures which animated a lot of pre-modern poetry but are still essentially different from them. I think the difference has, again, to do with authority: consciousness is switched off by subservience. Guessing what will please an authority figure calls for ingenuity, not real consciousness. Some critics will argue, I think, that Christian theology is a complex set of ideas, or even that free-market capitalism is a complex set of ideas, or that the Empire was complex (and so propaganda for the Empire was complex and rich in ideas). I disagree with all this, but I would accept that the ideas content of underground poetry (poetry by West-bloc dissidents) is the product of envy of hegemonic ideas, and so at some level an imitation of those who imitate the inarticulate wishes of the powerful.

Marxists also challenged every accepted idea. There is a structural resemblance between Marxism and critical poetry. This rhyme of positional value has been realised by a number of poets, and for example Macleod, Empson, and Madge were clearly men of the Left. However, it is just a "rhyme", and if you criticise everything you will most likely criticise Marxism as well. Left-wing poets sought an end to alienation, but the version of community which turned up first was pig-headed Party bureaucrats denying them the right to design their own work in favour of Party rules. It was the freelance outer Left which produced most of the significant poetry. I would be happy with the formulation that theoretical Marxism denied the real social order of class and property and wove an operatic new account of all history and all of the planet; this was wrong at almost every point, but its mixture of scope and detailed scenes excited poets into producing great poetry out of imitation.

Quite probably, Marxism produced after 1917 a state of anxiety about new ideas which also made new art into an anxiety symbol. *You are immoral and bad. Your knowledge of the world is self-deception. You are going to lose your property. And society is going to be taken over by people who hate you, who will take away your position, and who are very determined.* What a nightmare! How on earth are you going to sell that to anyone! One momentous British response to Marxist art was Stephen Tallents' reaction to *Storm Over Asia*, which he saw as a direct threat to the loyalty of the Indian Empire. The response, around 1928, was to invent British documentary cinema as counter-propaganda. Cinematic modernity (Pudovkin) was to be swallowed and eaten to neutralise it. Poets, too, strove to absorb the critical method, as a way of acquiring modernity and avoiding possible destruction by it.

Reflexivity is not enough on its own to make an interesting poem. If we took a neuroanatomical view of language, we might find two peaks, in particular, of its activity: introspective complex processing, and socially-oriented, turn-taking communication. I would argue that great poetry draws on both activity centres—there is a High Oral style which is intelligent as well as full of presence. What tends to happen in a given energy nexus is that the brain settles for one or the other and ceases to write interestingly. This combination is a skill and as such it can be acquired by a learning process involving repetition, social rewards, adequate models, protection during the stage of clumsiness, etc. The appeal of the Metaphysicals, I suspect, was that they had this desired combination. The Metaphysicals were pretty much the favourite asset of the New Criticism—they really hadn't clicked with the Victorian reading public, they did write great poetry, every fifteen-year old could feel a glow of pride as they "cracked" a Donne poem and began to say intelligent things about it in class. The social groups which allow the world of ideas to become part of daily life are found in particular places. Poetry of ideas has been written by people who were used to discussing ideas with their friends for whom acts of imaginative projection were congruous and not alienating.

Anxiety and hegemony are the key factors in our study. They are related — someone is anxious about originality because social reassurance is what makes anxiety go away. Any kind of group identification, faction membership, walking in step, reduces anxiety. A society based on individualism, where art is "bourgeois subjectivism" (to use Hauser's phrase), demands that the artist renounces solidarity and painfully develops originality. The winner is the one who is least vulnerable to anxiety.

Eighteen-year olds arrive in the university towns as strangers but also as susceptible to fantasies lurking in the air or in the subsoil. The process of acquiring a voice involves books as well as face to face interaction. Reading a poem is a momentary assimilation whereas acquiring a style is a profound assimilation. Indeed, if the behaviour modules in a poem are incomprehensible or impossible to mimic, the poem is effectively unreadable; we mimic the poem (whether the poem is a mimic of reality or not). There is an intimate relation between the ability of nervous eighteen-year olds to find means of building agreed terms of communication and play with each other and the ability to write poems which deliver a generous social space to a reader. You reach the poem as a stranger and somehow leave it as something else.

*Life Quest*, by Richard Aldington, may be the start of English poetry embracing modern ideas as its content. Another turning point was probably the collective experience of *The English Intelligencer* (1966–70), which made ideas the centre of poetics. The lapses of time we are discussing are very long, and the inhibitions that were dissolving were very powerful. Maybe the big story is, instead, "poetry is part of religion and relies on theology. Poetry loses religion. Poetry flounders. Poetry acquires ideas as a stabilising replacement".

And maybe the big story is, "poetry is part of institutional religion and relies on Christian myth. Religion loses national institutional status. Poetry goes through phase of secular barrenness and realism. Poetry moves over to personal myth". This isn't the one I wrote a book about. This is a big landscape full of figures moving around, and any patterns we make up are likely to be there somewhere.

Poets are afraid of writing didactically. There is a huge difference between poetry which shovels information over people's heads and poetry of ideas. Poetry by intellectuals is very clever about minimising information load in order to get to the ideas quickly. Modernity in poetry is about less knowledge and more ideas. Didactic poetry is associated with bureaucratic religions, loaded with rigid bodies of knowledge, and able to punish children who refuse to learn it. The Middle English poem *Cursor Mundi* would be a good example. Such knowledge has often been stored in poetry—thousands of volumes of it, in Europe and Asia—but is not sought after by modern poetry fans. Propaganda is recognisable in the fine units of composition because it is convergent; it is unambiguous and based on a circularity, and every part of the fabric is designed to support these principles.

Ideas are fragile things. *Ideas poems are fragile and slight things.* The way in which they break has to do with the speed of the brain processing; consciousness is only a temporary state consisting of intense processing which tends to solve the problem, so that consciousness ends as the brain reverts to more routine, less alert patterns. Totally routine poems (cf. the work of most of the English poets of the twentieth century!) are written by one of these. The cult of originality in poems has to do with seizing consciousness demonstrated by fragile, labile, incomplete, patterns of language. That fragile state of high awareness can be the content of poems, if captured. Ideas decay into organised knowledge corresponding to work, and, socially, to bureaucracy. As ideas, they are short-lived products. They survive only in short-distance traps, which detain them. Networks supply these short-distance traps. In the network, the idea is significant because the person you are talking to finds it important. It becomes a social fact. It is part of group process, not just an inner event, which disappears as that inner state changes.

Someone looking from a distance may say that these idea states are flimsy, volatile, insubstantial. They may prefer to look at what lasts a long time. We do not want to look at this because it corresponds to routine, bureaucracy, secure repetition. We want the poem on page 21 to be different from the poem on page 20, if possible. We value a network which values short-life states and short-distance processes. We want to be conscious and also to share consciousness.

All of this brings us to look at small groups as the home of poetry. Nations, as objects of study, offer no sustainable generalisations.

Individuals, by definition, do not support any generalisations. We want to find a level in between—the group. It makes sense to think that someone writing a poem thinks of the readers, and accepts linguistic norms which are liked and understood and recognised by a group rather than inventing a norm valid for one person. If that is true, the group's rules are part of the prehistory of the poem—the more stable part, which as we have just said is less valuable than the unstable, unique part. If we can find traces of these groups—and these may be much less public than poems, which are printed and available almost by definition—then they will help us write the history of poetry. We are asking things like what shape is shared sound? What changes during rapid brain processing? What size is shared attention? How do words make the inner outer, and the outer inner?

Suppose someone said, the brain talking to itself is what matters. The connections within the brain are massively richer than the connections, mediated by symbols, between separate brains. Symbols run down slow channels and are archaic. Norbert Wiener has said something like this. But it is of no interest to us because we are talking about poetry. Reading a poem is always a social act; it involves listening to someone. Having someone else there provides focus—a basic factor in attention and so in consciousness. A poem is a moving line of focus.

Art likes centres of prestige because these take social focus to the maximum. However, a scene may appear to be central because we are focussing on it—not just, focussed on because it is central.

The short lifespan is a problem, itself. Ideally, we would like consciousness to lose its object, its problem, and to become self-sustaining.

Richard Aldington's major poem of the 1930s was called *Life Quest* (1935) —a blast claiming to be in favour of life and against death. A's reputation is buried under tons of rubble, but this isn't at all a bad poem. For me, it is one of the first examples of an English poet writing at length about an intellectual idea—something which proved revolutionary in the long run. It is a much more carefully reasoned work than any of Lawrence's poems. As he helpfully points out, the poem is based on pages 23–35 of Grafton Elliot Smith's *Human History* (1930). I wish other poets were equally cheerful about their sources. The idea it dramatises has been even more discredited and forgotten than Aldington himself—a piece of bad luck. The idea is about the origin and diffusion of civilisation. Smith traces back the whole of civilisation to a Life Quest—the quest of men in Egypt to achieve life after death. The megaliths are "degraded mastabas" and their distribution along the Atlantic littoral traces the diffusion of

Egyptian cultural ideas, rendered without detail because of lower levels of technology. Aldington's poem shows

> Grimaldi bones smeared with red ochre
> That apes bright blood the life-giver
> Conjured in vain as age by age
> Rubble and drift and ashes built a tomb
> A stiff and rocky shroud
> > but saved no soul
> More splendid fantasy robed Osiris dead
> In gold and natron under pyramids,
> Furnished the palace-grave for an eternity
> The Ka has never entered.

The red ochre smeared on Stone Age burials is a forerunner of the gold and natron of Pharaonic mummies. Both acts were in vain, he says. The poem shows him at Gibraltar, gazing at the shore of Africa, musing on Egyptians coming West, also to Britain, in search of life-soaked substances;

> A white squall blew up from Cadiz
> Coming out of Portugal
> North-west from the uneasy bay.
>
> I stood on the last mountains of Europe
> Gazing at the first mountains of Africa
> Across the little straits

Egyptians sailed to blessed islands (of the dead) in search of elixirs. These concrete details illustrate the overall theme of the Life Quest. The poet is not merely retelling Smith's vast legendary narrative. Where Smith describes the domination of myth, the economy, the unit narratives of culture, etc., by self- admiring patriarchs, Aldington starts with the failure of these projects, which *saved no soul*, and goes on to achieve a glimpse of the emptying of the heavens. Having emptied the sky of the noise of human vanity, what we glimpse is the cosmos filled with non-human but living principles. The sun cult is a consequence of this. Aldington was certainly thinking of the lords of the Empire, who lost all credibility with him for their mistakes during the First World War, in which he was a front-line officer. Something this book clears up is the concept of "death cult"—it is true that some cultures devoted bizarre amounts of energy and raw materials to funerals, tombs and memorials. However, for Smith (who possibly invented this idea), this is also part of the Life Quest, and the "death cults" were also the great creative cultures. It is important to grasp this, as also that Lawrence thought the Etruscans were obsessed by death (! all the remains he looked at came from cemeteries) and yet hugely admired their vitality. Aldington says "An Etruscan tomb is gayer than the London streets". Somehow this phrase came to be the name of an enthusiastic but somewhat under-equipped rock band of the early eighties, Southern Death Cult. I do not understand the connection between WJ Perry's book *Children of the Sun* (a development of Smith's wrong core ideas), and the Asconan movement and the title of an archetypal classic sixties record by The Misunderstood. For Lawrence, the sun was alive, and the "dead cosmos" was Christianity and science—the European mainstream of the last 2,000 years, which is partly why he was so preoccupied with marginal cultures—Aegean and Etruscan.

Smith was a surgeon in an Egyptian hospital and as such had carried out many autopsies on mummies. He reminds me—even reminded himself — of Conan Doyle's anatomy teacher, his model for Sherlock Holmes—a man given to flawless chains of logic and dramatic revelations. I admit that Smith was wrong about everything, but *Human History* is still towering and impressive—he starts from the most physical details, of bodies and the layout of objects in tombs, to build up vast ornate theories, covering many countries, melodramatic and rich in detail, a kind of pulp archaeology.

I think Smith was unlucky; I came across an account of a Palestinian skull which had been decorated and evidently kept in the dwelling by the living—something which confirms his idea that the origin of human culture is the enshrining and adornment of the dead, yet at a site discovered after his death, and inhabited 5,000 years before the culture he focussed on. One could dispute whether the death cult energy was obedience to the wishes of the dead (who have no wishes), or to the mourning of the living; the creation of a father God seems all too similar to the practice of keeping a father's skull in the dwelling. The origin of realist art would, then, be in portraiture and in the wish to have the image of the beloved dead still in front of you. Sad to say, someone who developed this idea today wouldn't even mention Elliot Smith —his reputation is buried under his planetary mistakes. Wyndham Lewis drew on Elliot Smith (pp. 73-98 of *The Dithyrambic Spectator*) but has nothing of interest to add.

We can readily see the text as frozen words and so like funereal architecture; early writing is very frequently a way of storing the words of people in authority, and writing allows frozen authority, the self-perpetuation of a dead generation—much like skulls re-fleshed with clay. One stage in the creation of a book is a "primitive accumulation" of information, where information is not simply dissolved in every generation or at the end of every year. "Life Quest" anticipates the concern of *The English Intelligencer* with geography and culture, and the connection of an opposition between sacrosanct art and art that endlessly recreates itself, with the opposition between peasant and pastoral-nomadic societies. "Death cult" is not a metaphor for capitalism and inherited wealth as a dead force crushing society. Aldington does, however, seem to be contemplating the overthrow of petrified authority figures as elements of culture, preferring impersonal cosmological principles such as earth, sea and sky. The quest for immortality failed, and life is for the living.

It is striking that montage is already the great technical problem in Aldington, as with modern underground poetry. He is exactly poised on the ridge between being excitingly spontaneous and being choleric, abrupt, and gruff. Between drawing pictures with bolts of lightning, in his imitation of "The Waste Land", and cutting so quickly that the object isn't rendered at all and the poem doesn't let us in. He did attempt to write about the whole origin of civilisation here and had the insight that to do it in violent flashes, with intermediate and supporting detail ruthlessly wiped away, was the only way of opening poetry up to the rich information structures of prose. The way in which he adapts Elliot Smith's immense rational structure is fertile and essentially modern. Is this writing myth, as Treece and Hendry called for? Aldington went on being bad-tempered and became a character in *The Alexandria Quartet*.

There is a direct link between "Life Quest" and parts of *Lud Heat*, although Sinclair probably got his Egyptian diffusionist material from marginal occultist magazines. The theme of Sirius allows us to quote Martin Thom:

> wind from moon described
>
> lunar wind: sporadic blood whisper in the cranium
> or still's child on edge
>
> empty, happy, never there
>
> there by the dog star, a re-mark
>
> rattling the silver plates of the giant, still dying
> (FROM *THE BLOODSHED THE SHAKING HOUSE* )

He speaks of the signifier and reminds us that Benveniste said "Arbitraire, oui, mais seulement sous le regard impassible de Sirius". Later,

> Hieroglyphs in the Book of Zurich are monkey-goddess scratchings only. The pain does not arrive if tyrannical image as archaism is presented, rich in the layering of old oppressions, impressions.
>
> glow
> the dust
> lanterns
>
> sliding, only the wounded 'resolument moderne'
>
> This book is about 'water' and 'fear' and the rich light that so flies above a line dividing them.
>
> (FROM *The Bloodshed the Shaking House* )

Philip Jenkins, too, wrote about water and Egypt:

> In the Cairo Museum, a snake
> with its tail in its mouth
> symbol of the cosmic ocean
> the state of perpetual flux
>
> Porphyry in *De antro nympharum*
> identifies the solar barque leaving Memphis
> with its departed soul
> as no solid boat but the vehicle whereby they
> *sail on the moist*
>
> the rain which falls
> in central Africa
> the snow which melts
> on the hills of Abyssinia
>
> (FROM *Cairo, complete version 1981*)

Both works have themes in common with *Life Quest*. The scale of Elliot Smith's speculative errors does incline us to look more closely at evidence. Anatomy, archaeology, the invention of technology, do offer glimpses of the origins of human nature — glimpses we hardly benefit from if we add so many fantasies to the fragmentary real record. Because the academic discipline of Eng Lit largely identifies itself with making pupils question their reactions, question the poet's reactions, and seek for reflexivity, the products of this discipline will tend to admire those skills, as I do. Rather obviously, this discipline is implanted throughout the English-speaking world. The autocritique, the thing least welcome to adolescent poets, is also the most productive thing. The same thing damages people not being validated by the system and liberates people whose confidence is being daily pumped up by rip-open sachets of prestige.

~

The image bank of Christian doctrine and Classical myth has been closed down, poets seeing their credit cards on these banks taken away and sliced up in public. It wasn't much better with the delights of the patriotic history pictures—the fights for the flag, the naval melodramas. *Life Quest* dragged in archaeology and anthropology as replacements for this lost bulk. The formula of displaying the deep structures of the psyche through exotic and vital imagery drawn from non-Western and non-Classical cultures has moved to centre stage since. The dependence of poetry on myth has not really decreased. The handling of these exotic and fissile materials depends on protocols for dealing with acquired knowledge—something much easier to acquire from intellectuals than anywhere else. The dexterity of handling barbaric material begins with Jane Ellen Harrison, or with Nietzsche, well before Aldington's rewriting of North European prehistory. I am inclined, however, to see Marxism, with its lavish, starry-eyed, world-historical, faustian, moral operas, as the primal experience which so many great modern poems drawing on myth and history re-lived. While recovering the 1940s, we might look at two largely unrecovered Stalinist texts—George Thomson's *Marxism and Poetry* and Jack Lindsay's *Perspective for Poetry*. However authoritarian the methods, the way in which they integrate anthropology and myth into their theory of poetry is profoundly interesting and suggestive. This version of Hegel brought the dizzying historical series back on stage but allowed the poet to have access to all the previous terms of the series. It restored, in fact, the faustian parade, where the poet has access to all societies, all periods, and all states of mind. This, unsurprisingly, is what modern poets wanted.

## New Romanticism: a table

### Key names
JF Hendry; Nicholas Moore; Henry Treece; Norman MacCaig; Dorian Cooke; Edith Sitwell; GS Fraser; Stefan Schimanski; Douglas Young; Edwin Morgan; Christopher Middleton; Francis Berry; Philip O'Connor; DS Savage; Roland Mathias; Glyn Jones; Dylan Thomas; George Barker; WS Graham; Vernon Watkins; Edwin Muir; Adam Drinan; Os Marron; David Gascoyne; Herbert Read; Alex Comfort; Lawrence Durrell; David Jones; Kathleen Raine; Peter Yates; Nigel Heseltine; Hubert Nicholson; Patrick Anderson

### Key influences
Blake; Kierkegaard; Karl Barth; Mounier; Shestov; Berdyaev; André Breton; Kropotkin; Freud; Jung; Lawrence

### Some painters
David Jones, Cecil Collins, Michael Ayrton, John Minton, John Craxton, Keith Vaughan, Graham Sutherland, Gerald Wilde, Ceri Richards, John Piper, Leslie Hurry

### Some topoi
the religious dimension of art
the prophetic gifts of the artist
the blinding effect of materialist civilisation
the value of subjective feelings and of expressivity
the invocation of Blake and the Romantics
the adoption of Surrealist practices but replacing chance by self-expression
the preference for the eery, Gothic, and eccentric
the preference for landscape and the sublime
fear of destruction, and a preference for the ancient, the mythical, and the biological

### Some dates
1936 International Surrealist Exhibition at the New Burlington Galleries in London
1939 Apocalyptic manifesto
circa 1941 poetry boom, and boom of the New Romantic style
1950 eclipse of the school

1952 arrival of the Movement, deploying a concerted attack on the New Romantic style and on the reputations of their poets

### Key works
Collected poems, Dylan Thomas; George Barker, *Calamiterror, The True Confession of George Barker*; Edith Sitwell, *The Song of the Cold, The Canticle of the Rose*; JF Hendry, *The orchestral mountain*; WS Graham, *The Nightfishing*; Roland Mathias, *Break in Harvest*; Glyn Jones, *Selected poems*; S Goodsir Smith, *Under the Eildon-Tree*; Francis Berry, *Murdock and Other Poems*; Kathleen Raine, *The Pythoness*; Adam Drinan, *The Men of the Rocks*; Peter Yates, *The Expanding Mirror*; Patrick Anderson, *The Colour as Naked*

### Some magazines
*Seven, Poetry London, Poetry Quarterly, Now, Kingdom Come, Life and Letters, Transformation*

### Anthologies
*The New Apocalypse; Lyra; the white horseman; The Crown and the Sickle; A New Romantic Anthology; Modern Welsh Poetry; Sailing tomorrow's seas; New British Poetry*

Romantic prose Sacheverell Sitwell, *Splendours and Miseries*; Gwyn Thomas, *All things betray thee*; Northrop Frye, *Fearful Symmetry*; G Wilson Knight, *The Golden Labyrinth*; Robert Graves, *The White Goddess*; John Cowper Powys, *Porius; Owen Glendower*; Alex Comfort, *The Power-House*

# The dissolution of the horizon: New Romantic poetry

## The biomorphic forties

The specific style of the 1940s appears to have totally deceased, and even deceased *circa* 1948–50. I am referring to the "New Apocalypse" group, founded by Treece, Hendry, and Fraser in 1938, later broadening into a "New Romantic" movement. Look at this:

> One nightmare after cinderfall
> Idiocy in a slumber took me aside
> To see my friend in his golden fell
> Stumble at the handle of fiends'-hovel
> By the feral riverside.
> [ . . . ]
> And yet if all flesh was standing
> As thick as smoke from wall to wall
> And if love like gold was seen ascending
> Through the valley of the blood and the understanding
> What would suffice of it all
> To my friend in his fleshly desolation?
> (EDWIN MORGAN, FROM *"THE SLEIGHTS OF DARKNESS"*), or

> Here is her rigging bound
> Nerve, sinew, ice and wind
> Bowing through the night
> The starred dew of beads.
>
> Here her ribs of silver
> Once steerless in a culvert
> Climb the laddered centuries
> To hide a cloud in a frame.
> (J.F. HENDRY, FROM *"THE SHIP"*).

*The dissolution of the horizon: New Romantic poetry* [143]

(There is an excellent account of this movement in Robert Hewison's *Under Siege*.) A historical placing of the NR group is bound to note their affinities to other poets of the 1940s (i.e. formed in the 40s), such as Paul Celan, Johannes Poethen, and Nelly Sachs. These can easily be identified as updates of Expressionism; it is easy to find, in an anthology such as *Menschheitsdämmerung* (1923), poems which anticipate the New Romantic style. The explanation is non-exotic; certain Expressionist poets were adapting the sensuous and grandiose style of parts of the Bible; (some of them were Jewish, some Christian); and the circumstances of the 1940s encouraged poets to speak like priests, because the events of mass death and mass mourning asked for elevated speech to speak for them. This priestly function drove poets, both Christians and Jews, back to the Bible, and this common source explains affinities between different countries (Sachs in exile in Sweden, Celan in France). Affinities to Symbolism are also not strange, since that was also an era where poets saw themselves as priests and adapted the beauties of religious language in various ways. The basic rule within the school is to shift attention towards the prophetic books as the primary utterance of Christianity, and away from anything secondary, such as theological reasoning, sermons, epistles, canon law, and so forth. This is the overt meaning of the phrase "new apocalypse", and I think that an attempt to turn the inner rules of the *Book of Revelations*, of the books of Daniel, Esdras, etc. into aesthetic formulae, and then to write about the politics of the 1940s, about personal experiences, about the flux of ideas, strictly within those formulae, gave rise to New Apocalyptic poetry; and, less strictly adopted, to New Romantic poetry. The introductory essays to *A New Romantic Anthology* (by the Rev. EFF Hill and Walford Morgan) make this fairly explicit and judge the results by Christian standards. Starting points may have been either the artist's envy of the priest, or the priest's indignation at the secular State taking functions away from the Church. Envy of "primary" theophanic vision seems to be central for Hill. The movement fits within a historical pessimism about the Christian religion, whereby the termination of prophecy, with the Revelations of John, around A.D. 80, was a loss for the Church, perhaps even a loss of touch with true faith, which excluded "modern" Christians from a central area, and which would lead to the fall of the Church as a secular power. It must be reversed, and one valid sign of this reversal was a return in literary utterance to the directly theophanic genre of prophecy. We can see the NRs as an attempt to refound poetry with *Revelations* as the normative model, with generative textual strands like

Roman urban elegy, the ethics of everyday behaviour, and civics, cast into disfavour.

What we seem to be seeing is a shift of emphasis within committed Protestant poetry; the movements of the 1940s don't side with the secular historicism of modernism, and their great popularity was probably because they didn't offend the basic Protestant ideology of most of the reading public. They can be fitted comfortably within the traditional Protestant phenomenon of revivals, which include an attack on the complacency of the existing Church. All Dissenting groups, indeed, had an institutionalised nucleus of hostility to the State church. The contrast with the dominant literary style of the 1950s is not, then, a revival of religion after 1950; instead, it relates to a shift of emphasis within a broad Protestant spectrum of opinion. Externally, the mass public peril and mourning of 1939–45 stopped, and in fact the wartime collectivism was replaced, at least partly, by an individualist attitude encouraged from above; among poets within the Church, a sense of draining of the fluid of faith continued, but a self-vindication through claimed (private) prophetic gifts now seemed vainglorious, and the new response is an atmosphere of disillusion, where faith is preserved in shrunken form through privatisation. A return to reason, commanded by a common shift into a position of academic authority, allows the recuperation of faith: the teaching day is occupied in proving that the best poets are the Anglican ones, and one's imaginative life is occupied with a wish for people to be reasonable and act in a civilised way towards each other. The central texts are now not *Revelations* but the essays of TS Eliot, *The well-wrought urn*, and *Anatomy of Criticism*. The wish to take over the central State organs of ideology does not represent submission to their ideals but on the contrary a passionate desire for reform of them.

The forties have been done down by prejudiced propaganda, because "they produced no great poetry". Dylan Thomas, David Jones, and George Barker wrote undoubtedly the greatest British poetry of that time, in styles systematically breaking the accepted rules and yet following most of the particular rules of the school. However, its internal weaknesses are a sufficient obstacle to any attempt at revival. Perhaps the Apocalyptics never went far enough; they were an adequate basis for a truly revolutionary poetry, which never emerged because the movement failed to survive into a second decade. The attempt to extend the boundaries of poetic language was correct; the extravagant metaphors (e.g. Hendry named a poem "The orchestral mountain") failed to come off because of an internal disproportion: extremist jumps of imagery were undercut by much more orthodox verse technique all around them, which meant that they were contradicted by context. If you are going to apply sensational, almost psychedelic, metaphorical gestures, you must create empty space around them. Huge gestures need space. You have to discard the previous apparatus. Hedging them about with conventional syntax and the usual furniture of English poetry (in particular, even lines with regular line breaks) made them grotesque. The original aspects of Apocalyptic poetry appear almost as quotes, as something quite foreign stuck into a collage where every other component is fit for a drawing room.

Identifying a unified style implies a siting of each poet (or each poem?) in relation to the bounds, raised to cognitive dominance, of that style. I intend to ignore this rather long task. However, we can quickly note a transition during the early forties: the style became much less bizarre and illogical, much more organised, sonorous, ceremonious. Hendry's 1943 volume *The Orchestral Mountain* is a huge advance on his earlier poetry and Dylan Thomas made a similar advance. As the style matured, it became less salient. Edith Sitwell has to be comprehended in our picture of 1940s Romanticism, and certainly her poetry changed a great deal in the 1940s, but the style of her late poems can roundly be identified with the late nineteenth century, and with high-period Symbolism. The idea of Sitwell as a public and political (and religious) poet must have been amazing to people familiar with her work up till 1940. The prose activities of Hendry (1912–86) and Treece (especially) are essentially a response to poetry by Dylan Thomas which had been around several years before; they can be seen as interpreters of a style already worked out by Thomas and George Barker during the early thirties (Barker, *Thirty Preliminary Poems*, 1933; Thomas, *18 Poems*, 1934). There is no anthology of the school's best work; the ones that came out during the war were partial and rushed, while post-war anthologies have marginalised them in favour of almost every other group.

The theory of liminality developed by Victor and Edith Turner, and their associates, gives us a way of conceptualising the New Apocalyptic style. What they sketch is a zone outside the oppositions of social space, where social distinctions are broken down to give a communitas, a group whose purpose is solidarity (and which has no other purpose). There is a link between marginal sites used for pilgrimage and the marginal state of prophecy which is what the new apocalypse, permanently, was meant to be delivering. We can speculate that going to war may have occupied some of the functions of a pilgrimage, in which a communitas (with its features of lowness, unity, loss of personal interests, and comradeship) took over at least some of the time, and influenced the political mood of the country towards a collectivism and acts of benevolence (inclusiveness) towards the poor. This mood reminds us of the historical imperatives of Christianity.

Communitas likes to express itself through symbolic substances which cannot be divided, and which are often white (recalling milk), such as light, clouds, sap, or wine. I do not find such a symbol within the NR group; however, any census of their poems will reveal a very high proportion of body parts in the words they chose, and I would like to suggest that the body was elevated by them to be the shared indivisible substance, simultaneously the "liminal space" where integrity happens, and the source of prophecy. That is, it is as far removed from physiological reality as a cross is from planks. The style was not someone's private property, and its communitas status explains why so many poets felt the impulse to join it. This communitas group-state possibly explains why the movement died so quickly in 1950; it inhered inside a group identity, and once that dissolved, spilt from a broken vessel, it simply was not there for the individuals who had to go on to something new. It was a transformation of the universally familiar communitas offered by the Christian Church itself and could only come into being because the established church was felt to have lost some of its charismatic power, its symbols dying back into inanimate objects, chilling and expelling the forlorn creature (who becomes the individual as the outcome of a disaster). At one remove from the prophets is personalism, and at one remove from Personalism is the solemn self-definition of the underground poet.

Each poetic utterance is unique. However, we can set out a table showing parts of the conceptual field which governed the generation of those poems.

| (shunned) | (favoured) |
|---|---|
| reflexivity | emotion |
| 15–19 years old | 3–7 years old (in the sequence of development) |
| emotional | |
| group oriented | self centred |
| syntax | affective images |
| analysis & reason | teleology and appetite |
| categorisation | identifying with |

*The dissolution of the horizon: New Romantic poetry* [147]

distance closeness
even perspective distortion, high spots

In the work of WS Graham, "language" becomes a mysterious, timeless force transcending personal intention and social division. He uses two other symbols of liminality with the traits of communitas: the sea, sailed by fishermen; and, closely related, the ice pack to which Nansen sailed, and which he writes about in *Malcolm Mooney's Land*. The second of these also plays a central role in Hendry's long poem *Marimarusa, a Polar Sonata*; from a Greek term probably borrowed from Celtic, and describing, in one text of an ancient geographer, the "dead sea", the frozen sea of the very high North. This long poem was written in 1947 (or, perhaps, 1946–50) but published in 1978. Hendry's note relates it to accounts of exploration at both Poles, and the snow is that of post-war Vienna where the poem was composed, but there is nothing literal about it. In an interview he described the poem as being about a sensation of "nothingness", which he felt as "theological", and which involved dread, the vacuum, the abyss, infinitude, and freedom from all constraint. Thus fulfilling Turner's symbolic pattern, it is "trackless as the limbo all men seek,/ into a land of birds like the dead or the unborn". Outside, "The world of time was the world of becoming", but in the "dead sea", "(f)eatures of time snowbound in the clock-face freeze". The sea where the ice forms (underwater) has it "shooting to the surface/liquid stars and milk", a moment which Hendry compares to the birth of a cell. The freedom from time passing also means that the poet has great trouble giving his poem a forward flow. Two early long Edwin Morgan poems, of 1952 ("Dies Irae") and 1955 ("The Cape of Good Hope"), are about the sea, seen as a transcendent place that is boundless and contains all things. Nansen crossed the Polar Sea by allowing his ship, the *Fram*, to be frozen in, knowing that the set of the currents would take it west to Spitsbergen and the open sea; ice is thus a substance "within which" one can be. The agentless planetary drift of the Polar currents resembles the agentless action of language, in Graham's conception.

There is a link between the lack of differentiation between individual poets, the indifference to order and temporal flow inside the poems, and their lack of logical presentation and development. They generally don't use objects younger than 50,000 years old; the poems occur within a timeless zone (without before and after) which has, as a secondary rule, no objects whose origin belongs inside time. The popularity of parts of the body is a consequence of this rule. The relations of the parts of a body to each other are, furthermore, essentially simultaneous, not sequential. The organic imagery does not derive from Freudian beliefs, although it may have been helped by reading Freud. Although any New Romantic poem looks very much like surrealism, the gap between them and surrealism is important. NR poems were irrational but "motivated".

The forties style closely resembles a contemporary style of American painting, conveniently labelled "biomorphic" (as in Lawrence Alloway's essay). Biomorphism was a specific late form of Surrealism in which the artist reasserted the nonrandom meaning of imagery. Parisian artists like Masson, SW Hayter, Matta were its immediate precursors. Logically, the forties artists started from the horror of Europe being overrun (by tanks and also by madness) to develop a belief in eternal values, i.e. civilisation is bound to revive because values cannot die. The next step was to found these values in the human body, in its fibres and fluids, because these demonstrably are reborn in each generation. So, this is what Sutherland was painting, or Hendry writing about. If one looks at certain paintings by Arshile Gorky, or Jackson Pollock, or Stuart Davis, one sees successful biomorphic painting. Hendry states (*the white horseman*) that he thinks of the Image as a sort of fluorescent screen on which something of the deeper structure of reality is revealed. This corresponds remarkably well to the biomorphic painter's understanding of the canvas. My hunch is that Hendry and his fellows could have broken through into good poetry if they had been as radical as Gorky or Matta. The evidence, after all, was in front of them: there are photographs of two Matta paintings in *the white horseman*. Thomas' "Light breaks where no sun shines" is probably the ideal biomorphic poem.

Since the parts of our bodies actually are a million years old, there is an explanation for the body part imagery other than the influence of Professor Freud, a hypothesis which is quite misleading about the nature of this poetry. Physiology is just about the most easily manipulated of sets of imagery, and the recognition that it is not "imperious" or "stable" allows us the chance of working out what the poems actually mean, which a recursion to Freudianism takes away again.

Hendry was too attached to ego boundaries, syntax, and line breaks, to live out his own artistic vision. If feelings are "eternal", then you can jettison the self; you can produce a text which doesn't follow the rules of daily speech. You've got an empty space; the way in which you use it reveals the limits of your energies. The lines you draw will display what is happening inside your body. Subjectivity is frightening. Hendry was writing poetry so "archetypal" that it's altogether impersonal and yet still trying to cling on to the apparatus that points to a real person talking. Tense and sense die, the metaphors are everything, and yet the poems don't back them up, leaving objects in a vague and "essential" relationship to each other. Biomorphic painters seized on biological basics to express their own subjectivity; the Neo-Apocalyptics elected eternity and drained their poems of all local and personal reality in order to impersonate it. English (even British) poets have a habit of ignoring whatever in the landscape is less than 500 years old; the Apocalyptics make a reasonable attempt at ignoring whatever is less than a million years old. Because Poetry is Eternal, you don't actually have to write it, all you have to do to is Be A Poet. Eternity is a pusillanimous clutch at support from higher authority. Outside time there are no events. "Eternal" imagery is actually the complete denial of subjective choice.

There is a strange resemblance between the Apocalyptics and the euphemistic school of religious poetry, summed up in Christina Rossetti or Alice Meynell. Filtering out the transient is euphemism. Study of Kathleen Raine or of certain JF Hendry poems turns up a spindly language, resembling Anglican hymns. Religion is the greatest possible threat to writers discovering the subjective and supernatural. "Do not call up that which ye cannot send back". Their demon arrived in the form of a vicar. The mention of Raine brings us up to date, with the magazine *Temenos* and poets such as Jay Ramsay. This contemporary school is still confusing the strength of subjectivity with the existence of "eternal" symbols. Recourse to ancient symbolic systems is a call for help from the spiritual hierarchy and may in practice be a way of denigrating what is happening inside you. Any contest between "eternalists" and the approach of Picasso, jazz musicians, Action painters, all of whom accept the heat and transience of emotions, will reduce the former to mere phantoms. Subjectivity needs no justification, only realisation.

The block which held up the forties poets from realizing their own programme was the figure of the Poet, the pretty and sensitive and noble speaking voice. Let's just hint at the similarities between Francis Bacon and Ted Hughes—Bacon and Jackson Pollock gave up on painting pretty objects in ways that drew attention to their own sensitivity: Hendry and Treece and their allies did not. The avant-garde method is not an ornament to be pasted on; it is a demon that has to be wrestled with, and that breaks the weak in two.

## The International gang; or, how modern are you?

It is not quite fair to describe the activities of the New Romantics without admitting the existence of what they were attacking. The 1930s, stimulated by the international recession, heard a great deal of talk along the lines of:

out of date subjectivity
a systematic approach to problems of form
worn-out classes and equipment
inevitable historical imperatives
central co-ordination and planning
blind to the laws of history

which certainly suggested to nervous European artists that some kind of police was going to impose a set of rules for how art had to be done, put everyone through terrifying batteries of tests, and silence or exile anyone who didn't pass. The fantasy is fun to watch now, a kind of Hitchcock film full of jokes, shocking murders, and nostalgic glimpses of old architecture. Another group of people were sharing the fantasy, though with themselves in the role of police, sweeping away everyone who wasn't a modernist, a Nazi, a Marxist, or whatever it was.

It is difficult drawing a line through these activities to say, at this point they stop being acceptable, so to the left of the line they are still OK and win our approval. The uncertainties and complexities of the historical milieu scarcely lend themselves to this. Perhaps one should admire people who can achieve total polarisation and compare them to photographers who can seize a single moment of a teeming whole and realise that this will make a great picture. It's nice to know what modernity is, if only for a moment. The self-confidence of certain artists related to their failure to perceive almost every factor. If we consider that the virtues of English artists like David Jones and John Cowper Powys were put in the shade by modernist aggrandisement, a negative, we have to admit too that Britain would have done much better in the Second World War if it had more thoroughly adopted certain methods of modern war, for example the need to coordinate all arms, the ability of radio to give flexibility and coordination between units, the significance of tank warfare, and account this as a positive for the modernisers. If you said, in Liverpool in 1931, that people's jobs had been taken away by Dark International Forces, someone could well have replied that the jobs had been created in the first place by Dark International Forces, summed up as the Empire, in a town dependent on exports to give its docks a purpose. Since Britain dominated the world's exports still at that time, its prosperity stemmed from the "impersonal forces".

In every year since, say, 1914, there has been a line of opposition to be drawn between eclectics and fanatics, or if you like between conservatives and modernists, or the empirical and the theoretical. The line which favours machinery, technology, the elimination of individual subjectivity to be replaced by "mass impulses" or virgin theory, has been either capitalist or Communist or Nazi, rarely something else. The fantasy that only one style of art is "modern" and "significant" violates the consensus of today, since it puts monopoly power in the hands of one group and consigns everyone else to oblivion; fortunately, the defence of anything except pluralism is today unpopular. The fact that art in any year of the twentieth century is alarmingly diverse, and that this diversity seems to have increased, apparently makes any theory that "modernising" art is moving in any direction, or in one direction, or in the direction commended by any canonized theorist, invalid and even ridiculous. The preference for any current is aesthetic and subjective, rather than objective and exhibiting "the laws of history".

The New Romantics, then, were attacking a belief in a centralised reform of art, and perhaps society, which some of their contemporaries did talk about and believe in. The influence of the Great Depression, or of European dictatorship, or of the Second World War, on individual consciousness, even in its most subjective states, remained a fact not much affected by poetological pamphlets. The tenuity of artistic systems, or of Grand Wrong Theories, does not redeem the artistic weaknesses of the New Apocalyptics and their congeners.

We can consider Georgianism, Personalism, "pop" and spontaneous poetry, Green poetry, and feminism, as successive attacks on "technocratic" government and poetry. The differences are great but the need, for political effectiveness, to reach large numbers of people through imagery they understand means that quite a lot of the imagery is constant. A knowledge of the accepted distinction between "personal" and "impersonal" talk, for example can help us understand why feminism discouraged the avant-garde in poetry. A belief, that the impression of someone there talking with you represents the "organic" in poetry, tends to exclude documentary from poetry, and this may explain why poetry has tended to narrow down to the expression of one person's personal experience and to drop the larger subjects. Of course, the decline of the Christian Church as the source of a central cosmological framework inside which poetry could make large statements means that any way in which poets do now make such statements will seem unfamiliar, aleatory, personal, and factional.

# Moral man in an immoral society: personalism and authenticity in the 1940s

"Socialism in the name of the person, and Socialism in the name of the State: these are two distinct approaches, two schools of thought dividing the Left". Stanford, *The Freedom of Poetry* (1947), p.43.

∼

The New Apocalyptic programme involved rejection of the object-machine, which seems to have included much of the State apparatus, especially when making war, as well as industrial capitalism; rejection of mechanical imagery in poems (as attributed to Auden and Kenneth Allott); and a belief in the importance of myth as "the re-integration of the personality". The earliest known statement includes objectivity and logic, too, within the category of "the machine-world".

The most prominent idea behind the style seems to be personalism. This is a vague philosophy, but for its followers it offered two key lines of self-defence: against charges of indifference, since it was "socially committed" and saw itself as revolutionary, and against charges of collaborating with the State (seen variously as a war machine, an inhuman concentration of power, something impersonal and heartless, or as an impious erection of self-sufficiency which had no respect for God and His ministers). A broader distrust of the State within all Christian groups could refer itself to Reinhold Niebuhr, an American pastor very popular in the 1930s, in his book *Moral man and Immoral Society*. The stages of the way between those two concepts are of interest to us. If small groups can be moral, how large can they grow before they become indifferent to other groups, and so immoral?

Derek Stanford worked, during the war, with a battalion of Pioneers, conscientious objectors who were serving their country as labourers. This unit consisted entirely of artists. A significant split within the British intelligentsia was, then, between those willing to serve the State, fighting against tyranny, and those who considered that a State making war was already too close to a tyranny, and they could not take part in its operations without protest. The percentage of Scottish and Welsh artists making this protest was higher than the English quota. It is no more than reasonable to extend our view of the British State, as at 1943, to its overseas possessions and to recognise that these "conchies" were saying no to the Empire, and that they were in contact with other artists and intellectuals, saying no, in other countries, such as India, South Africa, and Australia.

It would be simple to write off the personalists as outside the great stream of collectivism. Certainly it's a good thing that pacifist ideas didn't catch on so infectiously that the population gave up, disavowed their leaders, and handed dirty State power over to Hitler. To counterbalance this knockout blow, let me flash forward in time and link personalism's attack on warfare and vast impersonal monopolies with, variously, feminism, Celtic nationalism, libertarian socialism, and Green politics. No one has ever said, all power to the Civil Service. Opposition to centralisation and oligarchy is virtually the consensus position, which makes it tricky to denounce personalism for arguing this position in around 1932.

There is a structural link between personalism and poetry, as we have it. Once poetry is enjoyed in solitude and through the medium of print, it has an individualist bias. The argument for withdrawing from public forums is that one has a "unique perspective", and the value of poetry becomes tangled up with the offset of that unique view from the "common" one, and this offset becomes tangled up with the critique of authority: whether ecclesiastical, academic, aesthetic, or political. This is all a fragile tissue, since (for example) Homer, the *Psalms*, *King Lear*, the hymn-book, and *Paradise Lost* are clearly public and impersonal. However, the problems of writing collective and "broad address" poetry in the twentieth century remain unsolved, and one can assume that many people who wanted to write in this manner left poetry and moved into less specialised markets. Having a "unique viewpoint" thus became a boundary-making divide between poetry and the audio-visual world, where the source of money also decides what the message is. This offset is either so mighty that it has to be expressed at all costs, or so tenuous that it evaporates when you try to express it in a popular medium. If the shared unconscious rule is that poetry has to be personal, about firsthand experience, interior, and in revolt, then poetry is inevitably personalist.

The Welfare State never achieved socialism, but this was part of its legitimacy, since the nation it served was not socialist either; what it satisfied was what brought it into being, a Christian nation replacing an irreparable system of parish relief, identifying the State (at some deep level) with Herod and Pontius Pilate, and regarding the individual soul as belonging to a higher order of being than the body or the group.

Critics generally ignore personalism when discussing the 1940s, so I will describe some of the evidence for my claims about it. In issue 1 of *Transformation* (edited by Treece and Schimanski, 1943), we have an essay on "The Political Implications of Christianity"; another on "Souls, Cannon-Fodder, or Robots?", by a Labour MP who had formerly been a Nonconformist minister; an essay by Alexander Blok, in the stage after he had become disillusioned with the Bolsheviki, called "The decline of Humanism"; an editorial called "Towards a Personalist Attitude"; an essay by Herbert Read called "The Politics of the Unpolitical"; an epigraph (to the whole volume) from Emmanuel Mounier, the leading personalist; a collection of essays on "The War and Writing", which mostly deal with the strain between the individual consciousness and the war-making machine. All of this can be classified as personalist; more, it would be indefensible to describe the policy and interests of the magazine without saying "Personalist". If I would detract something from that, it would be to note that Read was not (by this stage) a Christian, but an anarchist; to grasp the complex of anti-State affection (in a period of wartime totalitarianism, if I can use that phrase without any pejorative tone), we have to consider, also, anarchism and Celtic nationalism (which we could call "anti-imperialism"). I think there is also a category of fundamentalist Christian pacifism without personalism; David Jones was against the war, went round saying what good people he thought the Germans were, wrote the passage in *The Anathémata* about the brothers who killed each other unawares (Balin and Balan). Read was therefore a fellow-traveller of personalism. *Transformation* is 80% prose; the Christian component is larger than the poetic one. It's fairly clear that Treece was a personalist, but the case is less clear for JF Hendry, who was capable of considering myths other than Christian ones, and was, at least by his "Churchillian Ode", pro-war. Alex Comfort's poetry is not New Romantic, but he was a Christian pacifist and he published along with them because his politics are personalist. *Poetry London*, too, gave space to debates about anarchism versus commitment; we can take it that oppositions between classes, and between Left and Right, also existed, but there was probably no forum which both sides would deign to read, so that those conflicts were not "vocal" but "passive", settled before the domain of the written starts. GS Fraser's piece in "War and Writing" is right on the fault-line between a belief in the justness of the war and a sense of personal deterioration, emptying-out, and depersonalisation, under the stress of war service; he points out that the war aims of the Allies are to defend just that quality of individual liberty and self-determination which fighting the war snatches away "for the duration". Exaggerating, one could say that it is impossible to perceive that gap between collective imperative and inner emotional experience without accepting personalism in some form. It's good to have a strand of art which gives expression to such gaps. One may regard a split mind as one which only knows weak feelings, and these make for weak poetry; reflexivity weakens the central thrust, and this is one of the things which the mass audience finds difficult about modern poetry, that it's so interested in oscillations and fine nuances. This situation is only tenable for short periods; a modern poet who fears that identifying with other people (the "group") will mean forfeiting modern status, and who values political ideas to the extent that they are different from everyone else's, and so unlikely ever to become public policy, who makes the offset the main theme and the self-contradiction the content, is living in a state of unbearable tension. Another writer of the 1930s who used the word personalism was the Left theologian and anglophile, Nikolai Berdyaev. He also associated the words *object* and *Apocalypse*. In this passage

> What we fear in the future is not the act but the object, not what we can create but what we may have to endure. The future may inspire us with either hope or fear. Every man has to live his inner Apocalypse, which is based on the fundamental paradox of time and eternity, of the finite and the infinite. This Apocalypse reveals the ways in which we can realise our personality. Thus we are confronted with the ultimate problem of the personality. ( *Solitude and Society*, p.156)

we seem to see the direct antecedent of the Apocalyptic School, with the recognition that Apocalypse is the supersensitive membrane linking the eternal and the moment of time we are all living through. Since the writing of the New Testament, Eternity is present. Apocalypse is not a fleeting moment at the end of Time, but an abiding feature of human awareness since the Incarnation.

"Creative inspiration can likewise dispense with numerical time. It is always the sign of eternity's irruption into time, whose course it regulates. The non-eternal or what has no eternal origin or goal can have no validity [ . . . ] A time that does not participate directly in eternity is a degraded time[.]" This seems to have influenced the hostility of the school to documentary and objective writing, and news. This was their concept of degradation, their accusation of Auden and Allott. It is not clear to me whether the notion of Apocalypse comes from Berdyaev or Lawrence. These two writers are wholly incompatible. I think Goodland had read Berdyaev.

The period in which Savage shows a widening gap between the reading public and the best writers is the same one in which the development of national and imperial propaganda was creating a system in which everyone shared the same emotive symbols and the attachment of artists and writers to the glorification of public affairs was as close as it had been since the reign of Elizabeth. Savage tells us that contemporary society lacks all coherent standards and values, and so the artist is isolated from society, and has to find values inside himself. But meanwhile, the efforts of the Empire Marketing Board, the documentary movement, the British Council, the Exhibitions, and eventually the Ministry of Information, were creating a body of familiar imagery, embodying collective values, which the public understood and which artists could easily draw on and deploy. Derek Savage and the governmental artists are living in two different but simultaneous periods. His version of events works on many levels at once, even if it is wrong; without pausing for too long, let's note that political alienation, dislike of mass culture, and the urge for artistic originality are three different things, and that the attempt to equate artistic developments in Britain with those in France, Russia, or Germany really cuts politics out of the picture, since they were so different in those four countries. Finally, his observation (or decision) that work is the more modern the more completely personal and original it is, illuminates the last sixty years: people who follow this rule of taste (severing relations with the bourgeoisie, as he puts it) must reach completely opposite positions from those who do not.

The great defect of the New Romantic system, of which I believe Savage gives a reliable exposition, is that the poet, having emptied out all psychological and verbal bonds with the common life and with business and technology, goes on to a second stroke of the cycle in which he utters national destiny and duty, like the Hebrew prophets of old. This attempt to recapture public oracular office is compromised or doomed by the first stroke.

There is some resemblance in cultural geography between the situation of the anarchist and pacifist poet of the 1940s, making a life in semi-visibility, and that of the poet of the 1970s, locked out of "the structures" by a too uncompromised leftism, and seeking "alternative networks" of publication and distribution. We could draw an analogy between the personalism of the 1940s, which found absolute truth in subjective reality, as part of an attack on the insensitivity of modern totalitarian systems, including the Western World as war-machine, and the exceptionalism of the period 1965–80, when a resistance to sociology (as the fluid of centralised bureaucracy) combined with a compulsory statement of the bizarre, unpredictable, and irregular in poetry. The living quality of the organ metaphors of 1940s poets is a disguised critique of instrumental reason. As criticisms of the official psychology, the organic imagery can be compared with the exceptionalist social psychology favoured by the radical poets of the 1960s. The signified is "the government is wrong", and the signifiers have changed. These are remote analogies. Things really had changed an awful lot by the time "personal" poetry revived in the 1960s. In table form:

Guild socialism        - Georgian poets
Personalism-anarchism     New Romantics
autogestion and libertarian socialism      the 1960s poets

The leading personalist thinker, by the 1940s, was Emmanuel Mounier, editor of the magazine *Esprit* and linked to political parties of the Catholic Left. He was happy to describe his movement as revolutionary. He also divided up the spectrum of the intellectually "committed" into Marxists, existentialists, and personalists; I am bound to comment that this leaves out the Fascists, not the least significant group of French littérateurs, and that he was quite happy for Marxists and existentialists to be personalists at the same time. His writing seems quite without content to me, but it is high-flown and welcoming, and forming alliances is more fundamental in politics than having principles or policies. His philosophy seems to have no content except his prose style, and, although beautiful, this seems to come down to a refusal to see problems or indeed to stop talking. Persuading students that they had solved the crisis of Man of the mid-twentieth century seems to me to resolve a genuine anxiety. He could persuade himself of anything; his eloquent and joyful support of Pétain, in 1940, changed into enthusiastic support for the Resistance without pausing for breath.

Herbert Read was also interested in getting away from machine production, and we can observe, again, the set of analogies by which a dislike for State power implies a dislike of electrical power. He takes us back to the era of the Arts and Crafts movement, by whom he was surely influenced, while also pointing forward to the radical anti-industrial and anti-machine currents of the Counter-Culture. As founder of the ICA, after claiming that everything the State touched petrified and decayed, he opened the door for a new era of State-subsidised art protest. He was, in the 1940s, with Edith Sitwell, the only survivor of English Modernism in poetry; an early user of stripped-down free verse whose work is difficult to remember five minutes later.

The image-complex of authenticity seems to rely on a spatial metaphor with the body, as the seat of the self, being surrounded by concentric zones of different psychological charge. Alienation or disenchantment starts at a certain distance, where the eye is able to gauge distances and sizes accurately, and where objects are not immediately tangled up with our "selves" and their subjective feelings. Out there is the zone of detachment but also of separation and being cut off. Close in, a set of much more archaic faculties comes into play, unsteady and inaccurate, but still capable of reaction times, instinctive calculations, and cunning, which amaze the reason. Psychological "closeness" to another person also involves several concentric bands of space, perhaps the same ones, as the sense of sight is replaced by the parallel or divergent ones of touch and insight.

| 0 | 1 | 2 |
|---|---|---|
| intimacy | the rational world | the Liminal |
|  |  | the Remote |
| the subjective | the quotidian | the Sublime, the ideal |
| touch | sight | remote sensing |
| feelings | numbers | abstract ideas; formal learning |
| data of touch | tools | machines |

As these domains radiate outwards from some point (the soul?) inside the body shell, we have progressively less control over them, and they become more subject to reason, to discussion, and to the influence of other people. It follows that the more "inside" something is, the warmer, the more autocratic for us, the more subjectively free, and the less articulate, events are. A key manœuvre of the New Romantics is the projection of this inner domain into the "far outer" of the State and "history", so that particular actions by government officials re-enter the domain of passionate subjectivity. The projection of history into the anatomy of apocalyptic beasts provides them with allegories; we recall that haruspices predicted the fortunes of the State by cutting open the bodies of animals (a Babylonian and Etruscan skill). The withdrawal from this domain allows professional politicians and civil servants (and military leaders) to make decisions without reference to the citizen body, or to humane considerations.

I note that myths often involve the loss or acquisition of a body, thus offering us a convergence between zone 2 (the Sublime, Ancestral, etc.) and zone 0. This encourages us to find such a recursion in poetry, and to suggest that the convention (itself of vast antiquity) whereby the poetic excludes zone 1 also implies that zones 0 and 2 are both within the realm of the poetic. This certainly explains the tenor of New Romantic poetry, which is simultaneously, and cloggingly, physiological and mythical. A broad swathe of English (bad) taste is indignant at the introduction of any abstract notion, or any political notion, into the sealed precincts of poetry.

There is a problem with this model in zone 2, where my design co-locates the big abstract ideas and the Sublime. You are at liberty to find that this is a problem with my model, not with the British cosmology; but, as I have argued elsewhere, the realm of "high theory" shows an ominous coincidence between the Transcendental, the Sublime, and the Totalitarian. This is sometimes caught in the rather overloaded adjective "hieratic". The model predicts a struggle where the large views of philosophy also become the geographically unbounded and disproportionately large powers of the capitalist corporation; its clash with the small-scale lived world of the ordinary citizens is of course central to modern political discourse. It is the yardstick of zone 1 by which it is "disproportionate". I believe that the clash between scientific reason and fearful self-aggrandisement, including warfare, has to be left in: technology is adapted to self-aggrandisement, the State which makes laws and gives out justice is the organ which makes war.

Subjectivity in visual art is peculiarly traceable because of its association with object constancy. The capacity and stability of external space offer us a uniquely satisfying way of signalling expressivity or locating blurs and distortion. Modern painting shows a continuous band of variance around objective and subjective representation. It is not so easy with words, which are serial rather than stable. Visual artists have often proclaimed a belief in spontaneity which implies that the use of conventional and dimensionally accurate schemas causes a deterioration of the original, aesthetic, impulse: these schemas are those through which reflexivity occurs. The distinction between explicitness, convention, and reason is blurred. The conventional reason of a capitalist society, or of the political class that runs it, may not be compatible with reason *tout court* or with the primary evidence of the senses of the citizens of that society. Academic canons of painting have to do not only with correct proportion and recession but also with the political and moral meanings which are allowed to be painted.

Reflexive poetry is just the opposite of organic, biomorphic poetry. Terence Tiller wrote that the imagination is under conscious control, and that it is rational and precise in its operations; this was a deliberate protest against Apocalyptic credos. What he says is true, since the imagination is used for precise activities like designing boats and since its products are consciously designed, consistent, and exact, when they are (for example) paintings by Leonardo. Or are we to suppose that the word "imagination" does not mean "the capacity for forming images", but "the capacity for inventing or distorting"? the word seems to be used in both senses, an ambiguity which may have inspired a belief that art deals with the latter sense only, which produces disastrous artistic results. Tiller may have had Apocalyptic poetry in mind as such a disaster.

We are ready now to envisage how the preference for artisan production over machine production might correlate with a dislike for capitalism, for cities, and for large-scale reason. It is clear that we distinguish in affective quality between objects worked by mechanical reproduction, objects marked by first-person brushwork, and objects, such as pots, worked directly by the hands of the maker.

Reflexivity and handicrafts have one thing in common: the principle of feedback, the resistance by which we know the world exists around us, and we within it. The terms made by hand (and congeners) are incorrect, since the objects in question are never made by hands, but by tools, controlled of course by the maker, using his or her hands as the controller of pressure, direction, etc., and also as the neurological source of feedback, in combination with the eyes (and perhaps with sound?). Let's imagine an artisan who worked blindfold; or who worked only with hands, without tools. Or, one who was watching someone else work, and guiding them; relying on eyes but not, then, having the feedback loop of the hands and their rich sensory map. The implications of the differences between these sensory inputs are very important, as they are the primary channels by which the universe makes its nature known to our selves, but to draw a vital distinction between tool and machine production is fetishistic. The source of motive power (e.g. arm muscles, treadle wheel, wheel driven by steam) is distinct from the choice of control element, which actually determines how "sensitive" the feedback loop and how fine the finish is. The advent of computer-aided design, complemented of course by numerically controlled lathes and other "actuators", has transformed the world of production, without changing our neurophysiology or the laws of aesthetics.

There is a metaphor, unconscious and perhaps confusing, between these theories about handicrafts and the quality of sexual relations, where the difference between looking at someone, touching them (and being intimate with them), and having their image dear in one's "heart" and "mind", is of constant interest, if obscured by moral fulminations. Sexuality is controlled by a feedback loop between two people. This area of knowledge does not lend itself to generalisations. The "good objects" produced virtuously by artisans, who are happy because they are not oppressed, made from organic materials grown by healthy organisms, fit inside a "happy home" where no doubt the couple in residence look at and touch each other happily. The sub-theological discourse around the tactile experience of making household objects is coloured by the fact that we are also objects that need to be touched frequently. Intimacy is a source of anxiety, although it is able to calm this anxiety, and the discourse around poetry rotates around the quality of this experience, the sense of goodness and presence stored in certain forms of words, as a virtual caress and virtual love. We would think little of poetry that was not intimate with us, or which did not tell us intimate things about its human subjects. Culture simultaneously distributes this goodness and derives a surplus profit from selling the anxiety fantasies which are a kind of effluent or by-product of its production.

The association between ancient myth, valid insight, and arcane knowledge passed on at elite academies (and in linguistic codes remote from daily speech) gives us a topos of wide application. Theology, and the training of priests, dominated the universities still in the nineteenth century; the universities were then only for Anglicans, students had to subscribe to the Thirty-Nine Articles, and the preservation of Anglicanism was one of their functions in the eyes of many powerful figures. Clearly, there is a clash between this and the scientific notion of the university as a place which generates new knowledge by using mathematics and mechanical devices for sensing and recording. The opening of the universities to the disloyal—non-Anglicans, the lower middle class, perhaps people not loyal to the Crown—was a revolution, quite contrary to the sense of those institutions. Since belonging to the Church of England also means loyalty to the monarch, who is the head of that church, it also implies loyalty to the ministers of the Crown, and, for example to their imperial policy.

The New Romantic attack on machines is part of their attack on the state, and generalises the goodness of making by hand, where the shaping act is controlled by servomechanisms driven by feelings in the palms of the hand of the worker, to the goodness of personal emotional response, controlled by a servomechanism based on physical togetherness of two people, watching each other's faces and responding (not mediatedly but) with their whole hearts. The word "depersonalisation" adequately describes what they were objecting to; their concept rejects knowledge of society through statistics, knowledge involving thinking about a mass of people, knowledge mediated by theories (guaranteed by an instituted authority), or by measurement, as opposed to empathy and first-person accounts. Numbers and abstract ideas bear the same relation to intuition as making by hand does to machine production. Knowledge is inauthentic when it is the product of reflexivity, authentic when it is mediated through the palm of the hand, or through emotional intuition.

There is a connection between the dissolving of lines in an abstract painting, the dissolving of relative distance, and the triumph of subjectivity in poetry. The picture space represents either visible anatomy or subjective, inner-body, anatomy. The concentric zones we have described also involve a gradient between

(2) actions far away from the body governed by the eyes and "remote actuators"
(1) actions servomechanically controlled by feedback involving the eye:
(0) hormonal secretions.

How does the text of the poem fit into this radial spatial map? the NRs sited it in the "hot" area, where there is little differentiation; reflexive poetry sites it in the outer circles, where you have detachment and control.

To be more exact, the problems of correlating the different flows of data of which the self is composed (or, by which it knows itself) are those solved by reflexivity, and this moving between levels is the subject of the poetry of JH Prynne, Andrew Crozier, and Denise Riley, for example. For an ordinary self, the most acute ordinary problem would seem to be correlating "physical" sexual feelings about another person with "intellectual" perceptions and action relating to their feelings, on the principle that "everything profound loves a mask", poetry scarcely deals with this directly, but it is the "deep" subject of much modern poetry. Feelings are quasi-actions, which reflect the imperatives of the personality (or, compose those imperatives), but which are not under precise control, via measurement, comparison, recollection. There is a vital difference between building a shed and experiencing rage, although both are behaviour sequences involving physiological events and psychological programmes. Making feelings visible is a step towards conscious control of them, and this is why mirrors are a metaphor for reflexive "sight" of the emotions mediated through poems. Although critics rejected Tiller for being too controlled, he probably saw reflexivity as a way of raising feelings to a higher level, for example by reducing the self-projection in them and making more room for the other person, the loved one. The poem is like a mirror: if you write down your feelings, you can then "see" them. If this experience doesn't make you question your own feelings, there is something seriously wrong. Tiller was "looking at himself" but is unambiguously less egoistic than the New Romantics (who were avoiding self-awareness and merely expressing themselves the whole time). The NR method consisted partly of eliminating from the space of discourse all objects of known dimensions, and all comparisons, so that the true size and shape of "feelings" could not emerge and feelings could never be relativised.

Fear of reflexivity in art attaches to a certain form of linking the symbolic (art) to the involuntary and non-symbolic (everyday experience), and a powerful irrational sense of being betrayed if the two do not match up. Since they are different modalities of experience, they never can be equated with each other and the sense of betrayal is arbitrary.

FT Prince is a very different poet from those discussed here, but in a recent interview he expressed his great interest in "Christian anarchism". He wrote a poem on Thomas Campanella in this direction. His great poem *Dry-point of the Hasidim* is the product of his interest in Buber, another major influence on the personalists.

The constant misinterpretation of the political symbolism chosen by this group suggests that they have been historically hard done by (poets also believe that critics are intentionally hard of hearing, for reasons of ideological monopoly), but also that they framed their communication poorly. We would, I think, agree that there is an aesthetics of political communication, such that bad poetry is also bad political poetry. The design of significant speech is absolutely central to politics, not an add-on. However, I must also point out that critics today seem to have lost the ability to read the political and ideological messages carefully framed by poets, and the accumulated conventional knowledge seems to have passed critics by; the origin of this desperate situation is the stubborn dislike, back in the 1940s, of critics for (any) political messages other than national-patriotic ones.

# New Romantic poets

### Francis Berry

Berry, born in Malaya in 1915, published his first book of poetry in 1933, still a teenager. There followed *Snake in the Moon* (1936), *The Iron Christ* (1938), *Fall of a Tower* (1943), *Murdock and Other Poems* (1947), some new poems in *Galloping Centaur: Poems 1933–51* (1952), then after a gap *Morant Bay* (1961), *Ghosts of Greenland* (1966), and *From the Red Fort* (1984). *Collected Poems* (1994) includes a large extent of new poetry. (Berry, a professor of English, has also published numerous books within his speciality; a drama for Australian radio was published in the Collected. He died in 2006.) The word for his poetry seems to be expressionistic, with all that implies of surrender to the subject, a wild flow of vivid sensations, hypersuggestibility. He is prolific, inconsistent, constantly varying in technique, searching for material in several continents. His work is a tribute to the powers of the imagination. What an orchestra of verbal devices, as in this evocation of two Celtic horns found on a London site:

> They caw. Horns: horns. O very long and lorn, caw. The long bronze warhorns mourn:
>
> (Sounding from their asterisk, say conjectural, emplacement in the -
> Suppose any swivel, axis, handles, that you wish,
> Or logarithm dial for, in fact, I saw them not -
> Rampart of the old Sea-God's.)
> These horns had ample contours and a gradual supple spread and curve-
> away
> To flaring cup-mouths, where their glistening bronze skins
> Rolled inward with a burnished lighter hue
> From the glimmering rims or lips. And their throat linings

Are moist, have globule polyps, which dissolve and drip,
Then vapourize, and stain the mist with dunner veins.
(FROM *"In Honour of London Town"*, published 1952)

but one has to ask, how many poems actually bring the trophy home? (The horns stand for air-raid sirens.) (*asterisk*: standing for an uncertainty, hence conjecture; *logarithm dial*: a non-linear scale which we can imagine being used for range-finders on anti-aircraft guns, for example) He has consistently avoided the domestic autobiographical subject. The acceptance of material from reading implies a lack of the perceptual blocks which develop with a mature intellect, a lack of differentiation between the fixed self (alienated as that might be) and the unlimited mass of experience all around and beyond. Berry's wild enthusiasm for the material he is consuming in vast gulps is in danger of becoming exhausted, so that we have all the setting of a poem, all the details, but not a cogent artistic shape, which requires the integration and reducing to proportion of emotional impulses. There is always the question of how far he is involved with his material. The setting of his two books of the sixties, in Greenland and Jamaica (*The Red Fort* is set in India), brings up again this question of whether he belonged in his material, or whether it was merely exotic. One looks in vain for favourite and defining themes to emerge in his work: the constant quality is only that of hypersuggestibility, the ability to respond directly to emotions and sensations which so often precludes judgment and artistic control. I guess that this unmediated tumult of impinging stimuli retarded his artistic development. Exciting as his range is, Berry does not win a public victory over the drab domestic realists; his poems are not well enough designed in themselves.

Some Australian poets remind me of Berry; perhaps the tropical childhood preconditioned his work, a biologically active part of the world where growing and shaping processes take place with more energy than in the north. His vision of England is, then, exotic because he first saw it as somewhere strange and is interested in the weather and underlying biological regimes, the large-scale rather than the fine details which English poets normally home in on. He spent the Second World War in the Mediterranean and has since spent several years teaching outside Europe (and North America). The Berry tone is, not so much derived from exotic reading (though it is that), as a yearned-for reversion to primary childhood marvel, even ignorance and even disorientation. This combination of structural insight, erudition, and febrile dizziness, is his voice. His psychological landscape is not England but the Empire. One thinks of the equally drastic approach to biology in the poetry of DM Black, who was raised in East Africa.

Along with "Mediterranean Year", "Murdock" sticks in one's mind as his best poem. This, published in 1947 (and also in the *New Romantic Anthology*) seems to belong in the genre of English rural mystery and strangeness which flourished during the Second World War and was identified by David Mellor in his exhibition on the New Romanticism. It belongs with films like "A Canterbury Tale" and certain paintings by Michael Ayrton, John Minton, and Graham Sutherland. It is set in a village named Murdock, near a wood where two demon brothers fight nightly and cause terror to the villagers. It achieves a cumulative power which often evades the excitable and too inventive Berry. Periods of poetic optimism allow generosity of form and subject matter; Berry thrived in the forties and sixties, when he appeared to be in tune with the *Zeitgeist*, although he never made a permanent impact on public awareness. He missed the forties boom by being away fighting the war and the sixties boom by being too old and somehow cut off. He had anticipated the poetry of both decades.

One repeating theme is the grotesque, and this might be psychologically diagnostic as the polymorphous perverse; a pan-excitable stage before the infant has managed to sort out the bodies of other people into a stable form. In two adjacent poems of *The Galloping Centaur*, we find a grotesque treatment of female genitalia: first in the disguised form of the cloacas of Harpies, fouling the food; and then, in "The Honour of London Town", the eccentric treatment of the two hills of the City as buttocks: "(Two captured waxy trussed-down morbid moons)/ From those two trounced hills, with saucy and abominable cleft,/ Ever calling for some superlative colossal masculine shaft/ Your ramps-your rumps-Old Lady crone"). However, the grotesque is also a favoured device of poets who pitch their poems in historically and geographically remote places, as they try to persuade the reader that what they are imagining has sensuous reality and diversity. The passage on the Isle of Harpies suggests the Mannerist poets of the early seventeenth century (also called concettisti), such as Marini and Lubrano: Berry is determined to excel the classical descriptions of the Harpies, by Aeschylus and Vergil, by being more plastic, more illusionistic, more horrid, more graphic. Like the Mannerists, he succeeds; but the Classical writers got the episode over with quickly enough to move on to the next adventure, and expanding the scene to several hundred lines, as Berry does, is a victory which is also a defeat: his poem only treats that one episode. But, more pervasively, Mannerist poets are stuck because they accept standard Classical scenes as their model and perfect technique while ignoring the possibility of new invention. Somehow Berry's personality has not reached the surface, not articulated its essential themes.

> The Sun, a soldier-sovereign, hurls
> Brass balls through tubular halls
> Of light in Cyclades and Crete;
> Lands stutter in chequers, grimace then settle in whorls;
> The sulphurous plains start humping or flatten in heat;
> Stromboli itches with spray or crapular crawl of its soot;
> Goat, tethered to stump, nibbles and coughs at the root
>
> [ . . . ]
> Noon Sun, an Artisan at forge,
> Dins his hammer on targe,
> And Lipari Isles twirl whinnies of smoke;
> Land-slabs with cactus beards split wide with rage;
> The puff-toad stares and yawns midway his croak;
> Felucca's sail is slopped; the Libyan deserts crook
> Their violet snibbing mirage in cavorting mock.
>
> (FROM "MEDITERRANEAN YEAR")

What colours of language, what a fervent imagination! he seems to use a stratum of language before terms and proportions had been settled, when everything was teeming and mutating. (Note the combination of rhyme, in lines 3 and 5 of each stanza, and assonance.) (Cyclades: islands in the Aegean; crapular: crapule, a kind of drunken scum; felucca; Mediterranean sailing-boat; snibbing: rebuking, presumably of the deceived)

He has been championed by the distinguished literary critics G. Wilson Knight ("For many years now I have regarded Francis Berry as our greatest living poet") and Philip Hobsbaum. This merely raises the question, poignant for any reviewer, of whether it is better, faced with a poet of promise, to praise them audaciously and help their career, or give an honest surveyor's report and help them to grow. His work undoubtedly reached Redgrove and Hughes via Hobsbaum; it is significant that they concentrated on the Unconscious and on the artist's end of the work of art, however far they ranged geographically in finding myths. The search for an uncontrolled language, perhaps the search to get behind all the restrictions and polarisations of a class society which is also physically overcrowded, over-urban, etc., has typically followed the path back to the primitive artist and attempted to reach and re-cross the gap where language became civilised; the first choice was Highland bards, modified in the twentieth century to Siberian shamans, but already Gray was writing about Norse seers as an alternative Primal to Ossian.

The shaman-envy poem was a covert attempt to retrieve the eschatological grounds of the poetic sublime, alienated by stronger agencies who knows when during the sceptical nineteenth century; perhaps the first such poem in England was Berry's *Illnesses and Ghosts at the West Settlement*, broadcast on the radio and included in his 1966 volume *Ghosts of Greenland*. Was this his finest achievement? The immediate source was a story in *Thorfinns saga Karlsefnis*, familiar to all English students of Norse because of its inclusion in EV Gordon's standard primer of the language: Sù konr var þar i bygð er þorbjorg het; hon var spakona, ok var kolluð litil volva. Another source, perhaps, was Wilson Knight's *The Golden Labyrinth. British Drama*, where he makes out all drama to be based on the crossing of the gap between living and dead (and on bisexual innocent angel-figures, whom Berry did not take on); the story involves a witch and a second woman who is used as a medium for receiving the spirit-messages. This account of the demolition of the conscious mind, and of metric language from across, is frightening, enthralling, terse, and primal.

### Theology and sexuality: George Barker (1913–91)

The first thing I noticed about Barker was his resemblance to Pierre-Jean Jouve and (less so) René Char. (I remarked on this to a friend who was an acquaintance of Barker's. He informed me that Barker had lived in Jouve's house in Paris in the early thirties. I admit that information acquired in pubs is often inaccurate.) Certainly the influence of Char and Jouve is strong in the tone of absolute, liturgical exclamation: *D'extrême douleur vaste confusion!* I suppose that this specific moment, of exit from pure Surrealism while adapting the Surrealist approach to personal and lyric poetry, was common to many people. The poetic line itself is feckless and desperate, held together only by rhyme, and is only of use for railing against the limits of life itself. The sense of high risk at every point anticipates Hughes' use of kinetics, the threat to the body image constantly preventing the poem from slowing down. The threat I suppose is of poverty, or of damnation, or of compromise with the bourgeois order. The test of strength is poetic, either the local structure of the poem testifies to an inner energy which proves the ability to lead life at a higher pitch, or dull phrasing and timing gives the game away and makes the "rage against heaven" seem like immature bluster. When the binding of personal emotion and archetypal grandeur comes off, the poetry is extraordinary. Actually Barker had none of the rigour of thought and phrasing which Char had, or developed.

There is a depressing similarity between the weary Classical architecture in the paintings of Di Chirico and Delvaux and the religiosity of poems by Jouve and Barker. I guess the crux in Barker's poetry, for most of us, has been its limited lexical set, implying that the hyperassociation which his lavish style offers is crimped by too frequent recurrence of the same restricted set of ideas. His conviction brings on a lack of fluency with ideas. Predictability abolishes the sense of risk. Any wildly passionate style—in poetry as much as in acting, painting, or music—has to be backed up by a fertility and fluency of ideas, since after all excitement does generate many ideas. This limitation is compounded by his use of Christian imagery, since that is some 2,000 years old and is also under central control, not susceptible to Barker's creativity beyond a certain point. (He was a Roman Catholic.) This area brings us the complication that Barker was a non-intellectual, who however was able to put his total world-view and cosmology into verse for that very reason; his cosmology actually was Catholicism, so that this conceptual field has the double problem of potentially either making him the poet of the whole temporal and supernatural order, or of burdening the poetry with mediaeval thought whose relation to the real emotional events in question is remote and feeble. One has the suspicion that his religion was also a literary effect. The passionate tone and limited lexical range brought a problem of exposition; he likes to write long poems, and to put the protagonist in a situation requires an expounding voice which is informative and reliable, quite unlike the lyric voice; he solved this after a fashion, but was not strong at verse architecture, one is not always sure what is going on, which does cause the attention to flag in a long poem. He did a lot of obituary poems, a situation which neatly combines Eternity with concrete details about a named person; even this was by no means ideal, since the situation is closed and certain even before the poem starts. He liked to use words which carry their own teleology about with them, gobbling down the fix of cheap energy, little considering that this turned the text into a hostage and disabled him from any attempts to assert his own organisational pattern on it. His revolt against society is carried, or crippled, by his heroic revolts against the predictable courses of a text set up by himself.

It seems to me that there is a typical Irish, and a typical British, way of writing Catholic poetry, sacrosanct by the traditions and feelings of the audience; look at writers like Saunders Lewis, David Jones, and George Mackay Brown. Barker wrote in the typically and traditionally French manner of Catholic poetry.

Barker's reputation is now likely to depend on his location within the Soho milieu of the forties and fifties now made famous by such writers as Jeffrey Bernard and Dan Farson. This marketing ploy presupposes that the audience are more convinced by biography and legend than by poetry. If I thought poetry was obsolete, I wouldn't be writing this.

Almost all the anecdote about Barker is scurrilous. The story about Faber editors over 30 years telling him "we don't like your books, we can't sell them, but we can't drop you because you were signed by Eliot" is unconfirmable and probably fantasy. Barker in youth looked very striking in photographs; of course, good looks usually empty out a poet's work, because the poet is not dependent on verbal form and is not socially insecure enough to go through the punishing self-criticism which is the only path to style. Dan Farson's book *Fabulous Monsters* tells a story about Brian Deakin photographing Barker in a patch of nettles next to a public lavatory in Soho; as Farson narrates it, this is a skit on Barker's invincible narcissism, he was so convinced that he looked sultry and lean and saturnine that he had no sense of the ridiculous and didn't notice the irritated and malicious Deakin setting him up. B's later poetry is on the same territory as Deakin's photographs, Farson's reminiscences, and other Soho legendaries: it has strong biographical and realist bias, and the test is whether he could alter his style enough to show the characteristics of other people. Of course, D. was doing what every photographer does: using props to characterise the subject. There is a lot of Barker writing "from the outside in" to complement his earlier writing from the inside out. Writing obits is an ageing poet's way of marking time. Graham also did a lot of obituary poems, sometimes about the same people as Barker. Here we are inside the Soho legendary; it's useful, when reading *In memory of David Archer* (1973) to know who Archer was. Much information will be found in Farson's *Soho in the Fifties* about this poetry publisher and bookshop owner.

Barker was not an intellectual, which is why he was ignored by a generation of educated poetry readers; however, the structure of abstract ideas underlying his work is dense, because it is theology–his Catholicism pervades throughout. Readers who find complex non-empirical systems sleep-inducing (I count myself as one) will react badly to this. He was not a curious man and had relatively little information to vary and adorn poems with. Invocation of Christian poets of the past merely suggests that his themes are antique. Barker's belief in damnation makes each second potentially decisive in the battle for his soul but occasionally provokes resistance to his semantic labelling: no, we say, your soul is not at stake, this is not a decisive instant, this is not a moment of pure excitement. What is repetitive, cannot be decisive unless it was monotony that was being fought out and decided on. His social isolation then makes his poetry closed and useless. Perhaps the fate of the poem turns on its ability to reach genuine unpredictability; when it does, we believe that the fate of his soul is in the balance. When he stumbles through his usual themes in a ham-fisted and obvious way, no uncertainty is possible.

It seems possible that his exaggeration of phrase is based on boredom. The pan is too hot; everything burns up before it can be cooked. His rhetoric is on fire, its terrifying certainty contradicted by the cosmic uncertainty and risk he is proclaiming by means of it. If he is locked in a body and its drives, and construing the world within the terms of a Christian system 2,000 years old, boredom is a constant risk. At another level, this is the stress in leading a life without a job; between the daily freedom and the possibility of economic poverty being more constraining than a bourgeois profession. He was nothing but a poet; the function of a job is precisely to reduce risk and autonomy, which is why the poems of his tenured contemporaries are so shallow. Barker's direction came from inside, not from the corporation. He appears as an athlete and gambler, constantly raising his body to a pitch of performance to outrun risks, incurring a rapid loss of energy which brings on new risks. I take it we would rather watch an animal chasing for its life than one sleeping in a zoo or an office.

All of Barker's work is flawed; all of it is interesting. I would recommend *Calamiterror, Goodman Jacksin and the Angel, Two Plays* (radio plays, 1958), and *The True Confession of George Barker*. Certainly this leaves out a good many very interesting poems; but no one should try to read the Collected without medical assistance. Given the longueurs of his individual volumes, it is possible that his publishers' failure to bring out a selected until 1995 (some sixty years after their first dealings with the poet) was responsible for the obscurity which engulfed most of his life. He wrote in the 1930s several lyric, even mystic, novels, *Alanna Autumnal*, the texts in *Janus*, and *The Dead Seagull*, in a French style much influenced by Jouve's *Paulina 1880, Les aventures de Catherine Crachat*, etc. They aren't very good, but they do shed light on the domestic scene within which the furious arias of the poetry do their emoting.

Barker's personal problems must have grown less pressing when he passed fifty. The question then became whether he could expand into other areas without losing his furious drive, so achieving artistic maturity, or whether he would write occasional poems, full of the old tricks but desultory because his original fury had been so sexual and narcissistic. He obstinately went on writing: after the 1955 Collected came *The View from a Blind I*, the second part of *The True Confession, The Golden Chains, Poems of Places and People, In memory of David Archer, Dialogues etc, Villa Stellar, Anno Domini*. Even after the 1987 Collected, there came *Street Ballads*.

Only three of the poems in *David Archer* are actually about this patron, although the poems are numbered as a sequence; the unifying theme is an argument about metaphysics of striking dullness, like being stuck on an overnight train with a drunken and loquacious priest.

> The crisis of the word,
> the defeat of simply rational speech, is what
> the poem takes off in flight from [ ... ]
> the intellect
> of Europe sits on the banks of rational aggrandisement
> disbelieving all things, and repeats the same word.
> [ ... ]
> There is no crisis of the word. There is a crisis
> of the intellect and of the intellectual.
> It is the crisis that precedes the acknowledgement
> of the imperative of veneration.

So we hear endless turgid rational argument contending that reason does not work. Part of the tenuity of this discourse is its generalisation —as theology tends to make life itself uninteresting by dealing with the Eternal. Barker's poem editorials are dull because he does not evoke the drama of ideals and domestic life in the individual existence: mentioning editorials reminds me that Cyril Connolly could write such things and make them literature. Connolly's sketches were at least psychologically convincing; Barker wasn't good at evoking other people's characters; as his scope as a love poet is limited by his inability to write about women; so that we get declamations about love, but no poems about living together. *In memory of DA* really takes off when he describes people's actions concretely, without the theological blither. Poems 27 and 44 are excellent examples. 27, addressed to "my poor Higgins" (presumably Brian Higgins) says

> Then as hesitating you stood
> there, red-handed, caught alive, on went the flood-
> lights of Hammersmith Hospital and we saw the black book
> the perspex mask and oxygen tube and we knew
> it was the old cold bed for you.

This also reminds us that the young Jeremy Reed took up this part-medical, part-hagiographical way of writing about fantasists and losers, in his poems of the early seventies (*Saints and Psychotics*, for example). I would like *In memory of David Archer* if it were ten pages long rather than sixty-eight pages, which is pretty much true for the rest of his late volumes. Recalling Connolly's taste for the moralistes points us to Barker's failure to advance from the archetypal (the system of artistic psychology upheld by Christianity from, say, the third to the sixteenth century) to the empirical and differentiated (the artistic system which was beginning to take over in the seventeenth century). Moves away from the empirical in recent decades are partly based on the surviving strata of the stylised and dramatic which lurk within it; criticising art for not being purely empirical implies that this is a sufficient principle. A plural move away from the intact observed towards the observed-observer interaction, so that most of the interest lies in investigating the inherent rules of the mind and of systems, structuring the observation, has undercut realism; without putting Barker's pre-modern techniques in a stronger position.

Barker's manner is based on thermodynamics: heat forces humans into frenetic activity which is also high-risk; they indulge in risks to acquire enough energy to stay in uncontrolled, dangerous motion. *Calamiterror* is based on an image of the salamander as psychic anatomy: this lizard lives in fire, which in the poem exists within the human breast; the fire forces destructive, irrational, and erotic behaviour on the human, who is faced with psychic death if the fire slackens. The cynical reader may ask if this heat is simply alcohol, taken to in boredom and despair. The allegorical view of physiology explains why he can so rarely catch a likeness; he is stuck with a kind of thirteenth century medicine. The salamander image is static, and this explains his inability to set up a series of mental states differentiated along the time axis; this failure to deal with temporal series brings on a failure to differentiate successive pages of a long poem and the chaotic structure of his long poems such as the *Confession*. You can't undertake naturalistic observations of allegorical animals. The autobiographical poems may be about various love affairs, but you can't disengage anything like a sequential account of what happened in the affairs. Women were involved, love makes you perceive them vividly, but you don't get anything like a character sketch of a woman, in flesh and time. Since the detached activity of catching a likeness was essential to the Soho painters, Lucian Freud, Francis Bacon, and Michael Andrews, as the robust pictorial basis underlying their emotional effects, one can guess that Barker's failure to set up a realist-psychological framework limited his work. The *Confession* could easily be a Bacon painting.

The fervour of his poetry, if it is about anything outside poetry, is about physical attraction, tempestuous and rapidly repented acts of fornication in between uproarious drunken conviviality in the glitter and smoke of pubs. In fact, he may have spent much of his life in marriage, or at least in stable domestic cohabitation, and he had many children; but the poems are not about that, their tempo records liaisons which are fiery, shatter quickly, and are endlessly repeated. The history of his reputation is irrevocably tangled up with the theories held by other agents within the literary world about marriage and virtue. Sexual attraction in his poetry seems to be something that wears off, like drink, but then there is so much sexless English poetry which is too soggy even to burn. It is possible to view tumescent sexual attraction flaring up between two near-strangers in a bar as authenticity. This combination of high affect and short duration made the fortune, a few years later, of rock and roll. Barker's presentation of male sexuality in poetry evoked massed repressive forces, established to put down exactly that; his poetry and Logue's laid the way for a general upsurge of poetical male sexuality in the sixties, itself to some extent the groundwork for an upsurge of poetical female sexuality. Different people appear to live in different timescales, their vital substance stretched out along different lengths of time; Barker's poetic world may seem flashy and shallow, but an attachment lasting for five years may have little event to show in the exact time which a poem looks at.

The underlying contention is that *I'm such a highly-sexed bloke that I can't help chasing all these women and having all these children and all of us being poor.* He doesn't state this outright, but all the same it asks for a feminist reading that would turn it inside-out. Once you make your moral incompetence the basis for your poetry licence, you are asking for the reader to redesign your life for you. Of course, Barker saw this argument as a corollary of Original Sin and so as part of a pious illuminated legend of pride, sin, gin, bed, and eventual contrition. It was his starring vehicle, his claim to be like Baudelaire and like the lives of the saints, or even the Tristan and Iseult story. As perversely, the velocity and ardour of his style slily offers his sex drive as a form of behavioural beauty, the vigour of an untamed animal, and this is the artistic beauty around which his work is staged and which draws our attention. A masculinist reading of this would be pretty angry; his success with women in real life, or in pubs, resembles his success in presenting a romantic sex object to readers; unfortunately, this claim is too well staged, too densely fabricated, too virile and fascinating, to be easily cut down by scholarly austerity.

> Come, sulking woman, bare as water,
> Dazzle me now as you dazzled me
> When, blinded by your nudity,
> I saw the sex of the intellect,
> The idea of the beautiful.
>
> (*True Confession*, I, 3)

The masculinist objections to other men engaging in sexual display reek too much of envy and frustration to be advanced any longer. More pungently for his work, this thesis isn't present throughout Barker, and, even where it is (in the *Confession* and *Calamiterror*), it is mixed with contrition and a pessimistic anthropology (in the theological sense), not boasting at all. The rest of his early poetry, however lavishly it draws cheques on the poet's personal energy, has a different staging under it; he experienced the thirties not only through sexual urges, but also through hunger, and through the sick excitement of visualising how much society was blocking him from satisfying either one. Barker wrote the best English political poetry of the time; recording direct experience until its sheer directness wiped away any interest in society, and drove him back to morality as the way out, with theology as its science and law code.

Barker belongs with the Apocalyptics even if he began publishing in 1930; he is a melancholy example of the failure of that group to produce a second wave of mature art after the first wave of wild and confused originality. Barker and Dylan Thomas were born in successive years; they came between the Auden group and the Movement, both of whom came to occupy the Establishment and to impose their orthodoxy over decades. One could suggest that the Movement followed in the footsteps of the Auden clique, which eliminated personal subjectivity in favour of putatively ethical observations of public affairs, garages, bridges, and so forth; the Movement was equally opposed to emotions and imagination, but had further eliminated political enthusiasm, so that the depiction of dead reality had lost its purpose. (The point of transition would be the anti-ideas, anti-hope position of Auden's post-1939 poems.) But a more artistic, less inhibited, subjective kind of poetry had gone on flourishing. After realising how uninteresting Auden, Larkin and their playmates are, one comes round to a clear-eyed view of Barker, Thomas, Davies, Lynette Roberts, David Jones, and (in the earlier years) Edith Sitwell as the most important poets of the mid-century period. The selection of four of them by Eliot at Faber's was hardly eccentric. Perhaps their problem was partly that they weren't university educated and so didn't belong to the political class; a longstanding confusion between poetic art and social authority means that the reading public persistently grants a place to people with the social manners of the most prestigious class and the confidence that goes with prestige.

One of Barker's books is called *The Golden Chains*, and although he credits this to a "Cambridgeshire folksong" we can recognise in it an ancient Classical trope: the *aureae catenae* are the snares of rhetoric, irresistibly beautiful, binding the hearers. This wrapping up of a metaphor in a pictorial emblem is important in his work, and we can point also to the emblematic objects of a saint, devices dating to perhaps the sixth century A.D., an era of declining Classical traditions but when the Western folk tradition of piety was aggregating and being made ready for mass production. Pious prints and the Breviary spoke a lot to Barker. Another period of importance to his imagery is Mannerism, a peak period of Catholic rhetoric and painting, especially in Italy, leading in the Baroque, which gives him a vocabulary of paradoxes, cosmic combats, gravity-defying contradictions, rhetorical flowers, purple patches. The fourth period is, as we have mentioned, French Surrealism, especially its florid Catholic end. We could mention poets like Francis Thompson (of "The Hound of Heaven"), but I feel that they and he are merely local adaptations of Mannerist conventions, and unlikely sources for what Barker drew from Catholic literary tradition, which is of course cumulative. In "A Vision of England 1938" he speaks of "O London, magnificent monster [ ... ] I saw you astride the South in coils/ of insatiable economic appetite [ ... ] Where is the Cappadocian for that throat/ To cut the health and wealth of England loose?" The Cappadocian is Saint George ("Then a saint walked up out of the sea,/ Dragging his death behind him like a boat"), and so Barker is trying to deal with the problems of the world economy of the 1930s in terms of a Christian myth of the Late Empire, which in fact picks up a figure (the Horseman who slays the Dragon of drought) of Bronze Age antiquity. He uses this hoary machinery to get over the essentials—rage and distress—without error, but is handicapped in dealing with twentieth century reality. The rest of the poem is kitted out with allegories. Supposing that the attributes which Barker gives his tormented voluptuaries (and himself) are like emblems, and the sinners are like saints in torment, points to the limitation of Barker's technique: lack of the virtues of empirical observation, which of course had been in dispute with allegorical and mannerist writing ever since the seventeenth century. The pictorial clarity (like the smooth surface of a Delvaux) works against any psychological precision; in this picture-language:

I find
The voluptuous flamingo undulating and
Coiling in its female neck
The stringent flame the salamander.
My masculine salamander consume
The feminine flamingo of desire

(FROM *Calamiterror*)

it is as if sexuality refusing to allow any deeper psychological contact were like the physical objects of allegory refusing to allow more precise observation. The imagery of physiological organs closes in on the poem and stifles it. Justifications from such as Freud and Jung, to the effect that the unconscious thinks like a sixteenth-century painting, arouse the retort that the unconscious absorbs artistic conventions of the past because they are available in our visual world.

### Beautiful and Oceanic Bones: Dunstan Thompson

Let's imagine a poet who writes about emotions, who flows through breathtaking reversals of fortune without losing verbal balance, who can string together contrasting blocks of language with effortless perfection, who combines an unshaken belief in secular bliss and in poetry with a rush of darker notes perceiving the instability of the loved object. That poet is Dunstan Thompson.
Perhaps it's not necessary to say much else.

∽

"Deathscape with Megaliths" "Prothalamium for the Black Prince" "Dreams of the Barracks Emperor" "Thane of Ghosts": these are theatrical titles, indicating perhaps a love of fantasy or perhaps a great confidence in the audience, a sense of presence which means that the poet can stride to centre stage and enlist everyone's attention in his tiniest gestures, so that everything is heightened and intimate. Nietzsche said that everything profound loves a mask; Thompson's love of roles suggests both a deep faith in his own feeling and a deep trust in the reader. A steeping in Metaphysical poetry produced a twisted surface where everything is negated by antitheses and masked by metaphors.

Why like the scarab, a jewelled spider, weave
Silk from self centre, black blood catacombs,
To spin my hanging for bride brother's bed? How fast friendships grieve

> To hate. I see the swans float over the Thames
> With rotten garbage, sucked under by the Isle of Dogs.
> At hellgate bar, airman I cared for damns me; his decalogues
> Hail home, unman my epicene admirers proffering diadems.
> 
> ("THE THIRD MURDERER")

Thompson was born in 1918. He was something of a Barker clone. He went to Harvard and then edited a poetry magazine, *Vice Versa*, in New York, which attracted favourable comment; already we see a figure blessed by fortune, for whom the essential self-regard of the cultured elite is going to show itself as favour and indulgence, rather than as withering hostility. Poetry needs for its flourishing a sheltered space, where the pressures of realism are temporarily excluded; it then provides such a space for the reader. Universities can provide such protection, very exceptionally, for students who know the right people and who mature early. Close societies can produce hyper-socialised types, with developed verbal skills which provide the basic fluency without which a poem runs aground at every line. He published a book, *Poems*, in 1943, in New York; the book published in London in 1946 is in fact the same one, although with the addition of six new poems written in England. He served in the Army for three years, in an office job which sent him to London.

> Of those whom I have known, the few and fatal friends,
> All were ambiguous, deceitful, not to trust:
> But like attracts its like, no doubt; and mirrors must
> Be faithful to the image that they see.
> 
> ("LARGO")

I take this as a description of homosexual love, in a homophobic society, a poem describing disguise even while disguising itself as a costume piece about proud and treacherous nobles at some racked Italian court in a Jacobean tragedy. I have to point out why I consider that *like attracts its like* means exactly this. Titling a poem "Hyd, Absalon, thy Gilte Tresses Clere" (a line from Chaucer) is quite precisely coded to refer to male beauty, something stressed in the Bible, a universal reference, when it talks about Absalon. We could dismiss this, or say that a susceptibility to male beauty is merely a sign of sensitivity, but there are dozens of such lines and women barely appear. "Once /Bombs are as roses, will he kiss the blackheart prince?", never *she*. "In all the argosy of your bright hair" also specifically refers to a male head, of "This tall/ Young man, this blond young man, his mother's joy(.)" I can't really be bothered to stage a fight against the theory that the poetry of homosexuals is inauthentic because their feelings are too febrile and excitable, their passions too short in duration, their sexual switches too sensitive, their emotions unacceptably deep, etc. I mean, I've always enjoyed that fight, but I've humiliated my opponent too many times. By the way, if you're reading this, John Selwyn Gummer, fuck off. It does seem to me that Thompson was living in a big city full of lonely people, that the ones he mixed with were talented but rapacious, that they were attainable but optimistic and moved on quickly, that he was ripe and susceptible. It always surprises me how society can endlessly re-consume this mixture of susceptibility and quick recovery in adolescents and reject it in homosexuals. Thompson had his draughts of darkness:

> The goddess who presided at our birth was first
> Of those in fancy clothes fate made us hate to fight:
> The Greeks with gifts, good looks, so clever, so polite,
> Like lovers quick to charm, disarming, too well versed
>     In violence to wear weapons while
>     They take a city for a smile.
>     By doomed ancestral voices cursed
> To wander from the womb, their claws plucked out our sight,
> Who nighttime thinking we are followed down the street
> By blind men like ourselves, turn round again, and wait,
>     Only to hear the steps go past
>     Us standing lonely there, at last
> Aware how we have failed; are now the Trojan fool
> For all the arty Hellenistic tarts in plaster cast:
>     The ones who always rule.
>
>                                  ("Largo")

He'd been hurt, but I don't get the impression he stayed at home brooding and missed the next episode. "Greek" is one of those coded words for "gay", and "blind" seems to refer to inability to respond physically to women, actually heightening one of the other senses. The suggestion that other Greeks "plucked out our sight" does not make a lot of sense, and the bit about "by doomed ancestral voices cursed", although the orthodox wisdom of the time, is not quite borne out by the rest of the book. All the phrases have a straightforward emotional meaning, close to popular songs or Hollywood scripts, but the overall pattern is tense and elusive. "Arty Hellenistic tarts" were not a specific sector of the New York art scene but probably the goddesses who rule our fate; what a brilliant insult. If the goddesses were made of plaster, it makes no sense that they always rule, and their power is not fake, but then it all makes emotional sense, and the antitheses crackle like power lines. The Harpies intervened to punish violations of the law of the hearth, family morality, and the "doomed ancestral voices" may be the familial curse on those who do not marry. "Tart" is completely not an American word, but might suit a Catholic East Coast Anglophile, and sounds venomously symmetrical. It's hard to read these lines today without thinking of Tom Ripley and Dickie Greenleaf, marque-making forties preppies.

These poems bear quite strong resemblances to contemporary ones by Edith Sitwell and George Barker. When I saw "Largo", in Oscar Williams' terrific *A Little Treasury of Modern Poetry*, I assumed Thompson was British. The fact that he wasn't sheds some light on Neo-Romanticism in forties English poetry, a much more international and logical current than would at first appear. My impression is that an upper-class, north-eastern, and naval family might well strike other Americans as being English, in speech and manners, without doing anything else than continue regional and family tradition. Thompson was influenced, too, by late nineteenth century Romanticism, Manley Hopkins, Surrealism, and Elizabethan drama. The Hopkins touch is especially clear here:

> Sand-shifted Naiads never joined
> Largesse of arms so amorous: who, keeping, kelp-grown graves,
>
> Shrouded by shells, said Nay, said Nay, for no one, no,
> Would they unwind their glowworm hair. Grottoes of green
> Gold glittered his eyes
> ("IMAGES OF DISASTER")

It would be pleasant to think that a certain allegiance to Barker, and to melodramatic realism, links Thompson to our own Jeremy Reed. Complete concentration on a single personality affects the deepest and most subjective layers of the reader's psyche: we all respond to the history of a self because we all have a self, we all respond emotionally to emotions. If the self in the poem is projecting, wildly, onto another self, whose internal state is uncertain, and if that object of affections is simultaneously projecting onto the first self, then the emotional slope of the poem is oscillating wildly, all the time. This combination of immediacy, depth, anxiety and anticipation, sexual excitement, exaltation, is a good formula for poetry, perhaps better than any other. An interest in psychology, generally abnormal psychology, produces miserable poems where the poet appears as a health service manager and the feelings appear as inmate-patients, disenfranchised, administered and disavowed. In a business civilisation, great stress is laid on stability of judgment, on the ability of the official to separate feelings from analyses. This value is promoted in the educational system. If you are going to work for someone in business, you have to switch off your own feelings in order to be a good servant. Poetry, which benefits from constant instability, reversals, risks, conjectures, volatility, has just the opposite values from those of bureaucrats and academics, into whose hands it has fallen. If a lot of modern poets write as if they were applying for a mortgage, this is not a kind of artistic advance. All this has little to do with Mr Thompson, but may explain why he is not famous.

∾

"So swan in opera, queer/ But alto boy, exalts the imperial box of guilt". I am not sure what this means, but it's exciting; what is "the imperial box of guilt"? Can we see it?

∾

Since I first wrote this review, information has trickled in slowly and persistently, like a leak in a pipe. Dr van den Beukel, by some sort of conjuring trick, produced translations of his work into Spanish by Jorge Luis Borges. There was a second volume, *Lament for the Sleepwalker*, in 1947, which is great work, although not an advance on *Poems*. Confusingly, his English book is basically a reprint of his first American book, but with about seven poems swapped out and in and *Lament* includes the poems from his English book which were not in his first American book. Dr Jenner dug up a grainy reproduction of a portrait of our man, impossibly theatrical, more possibly the work of Leslie Hurry. A chance discovery revealed his travel book about Egypt, Palestine, and Syria, *Phoenix in the Desert*. By page 90 he still hasn't got off the plane, which perhaps explains why he never wrote a follow-up. His later poems were collected, as *Poems 1955–74*, after his death in 1975. These seem like cultured bric-à-brac to me; this argues detachment and serenity. He writes as if his whole heart and happiness were not at stake at each moment, and this is psychologically more restful, even if I can't identify such eighteenth-century *sagesse* with culture per se. They are essentially similar to his travel book, which reveals that he is a Roman Catholic, and quite pious. The late poems delve into cultures of the past, with a certain splendour, considerable curiosity about theology, rite, and error, and a fundamental detachment. The poet is just not there in the poems. Images of opening an antique shop and attending High Mass spring to mind.

∼

*Phoenix* also mentions that his father was a naval officer and wrote a book about submarine service in the First World War. This has a bearing on the persistent marine imagery of Thompson's poems. The death of Terry Brewster Thompson, US Navy, is recorded in poems in *Lament for a Sleepwalker*.

∼

James Keery's research has revealed the existence of an American end to the New Romantics as an institution (of a kind) called The Workshop, in Rochester, New York. This possibly chimerical entity (currently the subject of hot research by parties concerned with the forties style), run by Rae Beamish, was part of a, possibly even more chimerical, outfit called The International Workshop, and the only known reference to it dates from 1939. Studying Thompson outflanks all the line of disqualifications of the New Romantics: if someone could reach the same style in Harvard and New York, it can't have been merely a crazy aberration in England and Wales. I don't have enough knowledge of US poetry of the period to assess the extent of neo-Romantic poetry, or personalism, on that side of the ocean. It does seem that the belief in the unconscious as a source of poetic power was vital in the formation of Lowell and of Berryman, and that their unusual (and probably wrong) belief that madness gave them the keys to the kingdom of poetry was a modification of the New Romantic belief in prophecy and the release of the irrational unconscious. The influence of the NRs on the 1960s may have come about in this mediated form, with essential design changes and a rebadging, so that we can redefine Alvarez's preface to his 1962 anthology *The New Poetry* as a neo-Apocalyptic statement. He links the unconscious and history in a recognisably Apocalyptic way, making this link the key to a poet's legitimacy.

Robert Duncan was someone else writing in a high-1940s style in the 1960s, and it is easy to see how useful he found the hieratic and initiated manner of the English 1940s. To be sure, the influence of his work, florid and off-key, on the English scene has been a marginal and cultish thing, mediated through imports or through covetable and rare books like the Jonathan Cape issues of certain of his books. He lived for a while in the forties at the farmhouse in Woodstock where the magazine *Phoenix*, a close American equivalent of Personalist tendencies in Britain, was based. It was co-edited by Derek Savage, a pacifist, back to the lander, and New Romantic poet.

## *In the land of the not-quite day; or, the frisson of ruins. David Gascoyne*

The most controversial historical idea about British poetry is about the hidden links between the two repressed areas—the 1940s and the 1960s. This was brought to a head, about ten years ago, by James Keery's proposal of the thesis that there was only one main English style of the post-war era, and that it was based on the Apocalyptic style. Thus, Larkin, Prynne, and Dylan Thomas are all writing variants of the same style. This met with widespread incredulity. In 2000, Keery followed this up with a magisterial essay on *The White Stones*, Prynne's chief work, in which he traced in detail Prynne's use of imagery from Revelations, starting with the title—the white stones being the tokens which mark the saved at the time of the resurrection. This (as yet unpublished) essay set the poetry world by the ears. It came as the climax to years of undirected ferreting in second-hand bookshops and coming up with battered forties books—low-priced and largely a consolation prize for the real treasures still missing. Having acquired these forgotten books, we wanted to find some way of reading them. Witnesses to that lost era became precious sources. Few more than David Gascoyne (1916–2001)– a forties poet who had not only survived the purgatories of the 1950s to play a role on the modern scene but had also written extensive diaries—in 1937–39 and the early forties, which he lost, which were rediscovered in an almost miraculous way, and published in 1978 and 1991. If the new poetry was the final fruition of ideas originated decades ago, the evidence should be right there in the diaries.

## In the land of the not-quite day; or, the frisson of ruins. David Gascoyne [187]

Gascoyne's best poems, "The 7th dream is the dream of Isis" and "Elegiac improvisation on the death of Paul Eluard", are both Surrealist in inspiration. It's hard to focus on these two poems when there is such a wealth of first-rate Surrealist poetry from the other countries of Europe, but it would be unfair to deny Gascoyne his role as an emotional symbol for several generations of fans of modernism in Britain. "Isis" runs in part:

> little girls stick photographs of genitals to the windows of their homes
> prayerbooks in churches open themselves at the death service
> and virgins cover their parents' beds with tealeaves
> there is an extraordinary epidemic of tuberculosis in yorkshire
> where medical dictionaries are banned from the public libraries
> and salt turns a pale violet colour every day at seven o'clock
> when the hearts of the troubadours unfold like soaked mattresses
> when the leaven of the gruesome slum-visitors
> and the wings of private airplanes look like shoeleather
> shoeleather on which pentagrams have been drawn
> shoeleather covered with vomitings of hedgehogs

As it would be unfair to deny the impact of the poems—curated for later generations in mass-market Penguin anthologies (*Poetry since 1945* and *Poetry of the Thirties*). Of course, their isolated nature gave the impression to young poets of a huge unoccupied space—something that could belong to them, then. This was more exciting than a finished life's work, which would have given a feeling of a space owned and occupied. Yet, Gascoyne wrote surrealist poems only over about a four-year period. The other key English surrealists, Philip O'Connor and Hugh Sykes Davies, also published tantalisingly little.

We look at him in the context of the 1940s where prophecy was invading the realm of poetry and the dominant group called themselves Apocalyptic. He had consciously prepared for the role of prophet acquiring a programmed instability, loosened to shake as a telltale of distant, if rapidly approaching, energies. To be the dice thrown by the eyeless. Because you can sum up surrealism in a four-word phrase, we think we can sum up the surrealist movement without years of study, which itself is an incongruity. There is a street ballad element in the New Romantics, for example this piece:

> He built him a home, the rapscallion lad,
> In a turned-up boat on a lonely shore,
> And peopled it with a prince's dream,
> Was happy in rags if the fire burned clear.

by Henry Treece, from *Poetry London*. This manner is hard to place because it works so badly, but it did occur to me recently that it could be an attempt at imitating Prévert. Mention of Philip O'Connor at least raises the possibility that the practice of the poem as game, which was to take off in the 1960s, goes back to surrealism. Some of O'Connor's forties poems do seem to be using arbitrary procedures to create an autonomous world.

We can tentatively date Gascoyne's shift towards the Church as 1939. A group of poems in *Poetry London* no. 4, 1940, puts the matter, by then, beyond doubt. The shift may attach to his association in 1939 with Benjamin Fondane, Shestov's pupil, in Paris, and to the soirees at the house of Pierre-Jean Jouve and Blanche Reverchon, which were attended also by Gabriel Marcel, Pierre Emmanuel, and Jean Wahl. His diary epitomises one of his conversations at this time as "the Void—the end of History—the open tomb—the coming spiritual revolution—etc." Shestov now became his favourite thinker.

His poem to greet his own birthday ("Rondel for the Fourth Decade") seems to mark an exit into Christian poetry and the eighteenth century, as in the final couplet we find the word *ere* and the suggestion that the future is hidden by the veil on a mirror, removed as Time moves on. That is, he is writing inside a style which is itself a ruin, a ghost. The 1943 volume opens with a series of poems entitled "Tenebrae", "Pietà", "De Profundis", "Kyrie", "Ecce homo", "Lachrimae", etc., and it is clear that from now on we have to class Gascoyne, still only twenty-six, as a Christian poet. Logically, he ceased to be a surrealist in 1937, by his account. There is another book, besides the Apocalyptic flagship anthology, called the white horseman—*der weisse Reiter*, which I understand was actually an anthology of Catholic Expressionists. The decline of Christian hegemony is the central puzzle of the mid-century period. It was the Anglican church in crisis, not Anglican poetry in particular, so that the appreciation of poetry was basically damaged by the projection of a cultural struggle outside literature.

I think the only solution with tracing religious influences on literature is to lower our standards. Thus encouraged, let's claim that what Gascoyne got from his conversion to religion was a belief in prophecy as the most privileged form of speech. "(that) I have definitely been called to be one of those who are to announce the true underlying event taking place during this century" (*Journals*, p.254); "Am strongly aware [ . . . ] of being only the mouthpiece, instrument or reflection, of a higher power . . . " (*ibid.*, p.256) David Gascoyne thus saw himself as a literally Apocalyptic poet. I suspect that the other

Apocalyptics, too, struck on the idea of prophetic poetry first and worked out justifications (inconsistent and unconvincing, although fascinating) afterwards.

Joyce Cary supplies this perfect description of the Apocalyptor: "But how much more fearfully ghostly was this apparition that shook in every joint, whose enormous pale eyes were full of an excitement equally extravagant—whose very words sounded like the language of a world where meanings defied any common syntax". (description of Gerald Wilde, in *Nimbus*) Let's get this joint shaking! Wilde was the Screamin' Jay Hawkins of forties painters, wires jittering with the conduction of chaos. I wonder if we could see the tremble as a child relation of the physical gesture of an expressionist painter's stroke. The cumulation of slight but veridical strokes is a picture of—what? The unconscious of the universe? The world process? A quiverful of *frissons*?

My interest in religion and literature began with reviewing Geoffrey Hill's 1996 book *Canaan*. Hill seemed to me to be the best writer of anti-Thatcher poems, and the Anglican framework of that book persuaded me that neglecting Christian thought was a serious defect in a literary historian. We have lists of people at those soirées because Gascoyne helpfully supplies them in his Journals. These include Pierre-Jean Jouve (French Protestant, presumably Calvinist), Benjamin Fondane (ethnically Jewish but theologically Orthodox and a follower of Shestov), Lev Shestov (ethnically Jewish, theologically some kind of Christian Existentialist), Gabriel Marcel (Roman Catholic). Clearly, all that work I did on Anglicanism is quite useless here! And clearly, it's impossible to even sketch what was going on without "averaging out" and losing detail. However, what was going on between the interlocutors must have been a synthesis, something "averaged out". And what Gascoyne took away from these meetings—little less than the scheme within which he viewed the universe from then on—must have been less detailed than the "personal positions" of the theologians.

To draw a veil over my vagueness, perhaps I could draw your attention to some sources for modern Christian thought. To start with, most of the books are frustrating because they aren't specifically about the code for expressing Christian ideas in literature. Before carrying out this narrowing of focus, I suspect that we should suspect a significant transition here. If literature deals with the temporal and mundane, it is at one remove from the divine and the holy, which are timeless. Does everything change as we cross that line? Could anything *not* change? We could look at the Christian streak in poetry through a book like Kathleen Morgan's *Christian themes in poetry*, which conjures up a grouping of Eliot, Raine, Norman Nicholson, Charles Williams, Elizabeth Jennings, and Gascoyne, and even offers that as the ridge line of modern poetry, then in 1965. Some readers did not cease to regard that group as the ridge line, and this is perhaps where we should look for the later Gascoyne, as a thinker about poetry. Morgan's book is interesting, better is one in the Faith and Facts series by JR Foster, *Modern Christian Literature*. Another volume in this series deals with "Three Centuries of Christian literature". For Scotland, we have very interesting essays in two books by Craig Beveridge and Ronald Turnbull, suggesting a long-term resistance to the possessive individualism which vitiates so much of English culture, and the distinctive nature of the Presbyterian heritage. For Russia, GP Fedotov's work *The Russian religious mind* is illuminating. For the conservatism which rejects all modern art, Hans Sedlmayr's *Der Verlust der Mitte* is a revealing and concentrated statement, from a Catholic and Greater German standpoint (in fact, he writes off nineteenth century art as well). His position is rather close to Novalis. There is a Catholic literary magazine, called *Hochland*, which I have not been able to evaluate properly. Another approach is Karlheinz Deschner's, in his classic polemic *Kitsch, Kunst, und Konvention* where he traces the origin of kitsch, in many forms, back to religion.

The Christian literary thing collapsed like Enron. We have to consider the possibility that the decline of the Christian thing will be paralleled by the decline of the revered left-wing thing, to be succeeded by virtuality and consumerism without moral bonds.

Gascoyne's dream-poem "The Second Coming" mentions Rasputin, who here appears as a villain. Rasputin (as we learn from Zinaida Hippius' fascinating book of memoirs, *Zhivie litsa*) was in the habit of making prophecies, according to whose contents the Tsarina tried to influence Russian war policy. The significant point here is that this does not represent Russian spirituality, since Alexandra was German, not Russian. It represents, already, a "European" spirituality, in this case mixing Russian and German (as had already been the case for the mystic groups which arose after 1815 and which represented a policy strand of the Holy Alliance). Whereas the scene of 1820 shows us spiritual groups furthering State policy and, without any doubt, being funded by the Russian Secret Service (and others too?), Rasputin's career shows us more or less the opposite. The Russian Empire of about 1915 shows a massive State machine with at its head an autocrat being governed by a small spiritual cell, outside Church structures and more or less secret. Hippius says of Rasputin "At the beginning of the war he made a mistake: he had prophesied too definitely, he entered into "politics" and "geography": there will be, he said, victory, when Russian ships sail up to Vienna ... " (p.124) This real-world set-up is the model for Gascoyne's idea of his own message, as a diagnosis of the spiritual state of the world and advice for revitalising it. These messages are the content which his poetology is designed around. The question is what the source of his knowledge is—whether it is inspiration from God, or the voice of the Unconscious, or insight from studying the human race, or "prior knowledge" owed to a state of spiritual election.

Rasputin features in the poem as a villain—a nightmare. That is, not as a randomly chosen figure but as something which makes Gascoyne anxious because it is so close to what he aspires to. There is latent in this dream (!) a critique of the cult of personal aura and personal domination which had inspired the poet since his conversion. Maybe Gascoyne didn't have any more insight into "world history" than the monk Rasputin? I don't find major poems by Gascoyne in which he offers a critique of spiritual authority, but we can see in this very dense dream poem something like a critique of spiritual submission. The climax of the poem is a prophetic utterance in which he achieves his goal of defining the spiritual state of Europe—but only in a dream, being unsaid as it is said, surrounded by a sort of Fellini film of monks, grotesques, and manic little girls. If Rasputin stands for Shestov (or Freud), maybe the little girls from the Italia Conti theatre school stand for Gascoyne the poet?

Shestov was not right-wing in politics or even old-fashioned in religion. The *or* of *Athens or Jerusalem?*, his major work, is the key point: philosophy or theology, he asks, not wishing to plump for one or the other. He was an Existentialist, as Gascoyne thought, but one not interested by the absolute decision (which really brings intellectual life to an end). His status as a lay theologian makes him remote from anything within the Orthodox tradition. His attraction to Christianity is more because he was a good European than because he accepted the dark authoritarian heritage of the Russian Church. The *or* also means that his secularism and Christianity didn't really amount to a rejection of Judaism. He was an attractive thinker.

The most obvious thing about Gascoyne's *Poems 1937–42* (1943) is its dependence on Eliot. The whole thing is a follow-up to *Ash Wednesday* and *The Hollow Men*. Nobody remarked this at the time, presumably because of the imprecision of his technique. The similarity is at a more abstract level. Of course, the mood is also different—Gascoyne immature and full of hope, Eliot sober and pessimistic. We grasp the whole project of being an Apocalyptic when we look at Eliot's poems from his great era and see that most people naturally regarded him as a voice of the Time, a symptom of the world's malaise. "Most people" could be an exaggeration but, even his enemies saw him as hyper-modern, they objected to him partly because he reminded them of the times and they disliked the times too. The shared vocabulary of the two poets is from Christian literature, which inevitably links the universal — God — with the individual and personal. An exit from this could lead to much less important poetry, for example the *Choruses from "The Rock"*, which are no longer personal and just don't arouse so much interest. Gascoyne's project needs less explanation — it's just Christianity. The tortuous trail was his attempt to persuade himself that he was the chosen one, the era's throat.

It's only fair to recall Gascoyne's great return to surrealism for his "Elegiac improvisation on the death of Paul Eluard", in 1952, of which I can quote only a brief excerpt:

> Wind of the secret spirit
> That breaks up words' blind weather
> With radiant breath of Logos
> When silence is a falsehood
> And all things no more named
> Like stones flung into emptiness
> Fall down through bad eternity
> All things fall out and drop down, fall away
> If no sincere mouth speaks

I keep circling back to the foundation of Mass Observation. Gascoyne was present in the house in Blackheath — he either was part of the founding group, or he wasn't. The other three founders all wrote poetry — I think Harrisson only wrote one poem, but it was a very good one. MO was founded in 1937 with the objective of recording national life by getting hundreds of observers to record their own daily lives. It also sent teams of observers to study entire communities. The results are generally agreed to be wonderful. The programme stopped in the late 1940s and so its documents reveal a society that isn't there any more. Of course, it was a direct threat to literati who were willing to blither all day about "national character" without any basis in observation. MO eventually became a market research firm. What I think the story is, is that poets seized on sociology as a way of repeating Christianity, linking the story of the nation with the story of a human in a poem. They worried a lot about being typical — misplaced energy, since the real error was assuming that anyone could ever be typical of a whole society, underestimating the complexity of society by several orders of magnitude. The romance with sociology was one of the imitations of Christianity after the latter made its exit as a credible literary schema. Thus, it's not feasible to completely separate Gascoyne's interest in sociology from his interest in religion.

Why do I recognise a scene in a poet? Possibly not because n million households just rerun the same couple of dozen scenes but from my exposure to the didactic energies of the State. If you want to make WWI propaganda in favour of Britain, you have to devise typical scenes. The message just won't travel without this. If you accept that this propaganda was expert, produced thousands of times over, saturated the audience, clung to the memory, pervaded the imagination—it becomes depressingly clear, if this is true, how it could swim into poetry. The sad thing about MO is that their achievement rediscovered the knowledge which a professional group already had—the opinion makers, secretive and dictatorial people who during the world war co-operated to produce the fantastically memorable scenes which whipped up such enthusiasm on the "home front". Indeed, the disillusion of the 1920s was a hangover from this collective fervour cranked up during the war and which today we forget (because it seems so ridiculous). Trench battles were being re-staged far behind the lines for the benefit of the camera. It's arguable that the awesome techniques of psychological mobilisation (which were ready already before 1914) are more impressive than the brute technologies of machine gun and high explosive.

This helps to explain the bizarre match between surrealism and sociology in Mass Observation. If you associate the study of the collective with shared symbolism, stored imagery, patriotic propaganda, advertising, the popular press, etc., then surrealism seems quite relevant. Pictures ooze up from the unconscious—wonderful. What pictures exactly? They collect them, write them down. Surrealism spent a lot of time collecting popular imagery—dredging up the popular prints from the endless stores of the *bouquinistes* along the Seine, for example. They loved to recuperate the archaic, the folk, the floridly supernatural and pious, the garish, the occult, the unrespectable. When MO were looking for pervasive involuntary images, they were pursuing a surrealist project.

Poets are cowards fleeing from the realisation that the poem they write is not a version of the structure of the universe but something local and personal. The real reasons why someone is not interested by what you write are more interesting than the stubborn answer that you should be interested because it's about You. Gascoyne's artistic anxiety was well founded—his theory of typicality let him down.

[194] *Origins of the Underground*

## Romanticism and the 1940s

One of the salient facts of the 1940s was untimely death, and this cast the poet in the role of writing epitaphs, an ancient function which puts the poem alongside the eternal and so leads it to speak in timeless terms. The surrealists had marble statues as part of their shape library, in paintings and poems, and we can see the timeless forties poem as this statue taking over the whole picture and indeed seizing the right to speak. JF Hendry is a good example in English:

> In waves there leap upon her pallid eyes
> Loud, loud shapes of cloud.
> This is the entrance of great silences.
>
> Beyond the body of alabaster
> Over cliffsman death, white shrouds
> In a great fleet shine forth freedom in her majesty.
>
> A bird's wing is broken into their current.
> Across cerulean heights
> Starring the dark and fivefold continent
>
> The infinite allotropy of her spirit
> Eludes me still. Her voice
> Wanders on the wind with no wit in it.
>
> Speak! Speak to me, o aerophyte!
>
> ("ORCHESTRAL MOUNTAIN")

Surely I can't be the only person to see this as a fundamentally French poem in English. Hendry was writing to console himself, after the death of his wife in an air-raid. The timeless objects are there because what was immediately present to him was desolation. Because poets were writing as consolers and prophets, the question of their spiritual authority came up, and this is where theology comes to mean so much to Gascoyne.

If there is a staple narrative in modern Christian literature, it is this:

> heedless person adopts materialist beliefs & claims independence from authority
> goes to live in the city
> causes damage to other people
> becomes miserable and confused for lack of authority
> repents and reaches fulfilment in the bosom of the Church (*this bit is optional*)

Of course, a writer could implement this concept simply by writing about someone miserable and rebellious — the Christian reader could fill the rest in for themselves. My problem with this scenario is that, during phases of depression which are entirely natural and even inevitable, the schema reinforces the doubt and misery by challenging the victim's basic life assumptions. The promise of contentment so long as you give up the right to have ideas is dreadfully effective, but it also inspires scorn for the Christians. Gascoyne was handicapped in writing out this schema, because, so far as we can tell, his conversion to Christianity and the beginning of his drug addiction more or less coincided. The period of exalted religious fervour occupied the same time as the amphetamine abuse and looks uncomfortably like a symptom of it.

Another arm of Christian art theory followed on from the thesis of "tries to follow her or his own ideas & comes to a Bad End". They were happy to give modernist artists close attention so long as these could be represented as miserable, confused, and generally martyrs to personal choice. This attention is like that of doctors or policemen. Modernist art was welcomed so long as it could be presented more or less as symptoms of syphilis — tremors of a damaged neurology. Soup bubbles of an enfeebled and over-stimulated brainpan.

The 1940s were a period of crisis for the European aristocracy and so also one of waves of conservative ideology. These were returning to themes developed during the declassing of the French and Russian aristocracies, stored in the magazine of ideology. What is the link between occultism and the Right? I think the connection may go back to the Holy Alliance's use of mysticism as a defence against revolutionary ideas; an aspect of Romanticism which we have tended to lose sight of. Nicholas Goodrick-Clarke has written masterfully on the occult roots of the Far Right in Germany. Shestov wrote an essay, in 1908, called "The prophetic gift", which turns out to deny the existence of prophecy altogether. It was written for the twenty-fifth anniversary of Dostoevsky's death and kicks the idea that Dostoevsky foresaw anything, or understood politics, into the long grass. He points out in some detail that Dostoevsky got his political ideas by imitating the policies of the powerful and autocratic. This theme of imitating the powerful, and relying on deep memory, points us back towards the era of the Holy Alliance. In 1816, democracy was abolished from the continent of Europe. The educated could find lucrative niches as censors, spies, publicists for the regime, mediaevalists and mystics. The moment of the Holy Alliance saw a flurry of mystics and prophets in Europe; paid for, in all probability, by special staffs of the autocratic governments, as a counter to reason and the call for civil rights. Shestov says that the powers would tolerate the singers if they knew their perches, *yesli pevtsi znayut svoi shestki. D. soglasilsya na etu rol'*, Dostoevsky said yes to this role.

The ruins we have looked at in Gascoyne point to Gothic and so to the mediaeval imaginary and submission to a universal authority. There was a whole school of late Romanticism in Vienna and Munich, which was attached to the Catholic Church and to feudalism, in opposition both to the Revolution and to the Protestant Prussian state. The Occult Revival of the nineteenth century was intimately intertwined with Ultraright politics, royalism, and Catholic revanchism. A return to romanticism, and the cultivation of theologians, may both be expressions of this conservatism.

This clerical reaction was the voice of a dying class thrashing around —as the biggest landowners in pre-Revolutionary Europe, they suffered from every nationalisation of land and from every advance of the trading and manufacturing interests over the landowners. This applied less to the non-established churches and more to the ones where the prelates were younger brothers from the major landowning families, themselves slowly losing a grip on political power and on the summits of wealth. The art forms bound to them decayed along with them—a pervasive anxiety about the future being enough to corrupt the imagination. I am not quite certain that the avant-garde was born inside the French Revolution which had a severely classicising, Republican or Doric, taste. Instead, I think we should at least examine the role of the French royalists—a remarkably cultured and disaffected group, already in the 1790s, who could inspire cultured and disaffected groups over the following century. They had self-esteem and lots of leisure. We find a puzzling number of French avant-garde pioneers who were right-wing, anti-democratic, and inclined to spiritualism. Just as we find influential Socialists whose taste in art was civic and anything but "formalist". The Second Empire, without doubt the site of origin of the modern avant-garde, counted disaffected republicans, to be sure, but also disaffected legitimist monarchists, certain of not having public careers. They had a private system of values, upheld with perfect seriousness by small groups, indifferent to the institutions of the government. Isn't this a model for the avant-garde? If you expect sound left-wing opinions from the Impressionists and Symbolists, you're going to be sorely disappointed.

David Gascoyne had virtually ceased to write poetry in 1950, except for the long radiophonic poem *Night Thoughts*. Thus giving us a problem in finding something to talk about. However, that streak of sensibility didn't go away, and he was associated with the journal *Temenos*, edited by his old friend Kathleen Raine from 1981 to 92. It was subtitled "a review of the arts of the imagination", and Raine has defined its position as being against the secular. The title page of the first issue shows an amazing number of writers who had been associated with New Romanticism in the 1940s. We can probably find here a living continuation of the movement, if we accept that ideas have a life and that the ideas of the forties had been repaired and refreshed, reappearing in new garb. There is an overlap between prophecy and spiritualism and this is why we find Raine as editor of *Light*, a Journal of Psychic Studies. Did forties ideas have an occult influence on the 1960s, as James Keery suggested for Prynne? G Wilson Knight published his article "Poetry and Spiritualism" in 1956, in *Light,* and republished it in 1959 in the 2nd edition of *The Starlit Dome*, which is about eternal forms and symbolic architecture (the dome in question, and in general "orbs, domes, urns, wheels"). He likes to talk about "musical buildings", for a partly real, partly imaginary kind of edifice which his favoured poets (Coleridge, Byron, Shelley) dwell on in their work. He uses the term "hermaphrodite-seraph" for a partly human prophetic type of creature. In 1940, Knight wanted to launch a movement for a revival of the monarchy as a focus of propaganda, surrounded by a mystic symbolism. He said "a king is [ . . . ] the focal point of the nation's romantic and creative instincts". The centre point of this was Cranmer's prophecy over the royal infant Elizabeth in *Henry VIII*.

Gascoyne wrote a poem, in 1949, for the infant Prince of Wales: "Birth of a Prince". Today, the Prince of Wales funds the Temenos Academy (sited inside his Institute of Architecture, in Bethnal Green). It promotes symbolic architecture and a cult of leadership.

Knight "insists", in that article, that the specifically dramatic involves inevitably the specifically spiritualistic. An eccentric claim — but a pattern which seems close to "The Second Coming", which boldly mixes theatre and spiritualism.

There are reasons for believing that the Prince of Wales, the most influential relic of sixties ideas, read *Temenos* and was influenced by their ideas on the representation of authority in buildings and the discouragement of change. When people start talking of the dangers of materialism, the monarchical principle generally isn't very far away. Raine and Gascoyne had been poets in the 1940s, but *Temenos* was really a heavy magazine dedicated to creativity which defined what creative people were doing, then in the 1980s, as illegitimate and procedurally flawed. Reading *Temenos* was a numbing and alarming experience, rather like having someone beat you over the head with a telephone directory while yelling "It's your fault that they beheaded Marie

Antoinette!". Maybe you don't have to believe in God to make great art, you just have to believe in other people. They were strong on architecture containing cosmological symbolism, and the rigour and geometrical elaboration of Islamic architecture probably did have something to offer a poetry not strong on either. There is some link between the ruins which loom as the principal architecture of the 1940s, the musical buildings of Wilson Knight, and the symbolic and geometrically elaborate architecture we read about in *Temenos*. The argument is roughly.

(a) large expensive structures incorporating thousands of man-hours are a symbol of power and submission
(b) because of the way the human brain uses geometry, complex geometrical structures are similar in many cultures
(c) therefore this geometry is eternal
(d) therefore there are eternal invisible powers mightier than mere commoners
(e) therefore there should be a monarchy

Before the Second World War, Gascoyne read Henry Corbin's translations of Heidegger. Raine's magazine was an imitation of the *Eranos Jahrbuch*, which frequently (1949–1980) published Corbin's work on Islamic mysticism and architecture. Later, he became one of the guiding lights of *Temenos*, and, later still, the Institute of Architecture was set up in a largely Muslim area of inner east London and found in these high-Islamic geometries, in its *chahar-bagh* garden, a way of reaching Bengali schoolchildren.

The Eranos was little less than the laboratory where the New Age movement was developed. More locally, Blake was one of the presiding figures of the 1960s in Britain (and an influence on Led Zeppelin lyrics). The poetry publisher, Enitharmon, was probably open to Gascoyne's suggestions and draws a certain sensibility from Blake and surrealism. With Gascoyne, we find a link between spiritism and conditions of high nervous sensibility, acting as an amplifier for beams from the otherworld. The doctrine of "heightened sensitivity" is part of the attack on materialism: the materialists don't believe in spiritual matters because they are (something like) tone-deaf. It serves a variety of beliefs, from a spiteful aristocratic outlook (jumped-up peasants don't recognise the superiority of the blue-blooded because they are insensitive) to homosexual propaganda (where conventional men are too coarse to *hear the music*).

*In the land of the not-quite day; or, the frisson of ruins. David Gascoyne*

## Nympholepsy

G Wilson Knight published, in 1962, a book called *The Golden Labyrinth. A Study of British Drama*, whose central theme is that "seraphic equivalents, often in what we may call bisexual disguise, with suggestions of a state beyond sex, like 'the angelic heaven'" are figures which run throughout the history of drama, from Dionysus on down. Through it all "runs the one golden thread of the seraphic". This view is also based on a belief that the vocal spirit creatures really exist. The bisexual spirits of the blest are the voices who speak through spiritualists. Further, "The most striking advance of modern drama is its use of Spiritualism or other kinds of extra-dimensional insight".

Another window may be found in an essay of Edward Carpenter—socialist, vegetarian, and sexual reformer—where he seized on early accounts of cross-dressing medicine men to produce a theory that all cultural creation—all social progress, actually—was due to holy individuals of a third or intermediate sexual status. This, *Intermediate Types Among Primitive Folk*, 1914, was the first real entrance of shamanism onto the English literary stage. It was also where Knight got his image of sexually intermediate prophets—one chapter is called "The Intermediate Type as Prophet or Priest". It seems Wilson Knight lived in a world of besetting erotic projections which texts either prepared the way for, or were simply ignored. This shows the courage of self-revelation and setting aside the reality other people see. For, no one else sees drama as centring on prophetic hermaphrodite-seraphs. We would admit a link between hysteria, ecstatic religion, prophetic trance, and early dramatic performances. Spirituality and normal sexual activity do seem to shun each other's company. But Knight's nympholepsy is private to him. This sexual vision could be recaptured as a surrealist text, an authentic example of *l'amour fou* and erotic hallucination. Beyond the perimeter of the affable eccentricity where I like to hang out is the realm of the truly Cracked Pot—a jungle of insane fertility and rife variety.

Denis Donoghue has allowed us to view Knight through another window; for his essay on Pater's essay *Diaphaneitè* (1864) explains a homosexual code used by Pater and referring back to a dialogue of Plato on the transparent flame. The seraphs physically resemble that flame—and the fabric of Time is diaphanous to their eyes. Pater speaks of how "exotic flowers of sentiment expand, among people of remote and unaccustomed beauty, somnambulistic, frail, androgynous, the light almost shining through them". He also gives these beings powers of anticipating the future. Perhaps Gascoyne understood himself as a hermaphrodite-seraph, able to see the torn curtain. Perhaps his patrons, also, recognised this quality in him.

This imagery does not only give a background to Gascoyne's belief in prophecy but also to the popularity of shaman poems since the 1960s.

## Frissons and ruins

Gascoyne says in the introduction to the 1988 Collected Poems that it was sixteen years of amphetamine abuse which prevented his poetic ability from unfolding. "On the corner of Bleecker and nowhere/ in the land of the not quite day/a shiver ran down my backbone/ the face in the mirror turned grey". Sound familiar? Actually it's from a Led Zeppelin song. What we seem to detect here is the eighteenth century roots of the blues, in melancholia brought on by alcoholism, cheerily known as Blue Devils. It's from their traumatic 1976 album, *Presence*, whose aura of deathly weariness may remind us of Gascoyne partly because the principals were royally strung out. It's generally agreed that benzedrine in the short term enhances your attentiveness and makes you feel ten feet tall, but after three days up you have to face five days of feeling faint and ghostly. Distorting the body's natural rhythms can lead to an unnatural state with no rhythms at all, where you can neither fall asleep nor wake up. This then is the background for Gascoyne's *Night Thoughts*, the permanent insomnia he seems to live in. In "ash-pale against a cinder coloured wall, the white/ pear-blossom hovers like a stare", the grey colour is a projection of a wan human face, its stare a focus on nothing. ("A wartime dawn".) Ruins look best by moonlight, and the poet's ambitions are a castle that vanishes in daylight. After a *nuit blanche*, the world crumbles to ash in the affective state of sleeplessness and exhaustion.

The drug makes its takers prone to anxiety attacks, and this could relate to a historical attitude which projects feelings of organic decay onto the outside world, detecting in it spiritual malaise and secular decay. The mixture of feelings of weariness and inadequacy with projections onto superior beings (who have improbable levels of energy and coherence) may remind us of the alternation between comedowns and throbbing highs. Deep sensations of inadequacy go *pari passu* with projections of super-adequacy onto figures identified as spiritual masters. The benzedrine produces a distinctively blank energy, impossible to put to use because it is outside a situation, asocial because it is disconnected from other people around you, and their states of mind.

This may account for the curiously papery quality of his language in those forties poems. If we want to use the word *existential*, this is probably the least existential poetry we can imagine. This divided state is related to the projection of cosmological architecture—the split between the divine and the mundane.

### This Sporting Life

There is an old French Catholic motif about the sinner who achieves redemption through excess of sin, which cuts his earthly bonds. The poet and novelist Pierre-Jean Jouve (a Protestant, as Alan Munton pointed out to us) was one of the supreme exponents of this, where a basic assumption is that debauchery focusses the willpower of his characters and makes them capable of salvation. I suppose this is the context in which existentialism found popular favour.

The blues song emerged, so far as I know, out of Evangelical songs about the evils of alcohol and staying up late. Musicians generally had to work in a religious context in this largely Protestant Fundamentalist Southern community and they learnt these songs. In a secular context, they adapted the songs by taking out the repentance and redemption stripping them down to paeans to debauchery. These simplified songs were really very suitable for jobs in halls dedicated to drinking and dancing. Can we pause for just a momentary fantasy of David Gascoyne taking his drug highs and sexual adventures and presenting them as wilful acts of pleasure, as thrills? Poetry is less popular than rock music partly (mostly?) because of its burden of morality—constantly squeamish about pleasure. The clergy called the blues the devil's music partly because it had incorporated so much religious imagery and made so many cuts.

Stephen Spender wrote about Gascoyne's first mature volume, of 1943, in these terms: "Perhaps tragedy through a veil of self-pity and drugs is the only tragedy we are able to write of today, because it is only people who are disqualified from belonging to the totalitarian conflicts, by ill-health or by neurotic hypersensitivity, who are able to devote themselves completely to poetry". "An Elegy", on the suicide of Roger Roughton, in 1941 and at the age of twenty-five, opens an entire genre of English poetry which one can only describe as the Sporting Life song, as in *I'm getting weary, hard to carry on, most of my friends are dead and gone, this sporting life, this old sporting life is killing me.* We can see large swathes of the later work of George Barker and WS Graham as members of this genre, where the death of a friend seems necessary to get them writing.

The strand is partly a way of smuggling the melancholic hero back in, in the third person. With foresight, I don't think anyone would have voted for this genre of poem to be so favoured. But, English poets have a problem writing about things actually happening. Retrospect does work to some extent, although compromised by visual memories from moral prints of Methodist inspiration, showing the Drunkard, the Prodigal, the Speed Freak, the Surrealist, etc. The shadow of Methodist engravings seems to hang over them. Spender further pointed out that "The atmosphere of Christian conversion, in Gascoyne, is seen through the same veil" — the last act of the tragedy is the refuge in God. There is an eighteenth century song called "The unfortunate rake" where a ghastly cortege symbolises, in stately personification, the life and errors of someone who died of mercury poisoning as a near cure for syphilis. Mourning for debauchery is generally a mixed feeling. Jeremy Reed's work, of that period around *Saints and Psychotics* and *Bleecker Street*, seems like a continuation of one facet of forties sensibility. This is from "Folded", from his 1978 volume *Saints and Psychotics*:

> The light will slant moth-amber, angle
>                        books,
> and offslant frusk the tabid grey of slates.
> The manuscripts accumulate and circulate
>                 to accumulate
> rejections. The hour will still be static.
> Only the unseamed dust-stitches of hands
> that moved in deja-vu still bleeding. Ends
> are like this. Not confined to interiors
>                       or halls
> of moving hooks for limbs on plastic walls.

Reed was directly following Barker in those wonderfully macabre vignettes of decadents and obsessives, in a perpetual retox contained in a landscape of heroic degradation. Also, he was published by Enitharmon and by *Temenos*, and was a friend of Gascoyne's.

The overhang of Protestantism, which had such a tenacious grip on the printed word and on visual mass reproduction, seems to have decided that English confessional poetry would only happen through this rather morbid genre of funereal commemoration, where the devil has not only won but gone home. The late poetry of Barry MacSweeney is the classic confessional poetry from England but seems definitively merged with popular religion and the whole genre of evangelical accounts of alcoholism.

## On Night Thoughts

The theme of being awake all night facing a spiritual crisis is likely to remind us of another English poem — *The Everlasting Mercy*, by John Masefield. The hero is a debauched rustic character, a poacher by trade, who stays awake wrestling with himself and in the morning springs up, runs into the fields, and starts to plough — a symbol of effort and honesty. I really like this poem. It differs from *Night Thoughts* (1955) because it shows a deviant individual adapting to society, whereas *Night Thoughts* is about the wish of an individual for society to adapt to his ideal. Masefield's is rhythmically exciting, things are happening all the time, it ends with the basic situation being resolved — Gascoyne's poem is pretty much the opposite. I grew up in a town where there was no avant-garde literature or art and in a house where books like Masefield's made every room bulge. My English grandfather bought this book, I think, at a moment when it was still the most famous *modern* English poem.

*Night Thoughts* is an attempt to reach the plane of prophecy by freezing out personal biography but while retaining a grip on the world of objects and change. This is made clear by the documentary aspects of the work. Indeed, from a cinematic point of view it is very predictable — if you imagine it in visual terms, the "shots" are those much to be expected in documentary films or even the "scene-setting" of fiction films set in London. Gascoyne was in touch with the Mass Observation movement and had obviously absorbed the ideas of British documentary film. There was a powerful surrealist influence on MO — the links between surrealism and documentary become very plain if we watch Jennings' films or *Went the Day Well?* — and Gascoyne was the acknowledged expert on Surrealism, even at the age of twenty.

There are some interesting resemblances between *Night Thoughts* and *Fox Running*, by Ken Smith. Smith uses the phrase "night thoughts". He is writing about long nights of insomnia, a character ceaselessly loping the darkened streets of London, about the Underground. He writes about randomly spinning through night radio stations and about the "white noise" of detuned radio fuzz. All this sounds very much like *Night Thoughts*. I don't think Smith got this schema from Gascoyne, rather, that it is something present in the culture, a schema which to our good fortune has been described by the anthropologist Victor Turner. He describes the category of the *liminal*, as a zone of withdrawal where conflicts and oppositions are suspended, where practical purpose is absent, and where the eternal embodiments of categories are present, rather than local examples. My impression is that the majority of long poems written in Britain in the last sixty years have aspired to the liminal condition. This includes the non-Christian poems—secular poets still share this imperative. Indeed, one could talk of "competing over the liminal territory"—a fertile source of infertile quarrels, I suspect. The goal for the poet is presumably to reach a state above daily social conflicts by departing from their "role as themselves"; thus being allowed to say something which will not be invalidated by being referred to a position of partiality. The liminal voice is on no side; it is not a point on the spectrum but the whole horizon. In an era of class conflict, poets must strive for this. The music without pitch which accompanies *Night Thoughts* is what the liminal *sounds* like.

Christian theology is native to the Gospels. Its classic prose genre is saints' lives—always living out typologies from the life of Christ. Its classic poetic genre is the hymn, again tied to incidents from the Bible and to the feasts of particular days in the calendar. Anyone who writes Christian novels or poems is going to have Christ as the central character, almost nolens volens—it takes effort to drive him out. This is worse when the central character is the author—identification with Christ is obnoxious to all classes of possible readers. This was really a big problem for our poet, and many of his poems show a struggle between typology and autobiography. A prophet sees the world when looking into himself, and this equivocation is just the problem I have with his diagnosis of the spiritual condition of the world. For, in order for the world to have a spiritual condition, it would have to have a spirit. This is fine if we are talking about one person who does have a spirit but can only stand for the world if he is also Christ. If we take the people of the world as objects of knowledge, it is clear that their states are far too complex for an individual mind to apprehend—it would be like listening to a million phone conversations at once.

It seems that we can apprehend spirits one at a time. Soaring beyond that bounded knowable to emotional knowledge *general and also true* sounds dangerous and a delusion. Could we see the object, as a locally bounded resistant exemplar of the rules of the universe, as an equivalent in the dimensions of space of the moment in the dimension of Time? In saints' lives, it plays the part of the *tekmerion*, the physical evidence: anomalous objects prove the reality of visions. The poem might then be the equivalent of both of these in the universe of ideas. All are resistant because contingent—they are merely local. As they depart from the sacred archetypes, they become unique. The status of the object in modern poetry clearly derives from the collapse of a spiritual narrative, is the saving of shreds from that collapse. If we want to define Gascoyne's dislike of English poetry, we should look at the object as the site of one of the key differences between French and English poetry. A certain strain of English poetry has attached key importance to the cross-modal experience. For example, visible + tangible is "better" than visible only. An idea linked to a scene is "better" than an idea. It is felt that this cross-modality is a guarantee that the experience is authentic and not merely a product of fantasy and auto-suggestion. I don't think this proposal is wholly credible.

The poem is felt as a performable proof with proof status. It relates to a foregoing experience, outside it—a spiritual peak which is in need of evidence. The originality of the poem is the anomaly which proves divine intervention. Exceptionalism in modern poetry can be referred back to an essay in *Lux Mundi* (1889), where one of that Oxford group (led by Charles Spencer Gore) finds beauty in anomalies in the physical world and finds this beauty leading us to the existence of God. It is a very strange essay. But truly, we find originality in poetry driven to frightening extremes, and it is driven by a wish to convince readers of authenticity—a conviction whose foundation may not be there. Gascoyne's Journal is unsatisfactory because of its imitative status.

One can draw a distinction, in European poetry, between what repeats inherited central privileged norms and what abandons these norms in order to pursue originality. For a vast sector of literary opinion, originality has been proof of spiritual pride and of inauthenticity. The cult of exceptionalism in art has a geographical boundary to its distribution.

The gap between sublime and mundane calls for a link. To describe this mediation, I would like to use the term a relationship of the type R, where

{holy        R      temporal}
{     prophecy              }

It seems possible also that:

radio broadcast    R        local points
          antenna

or:
sound    R    language
     words

white noise   R   phonemes
    articulation

And so we can say that:

liminal space   R           documentary
        Night Thoughts

The white noise which appears in the broadcast of *Night Thoughts* (so broad-spectrum sound without pitch) is curiously important. It corresponds to the state of insomnia which is little less than the drifting into an egoless state where the poet becomes interchangeable with other people. The prophecy as violation of the laws governing the time-line of knowledge corresponds to the moment of repentance violating the rules of behaviour. Gascoyne wanted prophetic status to predict a spiritual reversal of the direction of European affairs. He had the problem of mediating his finished ethical vision in a poem which is doubly concrete, i.e. in dealing with a particular situation and in realising itself in a succession of particular rhythmic and acoustic moments. The saint is the eternal in temporally bound form, and prophecy is the perception of the confused succession of events in time elevated to the clarity of the divine.

Insomnia is a link to the young female schizophrenics described by Aaron Esterson in *The Leaves of Spring* (1972). He takes to the level of detailed empirical research the study of the phenomenon which produces ecstatic religion (in the phrase of Ioan Lewis). The image of the shaman, a besetting myth in modern poetry, drew in Britain primarily on the image of the journey through madness as promoted by Esterson's collaborator, RD Laing, at his Philadelphia Institute. The subjects of Esterson's study (composing volume 2 of the work *Madness, sanity, and the Family*, the first volume being written with Laing) had great trouble with insomnia and were much awake in the night. They forfeited reason—in a certain sense, one homologated by their doctors. They were representative of group events—in Esterson's analysis, which detected flaws in group process, embodied in the ways they communicated, the girls came to be the weak and sensitive points through which all the tension of the system came out. In this way they became the voice of huge impersonal forces, very much as Gascoyne expected to become, as he planned to base his life's work on. The group-based study of the Scottish psychiatrists followed up the work of Gregory Bateson and WR Bion in uncovering group dynamics, opening for us, in all probability, a better way of studying the genesis of a poet's style and work.

*In the land of the not-quite day; or, the frisson of ruins. David Gascoyne* [207]

## The Journal

The Journals are uniquely boring, but after all the last entry was made when David Gascoyne was twenty-six or twenty-seven. No one of that age has ever written an interesting journal about their *inner* experiences. The attack on materialism blames it for endless boring representations of mundane reality in the realist novel, but the Christian journal seems determined to offer at least equal banality and prolixity. I think the key influence on the Journal is Marcel Jouhandeau—his *Chroniques maritales*. He was a great writer, in my opinion.

I wonder if we could relate the documentary wish of the diary (repetitive, routine, unselective) to the spiritual wish to get beyond immediate self-consciousness and so discover something it had not produced and so, something not vitiated by human willpower. The urge to inclusiveness was meant to exclude trickery. This earnest, protracted, recording of data was the ancestor of the documentary camera (and of "conceptual art" based on rigorous procedures). Since the idea was to uncover the supernatural and what is beyond reason, maybe it isn't too surprising that *surrealism* came to feature in the documentary movement (via Jennings and Cavalcanti). Since the unconscious is that which tricks, this project seems basically flawed. So whatever is not our own voice, is the voice of God? This seems deeply flawed, too.

I wonder if what followed documentary, in English poetry, was the phenomenological school, with their earnest concern with visual perception. Important reference points for them were Merleau-Ponty's *The phenomenology of perception* and JH Prynne's essay "Resistance and Difficulty". A re-examination of Charles Madge's poetry showed a besetting interest in the relationship between 2D ocular perception and the mapping of 3D images.

Madge wrote two long "documentary poems" of which one came out forty-five years after its composition and the other ("The Storming of the Brain") has never been published. Gascoyne's romance with prophecy points to a gentler but unavoidable crisis in writing about personal experience in connection with the framework of abidingly true knowledge. We all want to think about society, even if we identify this with a small town only; the poet wants to feed our thought, but stubbornly offers personalised experience, with an individual or a small group filling the scene. The proposal that the great literary public should attend to a volume of poetry which is simply about one person's feelings has something staggering about it. After staggering, I would tend to support this line. The urge to be typical has vitiated large parts of modern poetic production and is really very similar to Gascoyne's drug-fuelled belief that his inner state mirrored the whole age. More recent poets have operated by a rule of matching, where the moment when personal experience matches something that can be found in the works of prestigious philosophers is eagerly seized on as the justification for a poem and the winning ticket. My (unconscious) decision to identify with something is not restricted to things which are merely typical. In fact, I may find it impossible to identify with what is typical because it is too familiar and offers my brain no new information. The idea that one could write sociological poetry which is also about a few individuals is only one step advanced from Gascoyne's conceit of being the chosen witness to his entire age. It is not vital to write documentary poetry, but it is vital not to write poetry from which everything unusual has been removed. Protestant literature, notoriously, arose as a replacement for the Saint's Life, but I think its struggle succeeded and was even over a long time ago.

### The surrealist/psychoanalytical/Catholic triangle

One of Gascoyne's poems, "The Fabulous Glass" describes the Madonna attacking the face of the holy babe. This was a dream, based on a real statue in the house of his psychoanalyst, Blanche Reverchon. It is very hard to say whether this image is surrealist, psychoanalytical, or religious. Images do not divide neatly between these categories, so it is not very satisfying to classify poets into the same categories. Those schools would give different explanations of the origins of the images: for Freudians, a revelation of something structural, internal, and absolutely true; for Roman Catholics, an allegory of divine truth; for the surrealists, a moment of absolute spontaneity, perfectly free and so revealing nothing. These cannot all be true. Perhaps none of them is.

There is an old Irish tale where Finn sleeps and sees himself suckling two seals. On waking, he is told that this means his two sons are facing dire peril at the hands of a band of Norwegian invaders (=sons of the sea). This line of cryptic and involuntary images is obviously not confined to the twentieth century. However, the captions are all more or less dubious. It looks very much as if there were a preordained tendency to see involuntary images, — perhaps a basic by-product of visual processing, and that different schools of talkers artfully claim possession of them and hitch them to their own more or less dubious theories. These images mostly involve animate bodies, and perhaps this gives us a clue to the New Romantic preoccupation with physiological processes. I suspect that it is no good looking at or inside the body to find prophecy—the information isn't there. This is a wrong deduction from the prevalence of bodies in involuntary images. They prevail because the basic environment is bodies, not objects. I would rather see these images as a kind of white noise, than as a message. That is, the space of variation of visual forms is all full of shapes and all written over —the complex image stands still because it is where we stop and stand. If we went on moving, we would find significance in every direction. This phenomenon is visual rather than visible.

What Corbin says about the distinction between the imaginary and the imaginal may be useful to us here. He also says that the Reformation of the sixteenth century was the re-opening of the prophetic inspiration which had closed by the end of the first few centuries of Christianity. Knight seems close to the vein of fantasy which may—via Tolkien, Moorcock, or Knight's friend John Cowper Powys—be the most powerful stream of twentieth century English literature. Knight's hermaphrodite-seraphs are just one species of imaginary creatures. As a social phenomenon, this obstinacy about private mythologies is probably inseparable from Protestantism. Blake, and the whole background of Protestant sects, explain why surrealism never really took off in England and Scotland.

Gascoyne's talent was not so big you could use it as a doorstop. Also, though he recovered and managed to write some poems later in life, his position throughout most of our period was as an ex-poet—a martyr to his own personality. He is rewarding to write about because of the documentation of his inner life—with the two intimate and retrieved journals which were published forty years after they were written—and because he was a follower, adopting ideas from people who were themselves prolific writers. For more recent poets, biographies, autobiographies, and diaries are simply not available.

# Bad science, pulp topography: Iain Sinclair

Sinclair (1943–) began by studying film, in the mid-sixties, and the imperatives of fast narration, popular mythology, and alternative cosmologies have guided his steps ever since. American cinema has devoted itself to the two primal events of light entering the aperture of the camera and life finding its exit from the body. The New World trio of gun, camera, car have provided a whole mythology of kinetic disorder, which Sinclair has perhaps only extended to other forms of energy. It's not clear why he gave up the more modern visual medium for poetry, but perhaps one factor was that his desire to catch extraordinary high-energy events had got to the point where they were events that never occurred, so that a camera was powerless to bring them in and only words would do. Much of his writing has the quality of someone recounting a film—some lurid tale of shoulder-padded gangsters, alien craft violating traffic regulations in some small Mid-Western township, demons using a stone circle as an entry port to the material world—to friends. Film-making also demands technophilia, and he has brought to this subterranean world the unflecked smoothness of highly polished lenses and the relentless pace of an athlete or a film editor. Hell breaks loose in the streets of the East End, but Sinclair is concerned to have every meter and recording instrument synchronised and on mark: like Edgar G. Ulmer, "his camera never falters even when his characters disintegrate". The preoccupation with tracks and alignments seems to start out from the mystery of chalk marks and camera angles used in the planning of a shoot. After adventures in manual trades, recounted in *Lud Heat* (1975), he found a congenial and self-employed trade as a book-dealer, which he pursued for twenty years. The slews of paperbacks, which he absorbed cutaneously without exactly reading them, proposed a world of legends sufficiently visual for him to set his equipment out and switch it on. The mythologies recounted in his catalogues—dealing in the Beats, horror, gangs of London, the paranormal, underground poetry, London topography, diverted batches of industrial chemicals, archaeology, the occult—are the raw material of his poetry. In 1987, he published a novel, describing a solution to the Jack the Ripper mystery and crazed and burnt-out second-hand book dealers, which opened new outlets for his consuming energies; others (*Downriver* and now *Radon Daughters*) have followed. I think his interest in poetry waned after the publication of *Suicide Bridge* (1979), although a number of pamphlets followed, self-published in very small editions. These more recent works, partially collected in *Flesh Eggs and Scalp Metal*, add substantially to the world view outlined in the two full-scale works of the seventies. There was apparently another large-scale project, *Red Eye*, abandoned, of which some fragments were put out, in 1974, in minute quantities. The prose divagations (once described by Sinclair in a note as "essays") are essential to the feel of the whole; I am going to ignore the case that Sinclair is a prose writer and outside my purview, since on a number of scores he fits in very well.

"There are only a very few of the original Experiemental D-E's crew Left by Now, Sir. Most went insane, one just walked 'throo' his quarters wall in sight of his wife & Child & 2 other crew Members (WAS NEVER SEEN AGAIN), two 'Went into the Flame' IE they 'froze' & caught fire, while carrying common Small-Boat Compasses, one Man carried the compass & Caught fire, the other came for the 'Laying on of Hands' as he was the nearest but he too took fire. THEY BURNED FOR 18 DAYS. The faith in 'Hand Laying' Died when this happened & Mens Minds Went by the scores. The expieriment was a complete success. The Men were Complete Failures". (from a letter quoted in *The Philadelphia Experiment*, by Charles Berlitz and William Moore.) This pulp fiction presented as scientific fact is in just the same key as much of what Sinclair writes; we have to add to the Fortean "anomalies of physics" the speculations about the lives of the famous, equally a staple of the popular press and equally, in fact, prevalent in *The Philadelphia Experiment*, which drags in a lot of legendary and speculative material about Einstein and several more shadowy figures. It's perplexing to open this book and see a photograph of John E. Neumann, the mathematician who worked on the nuclear bomb project and invented the computer program. Famous people must appear in popular mythology ... and *Suicide Bridge* is largely about the Kray twins, Howard Hughes, John F. Kennedy, Mick Jagger, Stephen Hawking, JH Prynne.

Sometimes I think his style is largely based on the jackets of books, which are inevitably more intense than the books themselves. Sifting his stock was Sinclair's method of getting to know public opinion, a method just as legitimate as teaching or marking share prices. The jackets are false, both as descriptions of the weedy prose inside and as claims about man and the universe; but Sinclair has permanently suspended the Reality Principle. At the same time, he's plugged into a shared mythology; the public gobbles up UFOs, Grail mysteries, parapsychology, conspiracy theory. He plugs into collective hysteria with the adroitness of a mobile sound-man finding a mains supply. Like Dick Clark, when the shelves are empty, he fills them. The culprits are even listed in *Suicide Bridge*:

> Atum speaks plague on the followers of Peachey
>
> on the Wilsons, Sprague de Camp, Hesse,
> on the Blakean publicists, the boudoir astrologers,
> "the Taozer babbling of the Elixir", Amis,
> Gog garglers, Ripper tourists, transvestite druids,
> zoo builders, Campden Hill tantriks,
> Avebury photographers, stone thieves
>
> may locusts fall on their heads

Most of these characters can be found glossed in John Sladek's sceptical *The New Apocrypha*. One of the features of Sinclair's more recent writing is the uncanny vividness of his portraits of people. We could see the whole of Sinclair's pulp physics as an attempt to portray the people he was hanging out with, people who believed in an alternative cosmology. Sinclair evokes the damned authors of these teeming and incondite fictions: "There are forgotten men in small town temperance hotels & mining shacks, mid-continental inertia, who have literally been waiting in their rooms, sitting by the bed, looking out on meridian street traffic, bills paid by computer, for over thirty years—for the phonecall from Hughes that will activate them: & meanwhile they write, on typewriters, science fictions & horror god inventions, squeeze nature into aborted surgeries, work for WEIRD TALES, John Campbell's ASTOUNDING, or Roger Corman; they invent (or are made aware of) impossible literatures in languages that were never spoken, the Necronomicon, or Ludvig Prinn's 'Mysteries of the Worm'". The last-named work is not some suppressed work of JH Prynne's, but an imaginary work *De vermis mysteriis* cited in works by HP Lovecraft. The whole can be taken as an allegory of the small-press poet: "The invented horrors are literal. They alone see the shape-shifting of the windows. They alone stare, night after night, at the planets. They become part of the machinery. The flying saucers & Cayce-inspirations spiral from their apparent boredom". (Both quotes from *Suicide Bridge*; Edgar Cayce was a pharmacist and receiver of "spirit messages".) Of course the information is spiked: American pulp fiction wasn't really created by an army of undercover workers for Howard Hughes. Sinclair isn't dependent on shamanism within an academic definition: he uses every possible source, even though some themes are directly related to the corpus of shamanistic myths as defined by Eliade, and he has himself stressed the links of neo-mythical artists to the Eurasian traditions, in his "retrospective manifesto", *The Shamanism of Intent*. No, the importance of Sinclair is that his evocation of primal forces is not trapped inside an empirical, modern, academic matrix of gestures: he has engineered something that is as recklessly hyperbolic as heavy metal music, which is totally beyond the reality principle, and this is the only environment in which imitation of primitive religion could possibly work.

With the long works, the question arises: what is their structure? I think finally there is no external motivation for the concatenation of *Suicide Bridge*, it is driven by a purely aesthetic motivation; I think of the music of The Yardbirds (on live albums) or Led Zeppelin, where one number flows into another, just to keep the energy at its highest level, mysteriously combining intensity and free association. The book is a compilation, as the subtitle "A mythology of the South and East" suggests; like Ovid's *Metamorphoses* and a number of other Classical collections of myths, it strings unrelated stories together. The essential thing isn't connection but pace.

∽3

Catalogue of *Suicide Bridge* (Page numbers are in brackets because the Goldmark edition of the book is unpaginated.)

| | |
|---|---|
| (1–7) | essay on Myth and Place |
| (8–15) | "cosmogony" or origin myth of the twin gangsters, Hand & Hyle (the Krays). |
| ((18–23) | account of Hand & Hyle |

[214]  Origins of the Underground

(25–35) the story of Kotope, a businessman, bookdealer, and believer in mysteries; assassinated by six Arabs.
(36–39) Peachey, a pulp Egyptologist and mystic
(40–46) another tale of Hand & Hyle
(48–52) "Slade & the Tyrannicides", equating Harold Godwinsson and Slade, an associate murdered by Hand & Hyle. He is dismembered by Hand & Hyle; his severed head babbles endless strings of data.
(53–71) life and death of Hutton, an associate of the gangsters (corresponding to an axe murderer whom the Krays sprang from Broadmoor and then killed).
(72–78) a party given by Kotope involving Hand & Hyle and the (unnamed) Rolling Stones; this segment possibly derived from the film "Performance"
(79–94) Howard Hughes (and Joseph Kennedy)
(95–110) the tale of a mage Skofeld in Cambridge; his debauched manservant Kox (both names from two soldiers who got William Blake arrested); more weird cosmology
(111–129) the tale of Coban, "the unknowable", a lost "elder god", who conceives in his own hand Bladud (a figure from Geoffrey of Monmouth), who flies over all Britain and falls to die on the site of Lud Hill. He is the first victim of the Suicide Bridge.
(132–42) Skofeld & the Great Work; more cosmological experiments.
(143–149) another tale of Slade; his severed head becomes the prophet & tutelar of England.

Let's look at a passage from the work: "So the sitings fade beyond Thorpe-le-Soken & sink into tidal mud at Mersea island, flickering lights along deserted roads. Whirring spiral gyres above the recumbent victim. Myrrh Sea, initiatory Magi gift, resin. Merde Sea, waste sludge of salt dyke, haunt of coypu. Mixing. Inland gulls hover for industrial scraps: but the celestial wound passage is opened & Slade reads the history of his own death.
  The Tyrannicides arrive.
  Inside the enclosed tropic car heat, fans blowing out essence of jackal, chicken feathers, red mud, Olduvai bone fragment, is the oracular head of Alfredo Garcia: a whisper in fly swarm, in Muscat sand, in the swift tongues of decomposition. Excess of wisdom has made them mad; has dyed the skin, tanned then the colour of saddle leather. Dead meat is changed into sound, dense insect squabble, speaking in tongues. Their blood is malarial fast, Livingstone pallor, shivering, brandy & salt

tablets: Hand & Hyle, brass knuckled Tyrannicides". Slade is walking, driven by some unknown compulsion, out in Essex; in imitation of the conventions of topographical writing, various spurious etymologies of Mersea are given. The flickering lights are UFOs, "Overhead is the well-documented UFO track". (Sitings may be a misprint for sightings.) The spirals, implying a link between celestial and terrestrial complexes of events, may be part of a Vortex: a pattern of energy, favoured by the English avant-garde group of Vorticists, traced by Tom Gibbons' research back to Swedenborg, present also in Orphic writings, where the swirls are part of the mixing-bowl (in Greek, *crater*) which gave rise to our Grail legend. His killers are Tyrannicides as part of a literary diptych which started with an evocation of the death of Harold Godwinsson at Hastings: "The thin shaft in his eye-socket is the periscope we use; root tendrils & fine hairs feather the wood, lift towards the informing sun. The ash-scalded tip presses on his brain nerve: the feather has flowered. Autopsy of linked metals, corrosion, treachery, forsworn impulses of wrist, water hand, error of history enters the chronicle . . . " Alfredo Garcia is a character mentioned but not seen in Sam Peckinpah's 1974 eschatological ultraviolent Mexican *noir*, "Bring Me the Head of Alfredo Garcia": a million dollars have been offered for this head. The "oracular" head is imported from a quite different cultural complex, being in fact the head of Orpheus; although the cult of severed heads was widespread in the Celtic world, and the head of Bran was buried in London, where Sinclair associates it with Friar Bacon's legendary Brazen Head. Olduvai is a gorge in East Africa where fossils of apparent human ancestors are found; Muscat is a kingdom on the Persian Gulf. "Livingstone" is the African explorer and missionary. Sinclair goes on in the next paragraph to evoke another film: "The head is also the enclosed nuclear box, chest of desert secrets uncovered by Ralph Meeker at the end of KISS ME DEADLY" . . . in this 1955 film by Robert Aldrich, the "secret" is stolen radioactive material, which explodes at the end of the film.

It's an exacting task to track down all Sinclair's associations, because of their sheer speed. The faculty of association of ideas is one of the most personal and distinctive traits; it is crucial to poetry, because if the reader is tuned to the same wavelength as the poet, that is the basis of success: whereas, if the reader isn't, they won't even understand the poem, not if it's as rapid and free as *Suicide Bridge*. He isn't using associations as collations to investigate real phenomena, but as sensitised paper to catch and record delirium, stimuli to enhance and share a mood. Most of the information needed is explained in the text, which reads like a kind of commentary (on photographs?).

Sinclair is close to a traditional function of photographs, that is to show the impossible or monstrous. A photo which showed someone falling down the side of a skyscraper would be worth more money, for example than one of the same person about to jump. The more impossible the event, the more transient and high-energy the event, the more precious the photograph. This is where myth enters the text. To this extent, he has remained faithful to the camera, even while using words. Sinclair shows nothing but what is impossible, producing a body of testimony which holds as much water as the Gobi Desert. He thrusts into your hand an envelope purportedly containing actual photos of the ship DE-173 disappearing, due to magnetic resonance effects, but which in fact contains nothing but a verbal description of the event.

The other traditional function of anomalous events is to act as proof of the truths of religion. Prophecy, for example is set up as a proof precisely because it violates the laws of the familiar universe. A very broad section of Christian texts, and paintings, are collections of miracles. It is not surprising if the post-mediaeval mass culture which grew on the debris of this rich mulch of nonsense retained the taste for things incredible and countering the evidence of the senses.

The reality principle reins in and modifies the primary processes of the id: "It is the dark inaccessible part of our personality; [ . . . ] We approach the id with analogies; we call it a chaos, a cauldron . . . it is filled with energy reaching it from the instincts, but it has no organization, produces no collective will . . . the logical laws of thought do not apply . . . contrary impulses exist side by side without cancelling each other out . . . There is nothing in the id that corresponds to the idea of time . . . The id, of course, knows no judgements of value; no good and evil, no morality". (Freud, *New Introductory Lectures on Psychoanalysis*, no.31). The rules of this domain are also the rules of Sinclair's world. Charles Rycroft, quoting this passage, goes on to compare the id with God, who exists outside time, can only be approached by analogies, has infinite energy, etc. These rules, or this lack of rules, also order the most vital parts of saints' lives and the legends of shamans. These mediaeval energies were transmitted to the nineteenth century via the genre of Gothic horror, a scrapyard of broken folk narratives, which is where Sinclair found them.

Religion is also the prehistory of kitsch. The word Gothic, as used in the period from about 1760 on, referred to the qualities—real or imaginary—of mediaeval culture; part of this was the resurrection of tales of terror, the forces used originally for moral discipline brought back, once the literal belief in Hell had disappeared, in merely aesthetic form.

Christian culture, in the form which it had adopted by, say, A.D. 1000 in Western Europe, had localised its violations of natural law: that is to say, it suggested that miracles were more likely at particular places. This served to draw people to those places, generating income for the churches and foundations which were built to cap the energies, pilgrimage being the ancestor of tourism. Sinclair follows this belief in the inherent virtues of Place, even though he is also able to satirise it as a pervading myth of documentary film-makers, that if you take the camera crew to where someone lived, you will say something more revealing about that person than if you stayed in a studio talking about their ideas.

I think that Sinclair's view of topology is an illusion, insofar as he attributes supernatural and mythical events to the configuration of places, in the same way that configuration dictates the course of rivers. This is articulated in the first section of *SB*: "The land the animal. They have a location which is charged with an intense & continually reinforced personal magnetism, literally driven down into the granules of soil—so that each single grain is a charged particle of energy, forming a live carpet on which they stand & move, a cathode mosaic of infinitely detailed histories & archetypes. Past & present are coeval, equally radiant". "Myth is breech: faces backwards. The siamese twin is place. They are sown together & cannot be separated, dependent systems. Man is the messenger substance between them. He is a raised tube, opened at crown of head & base of feet—so that it flows through him, conscious or unconscious, the surge, the tachyonic voltage". "Place is a harpoon of the specific and has no name. It is not anonymous in the sense of witholding its location but is unknown & discovered only by a charge as powerful as death—in death-moment or some other heightened absolute, birth, climax, murder (that false trail of secret savage acts seeking to pin down place by isolated sacrifice, undirected hand, ritualists of the locked room hoarding their pathetic equipment, chainstore magic kits & cheap cameras)". "Myth is what place says. And it does lie. It spreads a seductive field of pits & snares. You go mad if you try to pursue place through myth: your path will disappear over the nearest cliff. Place is fed by sacrifice of the unwary ... " I can't believe any of this—it's just pulp physics, although it is splendidly evocative. Traces are not left in places but in human culture, you couldn't link Chatterton with the part of London where he dies unless you had been told the story: Sinclair is deliberately slighting the terrific suggestive powers of language because he uses them all the time: he makes us see things that don't exist, that is his function. When so many writers were fetishizing language and pretending that it had a volition of its own ("I am writing about language"), Sinclair is denying it any role at all, ascribing everything to Place. "Chisels of partially-initiated Masons constructed the trap, wound the forbidden lore into a maze of earth & water". His ability to suggest that place stores behaviour patterns, forces us to behave in archetypal ways, contains slumbering and overwhelming imperatives, is most impressive: but ultimately this is the physical theory of the ghost story. And it's just not so.

I think his use of place derives from an ancient anxiety of film-makers, that they would photograph places, the places would be most of the information appearing in the film, and when it was shown the places would impose their own indifference on the film, they would not be transformed at all, no meaning would emerge, the images would remain essentially empty. This anxiety makes the aspiring film-maker develop emotional muscles to deal with it. He makes the act of faith needed to regard place as subjectively charged; and there we have it, Sinclair is incessantly telling us that Place is so charged. All narrative cinema is trick photography, relying on the suggestive power of intentional perceptual cues. The Bates house in "Psycho" is not sinister of itself but only because we believe a murderer is waiting inside it: the director pumps the meaning into the dull timber and bricks; equally, London is not some labyrinthine device for storing and releasing psychic energies, it becomes so in *Lud Heat*, partly also in *Suicide Bridge*, because of Sinclair's mesmerising impresarial patter persuading us that it is. Place, genuinely, is important in the organisation of memories, it involves our body image and sense of location, which are far more complex (and older) than our relation to symbols: giving place a psychic charge is another form of total simultaneity, tearing the reader out of normal life to immerse them in the imaginative world of the poem. Subjective though it is, this whole-body experience is what gives Sinclair's constructions their immense evocative power.

The Gothic view is that virtues linger around the relics of saints, traces of the virtue they had when alive, which I suppose is the basis for ghost stories. In the Romantic era, the cult was transferred to poets: hence the Chatterton myth, used by MacSweeney as well as Sinclair. (It would be interesting to compare *Ranter* to *Suicide Bridge*.) This belief in powers emanating as radiation affecting the sensitive and prepared, rather than through poems, paintings, or other externalised symbols, led on to Symbolism and to the Occult Revival.

One of the most common types of Chinese book is the local history, faithfully recording local genealogies, legends, notables, and curiosities: these are never translated into Western languages, because they are too particularist. Such texts also include accounts of local anomalies, observations which later helped naturalists but which also anticipate UFOs and the like. Higden's fourteenth century *Polychronicon* gives a description of Britain in terms of miracles attached to places, for example a pool which turns everything thrown into it to iron. I suppose that these learned works are really compilations of folklore. Explaining the Gothic as an echo of the Middle Ages begs the question of why certain devices were popular in the Middle Ages, or why there are similar narratives in far-away cultures, such as China. If China has ghost stories (and even a notion of Hell, derived from Buddhist accounts), we can't just blame ghost stories on Christianity. Similarly, the use of Gothic devices by Sinclair (and Hughes, Jeremy Reed, Brian Catling, modern horror films, etc.) is based on their inherent aesthetic efficiency, not on some passive imitation of the sermons of fourteenth century friars.

Sinclair evokes contemporary poets in terms of a geographical pattern: "Behind him, & through the forest, the fen, the coast, is that ancient miracle, the Wall, the unseen guardian of value. It is pegged & gated by those high consciousnesses situated in the East of England, those wills, those animators of the actual, hidden in Cambridge, Brightlingsea, London, curving through to Sussex". One can identify the consciousnesses in question (the phrase is a parody of Theosophist discourse about 'masters' in Tibet) as Prynne, Ralph Hawkins, Andrew Crozier: the London end could be many people but is probably Brian Catling. Even though the link between poetry and space is mythical, one has to admit that the English public prefers to see poets in terms of place.

There are a number of tantalising coincidences of language and ideas between the avant-garde, of the High period between (say) 1890 and 1920, and the occult sensibility. Symbolism may have passed on to the avant-garde, its offspring, not merely a grand belief in the authority of the Artist but also a spiritual theory of how artistic communication works. I learnt this from what John F. Moffitt is reported as saying: "he has, like myself [i.e. Tom Gibbons], been led to the inescapable conclusion that we cannot begin to understand early modernism in the visual arts without taking into account the widespread 'Occult Revival' which began in Western cultures in the late nineteenth century, and whose influence continues unabated at an admass level in the form of contemporary 'New Age' enthusiasm". Gibbons states elsewhere that "Such [early modernist] movements routinely argue that mankind needs to return to earlier and allegedly superior forms of consciousness. [ . . . ] These movements are defiantly anti-materialist and show the strong influence of late nineteenth century transcendentalism, especially of the types of occultism associated with the Theosophical Society. [ . . . ] The desire for millenarian regeneration is of course the reason why early modernist movements are self-consciously avant-garde, deliberately breaking with older and allegedly decadent forms of artistic expression. [ ... ] In order to evoke complex states of mind as accurately as possible, early modernist writers and painters aim at 'simultaneity'—the simultaneous evocation of complex thoughts and feelings. ... Overall, the effect at which early modernist communication aims is to be as close as possible to telepathy — the instantaneous and non-material communication of complex perceptions and states of mind". Moffitt wrote a book tracing the whole of Josef Beuys' ideas back to Rudolf Steiner, the Anthroposophist (who formed his movement in 1913 as a breakaway from the Theosophists). Sinclair's use of bad science may be simply a kind of local colour, authentic period detail, for dealing as a fan-documentarist with Modernism. I don't think the thesis put forward by Moffitt and Gibbons has won its spurs yet. For English poetics, it's very illuminating about Graves and Yeats: if we see them as squirming around trying to acquire a millenarian religious system of an occultist-Symbolist type, because that was the ideal they had accepted in youth, we shall be better off than if we write off their hierophantic conniptions as mere aberrations. In studying poets whose formative period fell in the 1960s, we shall inevitably fail if we ignore millenarianism, religion, and alternative cosmologies. Granted that the religion of the Palaeolithic, or any "shamanism", could not have been a real influence on that poetry, it's useful to recall the far less alien Symbolism and Occult Modernism whose embers were still lying around in the sixties (cf. *The White Goddess*) and warm enough to be rekindled.

Sinclair's later material does not fit into cycles like the sections of the large works; he has given up the prose essays or demonologies. These poems have the effect of snapshots, intense moments seared onto the paper, catching the energy of a transient alignment of parts.

> I had thought St. Vitus' dance as
> much of a back number as the cakewalk:
> it's stomping here in full fig,
> velveteen jacket worn to flesh, pocket
> torn out, like a split cheekbone
>
> try and flit from the coop
> of Old Holborn, phlegm, twitchy
> parrot moods: they've even
> picked up on bird diseases and foul pests
>
> the lolling sheepheaded beaten
> men, the form-filling

dole-scratching, ill-tempered lumpen
mess of what we are become
> ("Serpent to Zymurgy", *from Autistic Poses*).

This is an example of a new theme in his work, that of social comment; this started when, during the Thatcher era, large numbers of people began perceiving the public realm, the streets, in terms of horror and disease.

Religion, as was, has been split into two parts: the attempt to appear a good person and to exhort moral restraint, and the co-operation with the supernatural, where the stress is on demonstration, on the working of wonders in full view and without losing rhythm. Audiences are credulous but they want tangible proofs. It seems that these are supplied by brilliance of language: for the ordinary run of poet, pretending to theurgy is merely a source of self-humiliation. The poet who preserves the apparatus of reason, embedded in vocabulary, syntax, and lineation, cannot persuade anyone that they are in a state of mad exaltation and spirit possession. It is not enough to make a single gesture towards wildness; every word has to become theatrical, alogical, mythic. Even a page of Sinclair and O'Sullivan will demonstrate the extraordinary density and intensity of their work, the stunning degree of its co-ordination to a single purpose. The leftover apparatus of realism seems in comparison to be stodgy and dull, incapable of any kind of ornament.

Sinclair frustrates generalisations about *A Various Art* because he has so little in common with the other sixteen poets. The huge apparatus of narrative, with stage sets, character, and complex actions, is just the opposite of the intimate and indefinite approach of the others; although of course Doug Oliver has written book-length narratives. Most of the others are sceptical; Sinclair makes us believe things which are palpably not true. I have decided not to draw a set of Venn diagrams which would exhibit the overlaps and non-overlaps between the seventeen poets because the results are too specialised. Connections between Sinclair's romantic mythology and the Romantic poetry of the 1940s produced equally specialised results: the similarities could not be more tenuous. The choice of Sinclair to complete the anthology was natural because of a commonality of sensibility, a set of shared tastes in little magazines which, in pressurised times, amounted to participation and solidarity. Decades later, Sinclair put these marginal poets into the High Street: via *the new british poetry* and *Conductors of Chaos*.

## Radical toxins and lingering hallucinogens: Counter-culture and New Age

Where there is a fundamental dividing line between people who insist on every line being original and people who have trouble scraping up even one original line per volume, we may look outside poetry to an intellectual geography where people are questioning everything and originality is cheap and abundant. Along with the arbitrariness of the socially agreed sign, goes the imperious quality of conversation—you stick to the topics that other people can follow (and find acceptable), and academic classes stick to what is on the syllabus. As this might imply, if you go to the right place, you find people who insist on you talking originally. This is quite a wrench—it is hard to know which the problem is, being so intellectually quick, or breaching the alliance with people who have invested in conventional ideas. Because language flows along social networks, so does knowledge—originality follows naturally once your identifications with authority figures fade or die. Indeed, originality and damaged relations with the institutionally powerful seem inevitably associated.

Is there an underground press to go with underground poetry? The catalogue (for June, 2003) of the distributor Counter Productions offers us "Secret Black Projects of the New World Order", capitalism and schizophrenia, the heroic years of Spanish Anarchism, psycho-physiological investigations (into: auto-erotic fatalities, trepanation, cargo cults, self-mutilation, infrasound, and "a botched sexual encounter with a Volkswagen Beetle"), the aesthetic fascist fringe, the Situationist International, technical topics such as "Tesla's Wireless Transmitter, Cancer & radio, the Fisher engine, scalar fields", the Vril stick; auroral energy receivers, non-retinal vision, memetics, the digital economy,

### Radical toxins and lingering hallucinogens: Counter-culture and New Age

post-human rationality, nanotechnology, the engraved stones of Ica, the bloody rise of the Satanic metal underground, the failure of symbolic thought, current affairs as a system of control and disinformation, secrets of Cold War technology, the space scientist and occultist Jack Parsons, psychedelic shamanism, ley lines, the archaeology of violence, the rotting goddess, Montauk's Nazi-Tibetan connection, psychogeography, mammalian raptures, Dealey Plaza. All this along with plentiful amounts of avant-garde literature.

Apparently, around the instrumental knowledge used by business, the mainstream media, the education system, and the government, there is a periphery of other knowledge. Apparently, where the official knowledge validates itself by accounts which refer back to key sites, there are other accounts of what happened at these sites which do not agree. Apparently, underground poets were not simply reading The Times and academic journals every day.

The reason for choosing Counter Productions (reachable at PO Box 556, London SE5 0RL, UK) is that they are the closest thing to Compendium Books still existing. Compendium is now closed, but for thirty years was the most vital radical bookshop in London, and for most of that time the only shop which consented to stock a wide range of small press poetry. The experience of being in Compendium, recklessly flicking through the wonders of their stock, is what I am trying to re-create here. This kind of writing mushroomed in the 1960s, but study of the catalogue mentioned shows all kinds of work which goes back to the early twentieth, the nineteenth century (especially Decadence), or even to the eighteenth century.

Apparently the rejection of official wisdom creates a huge void, and the effort to fill this swirling fog with definite facts brings a special state of mind. I call it hyperassociative. The kind of knowledge this develops—teeming with new associations, speculative, critical of authority—is in grand contrast to the organised knowledge ratified by university courses and textbooks. It appeals to people who are psychologically loose—dissatisfied with their given social position, more excited by discovering the new than by acquired competences. The point here is not the validity of particular fragments of information but the startling contrast between two different states of the brain—hyperassociative (and unstable) versus cautious, submissive (and stable). The question is whether modern poetry can only be written by people in this state of looseness where they are breaking free of old and set associations, and forming new ones, all the time. This would incite us to study such counter-cultural knowledge as a necessary step towards the origins of this poetry even though this knowledge we want to acquire is itself substantial, testable, and not at all counter-cultural. This project would require us to gather alternative knowledge available at the times when poetry texts (that we are interested in) were being written—a simple exercise which rapidly reveals that maps of this influential material are unavailable. The thesis that the core of modern poetry is the Symbolist heritage, and the unifying factor is the surrender to hyperassociation, is elementary—but we need to gather a lot of raw material before we can even test it.

The hyperassociation thesis implies that creative individuals go at will into bewilderingly brief associational landscapes in which everything changes all the time. This programme of evanescent complexity offers devastating ammunition to anyone who wants to say that our knowledge of it is unsatisfactory. Obviously, we can't supply a recognisable and predictable pattern. Simultaneously, though, this notion offers us a way of describing amazingly disparate literary works with remarkably brief, pregnant, statements—even the phrase "loose joints" gets us a long way.

There was a moment in the 1930s when David Archer's Parton Street bookshop was publishing Barker and Dylan Thomas, and the most exciting young poets were hanging out in his bookshop. What I think this offers us is a glimpse of the febrile activity of the socially dissatisfied. Although specific claims of continuity from this hot-spot to the Counter-Culture cannot be made, I would claim that the state of feverish thought and dissatisfaction connects the two moments in its effects; and that this emotional state is the basis for effective modern poetry, with its free association and self-questioning. The formula was not politics but a combination of personal sexual dissatisfaction with a wish to project these problems onto the social order and to redesign that. We only become conscious of things which are unstable—the capacity to put the basic issues of human existence into words follows from a state of instability, which makes huge demands on the writer's energy but also endows the poem with that energy. Instability is productive—in the long run, it is likely to produce stability, a calm frame of mind which is, of course, incapable of producing the discontinuous and self-mutating artistic work which drew us here in the first place. People who search generally find what they want—and become the kind of intellectually conservative, law-abiding, stay at home culturati who produce the immensely numerous tedious books which incite us to revolt. This anticipates another point—immature and confused writers may be infinitely irritating and simply unbelievable. All the same, we are addicted to the work of the malcontent because a small percentage of it is both radical and intelligent, and we can't live without it.

I would like to offer, as a hypothesis, the idea that the avant-garde did not happen in Britain because weirdness, in this part of Europe, was too distracted by Protestant sects (and a kind of Protestant occultism), and blossomed in a neo-mythological form. This is an alternative to the theory that British artists were too firmly attached to their belief in property, the family, and Christian moral values. Another hypothesis is that the best modern poetry in Britain is quite rational—its leaders are actually quite contemptuous of the New Age/counter culture circus. The criticism of organised knowledge which fuels it is conducted on a rational basis. This would threaten the basic "everything is post-Symbolist" thesis.

The pendant to the thesis that official knowledge keeps the powerful in power is that irrational knowledge keeps cults in being and sustains the position of sect leaders with their semi-domestic, petty power. Everybody knows that the modern underground has shown a quite astonishing level of interest in the cults of the Roman Empire (following a comparison made by GRS Mead already in 1913). The reason for this may be a sociological parallel—the knowledge was produced by cult leaders as an organic function delivered to them by the emotional bonds of the cult. In fact, knowledge is part of group structure, and it comes back to life after 2,000 years because there is a group structure which offers it the right milieu.

Anyone can get from the counter-culture to the New Age movement. And it's not so hard to get back to the New Left, radicals with an ex-communist *carte blanche*, beatniks, and CND. But can we take a further leap, through passages not nailed down by lifestyle journalists and classic photographers, not caught by any TV camera, without publicity agents or clothes designers, and link CND back to the 1940s, to the *Peace News* which pacifists read while doing forestry work rather than fight Hitler, to back to the landers, anarchists of the Herbert Read vintage, personalist Christians, craft radicals in fungally assaulted cottages, Celtic nationalists, sellers of fugitive magazines, and to the readership of New Romantic poetry? I am not sanguine about the firmness of this path back, and as a sociologist I would point to the discontinuity inherent in a society based on the nuclear family: everything has to restart in every generation, there is no permanent household. I feel this is also why England takes so badly to the continuity of technical discussion and learning on which modernism is based; every generation starts from scratch. However, turning over the fragments of the past does show a few possible lines of continuity. If these are real, the great way of transmission would be the second hand bookshop, or, even better, the stall, where the dreams of the past are sold cheap to the dreamers of the present.

I offer, as a document of the era, extracts from Dave Cunliffe's "The Total Revolution: a Manifesto, Statement of Intent & Beyond", published in *poetmeat* (number 12, for Autumn, 1966), out of Blackburn, Lancashire:

∽

I see the Total revolution, at this moment in time, as a sustained assault, in depth at all levels, on the basic concepts & realities of technological society orientation. The real global anarchist impetus.

∽

I believe that technologically oriented societies are suicidal in that they germinate their own complex systems of self destruction. [ ... ] I am working for the destruction of machine society & would replace it by societies based upon universal love, peace & inner search, awakened awareness.
[ ... ] The sophisticated Western State Authoritarian Machine rules by a complex system of force & consent with censorship its root-tool. [ ... ] Establishments are using communication network control to create vast Brainwash Machines. That is by a subtle suppression & distortion of history, ideas, facts, news, opinions & events.
[ ... ] To fully destroy or weaken technological society we must fully engage it &, as far as possible, contract out of it. To defeat Brainwash machine systems we must develop an underground communications network(.)

∽

The true contemporary avant-garde poet's role is as shaman, prophet, priest, guru. [ ... ] I have no illusions about having a potential mass audience, valid large-scale two-way intercourse or vast reciprocal idea exchange at this stage of human growth & poetic awareness. Rather, presently seeing true avant-garde poetry as finely distilled communication for a small specialist audience. Only meaningfully involving that readership with a developed, receptive, open inner-ear.

∽

## Radical toxins and lingering hallucinogens: Counter-culture and New Age [227]

Some themes do seem familiar from the 1940s. For example, the idea of the war machine, involving both governments and machines themselves; the belief that wars are the product of psychological conflicts within individuals, advanced so clearly by Hendry in his essay in *The Crown and the Sickle* (and adapted as "the personal is political"); the rejection of discursive logic in favour of prophetic intuition; the belief that the poet has this intuition, can see eternity through introspection. The rejection of the (mass) media because of its link with propaganda also rings a bell. (Violent) history is a screen where the human psyche is expressed, yet is also a wrong expression of it. He believes in a group soul but is completely against the mass media. So maybe Cunliffe had spent time with people who were living archives of the 1940s. Or maybe he just read Kenneth Patchen, Henry Miller, Lawrence and Vedanta.

Let's take a closer look at one of the forties originals, in fact, at a prose-poem by Henry Treece, published in *The Crown and the Sickle*, called "To the Edge and Back". What struck me about this dream-poem is how it anticipates the acid trip: the poet goes into a trance state, sheds the trappings of space and time, goes back to the beginning of Time, sees a bird which was the beginning of life, worries about man's ethical destiny, has world history enacted inside his body, is taken by a shrouded figure to a place where secret things are seen, becomes at one with the archetypes, his eyes leave his body and fly over the City without him, he visits exotic (non-European) places, and wakes up exhausted. That is, the acid trip (with all that implies for the poetry of circa 1966–75) is an apocalyptic experience. You can see History without leaving your bedroom. The link between inner-body sensations and the real and extensive outside world has been much on people's minds since the addition of hallucinogenic drugs to the cuisine. I suspect the existence of a whole stratum of the psyche, delighting in such primal imagery, and fertile in it, which poets (generally) choose to switch off, believing its imagery to be crude, garish, and repetitive. It could well be true that it is relatively less personal than reflexive imagery, that is, everyone sees the same *primal* images; as well as being physiological in its imagery, because bodily sensations have there not been clearly separated from representations of ideas, or things outside the body. We might well compare it with the epics of Blake and with the "scrying" visions (recorded at such great length) of Edward Kelley, John Dee's medium, as well as with the imagery of rock lyricists and designers of album sleeves. The fact that poets of the 1940s composed by improvising, training to switch off the censor which asks for logical meaning, is also significant and may remind us of the 1960s and an improvised form of music, where songs emerged from long, ecstatic, "jams". The sensation of history penetrating his body, going inside it, is feverish, and yet it is just a pictorial account of a belief which many poets of the 1960s shared, namely that going deep inside themselves, beyond the plane of the conscious mind, brings them into contact with the truth of history. Almost, this might be the Prelude to *Crow*.

A further issue is, can we separate the "intellectual" poetry of the counter-culture (for example, the poets in *A Various Art, Floating Capital*, and *Conductors of Chaos*) from the psychedelic style which runs across all the arts, and which was the "native" or domestic style of the Counter-Culture? Can we equate "I fell across the plains of Tartary" ("To the Edge and Back", part 8) with the Inner Asia of Prynne's "Aristeas"? I suppose not. At one level, Sinclair's entire œuvre is a satire on the hippies and their anti-rational systems of thought. And, from most angles of approach, it's obvious that the poets in *A Various Art* were in conscious reaction against the hyperassociative, extravagant idealism which Cunliffe stood (and stands) for. They belong with a different strand of forties poetry, represented by Tiller, Madge, or Graham. But, if we put a mirror on the ceiling, we can see some threads that come from a different pattern. Sinclair is *tapping* the energy of those eloquent cultists throughout his work, in the same way as his favourite gangster films *tap* the violence of their criminal subjects, as captive heat. There are two poems by David Chaloner in that same issue of *poetmeat*, Cunliffe's own magazine. Ian Vine also appears, a sometime associate of John James in the Bristol poetry scene. There are poems by Chris Torrance and Lee Harwood—both later built into monumental volumes from Paladin, under the reign of Iain Sinclair. Torrance, a footsoldier who marched from beat to hippy to New Age, published a book with Ferry Press (and it had a favourable quote from Prynne on the cover). As we said before, four poets from *A Various Art* also appear in *Children of Albion*, a hippy's hip-flask. But I think we'd better stick to stylistic analysis; a poet and what he writes are in the same boat. Cunliffe went on from *poetmeat* to edit *Global Tapestry Journal*, which when last heard of in the late nineties was still going. One writer who doesn't seem to have influenced Cunliffe is Blake. The sixties arts world lived under the aegis of Blake, and poets, equally, all had to learn the lesson that imitating Blake doesn't work.

Somehow I "knew", already at an undated time, that small press poetry was linked with the New Left and the Counter-Culture. This was simultaneously first-person and inexplicitly transmitted knowledge; it was in the interpretative community of the poems (and I was in that community, and the poems were in the meanings of that community). Coming to a different linguistic regime, a book written as if for outsiders, where things have to be made explicit, gives me considerable problems, but I also don't want to prove, laboriously, something everyone knows.

One of the first things an outsider might ask is, given that both New Left and Counter-Culture burnt out or at least culminated in the 1970s, is it true that the poetic "underground" also culminated then, and that its energy ever since has derived either from the later careers of the original generation (transformed as individuals in a small-scale revolution that cannot be rolled back), or from poets faithfully following in their wake, heirs rather than revolutionaries? I don't have to answer this, since it falls outside the dates set for this book.

Other research questions: were there any "underground" poets who were not committed to the New Left? Can we draw a dividing line between anarchists and socialists? Given the rapid evolution of the New Left, as a community that debated and continually changed its ideas, can we connect changes in the poetry to changes in the shared ideology?

Speculative ideas must be tempted by the possibility of becoming practical reality, and so of taking on the values and language of politicians, of the actual power elite as opposed to the virtual ones. In the former dispensation, the Church looked after the sick and the poor (and schools): anyone who seeks spiritual authority is also interested in government, and this inevitably leads into business issues and business virtues; desks, files, budgets. As a civil servant, in 2001, in a part of the department which was closely geared to government policy statements, I was recommended to read Anthony Giddens as a source of the ideas which were animating government and, eventually, telling the department what to do. Giddens? but he used to be part of the New Left and is personally known to many of the Cambridge poets. His attempts to combine philosophy with sociology, dealing with the incomprehensibly complex surface of everyday reality, are not very far removed from that of the poetry recorded in AVA. Is the Third Way a crypto New Leftism? Or is it just the other way around—thirty years of getting jobs, and putting policies, even designs for courses, over with suspicious and conservative colleagues, have flushed all the radical toxins out of the system of the generation of sixty-eight. The finding of radical toxins lingering on in the waters of people who haven't got jobs, haven't had jobs, haven't been published, haven't been allowed to teach, seems to recover a fossil—something that didn't evolve. For me to define what Blair, Giddens, (or Prynne, or Denise Riley, or Iain Sinclair, or Tariq Ali) should be doing, would be overstepping my rights. No uncontroversial statement can be made defining what they sacrificed, what their "real" project is, what the compromises were and what the "core values". Summarising people's views on modern history would presuppose that we could summarise modern history.

Now, writing ideas that can become legislation (or, policy as laid down by directives to civil servants, etc.) demands certain qualities. You have to be serious, rational, and fair. It is possible, not only that underground poetry denied its links to psychedelia in order to appear fit to govern, but also that some creative writers forfeited their creativity in order to be sober and credible witnesses. The background here is one of casting doubt on the credibility of witnesses, something all barristers are expert in, and which we suspect most scholars are expert in too. If you want to write political poems, you want to be believed, and you want the poems to have a likeness with what is really out there. Suppose you write autobiographical poems. Suppose they are about a sexual relationship that goes wrong, where you present your behaviour in a favourable light. If the audience disbelieve your version of events, it is a very serious matter. Suppose you write about a relationship which goes well, and you were happy—they disbelieve this as well, and this has serious consequences too. If you want to write true autobiographical poems, then other poems based on play, fantasy, and fiction can be used to undermine your testimony.

Suppose the rule of academic discourse is you start out by disbelieving everything and build up patches of credibility from there. This is the most negative thing possible for poetry. It forbids everything. First-person, autobiographical, poetry cannot present evidence except first-person evidence. The reader must either admit this or not admit this. In the latter case, either the reader or the poet has to vacate the poem. To acquire credibility, you might exclude the imagination and intuition as sources of knowledge. This would seem to make it impossible to write good poetry—moreover, most of the very cultured people who can't write good poetry are, we think, inhibited by this acceptance. Bluntly: by accepting these two inner sources of truth you become a creative writer and have to accept that the Select Committee hearings will not call you.

Everyone would agree that the terms are these:
New Left
Pop culture

Hedonism & consumerism
Counter Culture
New Age movement
Shamanism & non-Christian religious apparatus
Irrationalism, intuition, personal myth
Identity politics e.g. feminism
New Right
Academic jobs
Depleted subjectivity and emptied communicative space
Mainstream poetry
privatisation
compromise
Blairism
Avant-garde
New Criticism and reasoning in poetry
Underground poetry

- but no two people would fit them together in the same way. There are two datings of the New Left. One is the wave of post-sixty-eight radicalism (which would have to include the Counter-Culture, New Age, etc.), another is the wave of intellectuals who left the Communist Party after Hungary (in 1956), generally supposed to be represented by the *New Left Review* (formed as a fusion of the *New Reasoner* and the *Universities and Left Review*). The problem here is that people who were in the Party in 1956 were Stalinists and by leaving they simply became Stalinists without a dictatorship. The newness of this "new Left" is not visible to me. The *New Reasoner* (edited by EP Thompson, from Hull) included quite a lot of poetry. I have examined some of this poetry rather carefully, and it is no good. It is Stalinist poetry: pompous, monumental, world-historical, and solemn. It was a whole bad decade for Left poetry, and Randall Swingler or EP Thompson, loyal to the 1930s, could not be influential in sixties poetry. The poetry of the underground cannot be attached to the first New Left. It must belong with the later current, which was interested in politics and depth psychology but rejected Marx and Freud as too rigid and counter-factual. The *New Left Review* eschewed poetry altogether.

English poetry was re-founded in the 1960s, especially from around 1966. There are few significant publications by new poets before this date. The new wave differed from its American models by being on the Left and differed from the pre-Budapest Left poetry by a whole battery of new attitudes and techniques. Everything important in the poetry of the 1960s and 1970s came from this package of differences from the standard Left poetry of the 1950s. However, if we unpack the package, we find it bears unmistakable resemblances to the traits of the psychedelic style. Briefly, we find an explosion in popular culture in 1966–67, then a political explosion in the universities in 1968, and then a take-off for poetry in 1969–70, with the publication of *The White Stones* and *Crow*. It is simplest to see these as phases of the same event (the pop world getting there first), and it is extremely difficult to see them as wholly unrelated. I know from in-group reactions to what I say that this link is very unpopular with the Cambridge poets. This is because they see it as invalidating their testimony. There is a background of infiltrating university life (against administrators who remembered the student revolts of 1968–73 and are keen not to employ anyone "unreliable"); of wanting to influence local or national government (against a background of witch-hunts, by the Labour Right, of the Labour Left); and wanting credibility in poetry when "hippies" or "psychedelics" were being identified with all kinds of nonsense. There is even a context of feminist critique of men for being irresponsible and hedonistic, leading to male poems being steady, serious, and boring.

The problem with being so very serious and sober is that your difference from the Movement vanishes. Winning this game makes you lose a row of other ones. Just as you win a war against a blitzkrieg army by intensive development of air power and tank warfare, so also the new wave of poetry gained some kind of academic standing by assimilating to the conservative, parsimonious bureaucrats of the old academy. Hedonism, the link with popular culture, the possibility of refounding culture on a new basis, the grasp of an overall lifestyle from which partial disciplines would flow, the love of play, conjecture, and improvisation—these fell by the wayside. The goal of the long march was abandoned.

We are still interested in the difference between alienated people and non-alienated ones. It does seem possible that the gap between impulse and fulfilment implied by rational study could account for the difference. If you believe in objectivity, this damages your powers of intuition, imagination, and impulse, so that they become feeble and don't work properly. Art is a park where these faculties recover, but in order to create art, you must first have undamaged emotional organs. Apocalyptic poetry was an attempt to develop intuition by forcing it to become dominant, by switching instrumental reason off. This was too violent to be good pedagogy, but still any art must open the sphere of imagination and intuition to some extent. Good poetry is all surrounded by a wrecking yard of bad poetry, and I think we are interested in asking why it's bad. This might, even, help to define reflexive poetry for us. It *was* like three-minute pop songs, where everything was perfectly timed and resolved. It was cool, something else prized in the sixties. It started from the realisation that it couldn't be like Blake.

If we look around for poetry which was less reflexive, which did let myth on board in a big way, we could mention the names of Martin Thom, Michael Haslam, Sinclair, Asa Benveniste, Peter Redgrove, among the successes. Perhaps we can shed light on the question by analysing a forgotten work—a forgotten classic, in my view—of the 1970s, in which the Counter Culture and the analytical intellect come close together. Martin Thom wrote:

> and have no shy
> nervous origin. Mirrors none
>     the map streaked
> with present joy. Jet, Iron
> Amber/ from the North in
> long trade across Mesopotamia
> delirious in no-home, days and
> weeks, a manic loop of assimilation
> writing these journals to hold time
> against all loss of shadow. A true
> night of pale registrations
> spread out coldly above
>     the nomadic line spilt through sand
> sinking in the impossible
> and no relief
>
> Blankets burnt at the Indus source
> far from any german sky-pole of the world
> raw with all change in nerve and loss
> of known quality
>     Until the moment breaks
> rain to earth, valley to range of hills
> rich off the dead structures they
> build terraces, splint earth with kindness
> and gather quiet and dark
> the quiet and the dark flower
> Persephone was
>     Not in cruelty. I do not live
> to rise from sleep to strike
> these birds of impossible design
> held by no poem to sing in ears
> sharpened to receive
> below the threshold, as in that unity

    spoken of in trance
        The bird-dancers
    all crazed in head and holy
    sick with images since thirteen years old, now rich
    in poetry and hidden chants
    whirling their iron dress, taking blood from the ear
    and waxy gold
                Now we are blue with the reflected coldness
    of strangeness affecting us.
                In night
    the glass of the world does not speak
    washed out to the image of the
    disappearing axe
    to every sign on these hills, and no call to

    and all tired herds sink in rain
    to ashen valleys, lie there
        to the left of your optic range
    sand sweet as grass, from red and blue cinnabar, rivalling
    the Linnaean geocracy
          bright with dew and quick bees
        all light burning, not damned or lost
            in th'imagined breath
            to live in the flight of shy nervous origins
          loving their origin
    (FROM *The Bloodshed the Shaking House*; DATED 1974, PUBLISHED
                                                                                  1977)

The passage evokes the shamanism of Inner Asia—an ecstatic, irrational, practice, associated with wild dancing and repetitive drumming. The theme is also nomadism, used by these poets to get away from rootedness and its mental consequences and the equivalent in poetry of cosmic flight in rock. The realm of anthropology was coded at that time to switch on thoughts about the function of social institutions, the possibility of changing them. The relaxation of rational boundaries acts to release impulses—both Freud and anthropology are used as windows on a hidden inner self of metaphors, analogies, wishes, fantasies, and pictures. The self dissolves its contracts with the outside world and finds a way of grasping what *reason* is. This unbearably rich formal world reminds us of the undisciplined sonic world opened up by the "free" guitar solo. It is spontaneous, improvised, led by affect, constantly shifting. This is why I find it hard to paraphrase—just as Sheila Whiteley found freestyle guitar passages hard to transcribe. Reducing it to order damages something integral and perpetually moving. The attachment of anthropological and Freudian imagery serves as a "frame opener" to key the kind of free association we are supposed to carry out while reading the poem. It is there as a window, opened through convention to show our inner selves: *Now we are blue with the reflected coldness/of strangeness affecting us.* This is really the opposite of didactic writing, although it is very erudite and rich in ideas. We have to mention Deleuze and Guattari, because they also wrote about nomadism, and because Thom's later career was as a translator of French psychoanalytical works — he was probably very early in reading avant-garde psychoanalysis, such as Guattari, in the early seventies. So the breakthrough in connecting free association, vagrant thoughts, with nomadic wandering, may already come from *Traité du nomadisme comme machine de guerre*. But it may come from *The English Intelligencer* circa 1966. *delirious in no-home* is really a metaphor for wildness and freedom, for the boundless expanses which the new poetry is going to gallop over; the jumps between personal experience in the now and the deep time of the ethnographical descriptions evoke this wildness and are the match of psychedelic disorientation. There is also a theory of Indo-European origins (a phase before the Saxon identity) among South Russian nomads, which has lost most of its credibility over the last sixty years. The material of the poem is like soft sand, fit to record the finest ripples of the medium passing over it, passive to autosuggestion. Poetry sited boundlessness in the free reaches of Inner Asian space (or, the North Atlantic, or, the prairies of the north-western USA) rather than in space beyond the earth's atmosphere or under the ground. Yet the dry air and flat horizons make the stars perilously close: *A true /night of pale registrations/spread out coldly above /the nomadic line.* The "icy waters underground", of "Astronomy Domine", the first track on the first Pink Floyd album, (so close to *blue with the reflected coldness of strangeness*) bear a puzzling resemblance to the imagery of Northern icy waters in *Malcolm Mooney's Land* and Hendry's *Marimarusa*. The ocean was evidently chosen as the expression of "lifting" of the body image into the boundless and weightless, which relates to 1940s radical use of the body as the source of all imagery.

I think we are entitled to think of some other anthropologically based works of the period — *Crow, Where the Arrow Falls* by David Wevill, *Filibustering in Samsara* by Tom Lowenstein, *Aristeas: in Seven Years*. Why was Thom not included in *A Various Art*? this is still a subject of debate.

## Apocalyptic foreglow, and origins of the Counter-Culture

the white horseman starts with a big juicy quote from Lawrence's *Apocalypse*, and the essay material in it is a direct continuation of this first text (which is, actually, a commentary on the last book of the Bible). Lawrence's irrationalist critique does not lend itself to clear explanation — the strips I follow can't really give an overall impression of the universe he moved in (which itself was much vaster than the explicit content of his books). The first salient point is what Aldington remarks in his preface to the *Apocalypse*-work, that there are some closely related works from very much the same time — *The Man who Died* and *Etruscan Places*. The second point, a rather exciting one this time, is the case Martin Green makes, in two books, that Lawrence's culture-critical work was very much influenced by his wife, by the radical libertarian Otto Gross, and by the milieu she came from, which was the "counter-cultural" colony at Ascona, in Switzerland (near the Italian border). The point was first made by Bertrand Russell: "Lawrence, though most people did not realise it, was his wife's mouthpiece. He had the eloquence, but she had the ideas". This means that we can get past Lawrence's isolation within the English-speaking world and find sources for his thought (? unthinking) in the German-speaking world. (A German focus can mislead, since the colony included Swiss-Germans and quite a few "ethnic Germans" — Rudolf Laban, a German-speaker from Hungary, and the Transylvanian Gusto Gräser, are examples.) It follows that the ancestry of the Apocalyptic school may be in that rich and heady mixture of ideas which animated the unofficial culture of Central Europe before the First World War. Ascona, a natural Paradise, home of a Theosophist colony from around 1889, a realm of cheap land because the vine-louse had destroyed the vineyards years before, was a *Schwabingsfiliale*, an out-station of Schwabing, the Bohemian quarter of Munich—a kind of clearing-house for visionary exiles. Harald Szeemann describes the radical (possibly, radically wrong) ideas as "anarchism; theosophy; life reform; anthroposophy; free land; free money; agrarian reform; the social utopia; the myths of the Youth, the Mother, the Old Wise Man; the reform of body, mind, and spirit; the reform of the arts (.)" The disciples were known to the locals as *ballabiott* or "naked dancers", and lived on a mountain near Ascona christened, after a mountain in a mediaeval romance, Monte di Verità—the mountain of truth, and this gave Green the title of his book. (Also the title of the German collection, *Der Berg der Wahrheit*.) The subtitle of his book goes on to label Ascona as where "the counter-culture begins", and I think Green is quite right about this. What we are looking at in Ascona is not only the milieu of ideas which produced Jung (Otto Gross being the classic example here), but also the one which produced Lawrence's most radical ideas because he was married to Frieda von Richthofen. The apocalyptics were the direct heirs of late Lawrence, the New Age poets of the seventies were the direct heirs of Carl Gustav Jung, but the overall conceptual space in which these ideas blossomed was perhaps the same and was perhaps not produced or owned by either of those prolifically writing individuals.

Something else Green tells us which has wide resonances within poetry of the last fifty years is about the Eranos group for the study of the history of religion, which met in Ascona right from its foundation in 1933. It was organised by Olga Froebe-Kapteyn, and the themes— "ancient sun-cults and the symbolism of light in Gnosticism and in early Christianity", "Man and the mythical world", "Man and energy", "man and earth"—are clearly inspired by the world of Asconan mysticism, besotted with the sun and energy. It was a mighty means of publicity for writers like Jung and Eliade and was one of the primary sources by which their ideas reached an English-speaking public. That is because the people who read the originals then wrote New Age foundation texts producing thousands of credulous works which reached a vast audience in Britain (and America). The Eranos books did not reach a wide audience directly but they were widely quoted. What we seem to see here is the neo-religious currents which had flowed so richly in Theosophy, in Yeats, Lawrence, Graves, etc., being re-normalised by a compulsory passage through Jung, and then starting to diversify again. It is impossible to draft an overview of the New Age movement—its dimensions are too vast. Further, a survey of para-religious currents flowing in the 1940s or 1950s is not something I am equipped to carry out—the links between Eranos, Eliade's shamanism studies, and the New Age are quite palpable but that does not mean that they were the only links between (roughly) the Symbolist revaluation of religion, the Occult Revival, and the culture of the 1960s.

Just as the Green strand of the New Age has clear links with the Back to the Land movement, so the globalisation of culture demanded by cultural managers today has clear roots in the opening of Protestant theology to non-Christian traditions (which we can associate especially with Rudolf Otto and Paul Tillich). It is also related to the documentary treatment of "picturesque peoples of the Empire" which was such a feature of High Imperialism, and which took so many forms in the second half of the nineteenth century, being a main preoccupation of European cultural figures (and, yes, cultural managers) for a whole century. One of the magazines which James Keery recommends as continuing the New Romantic impulse into the 1950s is *Nimbus* (1949–58), which was founded by Green and Tristram Hull. Now, the official translator of Jung into English was RFC Hull, who I believe was this Hull's father. One of the non-poetic essays in *Nimbus* is an account by Mircea Eliade of the Eranos gathering. Now, one of the things Eliade (populariser of shaman lore in the English-speaking world) reveals is that the Eranos was founded by Rudolf Otto. Otto was the author of *The Idea of the Holy (Die Idee des Heiligen)* and one of the most distinguished Protestant theologians of the century. Something which one could almost fail to notice in his masterpiece, distracted by the beauty of its language, is that he puts non-Christian religions on the same level as Christian ones, writing a kind of phenomenology of the holy. He was a Sanskrit scholar, and founded a museum for the history of religions, at Marburg, which had a worldwide perspective. The Eranos had a pro-Jungian stance at certain moments and its yearbooks provided intellectual material for the Jungian expansion into comparative mythology. We should not be surprised to find that this non-Christian movement was an offshoot of an intellectual current within the Christian Church, just as comparative religion in general was an offshoot of Old Testament studies, as more and more related texts turned up in the subsoil of the Near East. We can see multiculturalism as a phase of radical Protestant thought, moving away from the institutions and towards inner intuitions as the direct persuasive utterance of the Holy Ghost, which goes back to eighteenth century missionary activity. Multiculturalism in poetry has to be compared with the "Sea of Faith" movement within the Anglican Church, starting in the 1980s and associated notably with Don

Cupitt and David Hart, apparently dredging out of Anglicanism everything specifically Christian, to reach a depth theology, formless but building all forms: no holiness which is not a ghost. As Hart suggests, there are linguistic universals because the Holy Ghost does not need to use words. The belief that the New Testament contains a mythological element, which is bound in time, and a doctrinal element, which is firm and constant, preoccupied twentieth century Protestantism and as a by-blow made the mythology of other regions acceptable because non-binding. This agony of emptying out and vaporisation is something all poets have to undergo to enter the promised deculturated world, a kenosis in kind.

The Apocalypse of Lawrence has a great deal about the living cosmos (as opposed to the mechanistic, dead, one) and about the sun as a living thing. Rejecting a split between an outside world and an internal, psychological one, Lawrence thus pushes the subjective world out as far as the orbit of the sun and sets aside the real world. This is a vitalist universe animated with life force as living creatures seem to be animated by their life. This is urged by the Vitalist philosophy of Hans Driesch. In the physical world, it corresponds to the sun worship of the colonists at Ascona. They sought as much sunshine as possible. In medical terms, it is related to the treatment of tuberculosis — in the days when no antibiotics were available. Lawrence in fact spent much of his life in sunny climes because this was supposed to delay the day when he succumbed to his own TB. Geographically, Switzerland had made a good thing of sanatoria where the sick of Europe (the well-off sick, probably) were supposed to benefit from clean air and the rays of the sun while recovering from TB, nervous disorders, or whatever else. It may be that the cult of beach sunbathing, such a feature of the 1960s, was a replacement in Europe for sunbathing on mountains. The beach holiday would be an example of a mass leisure activity taking over from what had been an underground, religious, even cultic practice — the sunbathing of Ascona.

There is a metaphorical link between the vital flow which filled the whole great sphere between the sun and the surface of the earth, in vitalist thinking, and the idea of the soil as a living organ, which gave rise to biodynamism, fear of chemical fertiliser, and the organic farming movement. This is an aspect of fear of the object-machine which the Apocalyptics didn't get into (with one exception) but which shows us a much wider movement which shared the metaphors of the Apocalyptic and, partly, their attachment to Lawrence. However tiny the fraction of the population which shared the metaphor, it was consistent to wear textiles woven by hand, eat food grown without artificial fertiliser, and to write poetry not using knowledge which didn't come from sense experience (or from inner intuitions). Their aesthetic was closely related to the Back to the Land movement and in general to opinions which were against large corporations, centralised government, and bulk trade.

Were the 1930s all audenesque, or was there a tendril of lawrentian pupils? Candidates are Richard Aldington, Lawrence Durrell, FR Leavis, Glyn Jones, Joseph Macleod, and (Henry) Rolf Gardiner. Gardiner is the joker in the pack — an eccentric, right-wing, landowner, with intuitive sympathies with Nazism, a dislike of the "object-machine", and an amazing range of Anglo-Saxon/ arts and crafts/ ruralist prejudices, which he promoted vigorously through societies with very small memberships. Gardiner appears in virtually every book I read about the thirties — he is a favourite with historians because he was so florid and so strange. These qualities were not unrelated to his remoteness from power and lack of allies. Tanya Harrod, Anna Bramwell, James Webb, and Georgina Boyes have all written interestingly about Gardiner. He was a star Morris-dancer who sincerely tried to solve the problems of the world economy from the perspective which Morris-dancing allowed.

Joseph Macleod (1903–84) wrote *Foray of Centaurs* (1931, rewritten 1935), a book-length poem about vital energy (especially sexual), represented by the part-animal centaurs, and England, as a land sterilised by the machine and by the repression of sexual energies, which is brought to the brink of revolution by the Centaurs' foray. The plot is lawrentian, the idea is related to his many animal poems, but the stylistic and mythical detailing is elaborate and amazing. Macleod's chief poetic influences were Lawrence and Aldington. *Foray of Centaurs* was turned down by Eliot and today still exists as a typescript (in the National Library of Scotland).

It seems hard to get from Lawrence to a finicky and sanctimonious, basically frustrated, crank like Leavis, yet the Cambridge don defined himself as a disciple and publiciser of Lawrence — he had the Lawrence franchise. It doesn't seem possible to get from Leavis to the New Romantics. Yet the social wing of *Scrutiny* unmistakably partook of the resistance to the machine which Treece and Hendry summed up with their object-machine doctrine. Georgina Boyes cites a little-known 1933 *Scrutiny* article by Adrian Bell (a farmer and writer of books on farming, *Silver Leys* etc.), "English tradition and idiom", in which the whole pro-craftsman, back to the land, doctrine is trotted out. Francis Mulhern's classic *The Moment of Scrutiny* had already explained, with great clarity, the attachment of the magazine to George Bourne and to the world of the village craftsman which he extolled.

I don't even think Lawrence Durrell was influenced by DH Lawrence, yet he adopted the post of Sex Guru, a niche which Lawrence had invented. Durrell's poetry is forgotten today, yet his prose work mediated the typical sixties writerly pose of being an expert on sex whose whole grasp of human affairs was altered by this wisdom, which readers could acquire dollops of by buying his books. Perhaps the link is that Durrell was a close friend of Henry Miller, who was vitally influenced by Lawrence. Miller was a kind of living guru for *Phoenix* magazine, from upper New York State, a totally pro-Lawrence magazine.

I end up with the comment—almost an admission of failure—that Lawrence was remarkably uninfluential on English poetry although in the sixties he was omnipresent. Further, unfortunately—Rolf Gardiner was the closest, of all these stubborn and cranky figures, to the Apocalyptics.

### Digging for a New England

A certain issue of *Horizon* (no.56, August 1944) has an ad opposite the Contents page for books on "the Land and Farming" from Faber. The full-page ad lists forty-four titles. I suspect that they were making more money out of this than they were from publishing George Barker and Lynette Roberts. After reading Bramwell's careful tracing of intellectual and institutional links, we recognise, with a frisson of pedantic virtue, that the Earl of Portsmouth was the same man as the Lord Lymington who was an early inspiration of organic farming and got rather too close to the German figures—Darré, Hess, etc.—who were doing so much to make it thrive on the soil of the Reich. So what actually are (in the subtitle of Lymington's book) "the links between soil, family, and community"? The words *blood and soil* spring to mind here. Another book in their list is *The Life of the Soil*, by Lady Eve Balfour, an early star of the Soil Association and someone who saw it through to the 1960s—and the arrival of a new wave of smallholding weirdos.

We learn from WHG Armytage's book on Utopias (*Heavens Below. Utopias in England 1560–1960*) that the imagery of the Apocalypse was present in the thought of Utopians from the very first. This is an almost unbearably rich book. Just one flash from it is that the earliest Utopians dressed in undyed wool and got this from monks (who were still around at that time). The image of so many twentieth century commune-livers rushes to mind and now the hippies, Arts and Craftsniks, etc., briefly seem like monk wannabes. The phrase about "a new heaven and a new earth" inspired so many people to break themselves out of the old society without dying first. Armytage shows Lawrence telling Middleton Murry the land near Zennor where he planned to set up their commune was "a new heaven and a new earth"—when he wrote about Apocalypse, it wasn't looking forward to something, he was looking back at his own aspirations of around 1914-15. The "phoenix" image was about a new society rising from the ashes of an old England which was "dead". Armytage also discloses the existence of a large-scale movement of pacifists towards smallholdings and communes in the late thirties—he tells us there were several hundred of these. Max Plowman of the Peace Pledge Union was the most prominent spokesman for them. A series of metaphors supported this withdrawal into the small scale. Moving onto the land permitted someone to pull out of the state, while acquiring a community of face to face relations to replace the abstract (and corrupt) relations. It permits a similar pull-out from the exchange economy—no more commerce, you eat your own produce. A complex symbolic structure can be dismantled and destroyed. It is logical for an Apocalyptic poet to be into farming based on compost produced on the farm itself without buying chemical fertiliser. Smallholdings were "moral man, immoral society" at the level of food. The new England was there to be dug for.

Maybe we should see the invention of the monastery as the first utopian withdrawal also set off by wars, economic collapse, and a loss of belief in the state. Not just rough clothes but also the smallholding and the withdrawal from the exchange economy.

The rush of Faber books on the soil had perfectly simple motives—the system of international trade had not exactly collapsed, but it had ceased to carry ample amounts of food to the individual. In the middle of a world war, transport was largely withdrawn from the individual and from the consumer economy. People produced food in order to eat it. Self-sufficiency was a watchword of the 1940s even for people who wanted nothing to do with anarchy or communes.

## Prophets and archetypes

Norman Lewis, in his autobiography *I Came, I Saw*, describes the career of his father as spirit medium and a foremost member of the Spiritualist Church in Enfield. He tells us that, in the 1920s, one of the most popular groups of spirit guides were Red Indians. This mass movement is the forerunner of the "shaman" fad, and the helpful Red Indians are the forerunners of the fad for Third World spirituality. I believe there is a bookshop in Brighton which deals exclusively with Red Indian spirituality.

I don't know when Raine was converted to Spiritualism, but when she wrote her poem "The Invocation", she may have witnessed ecstatic and vocal trances, and connected these with poetic inspiration—the "gift of Apollo". One of the transformations in long time has been from the apocalyptor of the 1940s to the initiate imbued with shamanistic knowledge, popular in the 1960s, to the New Age poet involved with shamanism filtered through Jungian archetypes. This shared representation involves two strands, one of annexing Third World, non-Western, culture, and one of psychotherapy (which can appear in quite a different form, taking in science as a way of dealing with the irrational). The 1950s stereotype of the Outsider, incapable of following social imperatives, in a scenario of "moral man—immoral society", opened out onto a passionate interest in the motives for action which did not involve social imitation, compromise, or public argument: that is, dreams, intuition, aesthetic compulsions, the irrational, madness.

Jungian ideas have influenced Edwin Muir, Kathleen Raine, Ted Hughes, Peter Redgrove, Penelope Shuttle, David Black, Michael Haslam, Maggie O'Sullivan, Tom Lowenstein, Norman Jope, Vittoria Vaughan, David Harsent, and Elisabeth Bletsoe, amongst others. One could write an entire book about the effects of these ideas on poetry. All these poets fulfil the Apocalyptic idea of writing personal myth, yet it is doubtful that any of the recent ones were influenced by the 1940s period. (Raine, obviously, *was* a forties poet.) It would be difficult, looking at this list, to claim that the idea of writing personal myth was not a great idea and greatly fertile. Yet, amid all the difficulties of tracing influence, no one would claim that they got this idea from the New Romantics. Of course, there are many candidates besides Jung and his disciples—the New Criticism persistently announced myth as the tenor of the highest achievements in poetry.

When did Jungian poetry start? I am unable to uncover the history of the Jungian movement in Britain. A very early mention is a line in *Life Quest* which talks sarcastically of "being analysed by Dr Jung"—in 1935, then.
The Jungian doctrine does find eternal human values inside the individual psyche, does see history as the realisation of internal drives, does value the eternal and archetypal above the time-bound and documentary, and does see myth as central to modern art. All of this would be a good description of Apocalyptic writing, so to draw an equation between the two is not unnatural. The thesis that jungian poetry in the 1960s or

1970s absorbs and continues the imperatives giving rise to Apocalyptic poetry is also not unnatural or far-fetched. So I think the topic of interest shifts to other questions: was there a continuity from the forties, or did the "new mythic poetry" start anew, guided by the prose of Jungian doctrine? If this doctrine was strong enough to sweep up the survivals of New Romanticism (as indeed it seems to me), what were the transitional phenomena, and what was happening during the 1950s? what are the stepping-stones along the way, and what tangible cultural productions can we point to? Finally, what is the aesthetic merit of this current?

## Insecurity about myth

I believe that there was an amount of panic among mid-century poets about the inability to write myth, and that this was triggered by particular passages in books by authoritative critics, where they place "mythic" writing above other kinds and sternly point to failings of modern writers to live up to this ideal. This was just one panic among others in a writer's life, but it was successful because no one really put up a defence saying that, on the contrary, secularised poetry was more effective. It seems that the movement of the fifties which disparaged mythical writing also had an "inferiority thesis", a generalised belief that contemporary poetry was inferior and that this was too deep a problem to be solved by heroic measures by individual poets.

One has to separate the various types of myth used in literature: Classical myth; Christian myth; material from Third World mythology; personal myth invented by the writer and projected out into a public space of co-operative readers. The crisis can be said to start with the collapse of the first two types as codes for producing new literary texts; as a generalisation, the accepted outcome was a kind of poem which synthesised numbers 3 and 4, but which was only available to a certain section of the poetry world. The Apocalyptics were trying to develop a synthesis of numbers 2 and 4, with Personalism as the form of Christianity which explained their needs to them.

We can take it that the Christian faction were as aware as anybody else of the general decline of Christian cultural productivity since the early eighteenth century. The accompanying sense of anxiety created a lot of loose energy within the Christian camp. For want of counter-measures, the pain could be eased by an intellectual self-description, via a theory about a general decline of cultural creativity after an age of creative myth-making whose end could be placed in the fifth century B.C., the first century A.D., or the third century A.D. A trope of the necessity of myth was generously used by Christian critics to disqualify anything secular from being really great poetry. It also expressed a psychological threat to poets who could no longer write in passionately Christian terms. A counter-measure was to analyse the forces which had prevented, and were preventing, mythical thought, and puzzle out how to muffle them. One response to Bultmann's project (from 1915 on?) of demythologising Christianity is to retrieve and exalt the idea of Myth as a fundamental category of human language—beyond testing. For example, in the volume of debate about Bultmann which came out translated into English in 1960, Thielicke outlines such a revaluation of myth. Myth is so fundamental to the New Testament that this self-limiting of reason is always a likely path to follow when the pressure of comparing the Gospels with other Near Eastern myths, and of the ebbing of belief in miracles as a general category of event, put the Gospels in peril. Perhaps the line of prophets has never stopped. Mostly they are classified as simulators or schizophrenics.

Bultmann's point is that the myth of the New Testament is not specifically Christian, because it is borrowed from a common stock of Gnostic and Jewish-eschatological themes. God's use of the common vocabulary of south-west Asian myth suggests how He went to work—by thriftily sampling groups of signs which already existed. This takes us close to the core of the way Apocalypse works. There is something circus-like about the way God as author uses these animals as symbols in the vision He broadcast to John. Does God spend his time designing mythical animals, as He once designed the species of real animals? It seems as if He recycled commonly available parazoology in the same way that He used the human, local languages Greek and Hebrew to make His transcendent thoughts known to humans. The problem Bultmann identified is that although we cannot accept that the animals of Apocalypse are physically real, 3D creatures who ate and excreted, once we start rejecting the literal reality of parts of Scripture, we need concerted rules to tell us where to stop.

Christian exegesis aimed at people in northern Europe, in the mid-twentieth century, seems directed to use myths and emblematic actions, even animals, drawn from the collective store of that time and region. The scheme of the Apocalypse is not to teach beasts the use of reason but to use beasts as a language. Its symbols of divine history are closed within the boundaries of an animal's pelt. This is parallel to the falling or plunging of truth into the physiological bag or pelt of a human form, the horizon which closes around the organs of reason, tying them to neural channels of flesh. This is a preparation for the arrival of individual experience as the subject of art. The Apocalyptic poet is physically embedded in darkness and hopes by its light to make out a divine sign. Time, and the body, are dense matter which carry knowledge as well as blocking its rays out.

This debate within the Christian camp produces a "failure model" for secular writers who are stimulated by it to find their own mythical creativity. Hughes would be the most significant example of this, and his hesitations on a path towards autonomous myth show how difficult it was for less headstrong and gifted poets. He had to travel a long distance before writing *Crow* even if it was a step prefigured in his decision to study anthropology at Cambridge, twenty years before. The recourse to Jung may have been simply a step along a long path which began with dissatisfaction with 1950s Christianity—perhaps with an attempt to write Christian poems, in a way which did not succeed.

As the liberal line of theology drained out the divine and converged with secular thought, it stimulated to unnatural heights the energies of a supernaturalist current of theology, re-valorising the mythologically creative traditions within the Protestant world. This went hand in hand with a rediscovery of the political radicalism within the Protestant vision. There was within the Protestant ambit, although on its edges, a sector of mythical creativity which generously overflowed the supposed limits of the Age of Myth: Boehme, Swedenborg, Blake. All this is the background to the emergence of Blake into the mass market—why in the 1960s everyone tried to write poetry like Blake (and everyone failed). Blake's accounts of British antiquity were a great influence on the Sacred Geometry school: the great structures they uncovered were the physical setting for the myths of remote Albion and the gigantic, magically creative, creatures he conjured up there. His attack on Newtonian physics was an indicator of the kind of results they expected to harvest from the proper study of sacred geometries. The history of the poetic reception of Blake in the twentieth century probably peaked with the Apocalyptics, but runs on and on. Lawrence's failure to write prose visions (the frighteningly loony *Fantasia of the Unconscious*) was premonitory of a whole generation of Blakean hippies.

We can now gather some results about the development of Apocalyptic ideas during the adjournment of say 1950 to 1968. The developments occurred largely outside poetry, or the poetic evidence is of low artistic quality. They occurred within the speech communities of psychotherapy, Spiritualism and other fringe religions, and within the world of the Anglicans—the sector of it most affected by longing for the supernatural and "mythical". The key "opening" is probably the reception of Blake, and

Kathleen Raine's study of Blake (*Blake and the Tradition*) is a key text of the interim. Other key texts would include the publications of Eliade and Corbin, the *Eranos Jahrbuch* in general, and the authorised translation of Jung's works. Works by G Wilson Knight, and RILKO's *Britain. A Study in Patterns*, are also relevant. *Honest to God* (Bishop John Robinson's 1963 work) represents the climax of a Bultmannian wave which carried with it very wide sectors of Anglican opinion.

I mentioned Symbolism and the Occult Revival earlier on in what may have been a rather tantalising remark. In the late nineteenth century, art was seeing its territory under threat from science and religion. That is, most artists had liberated themselves from formal religion and didn't want to have priests supervising their imagination. As for the people who still believed in Christian doctrine, they were also becoming more original and were less and less happy at interference from the rigid central core of official religion. The reaction against science was called Symbolism, which developed pretty well all possible lines of resistance to the claims of science to describe inner psychological events accurately and completely.

It was accompanied by a movement called The Occult Revival, which was perhaps the attempt to seize the power of religion for artists (among other people), and face off the threat from the other direction. This has been less publicised than the symbolist revolt (acknowledged to be the basis for twentieth century art), less mentioned in the textbooks we were all brought up on, but was nonetheless integral to Symbolism as a process. James Webb's *The Occult Underground* is the great synthesis of all themes of this Occult Revival (a phrase he coined). Albert Hauser dates the advent of bourgeois subjectivism to the 1840s, and it is the era of art we are still living in. It offered a model of artistic greatness which was incompatible with obedience to organised religion. Consequently, every decade since then has seen a wave of "spontaneous" and personalised religious breakaways led by people who esteem their own subjective insights. We are helped to understand cult processes in the 1960s, or even in 2003, by going right back to the beginning of the era or even to Blake.

The religious currents of the twentieth century do seem very reminiscent of the nineteenth century, if you pay attention to such things at all. If the New Romantics remind us of the 1960s, this does not prove a transmission of cultural-genetic material. For, the NR critique of mediated and systematised knowledge hardly added very much to the ideas worked out, all over Europe, during the Symbolist era. Further, the ideas on myth, prophecy, etc., which they favoured, were present throughout the Symbolist inheritance, which you could find virtually everywhere, in any large stock of cultural objects. Sitwell and Robert Duncan, both active in the 1940s, had recourse to Symbolist techniques to which they had a direct link. Duncan grew up in a Theosophist household which had an immense store of Occult Revival books and ideas. (Indeed, we hear that Northern California had a whole tradition of occultist radicalism, from which Kenneth Rexroth and Harry Smith are familiar names.) Jung, of course, owned the same books. Jung was a collecting-basin for a vast amount of late-Symbolist anti-scientific thought. His doctrines were really a rewrite of themes from the Occult Revival, with some from the Symbolist milieu.

Works by Richard Noll (*Jung, the Aryan Christ*), Nicholas Goodrick-Clarke (*Occult Roots of Nazism*), Richard Griffiths (*The Reactionary Revolution*) and Richard Hamann and Jost Hermand, (*Stilkunst um 1900*) supply us with a great deal of very illuminating information on those times.

The core of the Symbolist critique of science is rapidly shifting mental associations. It is quite reasonable to say that science has not yet produced an account of these, and that they are important to the way human beings are. Poetry which does not use, or stimulate, these, might as well be prose and has little to fight with science about. Just as the arrival of photography pushed painting towards expression and subjectivity, so the irresistible spread of scientific description pushed poetry towards a range of techniques—basically, free verse plus the Symbolist heritage—favouring the personal, the fleeting, the fantasized, and the exceptional. Beside the intensely personal, this motive also favoured conjectural politics, thinking about events that couldn't be observed because they hadn't happened. Even though Britain had, all through this century, a democratic system with political rights for its citizens, the inner rules of art favoured writing which was outside conventional politics—very much like France under the Second Empire, where most aspects of modern art were invented. Huge sectors of French society were alienated, in that period, from the monarch, the government, and the cultural institutions they sponsored. Britain had no revolutionary art then because it had no (or, almost no) revolutionary politics. Hardly less obviously, modernity was always at risk, in Britain and during the twentieth century, because of the shallowness of the milieu which was wholly alienated from official institutions and available to explore new worlds of form and feeling. When we write the history of modern art (not, that is, the history of cinema, TV, detective novels, etc.), we have to develop the skills of political historians—even, of students of fringe politics. Expertise we may share with the detectives of Special Branch. The New Romantics cannot be understood without the anarchist and pacifist background even though no one has deigned to study it in this perspective.

## Temenos as a refuge for poets and ideas of the 1940s

The magazine *Temenos* (1981-92) was edited by Kathleen Raine, Keith Critchlow, and Philip Sherrard. It was succeeded by the *Temenos Academy Journal*. It was a successor to *Light, a Journal of Psychic Studies*, which Raine edited in the 1950s; and was an imitation of the *Eranos Jahrbuch*. The primary meaning of temenos is a royal estate, or the property of a temple, but a secondary meaning is sacred enclosure.

*Temenos* 1 includes poems or articles by David Gascoyne, Vernon Watkins, and Kathleen Raine, and issue 2 includes Peter Russell and David Jones as well, while invoking Herbert Read as a key forerunner. Clearly this is a reunion of forties poets, and an understanding of the later fate of the New Romantic aesthetic has to start with the study of *Temenos*.

During the time between 1945 and 1981, there were essential changes in the body of ideas to which Raine subscribed. One cannot map *Temenos* directly onto *Poetry London* or *Transformation*, for example Raine's ideas of the 1940s were distinctive to her, however rich the overlaps with other mythical and neo-Romantic thinkers of the period. This field was changed by the interventions of such a great scholar as Mircea Eliade, for example, even if it has passed through periods of torpor and disillusion, of blocked progress and an embittered loyalty to experiences which had faded and proved unrepeatable.

1. sacred geometry and occultist archaeology
Temenos is an *occultist* magazine. This is rather clearly signalled in issue 1, if you struggle through the rather tedious prose outbursts and look at the connections they point to. Raine boasts that the publisher is Watkins—set up to publish the works of Theosophy, an occultist movement. Raine bravely claims to belong to the New Age and draws collaborators from this supernaturalist movement. The appearance of an article by Janette Jackson, one of the officers of RILKO (the research into lost knowledge organisation), allows us to draw, again, a series of connections. The *RILKO Journal* is another magazine influencing *Temenos*, and *Temenos* claimed to own a stock of lost knowledge. Keith Critchlow was deeply into this form of architectural study and moved

from collaborating with John Michell at RILKO to co-editing *Temenos*. There has for a long time been a tradition of crackpot archaeology, running in parallel (and in loops) with the evidence-based tradition associated with the universities and with the Department of Works (now English Heritage), and carefully kept separate from it by the use of legitimation, review, and citation. RILKO recovered the crackpot tradition and surrendered to it. Jackson's article heavily cites RA Schwaller de Lubicz (Far Right occultist and "Egyptologist", husband of Issa Schwaller de Lubicz, who was reviewed in *Light* in the 1950s), and Frederick Bligh Bond. If we take the trouble to consult Bond's works in the British Library, we see that much of them consists of automatic writing, dictated to him by the Spirits, and that his method of investigating Glastonbury Abbey was to receive automatic dictation from a fourteenth century monk, who gave him the low-down. These clues make matters fairly plain—*Temenos* is based on the same doctrines as *Light*, and when Raine uses code-words their real interpretation is to be sought in Spiritualist and Neoplatonist doctrines.

The esoteric study of buildings of the past goes back ultimately to the speculations of Charles Piazzi Smyth (following John Taylor) about the dimensions of the Great Pyramid (1864), if not to certain elements in freemasonry, but was mainly fed, I think, by the Occult Revival. The forerunners (listed for example in the bibliography of Paul Screeton's *Quicksilver Heritage*) seem often to have had an interest in Theosophy or the Spiritualist Church. Sacred geometry uncovers, in trances or trips, an unreal world of energies, invisibly a local field of the geometries linking the stars to the earth in a Neoplatonic world-view, which carefully constructed buildings gather, focus, and guide. The ancients had "the ability to fuse cosmic and terrestrial energy through such instruments as Stonehenge, thus ensuring that a strong flow of 'Life Force' be directed wherever it was needed". (*Britain, a study in patterns*, p.55) I have been unable to find out much about the origins and dates of RILKO, but the ideas they studied are now familiar through the writings of one of their number, John Michell. Bob Devereux and the *Ley-Hunter's Journal* also deserve mention. Again, the most memorable literary expression of these ideas is in the works of Iain Sinclair. The revival of interest in ley-lines in the early 1960s was because of their supposed links with flying saucers. There has been a tendency to fuse "sacred geometry" with Situationist psychogeography. Critchlow is currently head of research at the Prince of Wales' Institute of Architecture.

The description of ideal forms reminds us of G Wilson Knight's iconographic work in *The Starlit Dome*, tracing recurrent and "ideal" geometrical forms in the poetry of the Romantics. "Musical buildings" is the phrase he uses. This is closely related to the ideal bodily forms of imagined and apparitional figures in the same poets. The popularity of such visions in the 1960s is not exactly unrelated to the use of psychedelic drugs; visual hallucinations do tend to follow a small vocabulary of form-constants (tunnels, spirals, cobwebs, and honeycombs), identified by Heinrich Klüver in the 1920s and related by recent research to convection patterns. The state of poetic hypersuggestibility is analogous to a similar state produced by partaking of laboratory chemicals. There is a further step whereby the size of someone's visionary power is the size of their artistic gift. This is the thesis of *Temenos*. If we look at the illustrations to Freimark's *Mediumistische Kunst* (art produced by people in mediumistic trances), we see obvious similarities to New Age art. For example, we see the "paisley" patterns, and scenes of contact with higher beings, or heavenly scenes. Some of these artists liked to draw in the dark as part of the automatic process.

2. Living universe

One of the preoccupations of Ascona was the living force of the sun, which became one of the key themes of Lawrence's *Apocalypse* and *Fantasia of the Unconscious*. The belief that inner feelings can be projected as myth was based on this understanding of the cosmos as a living thing, flowed through by currents of energy. The Eranos volume on the Sun Cult was an immense exploration of this theme. Kathleen Raine's poetry is preoccupied with the stars as the sources of influences which control human destiny. As a text on the jacket of one of her books says, her poems are often like a crystal in a crystalline universe, with strict geometrical axes reaching from us to the stars, conducting the most significant forces. It is hard to work out the role of the sun in this—it should surely dominate the scene, as by far the nearest star. If we concede that the sun is a star, we can align the Neoplatonic system (adopted by Raine) with the sun-cult of the Asconans.

One of the classic forms of psychedelic music was space rock. Drugs released an "inner space", without boundaries, which was associated with outer space because the Apollo Mission was flooding the media with awesome photographs of space, or from space. It is interesting to map the expanses of The Pink Floyd's "Astronomy Domine" or "Interstellar Overdrive" onto the astral channels of Kathleen Raine's *The Hollow Hill*, published a couple of years before. Psychedelic Britain floated into a topology which already existed, at least in viral form.

Iain Sinclair's *Lud Heat* has at its core, or close to its core, Stan Brakhage's film "Dog Star Man". This he links to the Egyptian architectural forms of Nicholas Hawksmoor's East End churches via the Dog Star Sirius, whose reappearance over the horizon in July allowed priests to predict the floods of the Nile and so to invent agriculture, in Egypt. This theory takes us back to Grafton Elliot Smith and to his preoccupation with vital energies, as taken up by Richard Aldington in *Life Quest*. Aldington was Lawrence's biographer, and this is the continuation of the lawrentian vein. Lud heat is a pun on blood heat and relates to a Swedenborgian way of healing, in which the energies of the sun, as the life force of the universe, burn out the flecks of illness. Egypt was the home of a sun cult, and *Children of the Sun*, the work of Elliot Smith's follower, W J Perry, refers to this. Harold Massingham, the chief among many writers on "the countryside" of mid-century Britain, adopted Perry's theories and spread diffusionist ideas to a generation of ill-informed writers on British antiquity. A key experience in Sinclair's poem is sunstroke, seen as a source of uncontrollable visions, and the link of a human brain to solar energies. Here again, the omnipresence of the sun is the gateway to a mythical universe. *Lud Heat* is also based on Brakhage's autopsy film; Elliot Smith, as a medical officer in Egypt, dissected many mummies, determined the cause of their deaths, and became fascinated by their amulets and elixirs.

In this vision of rays of light carrying the urgent forces of the universe fits, perhaps, the preoccupation of the Ferry/Grosseteste School with the quality of light. This is one of the most common tropes in *A Various Art*—something which helps to identify the group. It typifies the group to have light impinge with a controlled, discreet, aestheticised quality, in contrast to the violent and unpredictable solar surges envisaged by Lawrence. This suits, perhaps, a damp and oceanic climate.

(Brakhage's great film features a dog, a star (the Sun), and a man (Stan), and is called "Dog Star Man" for this reason.)

3. mundus imaginalis
At a certain point in *Temenos*, both Raine and Jeremy Reed refer to the imaginal world. This is a translation of mundus imaginalis, a phrase dear to Henry Corbin, and used by him to translate an Arabic phrase which refers to the visible and sensuous world of images, those which are apprehensible to our carnal senses but also reflect the world of the eternal and sublime Forms. I have to emphasise the value of Corbin— Raine, Michell, Critchlow, Blavatsky, Jung, Prince Charles, are

lightweights or worse than that. Corbin was a scholar of great learning with a philosophically trained mind. His work is very close to inexhaustible. *Temenos* was inspired by the wish to produce writing like Corbin's and nurture art justified by his ideas. Vain hope! Another idea he discussed is ta'wil, a Sufi method of interpreting sacred texts which involves improvisation, leaps of logic, reading against the literal sense of words. Allen Fisher chose the word ta'wil as the name of a publishing venture. I guess he got this from Eric Mottram, who cites Corbin in his own poetry and wrote a long paper on Corbin.

It is too simple to say that Corbin was looking for traces of Gnosticism and Iranian-Zoroastrian mythology in the symbolic structures of Islamic mysticism. He was doing that, but only as part of a vast project of reading unpublished manuscripts and producing translations into Western languages. He was an enthusiast for heresy— for the inspired personal interpretation of canonical truths. He was a connoisseur of esoteric Protestant writing, and his grasp of the formal principles of Islamic mystical writing gave him a way of talking about Boehme, Blake and Swedenborg—as sailors in the mundus imaginalis. He also studied such forgotten figures as Valentin Weigel and FC Oetinger (the author of *Cinnabaris exul redux in Pharmacopolium*). Virtually every aspect of Corbin's writings produces staggeringly new ideas and directions. Virtually every aspect sheds light on those heretics and misreaders of the twentieth century, the poets of the underground.

# Peripheral nationalism and collective disloyalty

The Scottish poets didn't exactly greet the Second World War with a Union Jack draped round their chests. George Campbell Hay, after several months on the run from the authorities in the woods of Argyll, gave himself up and served in a non-combatant role as a stretcher bearer. Ian Hamilton Finlay, an art student for part of the war, spent the later part of it in a Pioneer battalion, doing forestry work, also as someone who declined to bear arms, as did Edwin Morgan, serving in the Ambulance Corps in the Middle East. The tale of WS Graham is shrouded in obscurity, but it has been suggested that he avoided conscription by changing his address so often that the board never caught up with him. Douglas Young sued the government for breaching the terms of the Act of Union by conscripting Scots to fight overseas, a right they had specifically renounced; his fight kept him out of the war. Norman MacCaig refused to bear arms.

One of the unanswered questions is why the New Romantic movement was so big in Scotland and Wales. When we look at the organisation of *A New Romantic Anthology* (1949), with its separate sections devoted to Scotland, Wales, and Ireland, we are bound to look ahead to the revival of peripheral nationalism in the 1960s and the new devolution of the British poetic imperium. Most of the activity was Romantic, not apocalyptic, but we can't set aside the latter, because it was so dominated by Dylan Thomas, and because its two chief ideologues were Welsh and Scottish. In fact, the contact between GS Fraser and Nicholas Moore at Aberdeen University seems to have been influential in its development. It is simplest to account for Peripheral Romanticism in terms of a core periphery model, where processes in a cultural "core" from 1920 on involved interest in science, a critical attitude towards one's emotions, reflexivity, detachment, preoccupation with ideas, and interest in theory. Literary milieux outside this core shared these developments to a much lesser extent, and the word "romanticism" is a rather vague label for the stylistic result, lush and slightly dated in comparison with the "core", but ideally suited to readers who are themselves not fashionable. My impression is that the "centre" meant certain privileged sites, and excluded, for example people in London or Oxford who weren't part of the universities or the literary circles. Taking a degree was a more charged event in those days. The spread of the new, detached aesthetic to a wide readership was very slow, and took place only because of the development of mass higher education, and so the processing of hundreds of thousands of pupils through Practical Criticism and the mysteries of Eliot. As always with in-groups, there are signs of other close groups which had much less favourable access to print and influential magazines. I suspect that the feelings among the concerned at the University College of Bangor, at Glasgow University, or at Edinburgh University, were very different from those in Oxford, Cambridge, and London.

Peripheral regions were more able to produce "romantic" poetry because the anti-myth factors hadn't permeated so deeply there; because the idea of the nation/community hadn't been so damaged by disagreement; because the past hadn't been rejected (in the name of a generational conflict confused with the imperative to modernise and compete). Poets were able to draw on (accepted) notions of Celticity to establish, on the symbolic plane, a continuity with the past.

One of the factors seems to have been the broad consensus against war. The pattern seems to have been that a peak of anti-war feeling was reached around 1932–35, but was swept away by the Spanish Civil War, which made fighting fashionable again, and incidentally made communism, a militarised ideology, popular too. This shift was the basis for the eminence of pro-war effort, realistic, morale-building cultural activity during the war: the intellectuals, hot with anti-fascism, were already rapidly coming closer to the government line in 1940. This shift of opinion was perhaps later, certainly much less powerful, in the periphery, where fashion is always less influential. The peak of pacifism was there still unlevelled in 1939, or even 1945. The New Romantics were *de facto* the anti-government wing, by symbolic extension therefore the anti-war wing; not all NRs were anti-war, but anarchists, pacifists, and peripheral nationalists were certainly numerous in the movement.

Clever analysts may well spot pacifism as an updated version of the Nonconformist conscience; in Wales, the Nonconformist conscience was the dominant cultural and political fact, and resistance to the State was far more likely to be based on the Gospels (with the English as the Romans) than on the classics of anarchism. Political radicalism was missing a libertarian streak and was firmly concerned with greater morality and more bonds of community discipline.

One exhausting byway which Scottish poetry took in the 1950s and 1960s was the struggle with folk culture. Someone unwilling to write conventional poetry might not be sustained by a critical mass of likeminded supporters — where the critical mass might be two or three — and so get sucked into folk culture, instead of creating something modern and real. Tom Scott never realised himself as a poet. There is an interesting account of his state of mind in the late 1930s in GS Fraser's memoirs, which show him insisting on song and rejecting written poetry (and modern poetry) altogether. The blurb here shows him discovering himself in 1953 — a story which, as a narrative type, generally means the opposite. He did write a good poem — "In Auld Sanct Andrian's", from a sequence called *Brand the Builder*, recalling, probably, the time around 1930, and his father. The reasons for promoting him are obscure and deeply dubious; sociologically, his friendship with Pound and belief in Social Credit, poetically, his anti-modernism and translation of "pure lyric" poets of earlier centuries, usable as a polemic against modern poets (who "can't write lyrics"), although in fact Scott couldn't write lyrics either.

Within the realm of Scottish song, by its nature enveloping and, partly, collective, we can seize a few moments. Joseph Macleod, in the early 1940s, produced radio programmes on Hebridean folksong. These must have borne a strong resemblance to his books of that decade, published as "Adam Drinan": he abandoned Modernism and converged on a Gaelic folksong ideal, with results that make his fans uneasy. Hamish Henderson, author of a great book, *Elegies for the Dead in Cyrenaica* (1947), abandoned writing poetry to become a folklorist, collecting songs from tinkers, among others, and founding a folklore institute. Ewan MacColl, in the 1950s, led a folksong revival, which provided much of the cultural agenda for the next fifteen years. The folk revival achieved a lot in terms of musical creation in a folk idiom, against which we have to offset the degradation of poetry by incompatible folk models. So, even though the song thing was busily devouring the potential of Scottish poetry, and preventing serious poetry from being written, and making people feel guilty about writing poetry to be printed rather than sung, it was stronger in Scotland than in some other countries (say, England), and it was growing in those years; there was the possibility of a culture which was not divided between professional artists and passive audience, between literate poets and pop culture.

A few exceptional poets did emerge in Scotland who were not distracted either by imperious traditions of folksong or by its updated form of pop poetry. DM Black, George Mackay Brown, and Walter Perrie are examples. As for the others, the trouble with writing in strictly conventional and selfless terms is that you add nothing to the verbal pool and are invisible in retrospect.

Goodsir Smith did write the most impressive new romantic volume. His later career was disappointing. His poetry was libertarian, and consciously about the lifestyle it sported, with a theatrical richness and rascality that don't always hit the mark. We can suggest a relationship R, such that:
Folksong: R neo-folksingers
Celtic myth: R Scottish poets

~

The folk themes weren't part of the daily life of the singers, who in the 1950s or 1960s were often art students or middle-class dropouts, habitués of coffee bars. We might suppose that R also obtained between British rock bands and the blues, or between Eng Lit teachers and the poetry they taught. While poetry was so intimidated by song, we have to consider what folksong achieved, for example in 1960s albums by the Pentangle, John Martyn, and the Incredible String Band. By about 1964, the musicians in the clubs certainly were writing songs about their own lives and associates. Pentangle (circa 1967–72) were a folk group, with three Scottish members. The concept was a supergroup, composed of individual stars, which would be able to make concert appearances and records, rather than being tied to tiny audiences in folk clubs. There are lots of good things to say about them, I would recommend their records to anyone, but they had critical weaknesses which lay bare the problems in the modern folk ideal. Pentangle show, simultaneously, the lack of a central intelligence exploring the new possibilities, and the problems of developing folk tradition without becoming experimental, and so relying on individual intelligence. Many of their best moments came from the jazz angle: they had a jazz bassist, from London, who made their sound unique, and it's fair to say that they all liked jazz. So it's hard to decide whether they were an avant-garde group using a folk music vocabulary, or guardians of folk tradition. Some of their most effective recordings were simple country and western songs, like "Sally go round the roses", beautiful but not arresting our attention because of their lack of complexity and originality. They always had problems finding a repertoire that demanded a quintet: they kept reverting to songs for guitar and voice, not really needing accompaniment. They were nervous about their own originality, nervous about emotional projection and sharing as opposed to musical delicacy, and often sounded impersonal. The two guitarists weren't especially good singers, although excellent songwriters. It didn't surprise anybody when they broke up. I think that listening to Pentangle's recordings (for example on the double CD, *Best of Pentangle*) sheds a great deal of light on the successes and failures of modern Scottish poets, always tempted by folk ideals and always finding these cold, inflexible, and resistant. There are inhibitions about being individualistic, a manner which feels greedy in an atmosphere dominated by sociable and collective forms.

The Incredible String Band (circa 1965–74) were the other standard bearer of Scottish folk, equally dissatisfied with a straightforwardly traditional sound and repertoire, equally informative about the problems of poetry, equally far from the rock/blues vocabulary. They were most famous for being hippies two years before anyone else, and for signing to big time American label Elektra. They produced at least fifteen albums, not all of which I've heard, with something like 200 songs. *Earthspan* and *No ruinous feud* were the ones I liked. It's simplest to describe them as people who read *The White Goddess* and accepted it as the model for songwriting; they spent their whole career stringing invented myths (or "fakelore", as someone described it, in the sleeve notes to CD compilation *Troubadours of British Folk*, vol.1) together, with an empty space around them which is either evocative or incongruous. They are quite close to Alan Davie's later work, with numerous religious symbols patched together in an ingenuous, infantile, noisy composition. I listened to them a lot in around 1973, but although I've got the tapes I don't recall ever listening to them since I left school in 1974. The crux is whether you regard the singers' timing as free (and expressive), or whether you feel it as words that don't scan properly and singers who have no feel for meter. I lost my ability to believe in them; the albums are glittering junkshop collages of textures, endlessly changing, but quite uninvolving, the patterns are too vague or disturbed for my brain to lock into them. This illuminates the problems of poets using the montage effect: having access to a good library, you have endless cognitive and verbal patterns available as sources, it's simple to snatch them, but when you lay them out on paper they can all fall apart again and re-occupy their native identity, unless you have some binding principle that makes them all sing in the same key. Eric Mottram is probably the poetic equivalent of the ISB, an endless chain of montages that don't hold water. Some of the peripheral members were actually quite good musicians. The way the voices are miked makes them recognisable as people, alongside very poor pitching, as if professionalism was impersonal and inauthentic. There's something warm about their inability to carry a tune. The ISB sum up multiculturalism, New Age, collage, antirationalism. They were very literary ("In the evening reading Swinburne/ eating mightily, with some false lust"). Their style in clothes was arresting: brightly coloured, bold peasant fabrics, non-European, hurled together with gay abandon. The sleeve notes to a CD of a live performance in Canada, in 1972 (I don't think you would want to listen to this, but the original LPs haven't been reissued!) talk about rock groups withdrawing into "virtuosic distance"—a pivotal comment; the Incredibles, however friendly, seem to have abolished the depth that allures us in music right along with the "distance" of careful technique. It also says "the song structures were breathtakingly innovative". Although they couldn't actually write songs, they made up for this by using dozens of "ethnic" instruments, permitting constantly shifting textures: mechanical surprise instead of organic thematic progression. We may well link this to a drugged state, where textures are so irresistible, or to the infantile receptivity you reach by rejecting "Western reason" and purposiveness. The characters in the songs are equally exotic and disconnected; the ISB were a folk group with almost no trace of Scottishness, using communal forms sampled from communities they didn't belong to. They took the format of an art student's pin-up board, with a rich mixture of images, captured and butted up against each other, and stuck with it. The opposition of "free association" versus "structure" was probably linked with ethical arguments of the time, with "tight" and "loose" having symbolic values about behaviour. The ISB's lack of song structure probably was a statement about "freedom", recognisable to their hippy audience. A lot of people then saw being eccentric, whimsical, pastoral, and disinclined to effort as the path out of industrial society. A recent article in *Mojo* ("The sons of the soil", David Kenan; June, 2002) discusses an avant-garde folk scene, happening in East Kilbride, Japan, and New York, which seems to draw its references from the ISB and from a *really* obscure seventies group, COB, which included Clive Palmer (who left the ISB after their first album, of 1966). The phrase is "bedroom folk", which refers to the quality of the recordings and to the intimate, unhardened nature of the music. So someone still listens to the ISB.

In Scotland, the separate existence of printed poetry, to be read in private, was much more fragile than in England. While identifying the folk revival as the greatest enemy of Scottish poetry, we have also had to discuss some parts of it, in the interests of fairness. We are quite entitled to set poems and the words of songs side by side, this pinpoints the advantages and disadvantages of printed poetry, and it doesn't discredit something excellent like "John Franklin" or "Light Flight". When we see Walter Perrie patching a scene from a Scottish forest into a poem set in the desert, with a Biblical city beside it, we are entitled to think of the Incredible String Band. Perrie's two ambitious, large-scale poems, with their use of montage to juxtapose incompatible streams of events and reveal startling new relationships, stand above the poetry around them and have been more or less written out of Scottish literary history. Perrie (1949–) published *Lamentation for the Children* in 1977 and *By Moon and Sun* in 1980. There are certain resemblances between *Lamentation* (named after a piece of bagpipe music) and S Goodsir Smith's book *Under the eildon-tree*. In the line of our adventure, we are entitled to ask if this radical montage is related to the yoking of incompatibles, the discontinuities, of Apocalyptic poetry; the whole montage method is creative rather than representational, exciting rather than documentary. It may represent certain Apocalyptic impulses but so transformed by better control and technical understanding that they belong to a different world.

Perrie's use of myth can be compared to the revival of Scottish folk culture. What is significant is how far he has transformed it, reconnected it.

Although nationalists disagreed with the bipartisan consensus at Westminster, and with mainstream English poetry, their concern with reaching a popular audience and with putting across preset political lessons inhibited them from any stylistic originality. To generalise, the revolution of the sixties affected the smaller nations as a revival of nationalism and as a return to folk forms, leaving little space for the artistic experiments which were so successful in England. The most emotionally charged topics were withdrawn from processes of critical thought. A coherent ideological attack on the English mainstream did eventually develop (with authors like Conran, Hooker, Crawford) in the seventies and eighties. Because the nationalists of the late 1930s had resisted the war effort, as a function of being anti-English, and because they had picked up the ideas of war protesters at that time, they were "living archives" of such ideas in the 1960s, and, for various reasons, they were still on the scene, not having been wiped off the map by coherent and factionally aggressive in-groups. These traditions of resistance to technology and monopoly capital flowed seamlessly on into the green concerns of the 1970s, spiced with New Age ideas which were attractive because they incorporated fantasies about the Celts which dated back to *The White Goddess*, if not to the 1890s and Celtic twilight moonshine. In such writing, a society run by a military aristocracy was often portrayed as an anarchist feminist one based on magic and herbal wisdom. Resistance to the State, the mass media, and the machine has, in this way, always been popular with Welsh writers. The enthusiasm for devolution seems to have declined quite rapidly, as is the way with political passions. The realities of administration are incompatible with poetic fervour.

# The 1970s and Left versus Right in the Labour Party

We have to imagine a scale of radicalism and a game in which one becomes a better poet simply by moving more notches down that scale, while simultaneously disabling the jeers of radicals who insult every poet who is too compromised. This quite imaginary spatial object sums up the game of British poetry as the pitch sums up the game of football, but actually, it is only one game among many.

The constitution of the poetry world excludes Conservatives; the literary world is aligned with the portions of the middle class which look after people's welfare and so are employed by the State. The opposition of Left and Right in poetry is therefore between right-wing Labour and groups which include Left Labour, with a leavening of anarchists and Marxists. Our political analysis has therefore to be precise enough to register the differences between these two groups, on which public elections shed no light. The opposition expresses itself in poetry as one between reality, familiarity, certainty, and inactivity, on one side; conjecture, improvisation, reasoning, new learning and new associations, on the other.

The revival of British poetry which began around 1960 was tied up with the political protest and disaffection, among a minority which included many students and many readers of poetry, which began with the upsurge of CND in the late 1950s and quietened down in the despondent years of the 1980s. A large segment of the small press poetry world would have allied with Tony Benn only as a *pis aller*, as a difficult liaison with a force far more earthbound and slow-moving than they; but Benn was rejected by the upper echelons of the Labour and Union movement as far too abstract, up in the air, and fast-moving for their notions. In the upshot, the electorate plumped for a reformed Tory party so far to the Right of Labour that Conservative MPs of the 1960s intake saw their policies as outright class war. This sums up, then, the political situation of the leading British poets over the last twenty years; with horror, paralysis, and self-compensation always at hand. The power-holders in business and politics lack a layer of cultural creators to express their beliefs and memorialise their power; and the cultural creators lack a society, or even an imaginable society, to be the ideal dimension of their art.

Imagine the feelings of the Right about the Left: they're more intelligent than you are; they're more idealistic than you are; they are less compromised than you are; they always show you up in arguments; your ideas are a diluted version of theirs; and they always lose you elections. This pattern was, however, constitutive for the modern history of poetry: the experimental and innovative poets were and are easily identifiable as ultra-Left, and this closed the possibility of them being introduced to the public by the Labour-Right populists who have controlled mainstream publishing, reviewing, the media, and the teaching of poetry in schools. The latter groups are aware of their inferiority and so what they admire is partly defined by the ideas-rich radical groups whom they fear. The typical pattern is the "public" reputation of Roy Fisher: thirty years of being ignored, then they discover he's a major poet; a pattern of fear. Fisher is an intellectual of anarchist sympathies. The anti-intellectual, liberal-centralist camp chooses its favourite terms of praise from among the stylistic values of the intellectual Left: terms like "explore" "dissonant" and "innovate" are used to mean their opposites, because they carry prestige and a cachet. If someone actually did explore in poetry (which means going into the unknown and trying out many variations) mainstream publishers would not take their work on and you would never hear of them.

The interest in redesigning the microstructures of the Labour Party, invisibly changing its very fabric so that it evades problems by mutating, is a reflection of the deadlock in the parliamentary party between Left and Right; itself a reflection of deadlock between larger antagonists, in fact between the socialist State and local and international capitalism. This long-term intra-Party struggle was locked in its present state by the hard-fought contest for the deputy leadership of the national party in 1981 between Tony Benn and Denis Healey. The collapse of communism in 1989 could not bring any new flavours that the inner-party election of 1981 had not brought, and the votes were cast in that way as the climax of a long train of events, dialogues, and analyses. The contest was between setting out to transform the whole of society and tailoring party policies to meet electoral convenience; the defeat of the Left seemed to draw a concluding line under the historic project of overthrowing capitalism, so that there was no national institution which was even promising to put society right, and individuals had either to acknowledge that social disasters were coherent with the social structure and never likely to be reformed, or to "freak out" and secede to a point so far out along the spectrum that it was nothing like practical politics; and was essentially similar to an acceptance of no change. It was the capacity of the human mind for conjecture, for devising wholly new social structures out of philosophising, and then to persuade others of their virtue, and realise them, which was at stake. The symbolic defeat of the Left in its best chance of getting to hold governmental power resonated through poetry in a dozen different ways; the habit of devising ideal solutions to problems has become less popular ever since. Much of early feminism, for example supposed that there would be an alternation in power; that Labour governments would follow Conservative, and that at the appointed hour a Left Labour government would replace a Right one, and this government would enact legislation which would irreversibly alter the foundations of society. No one really expects such sweeping changes to come from a Conservative or Liberal Democrat government, and the Right of the Labour Party had been on the offensive against the Left ever since, apparently without ever suffering an internal defeat. Because the drama of transformation was abandoned, it was the death of the future: that is, as the object of overall human plans, rather than as the aggregate of many corporate business plans, adapted on a yearly basis to the shifting state of markets, passively drifting along with the thermal noise of social swirls, without purposes except survival and self-aggrandisement.

In the intellectual turmoils of adolescence, human beings transform their anxieties about the future into ideals, plans for personal and social life, against which all events in private or public realms will be judged; anxiety becomes theorising, and ideals absorb detail, from experience and study, to become great masses of information, able to become books. The death of the future could hardly help affecting literature; if the great imaginative schemes were taken out of storerooms and burnt, writers had nothing significant to write about, and few would want their books. The sheer triviality of mainstream poetry can be understood as momentary distractions from a huge psychological void and despair. The exile of the Left (i.e. those who supported Benn for deputy leader and leader, and, outside the Labour Party, the anarchists or Marxists) swept up British experimental poetry, almost all of whose practitioners, publishers, and readers belonged to those fractions. The inside of their poetry mirrored an outside and that outside vanished from sight. They were more given to prophecy and imagination than to passive recording of past experiences, and the shape of the future altered to falsify their hopes. The autonomy of the intellect from the weight of the past came under attack, but if the intellect was no longer of importance, there was no point reading challenging and information-rich poems of ideas, since neither the writer's journeys into the unknown nor the reader's speculative response to them could make any difference. The portion of the speculative unknown comprised in the poetry book you are about to read deteriorated in exactly the same way as the future of society, as if it was made of the same stuff and prone to the same diseases; it became attractive not to read it.

The Benn-Healey contest did not create a new era on its own but rather made public, in contest, the perception of a wide group of people, frequently in touch with public opinion, that a new era had already arrived. The situation in the 1980s may remind us of the tension between Left and Right within Labour during the 1950s, a period of extreme polarisation and consequent "dirty tricks" (evoked by Stephen Dorril and Robin Ramsay in their book *Smear: Wilson and the Secret State*) which produced a rich mud of political invective probably remembered and recycled during the 1980s disputes.

The Labour Left were obviously superior on grounds such as originality, far-sightedness, intelligence, idealism, radicalism, knowledge of history, capacity to arouse intellectual excitement; but the fight was carried out in other terms: politologists agree (with certain nuances) that many voters within the swinging vote (i.e. the one which decides whether you win elections or not) marked Labour down for internal disagreements, for being impractical and idealistic, for extremism, and for not running the government well as a (capitalist) business. Consequently, the Right was able to gun down the Left in the name of winning general elections and so being allowed to form a government. Denouncing "internal party dissensions" has, for many years now, been a code-word for muzzling the Left and preventing policy discussion. Politology, in fact, makes it clear that, for the last half-century, victory at general elections has depended on appealing to the central ground because it is impossible to win a majority without it; so an urge to the Right is built into the Labour Party, or at least the parts which study voting analyses. This means competing with the Tories, and, since socialism is not centre politics, forming a set of good capitalist policies which please the IMF and the City of London.

Dorril and Ramsay's thorough book evokes the intra-Party situation around 1960:

∼

"The party leadership had been covertly working against the left for most of the decade, often in co-operation with the secret state. [ . . . ] 'What we didn't know at the time', Ian Mikardo recalls, 'was that our leaders were using the National Agent's department in Transport House and the Regional Organisers out in the country to compile MI5-type dossiers on us.' [ . . . ] 'They were', says Mikardo, 'an eye opener. [ . . . ] Not just press-cuttings, photographs and document-references but also notes by watchers and eavesdroppers, and all sorts of tittle-tattle.' He was convinced there was intelligence input, possibly from Joe Godson, the Labour Attaché at the American Embassy".

You will understand that similar documentation for the last fifteen years is not yet in the public domain; all the same, for many commentators the prowess of Kinnock and Blair as leaders has been gauged by how hard they bashed their own Left. Dorril and Ramsay remark that the Gaitskell-Wilson leadership contest of 1960 unleashed a stream of dirty tricks, and an atmosphere of self-righteous paranoia, from the party Right, which broke inhibitions that never returned. We should note this primitive upsurge of anti-Left paranoia and examine its bearing on the reception of the great innovative poetry of the 1960s. The 1964–70 Wilson administration was fraught from start to finish with Left-Right struggles even within the Cabinet; Wilson only attained the leadership because many people felt that he could hold the balance between two blocs far more powerful than him. Wilson won, on the second attempt; the changes in the arts in Britain in the 1960s are inseparable from the presence of a Labour government which was led by a (conditional) left-winger.

Relations between Right and Left in the Labour Party were polarised also by the problem of economic dependence on the USA; exchange rate crises forcing the government to seek support from the IMF and the USA (which could control IMF decisions, too) were all too predictable, and the Right were paranoid about far-left elements ruining their standing with policy makers in Washington and so knocking down their whole economic and foreign policy. Wilson's deal with Lyndon Johnson was one of the major lines of sustenance which brought the success of his 1964–70 administration about. Modern Labour is, we could say, courting the middle class to bring it electoral victory and courting Washington to protect the pound and the balance of payments. The approach of sacrificing domestic reforms to currying favour with Washington is known as Atlanticism. This does not map so easily onto poetry, where, in fact, control of US assets was vital to the public image of most groupings, from Christian neo-formalist to Objectivist. Although the US is the world centre of capitalism, its poets are mostly anti-militarist in foreign policy, liberal in domestic politics, anti-racist, and (today) feminist and pro-Green. Confusingly, a strong stream of radical politics (and of politicising poetics) has come from the USA, Cruise missiles or no Cruise missiles.

Let us return to the forces which voted against Benn in 1981; the landscape is the product of their ideology and they were more numerous. Since the involvement of the Right is quite peripheral, poetry as a business—the mainstream—has been shaped by these groups; the readership they appeal to is the voters who, politologists say, are scared of a socialist Labour government but happy with a capitalist Labour government; and their concerted attacks on the experimentalists draw on the attacks of the Labour Right on the radical Left led by Benn or Livingstone, on the feminists, and on the Trotskyists. An attack from the Right within the working-class movement resembles any other attack from the Right; as if being in that political tactical situation produces the same range of invective, for example attacks on innovation, on thinking, reading, on open intellectual debate, on radical change, on speculation, on pointing out that social problems exist, on trying to do something about them; on remarking that a difference exists between the rich and the poor; on pointing out the basis of social values in arbitrary shared fictions, which change from decade to decade. These subjects are taboo in mainstream poetry. If you are opposed to social change, even tactically, you become a conservative—even poetically.

In 1981, the Labour Party split: fourteen sitting right-wing MPs left to join a new centre party, the Social Democrats, and the eventual total was thirty. This (described in Ian Bradley's 1981 book *Breaking the Mould*) was an episode in a long struggle between Left and Right. The provocation for the treachery of this tiny right-wing action was proposed changes in the Party constitution which would have allowed a much broader participation by the mass membership in policy making: a radical extension of the political class which could have mobilised the population in the political process and changed the face of politics. This was terrifying to a certain kind of politician; the Left critique of the individual personality here coincides with a poetics which rejects the personality in favour of hundreds of self-controlled mechanisms which are more or less public and subject to historical change; the centring of poetry on a personality cult of the poet can be equated with the bourgeois self-regard of politicians for whom politics is the story of their personal image, and policy a facet of their exciting personalities. The Social Democratic rejection of socialism was masked by soft and never clearly articulated ideas about change at the grass roots, so that nothing would change except people's behaviour; a glimpse of changing the shape of politics by altering its microstructure, which appealed to all parties at this period. Their discourse about "grassroots" can only be understood as a move in a triangular game between three groups: right-wing professional Labour politicians; left-wing activist ward, district, and constituency Labour Party branches; and an electorate which far outnumbers the others. The latter group were, during the seventies, attempting to impose party discipline on MPs and councillors to keep them to a left-wing line, compensating for the unconscious pressures of leading a middle-class lifestyle, enjoying power, and associating with the ruling class. Invocation of the electorate was really an attempt to evade any kind of control from voters and to get away with a prosperous lifelong gallop towards the Right. It was an attempt to liberate professional politicians from the need to have and defend ideas; to grant them job security. This renunciation of ideas went along with a new system of political communication, in which the most pressing need was to get rid of ardent discussion and of the activist, with his incessant questions and high expectations.

Given the CIA's tradition of forming and funding breakaway right-wing unions and parties to enfeeble resolute left-wing ones, we are entitled to ask who really funded the SDP, and how far they checked their actions with American allies (or handlers?) before they committed themselves. The "grassroots" claim is ironic, since there was a strong Atlanticist streak in the SDP, and they felt their moderation consisted largely in not upsetting the American alliance; their advantage would have been that they were much more plausible supporters of nuclear bases on Britain, and of nuclear armaments, than the "old" Labour Party, which had a left-wing membership. Shedding the membership was the way to political freedom and patronage from Washington.

We can equate the Social Democrat platform of "radical change by doing nothing" to a poetics which defines itself as modern but keeps every single element of traditional poetry in place; the fantasy of altering and dissolving the microstructures was expressed, and achieved, by poets who interrogated the fabric of language and of the self which speaks. The shift towards live arts tended to replace intellectual contemplation with imperious if fuzzy group moods. Reading is inauthentic because you are alone; the disco is authentic because collective. I am not denouncing disco music when I say that poetry which imitates it can end up as completely unsatisfying, and that private reading has quite a distinguished record. *Everybody say yeah! and put your hands in the air.* In the 1960s, it was possible to believe that Pop poetry was the progressive line, and that the new way for literature was simply to shed more and more literariness and become naive, spontaneous, rather birdbrained, and live. This current has now reached huge proportions and the mainstream has been profoundly influenced by it; in fact, the difference between the typical bad poem of the 1990s and the typical bad poem of the 1950s is precisely the injection of Pop banality. The enemies of the Labour Left were in favour of simplifying the message.

There is only a slight shift between taking politics back to the community and simplifying ideas so that everyone can understand them; the withdrawal of belief from the political class as a superordinate group communicating mainly within its own ranks was widespread during the 1960s (not only in Britain), but this downward shift, failing to bring mass participatory democracy, could mean the destruction of the political message and the departure of the politics of ideas from the scene. Certain elements of political idealism may seem, in retrospect, to belong to the world of words (of rousing platform speeches, and of print) and to be absent from the mainly visual media, such as television, magazines, and posters, in which politicians now primarily communicate to the public. (Communication the other way is not audiovisual.) The (disastrous) 1983 general election was the last time that Labour fought a campaign through public meetings and long impassioned speeches; Michael Foot was a past master at that kind of thing (he was certainly very exciting at the meeting I went to in Wood Green) but showed up very poorly on television and in still photographs. The new attack on the voter involves selling candidates like soap powder (a media cliché which I will take as true); the monitoring of public response to (media) events is so close that it diminishes the role of principles and ideas: you can't change these in the second, third, and fourth weeks of the campaign. The media are so uninterested by anything except the party leader that the election is lost and won on what he says: centralisation is imposed by the media, not by the party constitution. The rapid responsiveness to shifts of public opinion can be seen as democracy: a move which infallibly casts systems of ideas as undemocratic. So much for intellectuals with complex entrained sets of ideas which are understood at first by only a few people. Shifts in the regime of political communication systems, the market in which public power is allocated and exchanged, bring on shifts in the communicative regime of poetry; however transmuted and with whatever time lag. The differential between the full-time activists and the mass of the population is thus diluted or done away with. This can be seen (and this is the populist belief) as the erosion of the privileges of an arrogant and closed body of unrepresentative, if highly educated, people, whose specialised discourse to each other prevents mass participation; it often accompanies community politics, with phrases about getting rid of government bureaucracy because communities will do it for themselves. To others, it seems like reducing party headquarters to an advertising agency. Image replaces principle and redefines it as old-fashioned. The market-response analysis examines only the swinging voters; the issue of giving a bad and dissatisfying service to the legions of Labour loyalists is ignored.

The opposition of Left and Right inside the Labour Party over the past forty years has generally been one of issues versus personalities and personal victories. The former looks at the record of structural changes, the latter at electoral victories, as the evidence of "success". The first reference to the influence of television coverage on elections, which I have been able to trace, is in Vance Packard's *The Status Seekers*, of 1959. The Old Master of committed popular sociology reported that political professionals were already aware that the (male) candidate had to be young and sexy (to attract the female vote), and that the camera tended to reduce the issues to personalities. The question of being responsive to the market, and the devaluation of ideas, principles, or experiments as egoistic, have played a central and damaging role in poetry. Populists claim that whatever sells more is not only more appealing but also less arrogant, morally superior, politically progressive, aesthetically advanced, and virtuous. Because I have chosen to write about and praise the poetry which I enjoy, I will be denounced for being academic, intellectual, and puritan; and simultaneously for being selfish and hedonistic. The central discourse about poetry praises things which the critic does not like, but which are seen as not being elitist, not partaking of the old middle-class culture, and so as democratic. The tradition whereby critics act as a balancing force to the pressures of the High Street, the lying wordflow of publishers, by applying personal standards of taste, has been set aside for the last thirty years because it is seen as a form of authority. I cannot fathom why collectivism should be set aside in economics and imposed in art, where it does not work, but the aesthetic reaction of an individual has been made insignificant—and poetry with it.

The poetic Right has wanted poems free of ideas, and poems which are confident, smooth, and comforting; it has found the model for both in the works of WH Auden, once he abandoned critical thought.

It would be singularly difficult to say, in my case as in anyone else's, whether one had chosen extremist politics as a consequence of liking speculative poetry, or rejected conventional poetry because of its political complacency and unfitness. Certainly, if you are going to write poetry which rejects every banal statement, then being politically critical is a handrail; your poems might seem eccentric and even snobbishly contemptuous without that quality. This is structurally a given: whereas many of the decisions of radical poetry, and even of radical politics, are arbitrary leaps which only after their installation become recognition signs useful in deflecting attacks. The interesting point is not where one rejects convention but where one has acquired enough of the conventional signs of unconventionality to deflect attack from the enragés.

# Decentralisation: the ideal of workers' control

New Labour ideas on popular participation are a reduced version of an unrealised political vision of an earlier time. In the sixties, everyone believed in spontaneity, freedom from preset structures, freedom from authority, levelling of barriers, removal of hierarchy. These ideas, important also to poetry, were held by many people whose grasp on the world of ideas was nebulous but at their point of origin they may have been precise, well worked out, and part of a coherent system.

### Autogestion

The excesses during the thirties of capitalism in its various forms of Fascism and mass poverty, and the collapse of Western states and armies in the face of Hitler, led to a mass entry by intellectuals into the Marxist ranks. The news about the internal violence and oppression of the Soviet system, however much slowed down by expert Leninist propaganda, was bound to make a considerable impact on this group of activists. The most coherent response addressed the abuse of power by taking economic control away from the Party: if the ownership of the means of production rested directly with the groups of workers immediately involved with them, rather than with a remote Ministry in Moscow, then the workers would be genuinely free. A theory of autogestion (self-management) was worked out by Cornelius Castoriadis (a member of a small Greek Trotskyist party, in France from the late 1940s), and Claude Lefort, editors of the magazine *Socialisme ou barbarie*; the Arguments group, with Edgar Morin and Henri Lefebvre, followed after 1956. The source must seem somewhat dubious: Trotsky was a follower of Lenin, who had murdered Russian democracy, and at least a million of his fellow-Russians, in the first place; and Lefebvre belonged to the Stalinist Partie Communiste Française (PCF). Castoriadis did not address the problem of Marxism as legitimating authority, something which automatically biased power-structures in favour of a minority of theorists and of those, however few, who believed in Marxism: making everyone else second-rate citizens. Moreover, the radical nature of Marxism has usually meant that its adherents had seized power by force, whether opposed by the majority or simply by the mercenaries of the ruling class, so that a distortion, with the losing side being deprived of civil rights, was built into the moment of birth of the new order. Still, autogestion provided a brilliant solution to the political problems of all blocs of Europe, Communist, liberal-capitalist, and Fascist (which would have included Greece at this time): it solved the problem of alienation and boredom at work by giving the ordinary worker a say on what happened, it removed the necessity for a superior élite by giving the power of decision to works councils, it made the concept of someone else owning the means of production meaningless, and it made the revolution irreversible by giving everyone a stake in it. Less explicitly, it allowed for the easing of disaffection, the political co-option process, to take place in the easiest way, by dealing face to face; the outvoted faction was unlikely to become completely alienated from people who worked alongside them and were even their relations and neighbours.

The ideas of autogestion are not totally disconnected from the practice of self-management (*radnicko samoupravlanje*, in Serbo-Croat), set up as a partly genuine practice in Yugoslavia from 1950, after Tito called off the disastrous attempt to install Soviet-style command structures. The version of this which reached the West sounded rather exciting; a theoretical justification was written by Edvard Kardelj in *Socialism and Democracy*. A more recent, post-Yugoslav, assessment, is in Noel Malcolm's *History of Bosnia*: "And the natural breeding-ground for all kinds of discontent is a weak and malfunctioning economy—something which was also guaranteed under the Yugoslav Communist system. Indeed, the malfunctioning grew steadily worse as a result of the decentralizing measures of the 1960 and 1970s, since there were now redundant duplications of industries and infrastructure projects between the republics. The very worst kind of competition is the sort which happens when the competitors are operating on politically arranged loans and subsidies..." None of this invalidates the principle, it merely points out that the initial imposition of arbitrary authority, fatally allowed to carry on for forty years, vitiated the principle of self-management by limiting its reach. Heroic guerrilla leaders from an epic era of mountain camps weren't the best choices as managers. Unfortunately, it was Tito's arbitrary power which allowed him to impose self-management on Yugoslavia, as nowhere else in Europe. "This system worked as an overlapping set of mediaeval dukedoms, with networks of influence and patronage extending outwards from these privileged individuals through all areas of life. At its most benign, like any system of patronage, it could give assistance to deserving individuals; but the whole system was intrinsically corrupt. It was also stagnating, as the generation which had fought in the war passed retirement age. [ . . . ] The disillusionment of ordinary Yugoslavs was almost universal. For many, this took the form of a withdrawal from any kind of political life".

Another system of mass democracy was the soviet system, flourishing from 1917 until perhaps 1920, under which the soldiers in each unit, or the peasants in each parish, had absolute power, and elected workers' and peasants' councils (Soviets) to represent them. Confusingly, the Bolsheviks kept the name but destroyed the power of these soviets altogether, giving all effective power to the Communist Party. Lenin couldn't do with the Soviets because so many ordinary people voted for parties other than the Bolsheviks, and because while he wanted to make war, it was inconvenient to have the railway workers spontaneously decide not to transport his army, as this didn't fit in with the interests and ideals of the railway workers. The Russian people would have benefited if the railway workers had been able to throttle the Civil War by refusing to transport armies around, and there would have been no war if Lenin hadn't insisted on reducing the citizens to slaves and ignoring the way they voted. Approximately ten times as many troops were engaged at all times in repressing peasant revolts as in fighting the White-monarchist armies; Lenin refused to pay them for their grain but requisitioned it on a basis of force. The peasants had launched their revolution and shared out the land; the self-management system was working very well for them; prohibiting the grain trade removed the benefits of this and reduced them to serfs. Given that the peasants were 70% of the population, it was a little unfortunate to alienate them right at the outset of the regime. Who was wrong, the peasants or Lenin?

Another relevant system is that of the Spanish Anarchists in the Spanish Civil War; Orwell records his bemusement at their units putting every offensive to the vote before carrying it out. In the exigencies of war, the leadership put through new rules establishing a traditional system of officers and central command. However, the columns set up radical democracy in all the villages they liberated, which is one reason why they didn't advance especially fast.

The closest autogestion came to realisation was in the plan drawn up by General de Gaulle and submitted to the judgement of the French electorate by referendum, in April 1969. This would have allowed far-reaching control of enterprises by the workers. The electorate said no, and de Gaulle resigned. He came from a strand of social Catholic politics which had never accepted capitalism as a legitimate social formation. Certainly he was animated by the wish to destroy Communism by competing with it, but it is still a matter of profound regret that the French people did not follow the path he devised.

As with most Utopian systems, it's the blemishes which don't appear in the original theory which cause all the problems and suffering in the live version of the system; you might as well say that British liberal capitalism works perfectly, and the unemployed are just a blemish—imperfections due to friction which slows down the perfect adaptation of the system. As for the distribution of resources between workers' collectives, the fairest way of doing this is to give consumers control and let them spend them with which suppliers they choose; prices being set by bargaining; giving us something remarkably like a market economy. I can't imagine how you can avoid co-operatives going bankrupt and their members becoming unemployed; a modern economy is not based on self-sufficient agriculture. If a coal mine runs out, what does it matter that the miners own it? If half a million people leave school in a given summer, why would the self-governing collectives want to take on half a million recruits at just that time? Would the Centre reduce the principle of local autonomy, or would there be "frictional" youth unemployment, as there is now? Rapid expansion when a collective makes a brilliant innovation (surely new ideas have to grow, don't they?) is an acute problem: capital must be brought in, and many new workers, no longer personally known to the "owners" of the collective, must be recruited. What are the lenders of investment capital except part-owners?

All the same, this principle still offers the possibility of revolutionising the Western social system from top to bottom. Our social organisation is still imprinted by a recent era when most of the population were illiterate, and had little idea what was happening outside their town or village. We have to stop talking about real politics at this point, but the impact of this idea on artists has been immeasurable.

The theories worked out in isolation by Castoriadis and Lefebvre (*Les Structures de la Vie Quotidienne*) in the 1950s became the basis for the politicised elements of the Counter-Culture in the late sixties. The history of ideas is rhizomatic and doesn't show up in photographs, and the protesters of May 1968, when you can check, were often unreconstructed

Leninists or else Catholic radicals whose dislike of the State had rather different roots. The verdict given by a large French retrospective on the May Events is that their chief effect was to weaken the Communist party —the Left became much more concerned with spontaneity and liberty. The Situationists identified revolution with festival, *la fête*—allowing everyone else to remark that the May Events were a street party, and not a revolution at all.

A society where there are irreconcilable differences of opinion will cease to function, but that is only the end point when all debate has failed, the uncertain point is how much energy should be poured into debate, in order to find the best solution and reconcile the maximum number of people. In such a debate, the structure of society becomes visible, and the verbal domain becomes filled with an unheard-of energy: these are ideal circumstances for poetry.

I have reproduced the discourse of the neo-Marxist theorists, which is cast in terms of "ownership of the means of production"; this marginalises everyone—the majority of adults—who is not engaged in paid employment, or in fact everyone in the parts of their lives which are outside paid work. This excludes housewives and the unemployed; another group is students. The theory of autogestion was expanded during the sixties to collectives of tenants on council estates, of students, of claimants, of patients, of citizens, and generally of any group using some facility which brought them into contact with an authority which owned it.

At the present moment, political activity is in the category of leisure, and the time which citizens devote to it is regulated like a fashion, like a form of amusement. The laws of the land allow for participatory democracy; Richard Rose calculated the potential number of "active participants in politics", some thirty years ago, as about 2.75 million; (*Politics in England Today*); it is surely more today, and considerable power has been transferred to school governors, for example. The problem is of uptake; still more, of many people feeling themselves not to be the kind of person who is able to speak and to have a say and to run public affairs. It's hard to get figures on something so diffuse as local democracy, but clearly things have changed a lot since the mid-sixties, and out-groups like women, immigrants, and the working class are now far more common on local councils, as school governors, and as JPs, for example. Where there is no uptake from the citizen body, functions have to be devolved onto paid officials; the claim to represent a missing citizens' will can hardly be valid, and the delegated will can only be a kind of extrusion of the intelligence, animating a kind of Golem, clumsy and surly, at one end, and emptying out the intelligence of the originator, at the other end. I think all political fractions agree that spontaneous popular action is the best, and that only exceptional social functions can be run by paid bureaucrats, and then in an unsatisfactory way.

Autogestion was the political theory most favoured by the radical poets who emerged after 1968, and which most affected their style, for example in the use of indeterminacy, and in the critique of the immediate wishes and representations of the self.

Situationism didn't seem like a very English thing. The British radicals who fell in with Situationist ideas wanted to say goodbye to their personal pasts and didn't even want to normalise the new ideas by linking them with the radicalism of every generation, and I suppose the radical weariness of every generation in its decline. But if it all vanishes when you sober up, it wasn't even there in the first place, or it wasn't a thing that would hold you in its hands. So maybe it's worth looking at the Situationist International in the 1950s: the main man is Asger Jorn (1914–73), an abstract Expressionist painter, a Dane, a theorist of culture and the primitive. As chronology would suggest, he reached maturity and full voice in the 1940s: a problematic time for Denmark, as you can figure out. He was a complex man and a great painter, but there is a clear line in his work which has to do with intuition: that is, it belongs with the New Romantics, something that was happening here, which drew on DH Lawrence who was also happening here. The thing that goes right through Jorn's painting is the explosion of subjective space, the seizure of the canvas by a drama of the pulses inside the body, without scale and without detachment; this is a guide to Apocalyptic poetry, an illustration of it. Jorn was interested in primitive art, in a way quite usual for intellectuals in the countries which missed both Rome and the Renaissance; the great goal for someone like him was to re-learn the subjective quality of art (like Scandinavian pagan and folk art) which had never studied perspective or worried about proportion. What happens if you take this dissolution of knowledge and apply it to the language used in poetry? You get New Romanticism. Putting many autonomous individuals together would give a polycentric society.

In 1946, Jorn was fascinated by a teeming figure (*myldrande* in Danish) which appears in Islamic art and whose focusless nature he identified with a view of society with no centre of authority, and which he saw as the basis for his own abstract expressionist art, where line triumphs over figure and meaning is everywhere. The section, in Andersen's biography (volume 1, p.137), is titled "The Persian interlace and Scandinavian art"; Jorn found links with surface-filling, teeming, work in Scandinavia. This does give us a link between the forties and the sixties: we can associate this visual pattern with no centre and no resolution with the political model of a decentralised society built around autogestion, and with the polysemous and decentralised style in sixties poetry. Situationism is the link and was founded by Jorn. The modern poetry of the late sixties is not an exposition of an idea formed by philosophers; it is an associatively enriched area in which meaning flows in every direction. The space of Jorn's canvases is like the eye, sensitive all over: by being without objects, they open a space where there is nothing but our body-images; by being endless patterns, they offer no anatomy and threaten to drown our body-image.

By turning the canvas over to subjectivity, Jorn was suggesting frustration with the opportunities offered by the real social order; he was urging a far greater spiritual energy, a greater demand: the loss of disciplines and boundary lines of all sorts. When the Apocalyptics were abolishing the outside world, it's impossible they weren't attacking the system of political and property power as well. Why don't we know this? Because of a selective and centrally controlled memory, the same defective organ which has now forgotten the great poetry of the 1960s and 1970s.

The phrase I have translated as interlace is *ranke*, literally a vine. If you consider the greedy spreading of a wild vine, one not trained up sticks, you will notice that it resembles the underground spreading of a rhizome, as used by Felix Guattari as a symbol of decentralised teeming. It is like English *growing rank*. A vine has no central stem or main axis. The same figure is also discussed by Strzygowski, who calls it *das Muster ohne Ende* (the endless pattern). He associates it with the landscape patterns in certain Central Asian (Buddhist) cave paintings, which he claims are based on it: it gives an impression of complexity. It is a variant on the interlace, and bears a strong resemblance to the interlaces of Celtic manuscript decoration (which were clearly borrowed from further east). Drawing analogies between barbaric decorative art and abstract expressionism of the 1940s must be done with caution, because the intellectual presuppositions are entirely different, and the complexity of the geometry may produce a false resemblance (i.e. we associate what is too complex for us to read and what is non-figurative) simply because we cannot read the designs concerned. Personally, I am convinced there are resemblances between abstract expressionism and the barbarian art of the Animal Style, and that we can think about Jackson Pollock when looking at the endless interlaces of barbarian metalwork or manuscript decoration. Both represent an interest in soul above realism. Both, perhaps, deal with the world as something moving, rather than with the constant shape of something (when it is standing still).

Undeniably there is a connection between these teeming organic forms and fertility magic. We may well wonder about the dialectical relationship between the interlaces, magical depictions, and the later abstract quality of Islamic art. The Animal Style corresponds on the ideological plane to animism and its original home is on the steppes, or the steppe-forest zone, where people lived by animal husbandry and relied to a great extent on hunting.

## Non-hierarchical decisions

If we accept the metaphor of knowledge as property, knowledge distorts group decisions by engrossing purchasing power. Equity could only be achieved if everyone had equal purchasing power, and so could influence decisions equally. The project of giving everyone equal access to the decision-making process threw up a number of difficulties. The problem of decisions, taken in the past, disappearing from view because of habituation, and being untouchable, is one to which the non-explanatory styles of the sixties insistently draw attention. Something else which derives from the past is the expectations of the participants, on which they rationally base their calculations of policy; someone who has been excluded from the political process all their lives, or who belongs to a group which has for centuries been excluded from the political process, may not express their opinion, because they do not expect it to be listened to. If you put people in a meeting, it is unlikely that they will each talk for exactly the same amount of time. More cogently, people may not even turn up to the meetings. The study of what persuades people to speak or remain silent has been formalised to some extent; attention has been paid to so-called frame markers which label a situation and induce people to invoke a set of rules for behaving within it. For example, at the end of a formal meeting, there is a "frame marker" which marks the edge of a frame in which speech was constrained by rather precise rules; in the next semantic frame, information is certainly still being exchanged, as the meeting breaks up, but it is addressed within small groups, and may be of a social rather than an official nature. Usually, these frame markers are inexplicit, the rules governing speech within a semantic frame are inexplicit, and the construction of such rules is arbitrary and subjective. Much has been made, in the past thirty years or so, of attempts to bring new groups into the political process by positive encouragement of them. When someone says "The atmosphere discouraged me from speaking", it is usually difficult to determine what this atmosphere was, beyond a subjective feeling. The art of designing consultative institutions has a thousand refinements; for example, people are more likely to speak if in small homogeneous groups; the size of the meeting should not be left to chance. The concept of "frame markers" is more palpable, or more widely believed, in the debate over the unpopularity of poetry: people take the decision to avoid poetry on the basis of slight external signals, which might be called "frame markers". Reformers regularly propose that, if poetry could visibly be more warm-hearted, or more classless, or more entertaining, etc., then a huge audience would roll up. I am not able to decide whether these markers were set up by poets, or by the external enemies of poetry, or by the population at large; clearly, your view of who has this power of social authorship influences your views on reform.

The result of the consultation process is supposed to be the reconciliation of everyone to the final policy. This is the most tenuous, precious, and nebulous of processes. Autogestion theory is supposed to bring about a group identity in which all participate. Enthusiasm motivates people to provide, free, the extra hours of work which allow government to dispense with full-time professionals. In reality, the losing factions may be quite uncommitted to anything except sabotaging the winning policy so as to prove themselves right. In this way, the process of debate works if people surrender their individual predilections; if you adopt the general policy, you then see your wishes fulfilled. The decision is supposed to belong to no one and everyone, a kind of subjectless action. The boundary of the personality is unimportant for this purpose, since currents are supposed to pass right through it; everything belongs to the group, or rather, what does not, becomes unreal and obsolete. Abolishing "bureaucracy" would not speed up decisions: in general, the more people you consult, the more time the process takes. Also, the less of existing arrangements you take for granted, the more time everything takes. The decision process would be more expensive in terms of time, but, supposedly, if everyone on the housing estate goes to all the meetings, you get a better quality of decision than if some Town Hall bureaucrat in a suit takes them, swiftly and secretly.

One of the factors which could prevent individuals from co-operating with group decisions is strong internal desires. These become rigidity, almost conservatism: the radical democratic project must take on a critique of the self as part of its constitutive ideas. If poetry prescribes self-expression, rebellion, a strong view of the self, as part of an inheritance from an alienated society, then it leads away from social integration. A radical democracy in which every self retained an autonomous fief would look like our fragmented, capitalist society. The personality therefore fell under the same critical analysis as the other rules of nineteenth century art; it was identified as something ossified, repetitive, unfree, deterministic, it was dissolved and made fluent by the ideas of spontaneity and constant becoming. The libertarian Socialist poet jettisons the eristic pattern of thought, including all the structures of courtroom rhetoric acquired since Gorgias. This withdrawal from self-aggrandisement was particularly important for Ulli Freer and John Wilkinson. The notion of what makes language beautiful depended, essentially, on its conduct mirroring an idealised and imagined interpersonal process.

Conflict imposes a consistency of the will which may seem one-sided and unnatural when the conflict is solved. Instead, someone's wishes and attractions may turn out to be multiple and internally inconsistent. Indeterminacy thus applied at the level of the self. The shifting nature of internal flows, so beloved of psychological novelists and other stars of the "formalist" but also critical Western tradition, makes the individual able to respond to dozens of different situations without loss of integrity. This gives radical democracy the possibility of success. The way to survive in an unpredictable terrain of events was to become flexible and quick-reacting. Criticising the "theatre of the self" could actually help literature by freeing it from unnecessary polarisations and entrenched positions. Unmasking the trappings of a shell self could be liberatory also for the person unmasked.

An influential example, perhaps, was the Communist bloc, where the fearful silence of, say, 90% of the population, persuaded by recent demonstrations of mass murder of the nonconformist, could be blamed for the poor quality of decisions taken by the élite. The system could neither conciliate people by bringing them the good life nor get them to participate in its institutions on a mass scale. The project of getting much more participation in British politics would strengthen the system by making its policies better advised and with more general consent; although perhaps the system would be very different from what it is today. An interesting feature of the vanished Soviet system was people being compelled to attend meetings of the collective, something which was unpopular. Indeed, these meetings were very boring.

Public institutions would be far better run with a few million people contributing a few days a year to running them, having got to understand them, but this relies on those people giving up their leisure time.

Apart from a few hundred professional politicians, politics is a leisure activity: we have to understand, not art from politics, but political activism as a decision about leisure time. Mass participation in politics would come from a kind of communicable craze, like a craze for dancing or yoga.

Suggestibility may be the precondition of living in groups. How does it relate to the self? What is the self within autogestion? Who does the "autos" refer to? We see a shimmering between singular and plural subjects of chains of language. We assume that the psyche contains very strong forces leading it to imitate others, to identify with their emotional states, to seek their approval, and to feel anxiety when they disapprove; the political process has to satisfy these forces, which however guarantee its success. Satisfying these urges is not self-betrayal; they are not outside the self; pure intransigence is not natural or virtuous. The *autos* of autogestion is in fact plural, so that subverting the sovereignty of the self is essential to participatory democracy. The pair of *suggestivity: suggestibility* however suggests domination. The devices which allow us, in the theatre or in poetry, to have emotional sympathy and to cross the boundaries of the self, are infernally similar to the conjuring tricks of rhetoric which plunge us into dependency and illusion.

### The artwork as frozen fantasy and control universe

The relationship between the artist and the consumer of art was somehow analogous to that between the politician and the citizen, or the employer and the employee. This is the motive for loosening the internal structure of the artistic work: the belief that if what the artist imagines is too precise and too full of detail, that is analogous to an authoritarian government, which presents a community with a finished development plan, and allows no consultation during the process of refinement. The passive reader is supposed to be the analogy to a passive citizen. The attitude—perhaps rather late nineteenth century—of the artist's total dedication to a uniquely personal vision of life, acquiring virtue in proportion to His refusal to compromise, doesn't give an adequate explanation of the reader's, or looker's, experience; here it seems that co-operation, not rebellion, is the great virtue.

The person who sets the frame markers, concealing imperatives which shape the path along which decisions run, wields concealed power. This has influenced poets trying to erase all context signals to write books with "no expectations"; an abdication of sovereignty in favour of a protean "spontaneous mass acclamation". The power of drafting the propositions, setting the order of speakers, picking the delegates and the audience, or even switching the microphone off during someone's unwelcome speech (Gorbachev to Yeltsin) is part of the art of politics, but the subliminal imperatives sound like voodoo to me. In poetry, though, it's arguable that subliminal suggestivity about context and atmosphere is the one thing a poet must possess. Total intransigence possesses some readers, for whom refusal to identify with the narrator or the characters, and wilful misreading, are a matter of pride. As someone's intellectual pride swells up, their sensibility attenuates.

The analogy with property is also compelling; the artist's desire to work until every detail of a work of art is perfect is like the feeling of ownership, and what I feel as a reader about my favourite works of art is a fierce possessiveness. Art is wealth. Art which was not a possession, which deliberately avoided personal style, might lose all interest for the audience.

Julio Cortazar's novel, *Modelo para armar* (kit to assemble), asked the reader to assemble the fragments of a novel and work out what the plot and motivation were; an example of the illusion that you can leave autonomy in the artistic work and still expect it to work. This was a fashion of around 1962, although it followed some *nouveaux romans* which were slightly earlier. The thesis of these now totally forgotten novels was to do with misconstruing reality; a slightly later fashion turned that complete dropping-out of explanations to political intent, questioning why society is ordered in this way. Power is allegedly turned over to the reader. Vacuity is then cast as political superiority; the artist provides a series of unreadable blotches and then triumphantly accuses the audience of passivity.

The model of domination appears to include a rule of priority; if the artist presents an idea at time $t = n$, and the reader adopts the idea at $t = (n + 5)$, then there is held to be domination, and so the reader who is scared of being controlled resists the idea. Presumably there are other criteria for assessing ideas. Someone who resists poetic ideas eventually has to give up poetry altogether; of course, most academics don't read contemporary poetry at all. Poets whose sensibility is bizarre and marginalised, for example sound and concrete poets, are driven, into the corner where they can no longer make meaningful utterances, by a territorial contest with poets whom they hate; appropriation is inevitably accompanied by the negative affect of ejection, in someone else. One may well ask if they react against the semantic content and artistic devices because they hate the poets who use them, or if they hate the poets because they use the said meanings and contents. Rage makes it impossible to collaborate with other people; it is perhaps a claim for territory and resembles the contention for territory of male mammals. The work of art must be shared by two people, that is, the artist and the consumer; it is very unpleasant to be confined in a narrow space with someone frantic to assert their status and importance. The libertarian current of the sixties involved, importantly, the demand that artists should give up their struggle for status and control. The ideally free society would have to face rage, quarrels, status struggles, as part of natural human behaviour.

Intransigence is a tourniquet around the head which prevents anything from getting into it. But of course, rebellion may be the impulse to get up and go which takes the artist into a new space where his or her insecurities disappear and, incidentally, a new and generous art is created.

# Under the ground, into the Crypt

Having got this far, we can turn round and look once again at the patchwork of quoted poems with which the book opened. Yes, these are wonderful poems. Yes, there is a sector of British poetry all ignored by the national media. We have given some account of how it came about—not a history exactly, but information about some scenes which may lie along the way. We have looked at one sector of the Underground, so far ignoring other groups. There was a late seventies magazine called "British Underground Magazine Scene" (i.e. bum scene, *so witty*); the issues I looked at did not mention any magazines associated with either the Cambridge Leisure Centre or the Mottram group. It was I think possible for someone to be a full-time member of the Underground, in 1979, without having heard of either of these two groups.

There is a neglected biomorphic line in English poetry:

Dylan Thomas:

> Dawn breaks behind the eyes;
> From poles of skull and toe the windy blood
> Slides like a sea;
> Nor fenced, nor staked, the gushers of the sky
> Spout to the rod
> Divining in a smile the oil of tears.
> (FROM *18 Poems*, 1934)

D.S. Savage:

> As cottages from quarries of neighbouring stone
> We are built in our bodies and mortared with mud
> We are bolted with bones on a framework of bone
> And filled with a plaster of flesh and blood.
> (FROM *"Earth", from A Time To Mourn*, 1943)

[286]     *Origins of the Underground*

Kathleen Raine:

> His skull is a dead cathedral, and his crown's rays
> Glitter from worthless tins and broken glass.
> His blue eyes are reflected from pools in the gutter,
> And his strength is the desolate stone of fallen cities.
> (FROM *"ISIS WANDERER"*, 1949)

Jeff Nuttall:

> I stalk with the razorblade cranes, my pinhead reeling wingpower in the white light,
> Stilt legs reed legs red from menstrual delta.
> I stalk with an agate eye and a lunatic trapped in my fossilised head—My stare -
> My feathers are all the flash, the flash the dawn and finish.
> I am not outside the instant Being-Scream.
> (FROM *PENGUIN MODERN POETS 12*, 1968)

Maggie O'Sullivan:

> Ricochet, straw cauldrons, water sickle
>     rotting turbid Rails.
>     Pig gathers in the lemon.
>     Cow, later of wood.
> Lioness, 'twas all moon down in the brainstem,
>     tally-sticks -
> Jackal woke fresh, key made from Butterfly depths,
>     the Chrysalis,
>     the Spider.
>     Treasury Futures.
> Asterisms liced from the Skull.
>     Nerve Surge.
>     Expulsions to a Rope.
> (FROM *"BIRTH PALETTE"* FROM *PALACE OF REPTILES*, 2003)

Robert Sheppard:

> Tanned to stone, his mind rolled
> down her body; spermy milk
> in the whorls of her thumb. Cool
> as her exposures, mermaid homunculus, painted
> nails dug into her easy answers.
> The buckskin revolutionary fingers his vagina
> books, false eyes fallen on his
> speeches, the everyday facts of the
> seaweed's spermy grist(.)
>
> (*EMPTY DIARIES*, 1998)

The biomorphic preoccupation with physiology which all these poems share has implications for the use of syntax: as a rational function, it is closed down to be replaced by simpler, more ambiguous, more overwhelming pulses and gushes. Reliance on compound nouns, and on strings of nouns, replaces syntactic articulation; a pictorial quality takes over from the movement of argument. Nuttall wrote "Weather skull uterus, fleshlobe grown in a bone cave"—a fairly simple mutation of standard Apocalyptic imagery. "Empty Diaries" is in some way about the history of the twentieth century (with one entry for each year) but is also about nothing but sex—reducing history to physiology in the manner of the 1940s.

"Asterism" is a constellation—"stars inside the skull" being a standard Apocalyptic image. Indeed, the light "which breaks where no sun shines" is a light shining inside the skull. "Asterisms liced from the skull" may reflect Thomas' "Day lights the bone".

The resemblances between Nuttall and Dylan Thomas are quite detailed. For example, it has been claimed that ten of the poems in Thomas' *18 Poems* (1934) contain the word "worm". The first poem in Nuttall's Penguin Modern Poets selection goes like this:

> The corkscrew worm revolves
> Writhes its iron filing twist in the soft core of the rock ...
>
> When the worm curls
> Earth turns one reluctant revolution.
> All the older order of the planets
> Rearranges from this nuclear motor
> (etc.)

Nuttall has also been heavily influenced by Hughes—someone else drawing on the 1940s.

Christopher Logue wanted to get out of poetry and into live performances, inciting the audience directly, and so wrote songs; Nuttall suspects the power of the articulate word as an agent of Reason, and so gets out of poetry and into theatre performances where language is non-representational, and takes off into a world of its own. His co-design in 1965 of the sTigma, an environment which the audience had to crawl through, becoming involved with soft and even wet substances, brings art close to the fairground. The sTigma is described in *Bomb Culture*:

～

The entrance to the sTigma was through three doorways [ ... ] The last you could just squeeze through, but not back, no return. The corridor this led to was lined with hideous bloody heads, photos of war atrocities, Victorian pornographic cards, tangles of stained underwear, sanitary towels, french letters, anatomical diagrams [ ... ] After the living-room a corridor of old clothes, a red cylinder, knee deep in feathers, a giant tunnel of inner tubes scented with Dettol [ ... ]

~

(p.226). Nuttall is saying that an ideal of detachment and Apollonian equanimity prevents us from noticing the path to a new way of life or system of government; art could move all of our faculties, but we choose to remain outside it. We can say Nuttall is an enemy of the eye "If there is one mistaken concept [ ... ] it is that man is primarily a socially oriented political animal [ ... ] Man is a welter of fears, urges, needs, aspirations, appetites and emotions, on which his political rationale forms a mere crust(.)" Nuttall doesn't seem to have noticed the epistemological problems of defining these instincts, as he calls them. The successors to those tactile environments were in rooms designed for clubs and raves at which the audience were expected to be sensitised to experience by the use of psychedelic drugs. Nuttall reports in *Bomb Culture* that he set out from CND, the sTigma team came together through appeals in *Peace News*, and the reason for the wordless outfit was that he despaired of winning the argument by rational means: the grotesque images were a way of sweeping away resistance. Apocalypse without theology. Perhaps it isn't too surprising that there are links between this militant CND art and the poetry written by pacifists in the 1940s. Artistically, the sTigma is the realisation in three dimensions of the "physiological" poem of the New Apocalyptics, and its makers claimed prophetic, apocalyptic, status. It succeeds egoistic poetry like that of George Barker, where the centre of the poem is the mind/body complex of the poet, exploded to monumental dimensions: the reader no longer enters the poem by "identifying", but physically crawls into it. An "environment" resolves the distinction between personal and public. In the sTigma, the world has contracted to what we can touch: the inside of the body has become the entire diameter of the work of art. The existence of the abstract and symbolic is rejected in favour of immersion and tangibility; clear relations erased by the replacement of the eye with touch. As Anglicanism ceased to be the official religion of the whole society, it diverted its attention to the individual with a tragic sense of the disappearing *ecclesia*; Nuttall is pursuing the line of this desocialisation, the graph of diminishing diameter. He is literally saying that the state of your soul comes before politics. This individual drive was expressed as Personalism, and pacifism; this is where Nuttall comes from politically.

There is a style to which many of the poems in *Floating Capital* (as a keynote anthology of the London School) conform. It involves short clauses, simple sentences, noun clusters, primary physical sensations, a lack of categorisation, analysis of causes, and objective relational frameworks. One can imagine this as developing out of a primal compaction—a state in which there were no articulate words at all, but an unfocussed physical energy, not divided by the intervals which characterise articulate language. This void could in fact be sound poetry, the triumph of the physiological over the symbolic. When Bob Cobbing began doing it, sometime in the 1950s, we can see this as an origin of the style; a vacuity which was willing to be filled by something new. Nuttall and Cobbing were possibly the channels through which a mutated Apocalyptic influence flowed, to reappear in the London School and its traditions of the last forty years.

The interest in disorganised graphics, so common in Writers Forum publications, though generally omitted from anthologies, offers structural parallels to this brutish use of language. There is a key opposition between scaled, ruled space, and subjective, nondimensional space, which is dramatised by sprawling signs on the white page, which we are accustomed to see used in a very precise and regular way, by printing. This dislike for bringing objects into their true relation to each other is parallel to a use of language that rejects classifiers and classifying syntax, leaving things as a sprawling heap, throbbing with unpredictable waves of colour and heat. All of this is very far removed from Terence Tiller and from the poets of *A Various Art*. My intention is not to reduce things to their origins, nor to claim one strand of a potent poetic mix as central. Instead, this is an attempt to disengage one element for examination—this, against a background of void, as there is still no book about the London school, although a "scene", a swirl of self-replacing energy, has been there since 1963. This biomorphic line does offer us a possibility of considering how the ferocious internal development of London poetics removed the scene from groups elsewhere in the country and brought in features which certain other groups regarded as uncouth and grotesque. This divergence brought a certain froideur, and a post-glacial geology.

News of Nuttall's death reached me as I was correcting the proofs of this passage. It seems fair to point to his place in poetic history: in the sixties, he was one of the major players. The London thing didn't suddenly come from nowhere in 1980. Three poets—Cobbing, Nuttall, Mottram—were the founders of the London School, and were, each in their way, believers in the immediate instant as revealing the mystery of the incarnation of the soul in a bag of flesh. Each threw away the rational editing process to leave behind a chaotic excess of signs, lavish and circular. Each was, in his own way, an absolutely terrible poet. However, the irrational line as a whole includes extremely gifted poets like Dylan Thomas and Maggie O'Sullivan. Cobbing published about 500 pamphlets of his own work, in 1,500 publications from Writers Forum; an excess which indicates a fundamentalist faith in creativity and the instant. The clutter of his poems, or Mottram's, shows how productive the brain is when norms are removed. Because the rational levels of the mind are concerned with relations with other people, and so also with lawcodes and authorities, it is perhaps true that anarchism logically inclines someone to write about unmediated physical sensations, in a weak, non-mediating syntax, of repetitive and high-affect phrases. Mottram was not using the biomorphic style but, evidently, the theme of his 1986 poem "Peace Projects" takes us back to the longing for peace and resistance to the state and the interests it embodies; while the Corbin texts he is exploiting in "Peace Project 4" are about the mysteries of incarnation, the entrapment of the soul in the material world. Although he was an intellectual, his compositional line is acquisitive, uninhibited, and intuitive rather than cogent or concise.

## A split in the Underground

A recent email alerted me to the existence of Paul Gogarty and Philip Jenkins, two lost poets of the seventies. Rapid reading immediately threw up the problem of how both poets began with cool, reflexive and self-contained short poems and moved on to muddy, mythical, and primeval long poems (*The Accident Adventure*, and *Cairo*, respectively) and then fell silent. Their disappearance from memory points to the power of the groups which they did not belong to, and which have protected the memory of their own, through so many vicissitudes.

Poetry took a dramatic swerve towards the long poem as it left the sixties and entered the seventies, and took a less dramatic swerve back again at around the end of the decade. I recently made a list of fifty significant long poems of the 1970s, to which Jenkins and Gogarty were hastily added. My impression is that the long poem declined, not for artistic reasons, but because publishers wouldn't accept it and editors also, although they could have printed excerpts, or given whole issues to single poems, sheered away from it. Quite a few long poems waited on the shelf for a certain number of years—not being destroyed, but totally inhibiting the follow-up long poem. It is an over-simplification to suggest that the long poem had vanished by the end of the eighties. Allen Fisher's *Gravity as a Consequence of Shape* has been in progress ever since that time. But the record of the nineties just does not show such a list of long poems as the 1970s. A development was slowed down or stopped.

The function of length may have been to achieve local complexity without resorting to encryption. Pressure on space brought puzzle surfaces as a kind of defensive reflex. The missing space was furled up very tightly and inserted into a flat surface as a kind of infinite scroll—a denied surface.

Pop poetry too was a response to lack of space. Where space is money, poetry gets compressed. The responses may be more or less hand to mouth and may involve compromises and distortions. The long poem was an effective response artistically but it was unsuccessful economically.

Writing poems of the immediate present in the 1950s—and this is something hard to find in England, it's more in Germany that I find them—was exciting and subversive. Logue's 1959 volume, *Songs*, is in fascinating and beguiling contrast to what was around it. The long poem was a dialectical response to the shortness of Pop poems.

An examination of the Mottram *Poetry Review* (between 1971 and 1977) shows a high proportion of simple Pop poems. Alan Jackson features, for example. This is surprising, because it means that Simon Armitage or Glyn Maxwell could claim to be the heirs of Mottram and his heroic *Poetry Review*. There is a direct link between Simon Armitage and Brian Patten, Adrian Henri, and Roger McGough. *The Liverpool Sound*, remember, sold a quarter of a million copies. Almost by default, its succession became an inevitable style for naïve poets, over decades, as basic, really, as The Beatles are to pop music. Without pausing too long to reflect about the treacherous nature of all inheritance thinking, relying on bourgeois concepts of property and a contentious belief that time involves transmission of property and status but not change, I want to suggest that the Underground split in two in the late seventies, and that one arm of it went on to be a new cryptic and avantgardistic faction and to forget its former close links with Pop poetry (or, if you prefer, Beat poetry).

There are a number of checks we can make on the proposal that, up until 1977 or so, Pop and the avant-garde had not separated. We could, for example, look at the magazine *2nd Aeon*. Is this pop or avant-garde? Both. Just look at it. Its editor, Peter Finch, is a seriously underrated poet because he has clung on to orality and transparency, while pursuing experimentation and inventiveness. Another exhibit is *A Various Art*. Scattered through its pages we find direct address, spontaneity, parataxis, lyricism and philosophical analysis. This captivating mixture is a kind of frozen moment, of the 1960s (1966, the launch of *The English Intelligencer*?) — a time before loyalty tests. Consider now this passage from Eric Mottram.

Your assignment is to
Your assignment is to

    to my friend who ever
    studies me for death
    so he can live flat
    for cheerlessness so he
    can pitch mournful into the sunset
    best for photographing clouds over peaks
    it goes down each day so far

at Quarr
    hooded men appeared in the chancel
    to sing Gregorian
    the architect provided tall theatre
    for their process

"not to slip unconsciously into doing something which could, in a slovenly way, be described as 'living at second hand'"
    defeat by parents and education

to glimpse a possibility of relieving inwards tensions
    by telling stories which refused to resolve
    themselves in the usual way
without being explained

"home" no domestic establishment
a place where a man can collect keep and use
and hunt through his gear

to imagine Utopia steps to its founding
to imagine Dystopia marches to our enclosure
    imaging chains of prisons
    open on another
    dreams against choice

their gear emptied on a table top in contempt
    locked away lost away
an ice log hut in Siberia now enters
    dreams one beaten man
    not broken axing a trunk
    in cross snows
        (FROM "PEACE PROJECT 2", PUBLISHED IN ANGEL EXHAUST 6, 1986)

At first blush, this is both confusing and irritating. The quoted passage includes a self-description: the line about not leading life at second-hand explains why the labels have been left off. "Tall theatre" is an unrecognisable way of saying a church designed for spectators to see certain holy events; "hooded men" is an original way of saying "monks". "Open on another" is a literary way of saying "opening onto one another". I think the bit about the ice hut is an illustration of the word "pioneer". Every image is grabbed from reading—which some people would call "second-hand". "Peace Project 4", strangely, is based on a book by Henry Corbin and hard to follow unless you've read Corbin. In an interview in the same issue, the poet says "All I can say about this untrained, inexperienced fictive reader is—it's like going to sports events whose rules and regulations you do or don't know. If you don't know them, you don't go around abusing the event and lamenting This isn't for me—I don't understand it—in aggressive or mournful tones. You either take the trouble of learning the procedures, or stay clear". Whatever you think about the aesthetic possibilities of encryption, it's obviously hard to put it over to a wide audience. It's unreasonable to set up a demonic right-wing conspiracy against the "underground" when this new crypticity was able to make the audience stay clear all on its own. I say "new" because I really don't think it was there in the sixties. *The White Stones* is so clear compared to *Brass*. *The He Expression*, Mottram's book of 1972 is so clear compared to his work of 1977. I would agree that editors and critics were knocked down and overrun by the combination of complexity, montage leaps, removal of indicator signs, and length, but the same is surely true of the reader in general. The Underground split in two in the 1970s (which is why the word fell out of use). The Pop heritage went on, and went on reaching a large audience—the audience attracted by the spontaneity of the sixties, by live readings. This fraction has never gone off the air, although it has become more bourgeois and more middle-aged in line with its audience.

Conservatives hated Pop and intellectual work about equally, and the split between the two relates both to loyalty tests and to a situation of economic shortages. Galloping inflation meant continual fights over resources. The market for poetry shrank; consumers' perception of value for money lagged behind spiralling costs of production. The number of magazines shrank and the readings circuit wound down. There was contention over spare space. I suspect that this brought new polarisation—the mutual rejection of Pop and the avant-garde. This was complete by 1977.

I suspect that the atmosphere of contraction, contention and suspicion was repulsive to readers. In the sixties, new poetry had been expansive, insouciant, tranquil, welcoming. This was endlessly attractive. The atmosphere of de-legitimation, of assaults on existing cultural assets, also meant assaults on the reader and his cultural assets. This wasn't very attractive at all. Values of paranoia, Puritanism, hyper-criticality, seeped into the atmosphere and were slow to leave. The audience have been slow to come back. Of course, crypticity arrives because clarity is seen as the failure to pass a loyalty test. It is an open invitation to *outsiders*. If outsiders come into the room, they get a vote, and may "roll up" the distinctiveness of the group/style to deliver it back to conventionality. Mottram's poem is a sequence of captured images, complete in themselves, snatched from a media world seen as infinite and available. That is, he is very close to Pop techniques; part of the problem with his images is their immediacy. Pop poetry, originally, loved nonsequiturs—part of its genetic inheritance from Surrealism. "The He Expression" isn't even difficult.

Leaving out the signposts was taken as removing the perceptual filters but left the poem as perplexing. The cryptic style could simply be the switch-off of the oral faculty we discussed above. Because of this incomplete nature, it switches on only a partial response from our brains, which largely remain asleep. In this version, it would be symmetrical to the almost completely asleep state evoked by light verse and dumbed-down poetry. The extremes have symmetrical problems. Of course, getting rid of the pressure of communication and identification with other people was experienced by the experimental poets as a terrific liberation. Abstruse poetry felt much more direct, from the inside. This was an era which preferred spontaneity, when the unrestrained and instant quality of jazz was penetrating mass-consumption pop music. The preconscious phase of direct awareness is itself cryptic. You can't just sweep this fact away. Clarity arrives late and as a result of the action of reason—secondary by definition. Serious gazes at the complexity of unmediated consciousness, and of mediation, produce literature which is increasingly complex and difficult. Very simple verbal acts, including song texts, advertisements, pop poems, are heavily stylised rather than direct and primary. I believe that Mottram's poetry was very close to the surface of his consciousness—he had a fantastic ability to make associations and spent all day chasing and grabbing cultural goods to feed his brain. The difficulty is not the result of pedantic rewriting but of courageous spontaneity. The irony of courage is the likelihood of death. Eric certainly left quite a few poems strewn on the field of battle.

I want to float a notion of luminous complexity—a glass machine. This is my preference. To choose either banality or obscurity seems like intentional failure—a defect of the poetic faculties.

The Pop line shorn of linguistic experimentation includes *Iron, The North, Joe Soap's Canoe*, Bloodaxe, but also the *Poetry Review* of the Peter Forbes era and a whole ocean of live readers. It has remained popular. Its officials probably have never stopped regarding themselves as controlling modern poetry in general. In the interests of mutual understanding, I would propose a pragmatic sanction. Bloodaxe represents the modernity of the early 1960s. It postdates the Movement (although including large doses of Movement glumness to clog up the purity of Pop). Bloodaxe are different from the dominant style of the 1950s; but their list, and their anthologies, have systematically rejected innovations arriving after the early sixties. For me, these are the innovations which matter.

Conservative Pop poetry today likes to justify itself by reference to the New York School. That school were basically the local franchise of Surrealism, and I'm not sure they added anything that wasn't already there in the model. Conversely, someone who took on Surrealism today would probably be labelled as an offshoot of the New York School.

Why did the Pop line decay after the 1960s? Is this loss of legitimacy the effect of contrast or a real decay? If Henri is the legitimate heir of Prévert and Breton, and Armitage is the legitimate heir of Henri (and Patten), then Armitage is the legitimate heir of Breton and Prévert. Discuss. The question of the half-life of ideas is always hard to fix—why something comes off perfectly for Apollinaire in 1910, comes off not at all badly for Adrian Henri in 1965, and just makes you seasick in 1993 with Simon Armitage. In a way, it's more interesting looking for quality Pop work, because it's more hidden under the debris of time. If I look at contemporary work by Peter Finch, John James, Ralph Hawkins, Dan Lane—am I not seeing the heritage of the sixties, in the best way?

The underlying difficulty is the crisis of English popular music during most of this century, and the crisis of poetry's relation with song, and the virtues of song. In fact, there are two poles attracting poetry: the pole of lyricism and musicality (which seems to be timeless, since love and music existed in the Stone Age), and the pole of stylistic progress and intelligence. In talking about the mainstream, we may find it helpful to focus on their incompetence at dealing with the former area. For me as a reader, the heritage of the seventies, of Prynne, Mottram, and Allen Fisher, is endlessly interesting, while the Pop heritage leaves me cold. That's my subjective feeling, although as a historian I am well aware that Brecht, Prévert, Logue, also among my favourite poets, also wrote in an ideally simple way. I am fascinated by these long poems as a collector. We think that the 1970s are a lost decade; it's impossible for someone young today to find out what was happening in that unstable and unleashed decade. Anthologies systematically disfavour the long poem, which is a limit on a number of later anthologies featuring seventies poets. (There was no good anthology during the seventies.) It would be useful to have an anthology of long poems, which could at least show excerpts.

The last issue of Peter Finch's *2nd Aeon* (undated, but 1974) has a round-up of small press publications on pages 198–267. About 400 publications—it might be a good idea to read all of them. We can take our leave of the Underground at this point, now it has taken its definitive form, which was to remain remarkably constant over the following thirty years. The mystery of why this "poetry containing the future" failed to achieve market acceptance has now been cleared up—the emergence of a sector of readers favouring difficult poetry happened in parallel with the emergence of the poets writing it. The features of an arbitrary balance between assimilation to shared rules and mandatory originality, unnervingly precise analysis of someone's work, cursory and inadequate reviewing, a phantom distribution network, heroic feats of shopping, invisibility to outsiders, mutual ignoring by the Cambridge and London groups, were as much there in 1975 as they are now. And who are we to gainsay them?

# Conclusion

The current keeps taking us back to the notion of Myth. The picture retrieved is hardly clear but some loose observations may be made. The decline of Christian and Classical myth left a vacuum which was partly filled by documentary, something which had the didactic energies of the State behind it and whose portrayal of collective groupings and actions was to a great extent acceptable to the mass public. A staple of modern dull poetry is a sort of moralised documentary. When yet another poet positions an uneducated person digging a garden in a particular way, they are loyally following the syntax of showing authenticity as established by film-makers in the 1930s. These sequences are depersonalised and predictable—as Classical myths were. The reliance on objects and neglect of words is a sign of dependence on film. We have ingrained reactions which the poet gropes for like someone digging up potatoes.

Anyone objecting to administrative rationality is likely to reject the documentary style and go for irrational art. Both the romantic poetry of the 1940s and the New Age movement were the protest of the administered and offered a return to mythic thinking. These returns failed as a collective representation but they did raise themselves from the individual plane to the plane of self-selected groups—of cults, as anticipated by GRS Mead almost a century ago. Myth which is not orthodoxy can only be cultish, but because it is not tied to an ideological authority it can be invented and developed.

There is a line in modern poetry of personal myth. The fascination with the myths of other societies is a cover for the personal nature of mythic creativity, for example in the work of Iain Sinclair, Martin Thom, Walter Perrie, Philip Jenkins, and Paul Gogarty. Myth is presumably the record of prophetic insight, and the interest in Apocalypse was fundamentally an interest in the problem of generating myth. Releasing the powers of dream brought a flood of images of bodies, or organs, because (we suppose) this is the language which the unconscious thinks in. Myth is, perhaps, the extension of these confused but primal images into meaningful series of groupings.

The poetry in *A Various Art* is very little concerned with myth, with the exception of Sinclair's work. It mostly belongs with a secular and rational critique, whose goal is personal liberation. This liberation comes about by dropping out of what is felt to be a morass flow of popular illusions, rather than by opting into a cult with its proprietary myths.

Although this is a work about the past, the book has reached an end with significant questions left unresolved and irresoluble within the evidence available to us. The term "underground" is based on an economic test—simply, poetry which is produced by small (non-commercial) publishers, which is consequently not found in the High Street bookshops or reviewed in magazines read by a non-specialist public. It is a consequence of this test that, since the main evidence, *A Various Art*, was published by a mainstream publisher, the evidence melts and flows out of our hands at the moment we start to look at it. What was overground in 1987 had been underground in 1967. The real distinctions which we miss, however, are more subtle and more intimate than economics and have to do with the connection of poetry as such to social and political urges. I would like to know whether the poetry of Grosseteste Review (and later, *AVA*) was attached to demands for personal liberty and political change.

I have suggested that the poetry of *AVA* is quite incompatible with the neo-religious irrationalism of the Counter-Culture. So what was the poetry of that culture? And how does the Counter-Culture relate to the Leninist New Left, or to anarchist and libertarian politics or, these to various kinds of poetry? How many streams was the "underground" divided into, and what were the lines of disagreement? What pressure came from the audience, and were the splits in the audience the same as the splits among the poets? How were audience wishes mediated in an "anti-business", underground, environment? Did this reflexivity act to demolish facile visions of a new and equal society before anything else—cogent scepticism corroding the most proximate set of emotive ideals? I can't answer these questions.

A further line of questioning would have to do with the School of London—the associates of Nuttall and Cobbing. I regret there is no book which offers a description of their activities over the last forty years or so; apparently there is nothing written about them except by their own members. A synthesis on modern British poetry can only follow a number of specialised studies which we look for in vain. Where is the book on the 1970s, for example. Where are the biographies of modern poets.

Finally, the results of James Keery's research are about to transform our understanding of this whole area of history. I have not responded to them, or even summarised them, because they are too far-reaching and because they are not yet published. This book was written essentially in 2000. Keery's version of apocalyptic beauty has travelled a long way since then.

# Bibliography

More information on my website at www.pinko.org.

## Introduction
Macleod: see The Programmes of the Festival Theatre, copies in the Cambridge University Library.

## Occlusion
Mottram, Eric, *The British poetry revival, 1960–74* (London: Polytechnic of Central London, 1974).
D'Arch Smith, Timothy, *The books of the Beast* (Wellingborough: Crucible, 1978).

## Reflexivity
There is a great lack of sources on Tiller beside his books. An interesting statement is included in *Personal Landscape* (a selection from the Cairo magazine, ed., Robin Fedden; London: Editions Poetry London, 1945). A not very good book (*Many Histories Deep*, by Roger Bowen, Madison, NJ: Farleigh Dickinson University Press, c. 1995) does include something of his life when in Egypt. GS Fraser's memoirs, *A Stranger and Afraid* (Manchester: Carcanet New Press, 1983) include a piercing sketch of the English-speaking literary scene in Egypt.

## Cambridge, the Sixties, and A Various Art
Consult the bibliographies in *A Various Art* and in the Paladin *New British Poetry*.

James Keery's articles in *PN Review* (periodical: Manchester; numbers 93 and 95) and *Bête Noire* (periodical: Hull) are illuminating and carefully researched.

Riley, Denise, edited *Poets on Writing* (London: Macmillan, 1992), includes statements from many of the CLC poets.

*Grosseteste Review* (periodical: Matlock) issue 12 is a collection of explanatory prose. I have written elsewhere on John James, John Seed, and JH Prynne. The most revealing book about what it was probably like to be in Cambridge in 1966 is Nick Schaffner's *Saucerful of Secrets* (London: Sidgwick and Jackson, 1991), about The Pink Floyd, Cambridge's best band; their troubled odyssey between leftism, high-tech (the equivalent of Theory), and pure improvisation is of the first relevance.

## The Critical Tradition

There is a lack of books on the cultural and intellectual history of the Left in Britain. A special issue of Angel Exhaust (periodical: Southend), no.13, *Massive Transfers from Rich to Poor: Poetry and Socialism*, gives samples from the history of the Left in poetry. The essay on Madge is reprinted from there.

Croft, Andy, ed., *A weapon in the struggle* (London: Pluto, 1998), is about culture and the Communist Party.

See Madge's Mass Observation work in *Speak for Yourself: a Mass Observation anthology 1937–49*, Calder, Angus, and Sheridan, Dorothy, eds. (London: Cape, 1984).

Marks, John D, *The Quest for the 'Manchurian Candidate'* (New York: Norton, 1991).

On gestalt: Köhler, Wolfgang, *Gestalt Psychology* (New York: Liveright Publishing Corporation, 1947)

Gregory, RL *Eye and Brain* (London: Weidenfeld and Nicolson, 1977).

Roy Fisher interviews quoted from Fisher, Roy, *Interviews through Time* (Kentisbeare: Shearsman Books, 2000).

Crozier interview in Ryan, MP, *Career Patterns in Poetry*, 1982 doctoral thesis at the University of London, which also has vital interviews with Glyn Jones, David Gascoyne, and JF Hendry.

## Neo-Objectivism and Avant-garde Legitimacy

Zukofsky's statement in *Poetry (Chicago)*, 1931.

Quartermain, Peter, and Blau DuPlessis, Rachel, ed., *The Objectivist Nexus* (Tuscaloosa, London: University of Alabama Press, c.1999).

### History of the Ideas in Poetry
Smith, Grafton Elliot, *Human History* (London: Jonathan Cape, 1930).
*Experiment* (periodical, Cambridge)
*Cairo* is reprinted in Tony Frazer's anthology *A State of Independence* (Exeter: Stride, 1998).

### Documentary and Propaganda
Sussex, Elizabeth, *The rise and fall of British documentary* (Berkeley, London: University of California Press, 1975).
Vaughan, Dai, *Portrait of an Invisible Man* (London: BFI, 1983).
Taylor, Philip M, *The projection of Britain: British overseas publicity and propaganda 1919–39* (Cambridge: Cambridge University Press, 1981).
Constantine, Stephen, *Buy and build: the Advertising Posters of the Empire Marketing Board.* (London: HMSO, 1986).
Tallents, Stephen *The Projection of England* (London: Faber, 1932).
On the formation of foreign policy: Quigley, Carroll *Hope and Tragedy: a history of the world in our time* (New York: Macmillan. London: Collier-Macmillan, 1966).
On the 1937 Exhibition, see Woodham, Jonathan *Twentieth Century Design* (Oxford: Oxford University Press, 1997).
Wright, Patrick, *On Living in an Old Country* (London: Verso, 1985) Balfour, Michael *Propaganda in war 1939–45* (London: Routledge and Kegan Paul, 1979).
White, John Baker, *The Big Lie* (on the Political Warfare Executive) (London: Pan Books, 1958).
On the information research division: Lashmar, Paul and Oliver, James *Britain's Secret Propaganda War* (Stroud, Glos: Sutton, 1998).
Exceptionally interesting data on imperial naval strategy in Cain PJ and Hopkins, AG *British Imperialism: crisis and deconstruction 1914–90* (London: Longman, 1993).

### Neo-Romanticism: the Dissolution of the Horizon
Sinclair, Andrew, *War Like a Wasp: the Lost Decade of the 1940s* (London: Hamish Hamilton, 1989).
Savage, DS *The Personal Principle* (London: Routledge, 1944).
Stanford, Derek, *The Freedom of Poetry* (London: Falcon Press, 1947).
Gardiner, Charles Wrey, *The Dark Thorn* (London: Grey Walls Press, 1946).
Hewison, Robert, *Under Siege* (London: Weidenfeld and Nicolson, 1977).
Jackaman, Rob, *The course of English Surrealist Poetry since the 1930s* (Lewiston, NY, Lampeter: Mellen, 1989).

# Bibliography

There are by now many memoirs.

Mellor, David ed., *Paradise Lost: the Neo-Romantic Imagination in Britain 1935–1955* (London: Lund Humphries in association with the Barbican Art Gallery, 1987).

Yorke, Malcolm, *Spirit of Place: Nine Neo-Romantic Artists and their Times* (London: Constable, 1988).

The biomorphic: Lawrence Alloway's essay, "The Biomorphic '40s", reprinted in *Topics in American Art since 1945* (New York: WW Norton, 1975).

Personalism: Mounier, Emmanuel, *Le personnalisme* (etc.), in *Œuvres*, vol III, (Paris: Editions du seuil, 1962); Berdyaev, Nikolai, *Solitude and Society* (London: Geoffrey Bles, 1938) (published in Russian in 1934 as "The I and the World of Objects"); Niebuhr, Reinhold, *Moral Man and Immoral Society* (London: C Scribner's Sons, 1933).

Information on Pioneers in Stanford, Derek, *Inside the Forties* (London: Sidgwick and Jackson, 1977) and on Edwin Morgan's war service in his interviews, *Nothing not Giving Messages* (Edinburgh:Polygon, 1990); discussion in issues of *Transformation* and *Poetry London*.

Savage: D S Savage, ut supra

anarchism: Comfort, Alex *Against Power and Death* (London: Freedom Press, 1994); *Art and Social Responsibility* (London: Falcon Press, 1946) Read, Herbert *The politics of the unpolitical* (London: Routledge, 1943).

Data on the Arts and Crafts movement in Crawford, Alan *CR Ashbee, architect, designer, and romantic socialist* (New Haven, London: Yale University Press, 1985);

Naylor, Gillian, *The arts and crafts movement* (London: Studio Vista, 1980).

Pacifism: Taylor, Richard and Young, Nigel eds., *Campaigns for peace: British peace movements in the twentieth century.* (Manchester: Manchester University Press, 1987).

On the attitude of Christians towards total war, see Wilkinson, Alan *Dissent or Conform?* (London: SCM Press, 1986).

Info on Welsh refuseniks in Davies, D Hywel, *The Welsh Nationalist Party 1925–75, a Call to Nationhood* and the book on *Emyr Humphreys* by Thomas, M. Wynn (Caernarfon: Gwasg Pantycelyn, 1989); Griffiths, Heini *Achub Cymru.* (Talybont: y Lolfa, 1983).

Hendry's retrospective essay on the Apocalypse is in issue 31 of *Chapman* (periodical, Edinburgh); information on the dates of *Marimarusa* is on page 1 of issue 52. A slightly different date is given in Hendry's long interview in MP Ryan's important doctoral thesis on the careers of poets, ut supra.

[304]    *Origins of the Underground*

Information on the liminal in Turner, Victor *Dramas, Fields, and Metaphors* (Ithaca: Cornell University Press, 1975).

## Bad Science, Pulp Topography: Iain Sinclair
Gibbons, Tom 'Occultism', *Modern Painters* (periodical: London, no. 2:3, 1989), which is a review of Moffitt, John F *Occultism in Avant-garde Art* (Ann Arbor, Michigan, London: UMI Research Press, 1988).

## Apocalyptic Foreglow: Origins of the Counter-Culture
Ascona: Landmann, Robert, *Ascona Monte Verita* (Frankfurt am Main: Ullstein, 1982; originally 1934; new edition by Ursula von Wiese). Mühsam, Erich. *Ascona:* Muhsam (Zurich: Sanssouci Verlag, 1979). Green, Martin *Mountain of Truth. The counter-culture begins: Ascona 1900–1920* (Hanover, NJ, London: University Press of New England, 1986).
*Otto Gross, Freudian psychoanalyst, 1877–1920, literature and ideas* (Lewiston, Lampeter: Edwin Mellen Press, c.1999).
Eranos: See *Henry Corbin. Cahiers de l'Herne* (periodical, Paris), edited Jambet, Christian 1981. This includes two reminiscences of the Ascona gathering at pages 256–65 and 48–49.
Another account is in Webb, James *The Occult Underground*, (La Salle, Illinois: Open Court, 1988).
Occult Revival: the phrase comes from Webb.
biodynamism/organic farming: Boyes, Georgina *The Imagined Village* (Manchester, New York: Manchester University Press, c.1993). Armytage, W H G, *Heavens Below. Utopias in England 1560–1960* (London: Routledge and Kegan Paul, 1961).
Bramwell, Anna *Ecology in the 20th century* (New Haven, London: Yale University Press, 1989).
Multiculturalism: Cupitt, Don, *The Sea of Faith* (London: BBC, 1984).
Hart, David, A *One faith? non-realism and the world of faiths* (London: Mowbray, 1995).
Living cosmos: based on Green and Webb ut supra.
Macleod made this report on his influences in *The Festival Programme*.
Scrutiny: cf. Boyes pp. 125–33
Bultmann: essay by Thielicke in *Kerygma and Myth*, ed., Bartsch, Hans Werner (London: SPCK, 1953).
Temenos: info on *Light* in Görtschacher, Wolfgang *Little Magazine Profiles*, p.665 (Salzburg: Salzburg University, 1993).
Sacred geometry: Bond, Frederick Bligh *The Gate of Remembrance* (Oxford: Basil Blackwell, 1933).

Williams, Mary, ed., *Britain, a study in patterns* (London: Research Into Lost Knowledge Organisation, 1971).
Screeton, Paul, *Quicksilver Heritage* (London: Abacus, 1977).
mundus imaginalis: one of the texts in Cahiers de l'Herne is 'Corbin, théologien du protestantisme'.

## In the Land of the Not-Quite Day; or, the Frisson of Ruins. David Gascoyne

The papers given at the Gascoyne symposium in Cambridge, 26th April 2002, have been drawn on throughout. Besides the works of David Gascoyne (*Collected poems*, Oxford: Oxford University Press 1988), and *Collected Journals 1936–42*, (London: Skoob, 1991), these works were consulted.
Keery, James *Schönheit apocalyptica* (published on the web by Jacket magazine, at jacketmagazine.au.com)
Shestov, Lev *Athens or Jerusalem?* (Athens, Ohio: Ohio University Press, 1966).
  *Nachala i kontsy. Sbornik statei.* (Sankt-Peterburg, 1908).
Hippius, Zinaida *Zhivie litsa.* (Sankt-Peterburg: Azbuka, 2001).
 Heer, Friedrich *Der Glaube des Adolf Hitler* (Munich and Esslingen: Bechter Verlag, 1968).
 Jouve, P-J, *Diadème* (Paris: NRF Gallimard, 1970).
Victor Turner, *Dramas, fields, and metaphors.* ut supra
Goodrick-Clarke, N, *Occult Roots of Nazism* (Wellingborough: Aquarian, 1985).
Introduction to *Speak for Yourself: a Mass Observation Anthology 1937–49*, ut supra.
Foster, JR, *Modern Christian Literature* (London: Burns and Oates, publisher to the Holy See, 1963).
Spender's review is in *Horizon* (periodical, London), no.51
Schanze, Helmut, ed., *Romantik-Handbuch* (Stuttgart: Kröner, 1994).
Gore, Charles Spencer, ed., *Lux Mundi, A Series of Studies on the Religion of the Incarnation* (London: John Murray, 1889).
Smith, Ken, *Fox Running*, in: *The Poet Reclining*, (Newcastle-Upon-Tyne: Bloodaxe, 1982).
Masefield, John, *The everlasting mercy* (London: Sidgwick and Jackson, 1911).
Esterson, Aaron, *The leaves of Spring, A study in the Dialectics of Madness* (London: Harmondsworth, 1972).
Information on the website of the Institute of Architecture (www.princes-foundation.org).

Knight, G Wilson, *The starlit dome* (London; Oxford University Press, 1941).
*The Golden Labyrinth* (London: Phoenix House, 1962).
*A Royal propaganda* (unpublished typescript, dated 1956, in the British Library).

~

Acallam na Senorach (annotated and translated by Ann Dooley and Harry Roe as *Tales of the elders of Ireland*, 1999).
Information on the prince in Hutchinson, Maxwell, *The Prince of Wales: Right or Wrong?* (London: Faber and Faber, 1989), and Holden, Anthony, *Charles. A Biography* (London: Weidenfeld and Nicolson, 1988).
Henry Corbin issue of Cahiers de l'Herne, directed by Christian Jambet (1981).
Pater quoted from Donoghue, Denis, *The Practice of Reading* (New Haven, London: Yale University Press, 1998), quoting at p.221 from 'Poems by William Morris', a suppressed essay.
Spender quoted from *Horizon*, IX.51, 1944, p.212
There is a personal statement by DG in *Temenos* 1 (periodical: Dulverton: Watkins). Note that a notebook of poems from 1950 was discovered after his Collected poems came out, and these were published in the *Temenos Academy Journal* (London: Temenos Academy).

## Counter-Culture and New Age
*The Crown and the Sickle*, ed., Hendry JF, and Treece, Henry, (Westminster: King and Staples, 1945).
Whiteley, Sheila, *The space between the notes.* (London: Routledge, 1992).

## Left and Right: Labour in the seventies
Ramsay, Robin, *The Clandestine Caucus* (special issue of *Lobster* magazine, Hull, 1996).
Seyd, Patrick and Whiteley, Paul, *Labour's Grass Roots* (Oxford; Oxford University Press, 1992).
Wainwright, Hilary, *A tale of two parties* (London: Hogarth, 1987).
Bradley, Ian, *Breaking the Mould?* (Oxford: Martin Robertson, 1981). 'Who were they travelling with?', by Tom Easton (*Lobster*, periodical, Hull: issue 31, 1996) is a review of another book on the SDP.

Angel Exhaust Thirteen: *Massive Transfers from Rich to Poor*, is a history of British socialist poetry, as above.

Dorril, Stephen and Ramsay, Robin, *Smear* (London: Fourth Estate, 1991).

## Autogestion

Deleuze, Gilles and Guattari, Félix, *Capitalisme et schizophrénie* (Paris: les Editions de Minuit, 2 parts 1972-80).

Malcolm, Noel, *A history of Bosnia* (London: Macmillan, 1994).

Andersen, Troels *Asger Jorn en biografi* (Copenhagen, Valby: Borgen, 1994) Strzygowski, Joseph. *Altai-Iran und Völkerwanderung* (Vienna: ?? 1917).

Rose, Richard, *Politics in England Today* (London: Faber, 1974).

## Under the Ground

Nuttall quoted from *Bomb Culture* (London: MacGibbon and Kee, 1968).

There is some information on the School of London in my book, *The Failure of Conservatism in Modern British Poetry* (Cambridge: Salt), at pp.157-61, 195-201, 262-267, 280-285. The papers in Adrian Clarke's *Millennium Shades and Three Papers* (London: Writers Forum, 1998) shed much light.

# Index

A Various Art xxx, 23–45, 221, 298
acephalic patterns 278
Aldington, Richard 134–7, 252
anarchism 274
anomalies of the countryside 219
Apocalypse, Revelations, see Lawrence 112, 142–85, 186, 236–53
Archer, David 172
Ascona, Switzerland 236–7
associations for trapping and refining data see Ferry-Grosseteste School, Mass Observation, Eranos, New Romantics, classical heritage, social networks
Auden clique 177
autarky and withdrawal 242
authenticity xxix, 4, 93, 159, 163
autogestion 272–84

Balfour, Eve, humus occultist 241
Barker, George 170–9
Barnett, Anthony 40–43
beasts 160
Berdyaev, Nikolai 156–7
Berry, Francis 111, 166–70
binocular vision and 3 dimensional vision 21, 28, 60, 79, 207; superimposition 127
biomorphic art ; prophecies about beasts 148–9, 160, 245, 285
Blake, William 198, 209, 228, 246–7
Brakhage, Stan 252

British Empire 53, 84–6, 90, 97, 125, 154
Bultmann, Rudolf 245
Bunting , Basil 51–54, 113
Byzantium 105–6

Caddel, Ric 101–2
Christianity 105–7 155 156–7 171–2 178 188–92 194–5 201–2 204 244–5
cigarette cards 125
cinnabar 234, 253
Clarke, Adrian 44
classical heritage 117, 120–1
Cobbing, Bob 290
Compendium Books 223
continuity between 1940s and 1960s 186, 197, 225, 246–8, 278, 285–90
convection in visual hallucination 251; excitation spreading across crowds 279–82; the teeming figure 278; social networks 222
Corbin, Henry 198, 253–4, 293
Counter-Culture 27, 236–53
counter-knowledge 222–35
crackpot archaeology 136, 250
Critchlow, Keith 216–7
cross-modality 205
Crozier, Andrew 39, 70–77
data series, see diary; in cognitive feedback 19–20; in culture diffusion 134–6; historicism 113

[308]

# Index

depots of knowledge as primary material for texts 109–28; palace-grave 125; royal archives 137; cheap prints 110, 112; Classical heritage 115–7; great houses 121; cigarette cards 125; national museums 114; Alexandrian Museum 124
diary method 207
documentary 30, 45, 56–7, 60, 82–97; 181 (and whole chapter), and precision; rejection of documentary 112; see Mass Observation

Duncan, Robert 184
economics of information 90, 109, 111, 114, 123, 291

Egypt 16, 18, 20, 89, 135–8, 183, 250, 252
Ehrenzweig, Anton 104
Eliade, Mircea 237–8
Eliot, TS 44
Empson, William 49
encryption 291
English cosmology, see Shared Stories 68
Eranos gathering 198, 237–8
Esterson, Aaron 206
eternal forms 197
Euston Road school 96
exceptionalism 158

Farr, Florence 5, 54
Farson, Daniel 172
fear of transience 115, 121
Fedotov, GP 105
feedback see reflexivity 160–3
Ferry-Grosseteste School 6, 23–45, 70–81
film, cinema 30, 56–7, 85, 87, 90, 94, 131, 210, 215, 218, 252
Fisher, Allen 25
Fisher, Roy 62–70, 263
folk-music 256–8
Freer, Ulli 104
Froebe-Kapteyn, Olga 237

Garcia, Alfredo, agronomist 215
Gardiner, Rolf 240
Gascoyne, David 186–209
Georgian poets xv, 51, 117
Gibbons, Tom 195
glut of images; appropriation 114
Gogarty, Paul 290
Gothic: Claudian's Gothic war, 110 196, 216
Graves, Milford 41, 43
Great Exhibition 122
Green, Martin 236–8,
Grierson, John 85, 89
Grosseteste Review 24
group feeling (see autogestion) 91–3

Hall, John 34–5
Harrisson, Tom 49
Haslam, Mike xxviii
Hawkins, Ralph 35–40
Hebb, Donald, psychologist 57
Hendry, JF 142, 147, 194
hermaphrodite-seraph 170, 199
Higgins, Brian, poet 174
Hill, Geoffrey 189
Holy Alliance 195
Homberger, Eric, Art of the Real 66
Hughes, Ted 246
involuntary images 193, 227; see psychedelia, surrealism, sacred geometry, mundus imaginalis, convection form constants 251; nympholepsy 199;

Irving, Henry production of Faust 113; the Faustian parade 113–4

Jenkins, Philip 138, 290
Jorn, Asger 277; influence of the 1940s on the 1960s 278
Jung, Carl Gustav 243, 248

Keery, James xxx, 2, 25, 184, 186, 238
kenosis 117, 239; lost knowledge, see Rilko
Kluver, Heinrich 251
Knight, G. Wilson 170, 197, 199, 251

Lake, Grace xxiii
Lambert, Charles xxvii
Langley, RF xxvii
Lawrence D.H. ; 136, 157, 240–1, 246, 252; his Apocalypse 236, 239–42, 251
Lawson, Andrew 44
Lefebvre, Henri 50, 272, 275
Lewis, Norman 242
liminal 112, 145–6, 203–4
lithography 112
Logue, Christopher 287
London School 44, 289
looseness 224
Lux Mundi 205
Lymington Lord (Gerald Wallop) Fascist breeding expert 241

MacDiarmid, Hugh 12–13
Macdonald, Helen xxiv
Macleod, Joseph xxix, 56, 240
MacSweeney, Barry xxvi
Madge, Charles 58–61, 95, 207
Mannerism 178
Marxism 44, 54, 82, 114, 131, 139, 231, 272–3
Masefield, John 203
Mass Observation 30, 49–50, 95, 192–3, 203
Massingham, H J 252
medium see prophet 170
mirrors 19
modernist legitimacy 24, 51, 219
montage/rapid cuts ; personal montages 47; 121, 137, 258–61
Moore, T Sturge 3
Morgan, Edwin 142
Mottram, Eric 292–4
Muckle, John 118
Mulford, Wendy 33–4
mundus imaginalis 253 (see involuntary images)
myth: loss of myth 48, 160, 192–3, 210–21, 244–6, 298–9; folklore 256–8; personal myth 118, 245; closed off by literacy 121
national myth 82

naval policy 86, 89

New Age 222–35
New Left 229, 231
New Romanticism 1–2, 142–185
Newbolt, Henry 84
Nimbus, magazine 238
Noel, Malcolm quoted 273
Nuttall, Jeff 286–9

Objectivism 51–5, 93–4, 98–108
object-machines 151, 153, 226; Russia's greatest love-machine 190
obscurity 294
observer as object of study, see mirrors 71
occlusion 1, 10; and dissidence 91, 125
Occult Revival ; occultism 5, 176–7, 188, 195, 197–200, 219–20, 246
organic farming 241
organic values 239
Orthodox Church 105–8
O'Sullivan, Maggie 286
paradox 127

Pater, Walter 199
Perrie, Walter 260
Personalism 146, 153–65
photography 46, 216
Plowman , Max 242
poetry as documentary 98
Pop poetry 269, 291–6
Poundian scene of '50s 55
Practical Criticism 47–9, 93–4, 98, 255
precision 46–50
Prince, FT 164
Prinn, Ludvig, Baltic Ophite 212
propaganda 82–97, 137–8, 193
Prophet see spiritualism, apocalypse, shamanism, seraph
protestant mysticism 246, 253
protestants 143–4, 238–9, 246

psychedelia 227, 232; the Pink Floyd 235, 251; the Incredible String Band 257–9; the Misunderstood 136; see Iain Sinclair
psychoceramics ix

Quigley, Carroll 88

Raine, Kathleen 149, 196–8, 243, 249–251, 286
Raworth, Tom xxvi
Read, Herbert 159
Reed, Jeremy 202
reflexivity, see feedback 15–21, 76, 96, 118–120; classical models 119
repeatable scenes 85
richness of lexicon 122
Riley, Denise 44
Riley, John 102–108
RILKO 250
Rozanov, VV 103–4
Rudolf, Otto 238
Russian influence: see Berdyaev, Riley, Gascoyne, Tallents
sacred geometry 246, 249–51

Savage, DS 157, 285
Scots poetry 10–14, 254–61
Scottish nationalism 254–61
sensitivity 20, 161–2
serial images 19
Seymour-Smith, Martin xxx, 58, 66, 110
shamanism 169, 199, 206, 213, 220, 234, 242
shared scenes 123–6; stock imagery 27
shared stories 68, 84
Sheppard, Robert 286
Shestov, Lev 189, 195

Shklovsky, Viktor 63
Sinclair, Iain 210–21, 252
Situationism 277–8
Sitwell, Edith 145
Sitwell, Sacheverell 3
skulls 62, 285–7; oracular head 214–5; Palestinian 136
Smith, Grafton Elliot 134–6, 252
Smith, Ken 203
Smith, Simon 41
Smith, Timothy D'Arch 5
Solovyov, Vladimir 103
Spark, Muriel, quoted 63
speculative ideas 129–39, 262–71
Spender, Stephen 16, 201
spiritualism 196, 197, 199, 242–3
sun cult 136, 239, 252
surrealism 140, 148, 170, 187–8, 192, 193, 194, 199, 208, 295
Szeemann, Harald, Swiss exhibition organiser 237

Tallents, Stephen 85, 87, 89, 131
Temenos 196–8, 249–51

Underground, the 285–96
Thom, Martin xxv, 137–8, 233–5
Thomas, Dylan 285, 287
Thompson, Dunstan 179–84
Tiller, Terence 15–21, 161, 164
Tomlinson, Charles 61–2
Treece, Henry 227
Turner, Victor 203
underground press 222
van den Beukel, Karlien 183

Watson, Sir William 114–20
Wheale, Nigel xxiv
Wilbur, Richard 67

Printed in the United Kingdom by
Lightning Source UK Ltd., Milton Keynes
136762UK00001B/310/P